EXPLORATIONS IN DIVERSITY

EXPLORATIONS IN DIVERSITY

EXPLORATIONS IN DIVERSITY

EXAMINING THE COMPLEXITIES OF PRIVILEGE, DISCRIMINATION, AND OPPRESSION

THIRD EDITION

Edited by Sharon K. Anderson
Valerie A. Middleton

OXFORD
UNIVERSITY PRESS

Oxford University Press is a department of the University of Oxford. It furthers
the University's objective of excellence in research, scholarship, and education
by publishing worldwide. Oxford is a registered trade mark of Oxford University
Press in the UK and certain other countries.

Published in the United States of America by Oxford University Press
198 Madison Avenue, New York, NY 10016, United States of America.

Library of Congress Cataloging-in-Publication Data
Names: Anderson, Sharon K., editor. | Middleton, Valerie A., editor.
Title: Explorations in diversity : examining the complexities of privilege,
discrimination, and oppression / edited by Sharon K. Anderson,
Valerie A. Middleton.
Description: Third Edition. | New York : Oxford University Press, [2018] |
"First Edition copyright 2005 by Brooks/Cole, Cengage Learning"—T.p. verso. |
"Second Edition copyright 2011 by Brooks/Cole, Cengage
Learning"—T.p. verso. | Includes bibliographical references and index.
Identifiers: LCCN 2017013729 (print) | LCCN 2017031733 (ebook) |
ISBN 9780190617059 (updf) | ISBN 9780190617066 (epub) |
ISBN 9780190617042 (acid-free paper)
Subjects: LCSH: Students—United States—Social conditions. |
Students—United States—Economic conditions. | Privileges and
immunities—United States. | Oppression (Psychology) | Diversity in the
workplace—United States.
Classification: LCC LC205 (ebook) | LCC LC205 .A52 2018 (print) |
DDC 306.430973—dc23
LC record available at https://lccn.loc.gov/2017013729

To my children, you continue to teach me about the complexities of diversity. To my students, you have been gracious with me as I continue to work on cultural humility. To Jesus, my greatest teacher.

Sharon

Keeping thoughts of you on my mind continually helps me to persevere—God, Ma, Kia, Mudea, The Middleton & Mills Family, The Brodsky Family. Rest in Peace: Granddaddy, Dwight, Stefan, James, Kajka, Kody.

Valerie

CONTENTS

SECTION 2 STORIES OF ETHNIC COMPLEXITIES, PRIVILEGE, AND INTERSECTIONALITY

SECTION 3 STORIES OF ASSUMED PRIVILEGE

SECTION 4   STORIES OF SOCIOECONOMIC PRIVILEGE AND CLASSISM COMPLEXITIES

SECTION 5   STORIES OF SEXUAL IDENTITIES, GENDER, AND CISGENDER

SECTION 6   STORIES OF AGEISM, SEXISM, AND HETEROSEXISM

SECTION 7   STORIES OF DIFFERENTLY ABLED AND ABLEISM

SECTION 8   STORIES OF GENDER, RACE, AND IDENTITY DEVELOPMENT

SECTION 9 STORIES OF ALLIES, ACTIVISTS, AND PERSONAL COMPASSION

PREFACE: HOW THIS BOOK OF STORIES BEGAN

This book of stories first developed in because of a story or really multiple stories. One of those stories, Sharon's story, highlights her experience of coming to recognize her White privilege because of relationships and interactions with people who are not White and experience oppression and discrimination. At the same time this realization was growing, I (Sharon) wondered why the professional literature in my field of counseling psychology and other helping fields seemed to ignore the issue of White privilege. I asked myself, "Wasn't recognizing one's privilege and being honest about one's privilege an important part of being an effective, multicultural competent, ethical professional?" With this question in mind and a colleague, Val, willing to join me, we began the journey as coeditors of the first edition.

The first edition, *Explorations in Privilege, Oppression, and Diversity* (2005), was originally conceived as a resource for individuals and students in training in various helping professions, such as counseling, social work, psychology, human services, and education. We chose the title to draw attention to the invisible and elusive nature of privilege and the different statuses in which it is manifested. At the same time, we wanted to highlight the ever-present relationship between privilege and oppression. When one does not recognize her or his own privilege, others may experience oppression. We organized the first edition in two parts. Part I focused on stories of privilege within five different statuses: White privilege, socioeconomic privilege, able-bodied privilege, heterosexual privilege, and sexism. Part II looked at issues through stories related to privilege: assumed privilege; internalized oppression, acculturation, and assimilation; and personal compassion and being allies. The stories from our 27 contributors were real and raw. As editors, we were inspired and humbled by their authenticity and willingness to be vulnerable. Professionals in the helping fields were being honest about their privilege.

Six years later, we published the second edition, *Explorations in Diversity: Examining Privilege and Oppression in a Multicultural Society* (2011). We expanded the content and modified the title in order to draw attention to the practicality and necessity of the text for a broader audience to include any individual personally and professionally interested in understanding and uprooting privilege. The expanded content included ageism and the complexities of identities. The second edition assumed a general understanding of the concept of privilege and the ways privilege is expressed. We added new contributors who shared their compelling stories about privilege as well as oppression. Again, we were humbled and inspired by the honesty and vulnerability of the authors.

Another six years later we present the third edition, *Explorations in Diversity: Examining the Complexities of Privilege, Discrimination, and Oppression*. Similar to the first and second edition, the third edition holds true to the focus and tone of the first two editions. Again, we asked our contributors to speak from the heart (and the head) about privilege. Authors from the second edition, having updated their literature, graciously re-share their stories of coming to know and challenging their points of privilege. Additionally, new authors share their stories of privilege and/or oppression and discrimination because of different identities. In this edition, the issues of intersectionality and complexities come to the forefront as authors address their multiple identities. The third edition differs from the second edition in that we restructured the third edition to include nine sections with fewer chapters within each section. In addition, we provided an introduction to each section that highlights key aspects of each chapter.

The authors of each chapter represent real people involved in their struggles with privilege. Each chapter represents the authors' voices and their own way of sharing their stories. The authors use various means to describe their own positionality relative to ability, socioeconomic class, gender, race, ethnicity, religion, sexual orientation, gender identity, and so on. Although it is recognized by all of the contributors that the concepts discussed are socially, politically, and ideologically constructed, it is also recognized that these are the categories by which we name ourselves and others and the categories that make meaning of the narratives clear and accessible to the reader. The authors speak to the psychological costs of privilege rather than its benefits, as well as constructive methods for working through the dissonance that occurs when privilege is realized and acknowledged and the process of dismantling begins. Similar to the previous editions, we are humbled and inspired by the contributions from the authors.

As you, our readers, explore the topics in this book, we ask that you be open-minded and sensitive, for the sharing of these stories has not come without cost. Feelings of vulnerability, guilt, shame, embarrassment, and the like have all been part of the process of bringing this important topic into view in this way. In sharing my story, I personally am aware of my vulnerability and feelings of shame about my own journey. My lack of understanding and sensitivity seems abhorrent. However, I also recognize the value of disclosure in furthering my journey and the journey of others.

VAL'S STORY

Relying on eight years of public school teaching experience in the Chicago area, I smiled confidently upon entering my first university classroom as a teacher educator, in spite of the fact that nearly every student in the room sat before me with mouth agape. I turned my back to them to write identifying information on the board while I subtly checked to make sure I was buttoned and zipped. When I realized that I was appropriately secured, I assumed that the shocked expressions were a result of my being a Black female in a classroom of all White students. At my about face, the students had corrected their expressions and were awaiting my delineation of the syllabus for a course on diversity. That was the first time I taught a university course. Similar scenarios exist every semester when I walk through the door and lend themselves to teaching about issues of diversity, privilege, and oppression since my first position as an assistant professor in the School of Education at Colorado State University and in my present position as a tenured professor at the University of Northern Colorado (UNC) in Greeley.

My previous teaching experiences include Chicago and southern suburban area K–12 public school where students came from a variety of racial, ethnic, religious, and socioeconomic backgrounds. In contrast, my university experience has been teaching predominantly White, Christian, middle-class urban and rural graduate and undergraduate students training to be teachers, counselors, social workers, and the like. As a Black American, female college professor, I am somewhat of an anomaly. Typically, I am the only teacher of color many of my students have had, the only Black teacher they have had, or the only Black professor they have had. As a result, I find I must carefully and purposefully establish a level of credibility and authority that would typically come with the position, as it does for many of my White American male counterparts—a privilege they automatically have. An additional privilege they have is being called by the distinguished title of "Dr." 90% of the time, in face-to-face, e-mail, or phone interactions. However, students, upon making contact with me, generally address me by my first name or, when trying to be polite, call me "Miss," "Mrs.," or "Ms." Although these titles are not "offensive" to me, what does offend me is that none of my male counterparts are called "Mr." but are given the title of "Dr." or "professor," whether or not they have earned it.

These are the kinds of conversations I would have with Sharon, my friend and coeditor. We are both university faculty—one Black and one White, working in predominately White university settings with predominately White undergraduate and graduate students enrolled in education or counseling programs. Most of our students come from monoracial, White suburban or rural settings in Colorado or other states across the country, whereas fewer come from areas such as Denver, Chicago, or Los Angeles. In my position as Educational Foundations Faculty at UNC, which is situated in a town with a significant number of Latino and Somali families, the student population is still predominately White. This speaks to a situation that is also impacted by privilege.

Within the context of teaching about multiculturalism, many of our students say they support issues of diversity and multiculturalism; however, closer inquiry reveals that they mean "I am not a racist." They then go on to share scenarios of how they have a Black or Mexican friend, have dated someone outside of their ethnicity, listen to rap music, attend Native American powwows, and so on. When the burden of proof regarding the validity of their claims is placed at the forefront, many students become agitated, defensive, or resistant. However, rather than shy away from these reactions, I believe that they are necessary and critical steps toward deconstructing and reconstructing a belief system that addresses privilege and supports multicultural understanding.

Sharon and I have had many conversations about these aforementioned reactions and their connection to privilege. Sharon offers her own story, "An Awakening to Privilege,

Oppression, and Discrimination," which addresses such reactions in the context of her life. It is our hope that this book contributes to the resources on privilege, diversity, and oppression by encouraging readers to look within themselves—and rather than claim "I'm not a racist" or "I don't discriminate," purposefully examine and expose their statuses and actively choose to use the privilege they have to support those who may not be seen or heard otherwise.

In closing, Sharon and I believe that we selected accessible stories that allow for challenging one's thinking around the issues informing the transformative process of our students, ourselves, and others. We hope you will join us in laughing, crying, being angry, and gaining hope as you journey with us through our lives and add your own in uprooting privilege, fighting oppression, and affirming diversity in your personal and professional lives.

*It is important to note that the capitalization of certain terminology regarding ethnicity, gender, sexual orientation and other "naming" labels have been edited for capitalization consistency according to APA and publisher guidelines. It is also important to note that we, as editors and authors of the book, recognize the purposeful choices our contributing authors made in their work designed to address privilege, oppression and power. Each author provided their preference or view of how these terms should be treated. We recognize that at the publication of this book, we still have obstacles to overcome in order to tell these stories in the ways in which we would like them to be told.

ACKNOWLEDGMENTS

We wish to thank Sharon Hamm for her hard work in helping us make this edition happen. Sharon, your attention to detail and work ethic are astonishing and greatly appreciated. We also wish to thank Dana Bliss, our acquisition editor. Dana, your passion for and personal understanding of our topic was evident from our initial conversations. Thank you for helping us make this third edition a reality.

ABOUT THE CONTRIBUTORS

Allan Edward Barsky, JD, MSW, PhD, self-identifies as a proud father, a loving husband, a dedicated educator, and a strong advocate for social justice. Others may identify Dr. Barsky as a transplanted Canadian living in southern Florida where he is a professor of social work at Florida Atlantic University. Dr. Barsky teaches about conflict resolution, professional ethics, addictions, and conscious use of self. His book authorships include *Conflict Resolution for the Helping Professions* (Oxford University Press), *Clinicians in Court* (Guilford Press), and *Ethics and Values in Social Work* (Oxford University Press). He is past chair of the National Association of Social Work (NASW) National Ethics Committee and also chaired a national task force to review and update the NASW Code of Ethics from 2015 to 2017. In 2015, Dr. Barsky won the NASW "Excellence in Ethics Award." And, oh yes, he is gay and happy too.

Ruth Chu-Lien Chao, PhD, Associate Professor, University of Denver, teaches Diversity, Psychopathology, Counseling Theories, Counseling Practicum, and others. Her doctorate degree in counseling psychology (2005) is from University of Missouri Columbia. She has taught at a marginally Historically Black University, Tennessee State University, and is strongly interested in African American psychology, specifically on their distinctive well-being, support resources, and admirable resilience. She recently published two books. Her "Multicultural competencies in counseling: A statistical exploration" (2008) is concerned with contributing factors to multicultural competencies among the counselors. She also published "Counseling: An integrated approach" (2015) examined counseling theories and the integration with positive psychology. Her over 40 publications, presentations, book, and book chapters so far describe explorations, via counseling and research, into multicultural issues in counseling. She has won the APF Grant in Counseling Psychology for her research project, "Multiculturally Sensitive Mental Health Checklist" that targets mental health among African Americans. She won other awards and grants, such as APA PRODINS grant, ACA research award, University of Denver Curriculum and Diversity Grant, etc. She also received the American Psychological Association Grant Award in 2007, the Outstanding Research Award in 2005 from the Division 17, the Apple Award in 2008. She published in the American Psychologist, Journal of Counseling Psychology, Journal of Counseling and Development, Psychological Assessment, Journal of College Counseling, ACA VISTA, Encyclopedia of Counseling Psychology, Encyclopedia of Cross-Culture, and Handbook of African American Health. She served as faculty advisor to international scholars from Uzbekistan and Taiwan.

Kelly Costello has a long history of community activism and organizing, devoting his energy to supporting the work and interests of a range of historically marginalized communities—including a primary focus on LGBTQ issues. In 2003, he cofounded the all-volunteer-run Denver Zine Library (DZL), which features a lending library of over 15,000 zines, and has consistently worked as a coordinator and workshop facilitator since the DZL's founding. In 2005, Kelly helped to create The Tranny Roadshow, a group consisting of all self-identified transgender performance artists. The Tranny Roadshow toured nationally until 2008. Kelly's interest in promoting underground media and performance art is rooted in a commitment to ensuring access for voices not heard in mainstream media. As part of this commitment, he has served for the last two years as the Zine Coordinator for DINK, Denver's independent comics and art expo. Professionally, Kelly has worked as an advocate and coordinator for a range of community-focused programs. In his previous position as Director of Advocacy at Survivors Organizing for Liberation (formerly the Colorado Anti-Violence Program), he worked to fulfill the statewide organization's mission to eliminate violence within and against LGBTQ communities. Through this role, he oversaw a 24-hour crisis hotline, provided limited case management, and facilitated trainings for service providers. Since 2012, he has worked in the field of grants management at two private foundations and enjoys putting his love of spreadsheets to good use for social issues.

Kathleen M. Davis is a PhD Candidate at The Chicago School for Professional Psychology, and expects to graduate in June 2017. Kathleen received her Master's Degree in Counselor Education from Western Michigan University, and her Bachelor in Business Leadership from Baker College. She enjoys advocating for the rights of people with disabilities, and has dedicated several years to working in Rehabilitation Counseling. Beyond that, Kathleen has worked in higher education as faculty, and in mental health. As part of her studies at The Chicago School for Professional Psychology, Kathleen participated in Field Experience internships in South Africa, and Brazil. Her dissertation focused on male indigenous Mexican migrants, and the effects of transnational family separation and fear of family separation with mixed-documented families. Future research interests include indigenous health concepts, disability, vocational psychology, gender studies, indigenous psychology, international psychology, and qualitative research methods, particularly using focus groups. Kathleen lives in fabulous Las Vegas with her husband Paul, and two adorable pugs. She is originally from Michigan, and considers Battle Creek her hometown. She still has ties to the Great Lakes State through friends and family, and an enduring love for Lake Michigan.

Helen G. Deines is a professor of social work emerita from Spalding University in Louisville, Kentucky. A graduate of Stanford University (AB), Oregon State University (MEd), University of Louisville (MSSW), and Spalding University (EdD), Dr. Deines taught at the schools of social work at both Spalding and the University of Louisville, as well as the University of Louisville Medical School.

While teaching, Helen continued to work pro bono with clients one on one, facilitate support groups, and provide public and professional education. Over the course of her career, Helen received numerous awards as a university teacher, pastoral caregiver to and public advocate for persons with HIV/AIDS, and advocate for those who are poor.

Since retiring in 2007, Helen's practice has focused on the civil right to counsel for persons of limited means. Dr. Deines served as a founding member of the Kentucky Supreme Court's Access to Justice Commission. She is especially concerned with the need for zealous legal advocacy for parents and children on the abuse and neglect dockets of our family courts and "legal orphans" (children whose parental rights have been terminated but are not likely to be adopted).

Helen has been married for 52 years to Bill, a PhD organic chemist. They have three adult children and four grandchildren.

Edward A. Delgado-Romero, PhD is a professor in the Department of Counseling and Human Development Services at the College of Education of the University of Georgia. He is also a licensed psychologist in Georgia. Ed is a father of five: Javier, Isa, Nick, Emma, and Gil. He is blessed to be married to Angie who brings joy, stability, and love to his life and to the lives of their children. Ed is indebted to his mother, Isabel, and his in-laws Judy and Takis for their wisdom and love.

Ed enjoys mentoring graduate students and has actively presented and written with his advisees. His research team, BIEN! (bienresearch.coe.uga.edu), is a collaborative effort to fuse research and service. He emphasizes the need for psychological research to "give back" to ethnic-minority and immigrant populations. The BIEN! team and alumni are culturally competent researchers and their training is his focus.

Ed is a founder and past -president of the National Latina/o Psychological Association (NLPA). In 2016 he was recognized as a *padrino* (elder) of NLPA. Ed has written extensively in the field of counseling psychology and in multicultural psychology, specifically Latina/o psychology. He is proud of having written a book with his mentor Dr. Patricia Arredondo, *Culturally Responsive Counseling with Latinas/os*.

Devika Dibya Choudhuri is currently teaching in the graduate counseling program at Eastern Michigan University. A licensed professional counselor in Michigan and Connecticut, she has over 15 years of experience working with clients individually, as well as in couples, families, and groups. She specializes in cross cultural and diversity issues, as well as trauma, assault, and abuse and is a certified EMDR therapist. Her clinical experience has been in agency and university settings working with refugee populations, sexual assault and abuse survivors, and immigrant and multicultural populations. She carries the National Certified Counselor and Clinical Mental Health Counselor credentials as well as the Approved Clinical Supervisor. She teaches courses on cross-cultural counseling, advanced multicultural counseling, crisis, trauma, grief and loss, counseling skills, group work, couple and family, and counseling women, as well as lesbian, gay, bisexual, transgender, and queer (LGBTQ) populations. Her research and publications have focused on the areas of multicultural client issues, counselor supervision, and pedagogy. She has published a textbook on multicultural counseling and edited a set of eight monographs in the series, as well as published over 20 journal articles and book chapters and presented over 50 national and international presentations and workshops. She completed her undergraduate work at Smith College, her master's in counseling at the University of Vermont and her PhD in counselor education and supervision at Syracuse University. She has served on the National Board of Certified Counselors Board of Directors and has been the chair of the international counseling credentialing organization.

Barbara Gormley has been an activist in feminist, antiracist, and queer rights movements for more than three decades, and she facilitates interfaith dialogues. Recently, she participated in a Black Lives Matter protest in Chicago after Laquan McDonald, someone her students knew, was killed by the police. Dr. Gormley is an associate professor of psychology at Governors State University in south Chicago. She received a national teaching award for integrating diversity into a gender studies course from American Psychological Association Division 35. Dr. Gormley interned at Harvard Medical School and earned a doctorate in counseling psychology from Michigan State University. Before that, she worked as a social worker for many years, after earning a bachelor's degree in women's studies from the University of Michigan.

Michael R. Harris is a recent graduate of Farmingdale State College. He holds his Bachelors of Science degree in Applied Psychology. He is currently a full-time Teacher's Assistant for Eastern Suffolk BOCES. Following his graduation, he has been looking to teach abroad and is actively pursuing that goal. He lives in Long Island, N.Y. with his family and two dogs.

Marya Howell-Carter is an associate professor and chairperson of the Department of Psychology at Farmingdale State College. She is a New York licensed clinical psychologist with a specialization in adolescent, young adult, and family psychotherapy. Her teaching responsibilities include individual and group counseling, abnormal psychology, psychology of women, and cross-cultural psychology. Her current research interests and publications are in the areas of pedagogy, career development, and perceptions of people from multiracial backgrounds. Marya is the American Psychological Association liaison for Continuing Education for the Westchester Center for Psychological Education. Marya lives in Westchester County, New York, with her teenage children and husband of 25 years.

Karla Ivankovich, with over 18 years of experience in varied treatment settings, is a nationally certified, licensed clinical professional counselor, who has board certification from the American Psychotherapy Association and holds a distance counselor credential. In addition to being a counselor, she is an executive, educator, media personality, divorce mediator, and public speaker, and she serves on the Ethics Committee for the Illinois Counseling Association.

With a PhD in psychology, she possesses undergraduate degrees in business administration and psychology as well as graduate degrees in human development counseling (marriage and family therapy) and INO-disability studies and has completed additional coursework in educational leadership. Dr. Ivankovich attended Lincoln Land College, the University of Illinois at Springfield, and North Central University. She serves as an adjunct lecturer in the undergraduate psychology program at the University of Illinois at Springfield and the graduate counseling psychology program at North Park University.

Ranked as a Top Executive by the National Council of American Executives, Dr. Ivankovich serves as president and cofounder of OnePatient Global Health Initiative. In this position, her primary role is to provide executive oversight through outreach programming, mental health assessment, and clinical compliance.

Her research and publications have focused on body image, biopsychosocial aspects impacting health disparity, marginalized populations, millennial issues, obesity, self-esteem, and stigma. She has presented research findings at national conferences and is often called upon to provide expert opinion to national media sources. In private practice Dr. Ivankovich focuses on an individuals and couples; her scope of practice includes conflict resolution, general mental health, and intimacy.

Saliwe M. Kawewe, BSW, MSW, PhD is interim director and professor of social work with over 25 years of university teaching, research, and service experience. She has been at the Southern Illinois University School of Social Work since 1996 and has been interim director since January 2015. She earned her BSW from the University of Zambia in 1974; an MSW from George Warren Brown School of Social Work, Washington University in St. Louis in 1979, and a PhD in social work from the School of Social Service, Saint Louis University in 1985. Dr. Kawewe has a diverse international background experience in social work practice, policy, planning, administration, research, and child welfare in Zambia, Zimbabwe and the United States.

Dr. Kawewe has a commendable record of scholarship and various academic awards and honors for teaching effectiveness and community and professional service. She has published over 45 scholarly articles including book chapters, encyclopedia entries, and conference proceedings and is a consulting editor/editorial board member for several professional journals. Her research focuses on socioeconomic justice and human rights for Third World women and children, particularly in sub-Sahara Africa; economic structural adjustment programs; international social work and social development; HIV/AIDS; child welfare; cultural and human diversity; gender disempowerment globalization; and war and peace.

Allison L. Kramer, PhD, LPC, CAC II, is an associate professor of counseling psychology at Johnson & Wales University in Denver, Colorado. She has been a licensed professional counselor and certified addictions counselor in Colorado since 2001. In addition to teaching, she also a small private practice in Denver.

Allison has presented original research and reflections on ethics and best practices in counseling at numerous conferences, including the American Counseling Association, the Southern Association for Counseling Education and Supervision, the Association for Assessment and Research in Counseling, and the Colorado Counseling Association, and has published peer-reviewed articles in *Community College Journal of Research and Practice*, the American Counseling Association's *VISTAS*, and *Counseling Today*. Currently, she is the host of a monthly Ethics Highlight for the Thoughtful Counselor podcast (www.theth-oughtfulcounselor.com). Her hobbies include camping, hiking, and playing with her family in the beautiful Colorado outdoors.

Carol L. Langer, MSW, PhD, is department chair and professor of social work at Colorado State University–Pueblo. She teaches undergraduate Human Behavior and the Social Environment. This area of social work education is particularly important to her. She studies experiential learning, including immersions and simulations, and its role in erasing stereotypes and myths about diverse populations. In addition, she works with qualitative research methodologies.

Jessica Lloyd-Hazlett is an assistant professor in the Department of Counseling at the University of Texas at San Antonio. She earned a PhD in counselor education and supervision and an MEd in couples and family counseling from the College of William & Mary. She is also a licensed professional counselor. Dr. Lloyd-Hazlett's research interests include cognitive development, counselor preparation, and professional ethics. Further, she appreciates opportunities to learn with and from students and clients.

Colleen Loomis is a university-based scholar engaged in research, teaching, administration, and service. As an administrator, she has served as graduate program coordinator, research center associate director, and associate dean. Her research focuses on linking community, schools, government, and nongovernmental organizations to foster children's development to its full capacity. She has local, national, and international experience understanding the impact of programs and services on outcomes for children, family, community, and organizations, including cost savings to government and other funders.

Colleen is a critical, multicultural educator and has taught on the subjects of psychology, ethics, service learning, and community-based research methods. She has experience teaching at the undergraduate, master's, and doctoral level on campus and online with course enrollments from 3 to 200 students. Beyond educating students in the classroom and the field, she mentors students and colleagues around the world in grant writing, publishing, and professional development.

Colleen has a deep understanding of applied research and evaluation theory, in addition to having a strong theoretical and practical understanding of knowledge mobilization and exchange approaches. She has experience designing and implementing knowledge mobilization strategies and evaluating the impact of knowledge mobilization activities.

Having conducted research in the United States, Canada, Kenya, Madagascar, Laos, France, and Switzerland, Colleen is an active and effective listener, a strong communicator, and a compassionate project partner. Characterized by colleagues as gracious, calm, and principled, she is a compelling speaker who challenges people's thinking and inspires personal, professional, and organizational growth.

David MacPhee is a professor in Human Development and Family Studies at Colorado State University (CSU). His research and teaching focus on parenting, risk and resilience, and effective prevention programs. Related to diversity issues, he has been actively involved in work on feminist issues, including CSU's women's studies program and serving as a facilitator for CSU's Institute for Inclusive Excellence and its predecessor, the Multicultural Curriculum Infusion Project, which is a national model for teaching about diversity. Among his research interests are how best to recruit and retain underrepresented students into the STEM disciplines and cross-cultural comparisons of family systems and child-rearing practices.

Although he grew up in a fairly homogenous culture in Idaho, David has traveled, studied, and worked throughout the United States (particularly the South and Southeast), Belize, and Australia, all of which deepened his appreciation for diverse cultures.

Deborah Megivern Foster is a writer working on her memoir, *When We Were at Your Mercy*, focused on how social services were critical to keeping her family alive and intact. She has academic publications with the most cited being "Campus Mental Health Recommendations," about how colleges and universities can better treat students with mental illnesses. Other publications are on topics ranging from posttraumatic stress disorder to evidence-based quality of care to psychosocial rehabilitation. After receiving her PhD at the University of Michigan, Deborah taught social policy, mental health policy, and human diversity at Washington University in St. Louis. When she left academia, Dr. Foster became a mental health practitioner and then a college counselor for TRIO Student Support Services—the federal educational opportunity program for low-income, first-generation, and disabled students. Deborah is a proud alumna of TRIO programs herself. Deborah is outspoken about having chronic posttraumatic stress disorder, bipolar disorder, and binge eating disorder because she believes in breaking down the stigma of mental illness. She is proud of being in recovery from mental illness because she believes it is not shameful but courageous to tackle these disorders head on. She is also physically disabled by chronic pain of a back condition and fibromyalgia. Love them or hate them, Deborah has also written liberal political blog posts for years on Huffington Post, Medium, and other political sites, especially focused on racism, classism, and poverty. She adores Rachel Maddow. Dr. Foster lives with her beloved husband and almost-grown stepson, as well as an elderly cat.

Kianna M. Middleton was born in Chicago, Illinois, and was raised in the northern Colorado city of Fort Collins. Currently she is a PhD candidate in African diaspora studies with a designated emphasis in women, gender, and sexuality studies at the University of California, Berkeley. She holds two master's degrees, the first in ethnic studies from Colorado State University and the second in African American studies from the University of California, Berkeley. Her past research and ethnic studies master's thesis was on queer Black and Chicana narratives as a form of resistance and differential consciousness. Her dissertation theorizes the intersections between Blackness, disability, queerness, and intersexuality (also known as disorders of sex development) in the American medical and literary imaginaries. Her disciplinary interests include queer theory and queer of color critique, Black feminism, critical disability studies, intersexuality, African American literature, LGBTQIA literature, and critical pedagogy. When she is not facing the abyss of dissertation writing she enjoys running, hiking, reruns of the 1990s show *Living Single*, and writing poetry.

Geri Miller, PhD, diplomate in counseling psychology, American Board of Professional Psychology, is a professor in the Department of Human Development and Psychological Counseling (Clinical Mental Health Counseling Track) at Appalachian State University in Boone, North Carolina. In North Carolina, Dr. Miller is a licensed psychologist, a licensed professional counselor, a licensed clinical addictions specialist, and a Substance Abuse Professional Practice Board-certified clinical supervisor. She has also received a Certificate of Proficiency in the Treatment of Alcohol and other Psychoactive Substance Use Disorders from the American Psychological Association College of Professional Psychology. Dr. Miller has worked in the counseling profession since 1976 and in the addictions field since 1979. She is a volunteer with the American Red Cross Disaster Mental Health Services and works as a volunteer psychologist at the Watauga County Health Department.

Dr. Miller has published and presented research on counseling. In 2003 she published *Incorporating Spirituality in Counseling and Psychotherapy* (John Wiley). In 2015 she published a fourth edition of her book on addiction counseling, *Learning the Language of Addiction Counseling* (John Wiley). In 2011, she published *Fundamentals of Crisis Counseling* (John Wiley) and in 2012 *Group Exercises for Addiction Counseling* (John Wiley). She is currently a member of the American Psychological Association's Psychology of Religion (Division 36) and Addictions (Division 50) and the American Counseling Association's divisions of the Association for Spiritual, Ethical, and Religious Values in Counseling and the International Association of Addictions and Offender Counselors. She serves on the North Carolina Substance Abuse Professional Practice Board.

Matthew R. Mock, PhD, was born in Santa Monica, California, as the middle of seven children. He grew up in the west Los Angeles community, one of a few Chinese families in the area at that time. He remembers being "very Chinese" while in the family home and almost anything but Chinese outside of it. His father financially supported the family as a postal carrier for 50 years until he retired and his mother worked very hard tending to the needs of the children, all the while struggling to make cultural adjustments and adaptations in a community foreign to her. Matthew has memories of how his "resource-stretched" family had very little in terms of economic resources but a lot in terms of sibling richness and interactions with others forging his way into civic rights movements.

An academic scholarship took Matthew to attend Brown University in Providence, Rhode Island. While in school, he wrote short stories and poetry thinking he would follow his heart to work as a teacher with children with learning differences. Learning about disparities in mental health treatment reshaped his focus. He received a BA with a major in psychology and a minor in special education. In retrospect, attending Brown was a significant time to examine his cultural identity as well as the impact of social class differences.

Matthew moved to Berkeley, California (where he has since lived), to attend graduate school. While in school, he worked as the mental health coordinator at an Asian American organization. This crystallized his developing awareness of his own identity and significance in addressing all of the differences and cultural shock that he had experienced in his life up to that time. He received his PhD from the California School of Professional Psychology, Berkeley/San Francisco.

Matthew holds multiple professional roles including as a professor of counseling psychology at John F. Kennedy University in Berkeley, California, a private clinical practitioner, and a writer. He deeply appreciates being able to teach and train the next generation of mental health practitioners especially to infuse and integrate social justice and multiculturalism throughout their work. He proudly served as the director of the Family, Youth, Children's and Multicultural Services for the city of Berkeley for over 20 years.

Matthew still bicycles, writes professionally and personally, and travels, oftentimes as an invited speaker, consultant, and trainer nationally and internationally. He loves to teach and write and to break stereotypes by demonstrating to his audiences that he is one example of a "passionate, Asian-American man." Most importantly, Matthew has a 25-year-old, "full-focus" daughter who is his "gift to life, our jewel" who gently reminds him about social justice and gender issues on a daily basis. Having majored in Asian American studies as well as psychology as an undergraduate and now working in Matthew's field, she is a part of his legacy.

Jacqueline J. Peila-Shuster, PhD, LPC, is an assistant professor in the Counseling and Career Development graduate program at Colorado State University in Fort Collins, Colorado. She teaches courses in career development, supervises counseling internship and practicum, and serves as the internship coordinator. She received her PhD in education and human resource studies with a focus on counselor education and career counseling in 2011 from Colorado State University. Jackie also has a master's degree specializing in Counseling and Career Development and a BS in Occupational Therapy. Her areas of interest include career counseling and development across the lifespan, counselor education, and strengths-based approaches to career and life design. In a nutshell, Jackie has a passion for standing witness to individuals' unique life stories while encouraging their strengths and hope in ways that they may discover themselves and maximize their life designs. She implements this by translating theory and research into real-world application in career and life design counseling and student instruction/supervision.

Jessica Pettitt, MEd, CSP, pulls together her stand-up comedy years with 15+ years of diversity trainings in a wide range of organizations to serve groups to move from abstract fears to actionable habits that lead to teams that want to work together. With a sense of belonging and understanding, colleagues take more risks with their ideation, converse precious resources through collaboration, and maintain real connections with clients over time. For more information, visit www.JessicaPettitt.com

Sametra Polkah-Toe was born the middle child of three children to a Liberian father and African American mother in Buffalo, New York. Her interest in social equality formed at a young age while growing up in a city with two very striking reputations; that of "The City of Good Neighbors" and that of the sixth most segregated region in the United States. Passionate about studying the intersectionality of race, class, and gender, she earned a BS in applied sociology in 2011 and completed a master's in clinical mental health counseling from Medaille College in August 2016. She currently works as a rehabilitation practitioner at a mental health recovery center where she assists individuals with accessing the appropriate services to maintain optimal mental health and works as an in-home behaviorist for at-risk youth. Besides work, she enjoys volunteering her time advancing the cause to expand the scope of practice for Licensed Mental Health Counselors and maintains professional memberships with the American Counseling Association, Counselors for Social Justice, and the Association for Multicultural Counseling and Development. You can also probably find her cuddling up with a good book, whipping up something creative in the kitchen, or watching a good movie.

Paul E. Priester is a professor in counseling psychology in the School of Professional Studies at North Park University. He has a PhD in counseling psychology from Loyola University, Chicago, and an MA in rehabilitation counseling from the University of Iowa. His research interests include the integration of spirituality into psychological practice, the measurement of Islamic religiosity, evidence-based treatment and prevention of addictive disorders, culturally competent counseling practice, and the use of popular films as a form of adjunctive bibliotherapy. He lives in Milwaukee, Wisconsin, with his wife (Katherine), daughters (Caitlin and Margo), son (the real Paul), and his Treeing Walker Coonhound (Comet). He also owns and operates an organic orchard and berry farm (Happy Destiny Farm) in Two Creeks, Wisconsin.

Damien W. Riggs is an associate professor in social work at Flinders University and an Australian Research Council Future Fellow. He is the author of over 200 publications in the areas of gender and sexuality, family, and mental health, including (with Elizabeth Peel) *Critical Kinship Studies: An Introduction to the Field* (Palgrave, 2016). He is also a Lacanian psychotherapist and specializes in working with transgender children.

Linda Robinson, PsyD, is a graduate of the Illinois School of Professional Psychology. She holds a license in the state of Illinois as a licensed clinical professional counselor, is board certified via the National Board of Certified Counselors, and holds a Distance Credentialed Counselor Certification from the Center for Credentialing and Education. Dr. Robinson's clinical experience includes 25 years working in the field of community mental health providing both direct counseling services and administrative direction to various clinical programs. Dr. Robinson has served as assistant director of the Child and Adolescent Program for the Community Mental Health Council in Chicago. She has also held the position of administrative program director at the Bobby E. Wright Mental Health Center in Chicago where she provided administrative direction to their adult programs for the mentally ill. Her instructional experience includes associate professor at the Chicago School of Professional Psychology and assistant professor at Argosy University. She also has experience operating a private practice in the Chicago area. Her special interests include cultural competence and issues of bilingualism in the counseling setting.

Ying Shan (Doris) Zhang has obtained her Master's degree from the University of Denver's Counseling Psychology program, specializing in Clinical Mental Health Counseling. She is a Registered Clinical Counselor with the BC Association of Clinical Counselors in Canada, and she has engaged in research presentations at local, regional, as well as national conferences in the United States. Doris' research interests include examining cross-cultural competence in psychotherapy, as well as investigating the impact of cultural and social justice factors on minority health and development. Doris has been awarded by the Rocky Mountain Psychological Association at its 85th annual conference as the recipient of outstanding empirical research award, as well as the recipient of outstanding empirical research on diversity issues award. Outside of research, Doris is affiliated with the American Psychological Association of Graduate Students, and she is also a member of the American Psychological Association Division 17—International Section. Within the Division, Doris serves as a contributor on the International Student Mentoring and Orientation Committee.

Daryl H. Thorne was raised in Alexandria, Virginia, in the 1970s through the 1980s. She attended Seton Hall University as an undergraduate in the late 1980s where racism was very present. Her mixed Cherokee ancestry, creations of Blackness (and Whiteness) along with experiences of racism and supremacism—some of which are addressed in the chapter—continue to motivate Dr. Thorne to empower those most affected by socially constructed ideas of race, ironically, in a country built on racism. Her passions are firmly entrenched in matters of social justice as a mixed-ancestry Native American and as an educator. She has been married to her high school sweetheart for 25 years and has two beautiful, thoughtful, and intelligent children.

Dr. Thorne is currently an assistant professor and program chair of the human relations degree program at Trinity Washington University in the School of Professional Studies.

She earned a MEd in guidance and counseling from Bowie State University and an EdD in counseling psychology with a concentration in counselor education and supervision from Argosy University. She teaches interdisciplinary courses that explore and critically analyze race and racism, inequalities, and social justice issues in the United States to a diverse student body of historically oppressed and underrepresented adult undergraduates in the District of Columbia. Dr. Thorne previously taught Multicultural Counseling, Counseling Theories, and Principles of School Counseling in the counseling program in the School of Education as an adjunct professor. Dr. Thorne is a licensed clinical professional counselor in the state of Maryland, and a nationally certified counselor. Through her private counseling practice, Dr. Thorne continues her social justice mission through conducting antiracism educational seminars, pro-bono work with veterans and military families, and holistic counseling to individuals and couples.

Heather Trepal, PhD, earned a bachelor's degree in English at The Ohio State University, a master's degree in education (community counseling) from Cleveland State University, and a PhD in counseling and human development services from Kent State University.

Heather is a professor in the Department of Counseling at the University of Texas at San Antonio. She serves as the coordinator for the Clinical Mental Health Counseling Program. She is a licensed professional counselor and board approved supervisor in the state of Texas. Her primary academic and counseling interests include women and self-harm (nonsuicidal self-injury and eating disorders), supervision, gender issues in counseling, and counselor preparation. She enjoys giving back to the counseling profession and has served as the president of the Association for Counselor Education and Supervision and the Association for Creativity in Counseling, both divisions of the American Counseling Association. She is the proud parent of three children, Aidan, Mason, and Emerson, and a feisty Chihuahua named Ray Ray.

Meagan Voulo is a second-year PhD student in the integrative neuroscience area at Stony Brook University. She graduated from Farmingdale State College with a BS in applied psychology. Currently she is working in the Parsons Learning and Memory lab. She is studying sex differences in extinction learning and retention and how this can be applied to human studies of anxiety disorders, specifically posttraumatic stress disorder.

N. Eugene Walls is an associate professor in the Graduate School of Social Work at the University of Denver where he teaches courses in the master's and doctoral programs in research, issues of power, oppression and privilege, pedagogy, and community social work practice. His research focuses on modern forms of prejudice, multicultural pedagogy, and issues of the LGBT community with a focus on an intersectional analysis of risk and resilience. He lives in Denver, Colorado, with his primary partner, David, and two chihuahuas, Tito and Dita. While no longer square dancing, he currently enjoys line dancing, including teaching line dancing at a number of venues in the Denver area and at national line-dancing events.

Joy S. Whitman, PhD, is core faculty at The Family Institute at Northwestern University in the Master's Counseling Program. Prior to this position, she was core faculty at Walden University in the Counselor Education and Supervision Program, associate professor at Purdue University Calumet and associate professor at DePaul University. At DePaul

University she also served as the associate chair and then chair of the Department of Counseling and Special Education. She served as the president of the Association for Lesbian, Gay, Bisexual, and Transgender Issues in Counseling in 2005–2006 and as governing council representative of the division for six years. Her research focus is on LGBTQ counseling issues, specifically on training counselors to provide affirmative therapeutic treatment, and she has published and presented on these issues nationally and internationally. In addition to her position as a professor, Joy is a licensed clinical professional counselor in Illinois and a licensed professional counselor in Missouri. She maintained a private practice for 18 years in Chicago and served adults clients and couples. She has experience treating clients with a history of abuse, eating disorders, anxiety, depression, career concerns, and an expertise with LGB clients.

Heidi A. Zetzer is the director of the Hosford Counseling & Psychological Services Clinic and a lecturer with Security of Employment in the Department of Counseling, Clinical, & School Psychology at the University of California, Santa Barbara. Dr. Zetzer teaches practicum and supervision courses, supervises student clinicians and supervisors, and provides psychotherapy to community clients. Dr. Zetzer is the president-elect of the Association of Psychology Training Clinics and the chair-elect of the Supervision & Training Section of the Society of Counseling Psychology (Div. 17) of the American Psychological Association. Dr. Zetzer is a past president of the Santa Barbara County Psychological Association and previously served as the chapter representative to the California Psychological Association. In 2014, Dr. Zetzer received the Outstanding Counseling Supervisor Award from the Supervision & Training Section of the Society of Counseling Psychology of the American Psychological Association.

Dr. Zetzer earned a PhD in counseling psychology from the University of California, Santa Barbara in 1990, an MA in counseling psychology from The Ohio State University in 1986, and a BS in psychology from Denison University in 1983.

ABOUT THE EDITORS

Sharon K. Anderson, PhD, is a tenured full professor in the School of Education and teaches in the Counseling and Career Development and Higher Education Leadership programs at Colorado State University in Fort Collins, Colorado. She is also a licensed psychologist with a clinical practice working with the elder population. Her publications include six books and 50 book chapters and articles, which focus mostly on issues of professional ethics and issues of privilege and diversity. Sharon holds a bachelor's in English education and a master's in counselor education, both from the University of Wyoming. Her doctorate is in counseling psychology from the University of Denver. Before receiving her doctorate and becoming a faculty member at CSU, she worked in the TRIO program at the University of Wyoming. Most importantly, Sharon is a single mom of two children, Robert and Taya, who are now young adults.

Valerie A. Middleton, PhD is a tenured professor at the University of Northern Colorado teaching and researching the topics of equity, diversity, social justice, privilege and oppression, educational methodology, service learning, professional development school partnerships, and international education delivery systems. She holds a bachelor's degree in special education from Illinois State University, a master's degree in special educational needs from Colorado State University, and a doctorate in teacher education and staff development from Colorado State University. Previously, she taught students in grades K-12 in Chicago-area public schools as well as graduate and undergraduate students at Colorado State University and Northern Arizona University. Valerie and her daughter, Kianna, share passions related to social justice and seek to continue educating others via their teaching and professional roles in higher education.

EXPLORATIONS IN DIVERSITY

EXPLORATIONS IN DIVERSITY

SECTION 1

STORIES OF WHITE PRIVILEGE, WHITE RACIAL IDENTITY, WHITENESS, AND INTERSECTIONALITY

We live in a society that includes a population of people who are all similar yet "different" in how they move through this world, experience this world, and are perceived by others in this world. The color of our skin, the type of hair we have, the way we speak, the language we use, our intellectual capacity, our gender, our sexual orientation, our height and weight, and other factors determine how we are treated by others and how we experience our existence. This section includes stories of privilege. Sharon K. Anderson shares her growing awareness of her White privilege and others' invisibility and oppression because of their skin color. Heidi Zeter and Deborah Megivern Foster address the concepts of Whiteness, White privilege, White racial identity, and intersectionality. *Intersectionality* is a term that has been around since the late 1980s and is used to refer to the complex and cumulative way that the effects of different forms of discrimination (such as racism, sexism, and classism) combine, overlap, and intersect—especially in the experiences of marginalized people or groups (https://www.merriam-webster.com/words-at-play/intersectionality-meaning). In this section, our authors share their stories of privilege, oppression, and discrimination resulting from their varied individual and/or overlapping social identities.

Anderson in "An Awakening to Privilege, Oppression, and Discrimination" shares her story of coming to know her privilege as a White person. Her chapter highlights several experiences with people of color who shared what they knew first hand: oppression, discrimination, microaggressions, and invisibility. A defining moment for the author opens her eyes to her White privilege and the oppression of others.

In "*White*out: Growing Out of the Problem of White Privilege," Zetzer describes her White racial identity development in relation to critical events in her personal and professional life. These events include early racial socialization, teaching a multicultural awareness course with culturally diverse colleagues, and engaging in multicultural dialogue following an interracial conflict that was precipitated by her exercise of White privilege. Zetzer highlights the key ingredients to her transformational learning as awareness of the negative effects of color-blind racial attitudes and impact of microaggressions and the necessity of multicultural dialogue. Zetzer's story demonstrates shifting from "avoidance goals" to "approach goals" as a way to "grow out of the problem" of racism and White privilege with the benefit of engagement in warm and meaningful multicultural relationships.

In "The Challenge of Accepting White Privilege After Living a Life of Poverty," Megivern Foster shares her journey of coming to know her privilege as a White person having lived in poverty and hardship as a child and young adult. Being poor, she believed that privilege based on her skin color was not providing advantages, which is not an uncommon thought for poor Whites. Through a growing awareness, the author describes her transformation and new understandings of her intersectionality and Whiteness.

CHAPTER 1

AN AWAKENING TO PRIVILEGE, OPPRESSION, AND DISCRIMINATION

Sharon's Story

Sharon K. Anderson

My story begins many years ago, actually at birth, with my socialization process (Harro, 2013). I had a particular package of social identities ascribed to me: female, White, able-bodied, Christian, and heterosexual. I was born into a family that was of White European descent, Christian, middle class, and farmers/ranchers. My context included an all-White family of origin and extended family. I was raised in a mostly all-White, low- to middle-income, rural community. I grew up attending a country church where everyone was White and looked like my family. I attended a school, K–12, in which all my classmates were White. Within the grades above me and below me, only a handful of students identified as Mexican. The teachers, and the administrators and staff, with one exception—the janitor—were White. Needless to say, my worldview growing up was built on, socialized on, what I knew and had experienced as a White female.

As Harro (2013) suggests, the sources that socialize a person within a system of oppression are potent, and the socialization process is "pervasive . . . consistent . . . circular . . . self-perpetuating . . . and invisible" (p. 45). This was true for me. It wasn't after I had obtained my master's degree and taken a job that my world expanded to include people who didn't look like me. This was the beginning of my breaking out, or at least a disruption of the socialization cycle I had unknowingly participated in for the first 23 years of my life. Before I share about that part of my journey, I need to share about a conversation and my thinking that planted a seed in me for a defining moment some years later. It was a defining moment in which I could no longer not see oppression and not deny my White privilege.

BLINDNESS TO WHITE PRIVILEGE

During my doctoral years, a friend, an African American female, told me about a recent experience she had had at a fast-food restaurant. My friend was in the front of the line, ready to order her food, when the female employee, who was White, looked right past my friend and asked the next person in line, who was White, what she would like. As my friend told me about her experience and clearly shared her belief that the act was discriminatory, her view was that her Black skin made her invisible to the White employee behind the counter taking people's orders. Although I could hear the anger and hurt in her voice, I had a hard time believing my friend's interpretation of the event. I remembered thinking, however not saying, "I'm sure you're mistaken. People aren't that rude. I'll bet the employee just thought you were still deciding on your order and wanted to keep the line moving."

My blindness to White privilege and other privileged statuses most certainly originated in my socialization process. Although I don't recall ever hearing my parents or other adult family members make overt derogatory remarks about people of color, I also don't recall any discussions about inequality, discrimination, or privilege. My family's view on success and hard work was based on the Protestant work ethic and the "pull yourself up by your bootstraps" notion. I believed this too.

I carried this thinking with me into my early adulthood and college environment. My belief was that almost everyone in the United States spoke or should speak English and could gain entry into college if she or he just worked hard enough in high school and that *discrimination* was just a word that "angry People of Color" used to get their way or manipulate the situation. I was oblivious to the fact that having White skin, speaking standard American English, being able-bodied, being middle income, and supporting a Christian belief system were all "unearned assets" (McIntosh, 2000) that afforded me entry into places and opportunities less available or not available to everyone.

NEW RELATIONSHIPS—COMING INTO CONTACT

After earning my master's degree, I began working for the TRIO programs: Student Support Services, Upward Bound, and Educational Talent Search. While employed in these programs, I provided services to students from different ethnic groups (Asian, Hispanic, African American, and Native American); and I worked alongside colleagues who represented these groups as well. This was the first time I had genuine and sustained contact with people whose skin color was different from mine. My obliviousness to oppression and discrimination was challenged by the colleagues I worked with and the students I served. One female colleague in particular, who identified as Chicana, would share her insights with me about how students of color were being viewed and treated on our college campus. On a superficial level, I started to see some of the obstacles people of color face in achieving their educational goals, and I understood what my colleague was saying. However, deep inside I still held on to my ethnocentric worldview (Sue & Sue, 2016) of what was normal, valued, and expected. To say the least, my internalized worldview was different from those around me. For instance, the Native American students in our Upward Bound program often requested leave from our summer session to participate in powwows and other cultural events. When I became the director of the program, I honored the students' requests to be gone for a week or more, but inside my head and heart, I questioned and disliked the disruption. Sometimes the students would leave for the powwow and not return to complete the six weeks. I couldn't comprehend their choice to put their cultural and spiritual ceremonies above the summer-school experience on a college campus. Why wouldn't they choose what our program offered? My internal response was a view that supported a notion of cultural deficits (Sue & Sue, 2016). I began to think of these students as less able to succeed in our program.

Elizabeth Minnich articulates the thinking in which I was grounded this way: "whites are taught to think of their lives as morally neutral, normative, and average, and also ideal, so that when we work to benefit others, this is seen as work that will allow 'them' to be more like 'us'" (cited in McIntosh, 2000, p. 32). As the program director, I could have taken the opportunity to look at our program for ways to make the summer school experience more culturally sensitive and welcoming. Instead, I wanted the Native American students to fit into the program; that is, I wanted *them* to be more like *us*. When my students of color or my colleagues of color talked about discrimination, oppression, and feelings of alienation—the consequences of systems based on privilege—*I didn't really see it—the reality of their experiences. And I didn't see my privilege.*

HEARING BUT NOT SEEING

After seven years of working with Upward Bound, I left my job and attended graduate school to obtain a PhD in counseling psychology. These four years provided additional opportunities for me to break the cycle of socialization. One of my fellow classmates was a gentleman who identifies himself as Chicano. During these four years, he shared his passion of working with people who represented diversity, and he encouraged me to spend time reading multicultural literature in psychology and counseling. He shared his concerns about the inequality of mental health services for people of color and how people of color typically preferred to counsel with someone from their own culture. Again, on a superficial level I was able to take in the information from the multicultural literature and the concerns about the inequality of mental health services, but when his perspective and experience challenged my worldview of the "normative," "average," or "ideal," in which a White counselor might not be viewed as good enough, I became disconcerted and defensive. I continued to listen to his stories of discrimination, gross misunderstanding, oppression, and profiling by Whites in authority, *but I didn't really hear him—once again, I didn't get it. I didn't get his oppression. I didn't get my privilege.*

After I had completed my doctorate and spent a year in the Midwest as a staff psychologist at a university counseling center, I received a faculty appointment at Colorado State University, where I developed a friendship with Val, my coeditor. Our friendship brought together many differences. Val is Black; I am White. She was born and raised in a city; I was born and raised on a farm. She experiences oppression and discrimination because of her skin color; I experience privilege (a term I now use in retrospect) because of my skin color.

As I previously mentioned, I had been told stories of discrimination and microaggressions (Sue, Bucceri, Lin, Nadal, & Torino, 2007) by my students, colleagues, and friends of color without truly accepting the validity of their articulated experiences. Because of my friendship with Val and my curiosity to better understand multicultural issues, I accepted Val's invitation to attend a Women of Color conference. This was another opportunity to break out of the cycle of socialization.

Upon our arrival at the conference, I experienced the uncomfortable feeling of being one of a few White women in attendance. I remember thinking, "I'm the minority here." I began to wonder whether I had made a mistake in coming. Since I wasn't a woman of color, I assumed others would wonder why I was there. I truly didn't think or feel I should be welcomed, and I wondered what I was going to face or be a target for.

As the sessions progressed, I became enlightened but also more uncomfortable and frustrated. I remember during one session becoming particularly irritated when those in attendance, women of color, expressed anger and hurt toward White women. I felt like a target and wondered why I wasn't positively recognized for my presence, as a White woman, at the conference. Why wasn't I seen as a well-meaning White person (Wolfe, 1995)? Val encouraged me to listen and stay emotionally and psychologically present, even though I wanted to run away by mentally/emotionally disconnecting and focusing on other thoughts or feelings.

During this same period of time, Val and I would have what I call *difficult dialogues*. She wanted me to truly hear about the stories of discrimination, bias, and oppression. I wanted to deflect the issues by claiming Whites are treated poorly too. I would argue for what I called *reverse discrimination*. I was not ready or willing to break out of or away from how I had been socialized not to see oppression. I didn't want to see my own privilege as a White person and the invisibility of others. *I just didn't really want to get it. I didn't want to see her oppression. I didn't want to see my privilege.*

DEFINING MOMENT

As our friendship and work relationship progressed, so did our level of dialogue. Val and I would occasionally meet for lunch to discuss ideas relative to teaching our predominately White population of students about issues of diversity. When Val and I had ended one such lunch at a nearby restaurant, we decided to check into the possibility of using that restaurant as a meeting place for future conversations that would include more of our colleagues. We decided to find an employee of the establishment. The following few seconds disrupted how I understood oppression as an intellectual concept and made it, in my eyes, a reality for my colleague. Val approached the receptionist, a White woman, to inquire about the cost and availability of the facility. The receptionist craned her neck to look around Val, as if she wasn't there, and then asked me, "How can I help you?" As this scene played out before me, so did a flashback of the conversation with my other friend who told me about her experience of being invisible.

In that instant, my privilege failed to blind me in a way that had previously kept me from getting it. I could see now. I could see how my white skin made me visible, and how Val's black skin and my other friend's skin made them invisible. I could better understand why the Native American students I worked with in Upward Bound might not want to come back to summer school after their powwow or Sun Dance ceremony. I could see why a person of color might want to work with a counselor of color and not a counselor with white skin. I could see how being recognized is an event that I experience and expect as natural, and how not being recognized is disrespectful, discriminatory, and oppressive. I could see why I needed to be a believer that there is a system of oppression, and I can or do a play a role in that system if I'm not actively fighting against it. I could see how what I experience and expect in everyday life is based on my White privilege. Although I can't truly understand the experiences of people of color, the sum of my past experiences, united with critical incidents such as this, help me to see that privilege exists and that I am one of its beneficiaries.

Following this eye-opening experience, I began to explore the literature on multicultural issues in psychology and counseling. I looked for other professionals who were writing about how they came to know their points of privilege. In addition, I was looking for evidence of what was needed to help privileged individuals like me see it, believe it, and, most importantly, get it—the discrimination and oppression others experience because we are potentially blind to our own points of privilege. Finding little to nothing, my exploration ended with me deciding I could begin the discussion with my own story.

CONCLUSION

It has been more than 10 years since I made the decision to write about my experience. The result was the first edition of our book, *Explorations in Privilege, Oppression, and Diversity* (2005). Since then, having ongoing conversations with colleagues of color and raising two children who are multiracial have encouraged me to stay uncomfortable and aware in my White skin and the "unearned assets" I have in my invisible knapsack (McIntosh, 2000). By uncomfortable I am not suggesting feeling guilty or ashamed of who I am, a White person (Spanierman, Todd, & Anderson, 2009). I am suggesting that I remain vigilant to what I now see and hear from People of Color about their experiences. I am also suggesting that I be unwilling to slip into the cycle of socialization where I am a participating in the system of oppression again. Last, I am suggesting that my professional/personal self-narrative (Anderson, 2015) develop cultural humility (Sue & Sue, 2016). The self-narrative is an "organization of self-related information" (Anderson, 2015, p. 195) that people have about themselves that propels them to action because of who they are within their core or essential self (Anderson, 2015). I would suggest it is that part of us that truly hears and responds in a way that is coherent or congruent with the self. *Cultural humility* is described as an attitude and a "way of being" with diverse clients that values the presence and importance of cultural factors (Owens, Tao, Leach, & Rodolfa, 2011, p. 274) and works toward genuine respect and understanding of a person as a cultural being. I might add to this description that cultural humility could include being aware of my privilege and how, if I am not actively working to disarm the system of oppression out of my self-narrative, then I am participating in it.

DISCUSSION QUESTIONS

1. The cycle of socialization begins at birth. What social identities were you socialized into?
2. Through the socialization process, what messages did you receive, either covertly or overtly, about others who were different from you and your family?
3. The author described several experiences in which she denied or struggled to see the oppression and discrimination of others. What experiences have you had that were similar? What experiences have you had that were dissimilar?
4. Sometimes it takes a defining moment or a critical incident in our lives to bring about a new understanding in the area of diversity, oppression, and discrimination. Describe a time when this happened to you. What was the outcome of such an experience?
5. Consider your self-narrative, how do you understand who you are at the core? How does coming to understand your privilege become part of your self-narrative? How does having this knowledge now impact your self-narrative?

REFERENCES

Anderson, S. K. (2015). Morally sensitive professionals. In D. Mower, P. Vandenberg, & W. Robison (Eds.), *Developing moral sensitivity* (pp. 188–204). New York, NY: Routledge.

Harro, B. (2013). The socialization cycle. In M. Adams, W. J. Blumenfeld, C. Castaneda, H. W. Hackman, M. L. Peters, & X. Zuniga (Eds.), *Readings for diversity and social justice* (3rd ed., pp. 45–52). New York, NY: Routledge

McIntosh, P. (2000). White privilege and male privilege: A personal account of coming to see correspondences through work in women's studies. In A. Minas (Ed.), *Gender basics: Feminist perspectives on women and men* (2nd ed., pp. 30–38). Belmont, CA: Wadsworth/Thomas Learning.

Owen, J. J., Tao, K., Leach, M. M., & Rodolfa, E. (2011). Clients' perceptions of their psychotherapists' multicultural orientation. *Psychotherapy, 48*(3), 274–282.

Spanierman, L. B., Todd, N. R., & Anderson, C. J. (2009). Psychological costs of racism to Whites: Understanding patterns among university students. *Journal of Counseling Psychology, 56,* 239–252.

Sue, D. W., Bucceri, J., Lin, A. I., Nadal, K. L., & Torino, G. C. (2007). Racial microaggressions and the Asian American experience. *Cultural Diversity and Ethnic Minority Psychology, 13,* 72–81.

Sue, D. W., & Sue, D. (2016). *Counseling the culturally diverse: Theory and practice* (7th ed.). New York, NY: John Wiley.

Wolfe, N. (1995). The racism of well-meaning white people. In M. Golden & S.R. Shreve, *Skin deep: Black and White women write about race* (pp. 37–46). New York, NY: Doubleday.

CHAPTER 2

WHITEOUT

Growing Out of the Problem of White Privilege

Heidi A. Zetzer

IDENTITY AND SOCIAL LOCATION

I am an educated, employed, White, heterosexual, 50-something woman who is 5 feet, 7 inches tall and weighs 110 pounds. I am spiritual but rarely go to church. I practice mindfulness (Brach, 2003; Germer, 2009) and study Buddhist psychology (Kornfield, 2009). I have a husband and two sons, ages 23 and 26. I grew up in the 1960s with an irreverent, hippie, artist father and a sympathetic, conventional, artist mother. I attended integrated public schools in Cleveland suburbs with lots of Christians and Jews. I lived in the midst of racist jokes and interracial relationships. Like many of my White contemporaries, I was raised to see myself as a color-blind individual (Neville, 2009) living in a cultural mosaic.

I come from a flock of aversive racists (Bonilla-Silva, 2014; Dovidio, Gaertner, Kawakami, & Hodson, 2002). No one I knew would ever admit to racist thoughts or actions, notions of White superiority, or fear of "the other," but the subtext was often there. The explicit message was that we are all created equal and the civil rights movement was a good thing. The implicit message was that Whites just happen to be better than Blacks at certain things, and affirmative action was a questionable thing. Praise for Black achievements belied the expectation of few accomplishments overall. Concerns for safety, housing prices, and miscegenation were characteristic of the private conversations that White families had with one another. White privilege was far outside anyone's consciousness, while fear of being called a racist was well inside it. The psychological discordance between the text and the subtext was very confusing. How could I be free of prejudice and filled with prejudicial thoughts? How could I be color-blind and react so viscerally to cultural differences? How could my Black friends and White friends be so similar and yet so different?

As a graduate student in counseling psychology in the mid-1980s, I participated in a variety of cross-cultural counseling courses and diversity workshops offered by prominent psychology programs at the cutting edge of multiculturalism. These experiences helped me comprehend the discord and led to a tremendous growth in my intellectual understanding of cultural differences. But on a deeper level, I was left unchanged. In the language of the Multicultural Change Intervention Matrix (Pope, Reynolds, & Mueller, 2014), I experienced first-order, but not second-order, change. For individuals, first-order change is characterized by increased awareness, knowledge, or skills, whereas second-order change results in a paradigm shift. I entered graduate school as a naive "well-meaning white person" (WMWP; Trepagnier, 2007), and I exited it as a knowledgeable one, but I still did not fully and deeply comprehend the impact of daily racism on people of color and the part that WMWPs (like me) play in its perpetuation (Yancy, 2015).

It was not until I held my first job as a university professor and joined a diverse team of multicultural educators that my perceptions of the world and myself began to change. I began a journey that is endless and essential. I started to understand what my colleagues of color; lesbian, gay, bisexual, transgender, and queer students; working-class and Jewish friends; and large-bodied companions had been telling me: that there are no breaks from the work of living in a multicultural community. Oppression is real, and advancing social justice is a difficult job (Talleyrand, Chung, & Bemak, 2006), one that is fraught with resistance to multiculturalism (Mio & Awakuni, 2000) and political change (Toporek & Williams, 2006). Once, while speaking to a colleague, I said that I was weary of the resistance that I encountered while teaching a multicultural awareness course to graduate psychology students. My colleague wanted to support me and offered, "Well, you won't have to deal with it when the quarter is over!" That might have been true if I had retreated into my White privilege, but I had come to the conclusion that the comfort of privilege was not worth its price. The cost to me and my friends was too great.

The purpose of this chapter is threefold. First, I introduce multicultural dialogue as a key ingredient to transformational learning—the kind that sinks into your bones and is remembered. Second, I describe a painful and critical incident in my own multicultural development that illustrates the value of dialogue as a constructive response to multicultural conflict. Finally, I offer my reflections on where I am now and how I hope to continue to "grow out of the problem" (Conoley & Conoley, 2009) of White privilege.

EDUCATOR AS STUDENT: WHITE RACIAL-IDENTITY DEVELOPMENT AND MULTICULTURAL DIALOGUE

Models of White racial-identity development (WRID; Spanierman & Soble, 2010; Sue & Sue, 2016) provide educators with benchmarks for their students' growth. But what if I apply one of these models to myself? I agree with the basic premises of these models, which assume that "No child is born wanting to be racist!" (Sue & Sue, 2016, p. 406) and that there is no protection from breathing the "smog" of cultural racism (Tatum, 2003,

p. 118). White people benefit from institutional and individual manifestations of racism (Bonilla-Silva, 2014), however indirectly or unintentionally, and the accrual of these benefits creates a dilemma for fair-minded White folks. How can I see myself as a just person when I willingly participate in a system that is inherently unfair? This dilemma has motivated my WRID.

If I apply Sue and Sue's (2016, pp. 389–424) seven-phase process model of WRID to myself, I can track my evolution from the *naiveté* and *conformity* phases of childhood, high school, and college (Phase 1 and Phase 2) to the *dissonance* phase of graduate school (Phase 3) to the *resistance/immersion* and *introspective* phases of my early career (Phase 4 and Phase 5) to now. Now, I see myself in Phase 6, *integrative awareness*. However, to get here, I first had to resolve the confusion I felt in the *introspective* phase.

When I was in Phase 5, I was in an existential crisis, disconnected, isolated, and confused. I was roiling around in a developmental eddy, asking, "What does it mean to be White? Who am I in relation to my whiteness?" And "Who am I as a racial/cultural being?" (Sue & Sue, 2016, p. 411).

Sometimes I felt like I was in a *White*out—lost in a blizzard of White privilege and unable to discern my next step. Personally, what I lacked was contact with White folks who were expanding or questioning their worldviews. I often felt isolated and alone. I felt supported by my White colleagues, but few were actively involved in moving themselves or the institution in the direction of multiculturalism. We did not connect with one another very easily. My insights into myself as a White woman were often painful. The further I went in my WRID, the less I cried for myself (feeling shame for my mistakes), and the more I cried for humanity (feeling sadness for the acts of violence or indifference that we perpetrate on one another).

I started to see how the tears of my wounded ego silenced the voices of my colleagues of color. My colleagues took steps to relieve my hurt feelings by quieting their own frustration or disdain to take care of me. I learned that I could listen to their accusations and their requests for accountability and search for the ways that I contributed to their concerns. When I was in graduate school, I responded to my classmates' confrontations instantly and automatically. I gave myself only two choices. I could (a) swallow their accusations whole or (b) reject them outright. Now, I am better at allowing myself time to reflect on their words before leaping to a response. I am less defensive and more open.

What brought me to this place? Like Kendall (2006), the reason I have matured as a multicultural being is due to relationships with colleagues and the dialogues that we have shared with each other. One of the greatest surges in my multicultural development came with my collaboration with three diverse colleagues: Juliet Betita (Filipina American), Keith Mar (Chinese American), and Muriel Shockley (African American).

We sat around my kitchen table with the intention of revising our university's Multicultural Awareness course, but we serendipitously discovered that our reciprocal disclosures about all types of oppression and privilege were more powerful and more meaningful than the literature we planned to provide our students. The topics of our meetings flowed spontaneously between course design and personal revelations about race, class, gender, and sexual orientation. We revealed our vulnerabilities gradually. Keith, Muriel, and Juliet described how they felt when someone made a racist comment, treated them differently because of their appearance, or ignored their racial identities. I disclosed my fear of cultural differences and being seen as racist. We also identified and examined various sources of privilege. For example, Keith holds male privilege, Muriel has class privilege, Juliet possesses heterosexual privilege, and I have White privilege, just to name a few. The multiplicity of our identities became undeniable. We confronted each other with respect and compassion. We learned to tolerate the discomfort of our differences, which allowed us to gain valuable insight into each other's perspectives.

We transformed these focused conversations into an approach to multicultural counselor training, which we called *multicultural dialogue* (MCD; Betita, Mar, Shockley, & Zetzer, 2001; Zetzer, Shockley, Mar, & Betita, 2000). We defined MCD as an authentic conversation about what it means to walk in the world as a member of a multicultural group. The purpose of MCD is for people to hear each other's stories and perspectives so that they can learn from each other and grow in ways that promote their racial/cultural identity development (or WRID). We modified Swindler's (1983, p. 1) 10 principles of interreligious dialogue for use in our classrooms.[1] The principles of MCD were designed as guideposts for students to use as they listened and responded to each other's experiences of and perspectives on oppression and privilege. For example, three of the principles call for students to allow each other to self-define, to abandon "hard-and-fast assumptions" about "the other," and to aim to experience someone else's culture from "within." We observed that MCD nurtured the presence of Rogers' (1957) core conditions in our classrooms and led to broadened perspectives on oppression, privilege, and multiculturalism.

When we developed MCD, the notion of dialogue as an interpersonal enzyme was not new (Bohm, 1996; Isaacs, 1999; Patterson, Grenney, McMillan, & Switzler, 2000; Sue, 2013; Sue et al., 2011). Even the application of MCD to diversity training had been done before (Ford, 2012; Murray-García, Harrell, Garcia, Gizzi, & Simms-Mackey, 2014; Stephan & Stephan, 2001; Wilcox, 2000). But we did one thing very differently. Keith, Muriel, Juliet, and I started the course with a 3-hour demonstration of MCD. This was an exciting teaching strategy for me. The four of us sat in a fishbowl with 60 students seated around us, and we provided them with our own version of *The Color of Fear* (Wah, 1994). For example, during one of our dialogue demonstrations, I confessed that I felt guilty for being White. Muriel replied that she saw White guilt as an impediment to change and urged me to "just get over it." I felt relief at hearing this because I thought that I was *supposed* to feel guilty when confronted with my racism or White privilege. Muriel's comments made me realize that my guilt was paralyzing me. My shame prevented me from empathizing with people of color and stymied me from striving for social justice.

Our demonstration of MCD was followed by instructor-facilitated dialogue throughout the remainder of the quarter. Our hope was that MCD would raise *student* consciousness. For me, however, the most powerful result was a major shift in my White identity. After that, I was absolutely certain that I would never be the same. I achieved a fuller understanding of my racial identity and privilege and a glimpse of myself as an agent of social change.

---

1. I am indebted to Dr. Jim Malarkey, from the McGregor School of Antioch University, for introducing me to Swindler's principles of interreligious dialogue.

THE BLINDING EFFECTS OF WHITE PRIVILEGE: A CRITICAL INCIDENT

This critical incident occurred after we had been teaching MCD for several years. I was still in the introspective phase of WRID (Phase 5) but thought that I had it mostly figured out. I was wrong. I was still in a *White*out, but this one was my own doing.

My personal reflections on this critical incident and the dialogues that followed it led me to three important insights. Each insight was precipitated by a "disorienting dilemma" (Mezirow, Taylor, & Assoc., 2009, p. 7) that challenged my sense of identity as a WMWP and helped me grow. I am grateful for this experience and to another one of my colleagues for nudging me forward. Here is my story.

I was part of a multisite faculty conference-design team, and I was responsible for facilitating the opening session on leadership. The purpose of the session was to describe what motivates someone to serve as a leader. A participant mentioned moral indignation as a driving force. I thought this was a productive avenue for elaboration, so I invited more responses on this topic, but my inquiry was met with blank looks. My anxiety started to rise, and I feared that I had gotten off track. I felt I needed help. So in a room comprising mostly White people, I looked to an African American colleague from another campus who was also on the design team and asked her to talk about how anger motivated her work in the field of social justice. I hadn't known her for long, but I had already had several conversations with her about her passion for this work, and I thought that her comments might deepen the discourse. Her facial expression told me instantly that she was angry with me. She politely declined to speak. There was a long, awkward pause. I found myself thinking, "Please say something! Please help me out!" She looked away from me and didn't say anything more.

FIRST INSIGHT

I was surprised by my colleague's reticence—baffled, really. What could I have done wrong? I was relieved when the large-group discussion ended and I could stop facilitating and start reflecting on my actions and her response. My realization of wrongdoing was sudden and distressing. I experienced that sinking, awful feeling associated with failing to grasp the situation until it's too late and wanting desperately to take it all back. My initial understanding of this critical incident was that I had failed to step outside of myself and consider the situation in which I was prompting my colleague to speak. It was unsafe. At the time, the atmosphere on her campus was rife with racial conflict, and my colleague was serving as the sole source of support for African American students. She was politically vulnerable. I knew this when I addressed her, but I lacked the sense to situate her in that context. I was blinded by my own needs and unconscious of the privilege afforded to me as a White woman in that setting (Wildman & Davis, 2000). As a White woman, I was free to speak without someone attributing my attitudes to my race. As a White woman, I could be seen as an individual and not a representative of a racial/ethnic group. As a White woman, I could assume that my perspective would not be challenged because of my race/ethnicity. As a White woman,

I arrived at the conference unhampered by a history of endless questions about my race or my racial perspective that are both part of being a "racial/ethnic minority" in the United States (Johnson, 2005; Kivel, 2011; Sue, 2013).

I felt tears in my eyes. My distress stemmed from my dismay over my own ineptitude and my fear of the impending confrontation. At a minimum, I had broken any sense of trust that might have existed between us. I had identified myself to my colleague as a conscientious White person, and I had proven myself to be an unconscious, privileged White person. I tried to talk to her right after the morning session, but she refused. She was visibly perturbed. Others asked me, "What happened? What's wrong?" None of the White people I talked to seemed to know what was awry.

We did not talk until later in the day. My colleague was furious with me. We sat in the presence of other team members and engaged in an MCD about my actions and her response. The conversation was extremely difficult and extremely valuable. Both of us made explicit efforts to understand and articulate each other's perspectives. As we spoke, we saw the institution's role in building the context for what happened between us. The lack of faculty diversity and absence of support for African American students were two factors that made the campus climate stressful. I gained a fuller understanding of what I had done and the impact my White privilege had on someone I admired.

SECOND INSIGHT

I had been in these situations before and had resisted taking responsibility for the unintended impact of my behavior. I used to leap to my own defense. This time, because of my previous dialogues with Keith, Muriel, and Juliet, I knew that it was vital for me to *reflect on my actions first*. This stance allowed me to hear some of what my colleague had to say. However, it was not until a full year later, after an e-mail exchange, that I gained some deeper insight into my behavior. My colleague wrote:

> Heidi,
> One of the elements that I think is very important when peeling back the onion (so to speak) as it relates to unlearning issues of oppression and privilege is the false sense of superiority that whites adopt/construct in their relationships with persons of color. I believe that is what you experienced with me, stay with me on this . . . the more you learn about how oppression operates, you learn that anger is a natural state in the unlearning process. However, liberation can be achieved through cognitive dissonance, which is also a natural stage that can be achieved in the unlearning oppression process. Oppression work is a journey, and the work feeds into the quality of our lives as human beings. (personal communication)

After first resisting and then contemplating this e-mail, I reached a deeper level of understanding. I came to realize that I had assumed too much—not about my colleague's willingness to speak or what she would have to say. I assumed that I could *define her contribution*. I assumed that I was *entitled* to do that. This was more than a facilitator's mistake; this was a *White* facilitator's mistake, and, of course, it was my mistake. Certainly, I aimed to avoid making the mistake again. In the distant past, I might have vowed to protect myself by halting my participation altogether—to avoid the risk and stay away from multicultural situations in which conflict might occur. However, I realized that I would not change and grow unless I maintained my commitment to "difficult dialogues" (Sue, 2015; Toporek & Worthington, 2014). I understood that I was unfinished in my multicultural development, and, as a result, I remained committed to increasing my multicultural competence (Falender, Burnes, & Ellis, 2013; Inman & Kreider, 2013; Sue & Sue, 2016). This commitment required me to continue participating in a multicultural community, to recognize my fallibility, own it, learn from it, and remain open to other people's experiences of me.

THIRD INSIGHT

Before I submitted the original version of this chapter to the editors, I requested feedback on it from my colleague. I was grateful to her for continuing to dialogue with me about historical events. My last insight was the most painful one. I did not understand this until much later, but it's clear that I ignored my colleague's right to confidentiality when I used my sociopolitical location (Watts-Jones, 2010) to elicit her disclosure of experiences and viewpoints, which she had shared *privately and in the context of the conference design team*. This was a disturbing realization for me, and a perfect illustration of the way in which unexamined White privilege destroys trust in multicultural relationships. I privileged my needs over her rights regarding confidential conversations without even realizing it. This latent insight gave me an opportunity to move in the direction of even greater congruence between my actions and my identity as a WMWP.

ANALYSIS

For people of color, the costs of racism and White privilege are evident on macro and micro levels (Alexander, 2012; Delgado & Stefancic, 2012; Neville, Worthington, & Spanierman, 2001). On a macro level, there are tremendous structural-economic disparities in our society (Bonilla-Silva, 2014; D'Andrea & Daniels, 2001; Sue & Sue, 2016). The legacies of historical oppression are evident in modern-day inequities (Alexander, 2012; Collins, 2009; Gordon, 2015; Takaki, 2008) and have yet to be completely undone. On a micro level, there is increasing awareness and understanding of the physical and psychological impact of racism for people of color (Brondolo et al., 2008; Brown et al., 2000; Clark, Anderson, Clark, & Williams, 1999; Contrada et al., 2000; Hoggard, Byrd, & Sellers, 2015; Lowe, Okubo, &Reilly, 2011; Thompson & Neville, 1999).

The costs of racism and White privilege for White folks, however, are less obvious. On a macro level, there is an astonishing loss of productivity, which affects the quality of life for everyone (Neville et al., 2001). On a micro level, the costs include, but are not limited to, loss of connection to one's ancestors, condemnation for affiliating with "those people," discomfort with people of color, and witnessing or participating in oppressive practices (Kivel, 2011; McConnell & Todd, 2015; Nissim-Sabat, 2015). Spanierman, Heppner, and Neville

(2002, p. 3) identified three overlapping domains in which Whites may experience the costs of racism: The costs of racism to Whites may be cognitive (e.g., distorted perceptions of reality, lack of knowledge of others, confusion regarding the coexistence of democracy and racial inequality); affective (e.g., fear of others, anger, and guilt); or behavioral (e.g., having relationships exclusively with other Whites, censoring oneself to avoid a perceived tension, being rejected by other Whites when challenging racism).

The varied dimensions of the costs of racism to Whites are referred to collectively as psychosocial costs. Spanierman and Heppner (2004) devised an instrument designed to measure these costs—the Psychosocial Costs of Racism to Whites Scale—and researchers have examined these costs over time (Sue, 2010; Todd, Spanierman, & Poteat, 2011). In my view, the costs associated with each of these domains converge at the crux of multicultural relationships.

One cost of racism and White privilege comes through the periodic resurrection of racist double binds in multicultural relationships. According to Mahmoud (1998), racist double binds are perpetrated when a person with more power or privilege torments a less powerful person by conveying contradictory overt and covert messages, which leave the respondent with no cost-free alternatives. If the respondent confronts the instigator of the double bind by identifying the contradictory messages, the instigator is likely to play the victim and accuse the respondent of being hostile, argumentative, or hypersensitive.

A typical example of this occurs when students of color are asked by their instructors to offer the Black/Latino/Indian/Asian person's perspective on a particular issue. The students risk appearing uncooperative or overly sensitive if they do not comply, but abiding by the request violates their integrity. The instructors are using their position to define the students' contributions, and students of color must accept this definition or risk being silenced or censured for their resistance. Other double binds are expressed in White-proffered statements such as "I don't see you as Mexican/Indian/Black. You aren't like the rest of them." People of color are left with two choices: (a) deny their own identity and be seen as good or (b) own their identity and be seen as bad.

I exercised my power and privilege in my attempt to define my colleague's contribution to the discussion on leadership. The *overt* message looked like an innocent invitation to speak, but the covert message was "Walk into this minefield because *I* need your help, and *my* needs (or the needs of the organization) supersede yours." Granted, I did not consciously concoct this situation, but I did initiate the dilemma. My colleague had two poor choices: (a) comply with my request and disclose privately held observations and opinions, which would have the effect of reinforcing White privilege, or (b) resist my request, which entailed the risk of appearing uncooperative or overly sensitive.

Mahmoud (1998) argues that narcissism is behind the double bind, and I have to agree (Zetzer, 2015). I asked my colleague to speak because I was worried about embarrassing myself. Later, I could not accept my colleague's reaction to me because it would damage my well-meaning White identity. The risks to me both during and after this critical incident were strictly *personal*. I could either (a) take a close look at myself and feel empathic remorse for hurting someone or (b) defend against this insight. The risk for my colleague was *personal and political*. She could decline to speak, or she could speak up. Both of these options were confounded with individual and institutional ramifications.

Oppression and privilege flow beneath the surface of multicultural relationships like an underground river. All parties are aware of it on one level or another. Every so often, the river rises and we have an opportunity to witness its impact and change its course. The critical incident I just described provided me with multiple revelations. I realized that I was likely to persist in putting my multicultural relationships at risk if I did not unpack my invisible backpack of privilege (McIntosh, 1989, 2015) and engage in antiracist actions. I also realized that it was getting harder to live in a state of incongruence. The dissonance between my well-meaning White identity and the impact of my behavior was like mental tinnitus. I was in a chronic state of discomfort.

As I matured as a person, I came to realize that I am dependent on the positive appraisals of people of color. Somehow, if I was deemed a "good White person," I could relax my vigilance and breathe a sigh of relief. This was faulty thinking. Even if I got preapproval as a "good White person," I would still make the mistakes that I do. I would still struggle with cultural delusions produced by privilege, and I would still unintentionally trample on the rights of my colleagues and friends. I realized that I could not leap ahead in my own WRID (Sue & Sue, 2016). One of my former students expressed this wish eloquently. She said, "I just want to *be*." I often found myself wishing for this kind of comfort; but I came to know, deep down, that I needed to find my voice and work toward greater congruence between how I see myself as a WMWP and how I behave in the world.

A WAY OUT OF THE *WHITE*OUT

The incident described in this chapter occurred more than 10 years ago. I have grown since then. Now I see myself in Phase 6 of WRID, *integrative awareness*. I am committed to a nonracist identity and to dismantling oppressive practices (Sue & Sue, 2016). However, despite Peggy McIntosh's admonition to see teaching and writing about White privilege as "bravely taking action," (2015, p. 19), I do not yet see myself as engaged in the final phase of WRID: commitment to antiracist actions (Phase 7). This is my current growth edge. Fortunately for me, I have a diverse group of friends and colleagues who are pulling me along. Our dialogues on race, gender, and class have prompted new reflections on my previous insights.

REFLECTIONS ON FIRST INSIGHT: 10+ YEARS LATER

There is a wonderful pop-psych book on narcissism (Hotchkiss, 2003) called *Why Is It Always About You?* This book comes to mind as I reflect on my first insight. I notice that my analysis is about *my* lack of understanding and *my* growth and what *I* need to do to be a better individual. I also notice that, even though I became more cognizant of racism in my own institution, I did not try to precipitate organizational change (Hurtado, Engberg, Ponjuan, & Landreman, 2002). This response reflects individualism, perfectionism, and color-blindness writ large, and all are associated with lower levels of cultural awareness (Wang, Castro, & Cunningham, 2014).

Individualism separates White folks (Triandis, 2001) from each other and prevents us from witnessing the collective impact of our neglect of social justice (Gordon, 2004). *Perfectionism* is double-edged (Stoeber & Otto, 2006). It motivates growth but also paralyzes people. My perfectionism prevented me from *listening* and "tarrying" long enough to truly understand the impact and insidiousness of White racism on my colleague and the system in which we worked. The following quote from Yancy (2015) captures the notion:

> The unfinished present is where I want whites to tarry, to recognize the complexity and weight of the current existence of white racism, to attempt to understand the way in which they perpetuate racism and to begin to think about the incredible difficulty involved when it comes to undoing white racism. (p. 107)

Finally, I notice that, when I asked my colleague to share her indignation, I ignored our racial identities and social locations. It was as if I was color-blind! *Color-blind racial attitudes* (Neville, Lilly, Duran, Lee, & Browne, 2000) are expressions of the new racism (Bonilla-Silva, 2003, 2014) and frequently serve as a cover for microaggressions (Sue, 2010). *Microaggressions* are "brief and commonplace daily verbal, behavioral, and environmental indignities, whether intentional or unintentional, that communicate hostile, derogatory, or negative racial, gender, sexual-orientation, and religious slights and insults to the target person or group" (Sue, 2010, p. 5). When confronted, I could have easily said, "But I don't see you as a Black person. I was just asking you about what makes your angry!" This would have been a *microinvalidation*, a denial of racism and its effect on my colleague and me. Unquestioned White privilege allows White folks (like me) to attend to or to ignore race when it suits us. This is a dance of denial, and it is a barrier to individual and institutional change.

REFLECTION ON SECOND INSIGHT: 10+ YEARS LATER

It is still difficult to read the email from my colleague that referred to the "false sense of superiority that whites adopt/construct in their relationships with persons of color" and not cringe with recognition. My colleague was absolutely correct in her report of how I located myself in relation to her. I felt entitled to write the social narrative for both of us—to *control* the discourse. Underneath my words was an assumption that she would cooperate; hence, my surprise when she did not follow the script.

Sue and Sue (2016, p. 394) remind us that "being a White person in this society means chronic exposure to ethnocentric monoculturalism as manifested in *White supremacy* (Hays, 2014)." This socialization was the foundation for my entitlement. It is virtually impossible for me to have grown up in the United States and not internalized such beliefs (Gallardo & Ivey, 2014). "To believe that one is somehow immune from inheriting such aspects of White supremacy is to be naive or to engage in self-deception" (Sue & Sue, 2016, p. 394). Condemning myself and swearing off multicultural relationships would not have eliminated my unconscious entitlement. So what is a conscientious and well-meaning White psychologist to do?

REFLECTION ON THIRD INSIGHT: 10+ YEARS LATER

By asking, "What do you want to achieve?" rather than "What do you want to avoid?" a positive psychologist would encourage me to "grow out of the problem" (Conoley, Plumb, Hawley, Spaventa-Vancil, & Hernández, 2015). Translating *avoidance goals* into *approach goals* will help me find a way out of this *White*out. So rather than aiming to avoid being seen as racist, I want

- to embody the Ethical Principles of Psychologists and Code of Conduct (American Psychological Association [APA], 2002, 2010); the Multicultural Guidelines on Training, Education, Research, Practice and Organizational Change for Psychologists (APA, 2003); and related guidelines (e.g., Guidelines for Psychological Practice With Transgender and Gender Nonconforming People; APA, 2015), which are intended to protect human dignity;
- to engage in advocacy and activism for social justice (Fouad, Gerstein, & Toporek, 2006); and
- to develop a White identity characterized by openness, authenticity, and a willingness to tarry long enough to feel the true impact of oppression and privilege by engaging in multicultural dialogue (Betita et al., 2001; Toporek & Worthington, 2014), no matter how difficult.

I want to be part of a communitarian culture (Johnson et al., 2014) that is grounded in compassionate confrontation and collective action. Most of all, I want to walk out of this *White*out and into the warmth of meaningful multicultural relationships that are unencumbered by racism and White privilege.

DISCUSSION QUESTIONS

1. In what ways are you oppressed? In what ways are you privileged?
2. How have your experiences of oppression and privilege shaped your willingness and ability to engage in multicultural dialogue?
3. Do you think that the author is speaking from a place of White guilt, political correctness, or both? How do you contrast these phenomena with ethical growth and development?
4. Do you think that the author was honest enough in her interpretation of this critical incident? Is the author's perspective still limited by her White privilege? Explain your response.

5. If you are a White person, how would you feel if someone asked you to talk about your anger regarding oppression and privilege in a room full of your friends or colleagues? Have you ever tried doing that? If *yes*, what happened? If *no*, why not?
6. Have you ever been confronted by someone who experienced your behavior as a microaggression? In what ways did you respond defensively? In what ways did you respond openly and with a willingness to learn?
7. What role do color-blind racial attitudes play in the perpetuation of racism and White privilege? Is it really possible to be color-blind?
8. What do you hope for yourself as you engage in your own journey of racial/cultural identity or WRID?
9. What do you hope for the world?

ACKNOWLEDGMENTS

I would like to express my appreciation to Sharon Anderson and Valerie Middleton for their editorial comments. Special praise is due to Richard Whitney and Michael Loewy for their valuable feedback during the construction of the original narrative. I feel especially grateful to Juliet Betita, Keith Mar, Muriel Shockley, A. J. Thoroughgood, and Jesse Valdez for their contributions to my multicultural development. Portions of this chapter were presented at the 109th Annual Convention of the American Psychological Association, San Francisco, California, August 2001.

REFERENCES

Alexander, M. (2012). *The new Jim Crow: Mass incarceration in the age of colorblindness.* New York, NY: New Press.

American Psychological Association. (2002). Ethical principles of psychologists and code of conduct. *American Psychologist, 57,* 1060–1073.

American Psychological Association. (2003). Guidelines on multicultural education, training, research, practice, and organizational change for psychologists. *American Psychologist, 58,* 377–402.

American Psychological Association. (2010). Amendments to the 2002 "Ethical principles of psychologists and code of conduct." *American Psychologist, 65*(5), 493.

American Psychological Association. (2015). Guidelines for psychological practice with transgender and gender nonconforming people. *American Psychologist, 70,* 832–864.

Betita, J., Mar, K., Shockley, M., & Zetzer, H. (2001, November). *Challenging racism, privilege, & oppression: Building bridges through multicultural dialogue.* Workshop presented at the Multicultural Center, University of California, Santa Barbara.

Bohm, D. (1996). *On dialogue.* New York, NY: Routledge.

Bonilla-Silva, E. (2003). New racism, color-blind racism, and the future of whiteness in America. In A. E. Doane & E. Bonilla-Silva (Eds.), *White out: The continuing significance of racism* (pp. 271–284). New York, NY: Routledge.

Bonilla-Silva, E. (2014). *Racism without racists: Color-blind racism and the persistence of racial inequality in America* (4th ed.). Lanham, MD: Rowman & Littlefield.

Brach, T. (2003). *Radical acceptance: Embracing your life with the heart of a Buddha.* New York, NY: Bantam Books.

Brondolo, E., Libby, D. J., Denton, E. G., Thompson, S., Beatty, D. L., Schwartz, J. Gerin, W. (2008). Racism and ambulatory blood pressure in a community sample. *Psychosomatic Medicine, 70,* 49–56. Retrieved from http://dx.doi.org/10.1097/PSY.0b013e31815ff3bd

Brown, T. N., Williams, D. R., Jackson, J. S., Neighbors, H. W., Torres, M., Sellers, S. L., & Brown, K. T. (2000). "Being Black and feeling blue": The mental health consequences of racial discrimination. *Race and Society, 2,* 117–131. doi:10.1016/S1090-9524(00)00010-3

Clark, R., Anderson, N. B., Clark, V. R., & Williams, D. R. (1999). Racism as a stressor for African Americans. *American Psychologist, 54,* 805–816.

Collins, P. H. (2009). *Black feminist thought: Knowledge, consciousness, and the politics of empowerment* (1st ed.). New York, NY: Routledge Classics.

Conoley, C. W., & Conoley, J. C. (2009). *Positive psychology and family therapy: Creative techniques and practical tools for guiding change and enhancing growth.* New York, NY: John Wiley.

Conoley, C. W., Plumb, E. W., Hawley, K. J., Spaventa-Vancil, K. Z., & Hernández, R. J. (2015). Integrating positive psychology into family therapy: Positive family therapy, *The Counseling Psychologist, 43,* 703–733. doi:10.1177/0011000015575392

Contrada, R. J., Ashmore, R. D., Gary, M. L., Coups, E., Egeth, J. D., Sewell, A., . . . Chasse, V. (2000). Ethnicity-related sources of stress and their effects on well-being. *Current Directions in Psychological Science, 9,* 136–139.

D'Andrea, M., & Daniels, J. (2001). Expanding our thinking about White racism: Facing the challenge of multicultural counseling in the 21st century. In J. G. Ponterotto, J. M. Casas, L. A. Suzuki, & C. M. Alexander (Eds.), *Handbook of multicultural counseling* (2nd ed., pp. 289–310). Thousand Oaks, CA: SAGE.

Delgado, R., & Stefancic, J. (2012). *Critical race theory: An introduction* (2nd ed.). New York, NY: New York University Press.

Dovidio, J. F., Gaertner, S. L., Kawakami, K., & Hodson, G. (2002). Why can't we just get along? Interpersonal bias and interracial distrust. *Cultural Diversity & Ethnic Minority Psychology, 8,* 88–102.

Falender, C. A., Burnes, T. R., & Ellis, M. V. (2013). Multicultural clinical supervision and benchmarks: Empirical support informing practice and supervisor training. *The Counseling Psychologist, 41,* 8–27. doi:10.1177/0011000012438417.

Ford, K. A. (2012). Shifting White ideological scripts: The educational benefits of inter- and intraracial curricular dialogues on the experiences of White college students. *Journal of Diversity in Higher Education, 5,* 138–158. doi:10.1037/a0028917

Fouad, N. A., Gerstein, L. H., & Toporek, R. L. (2006). Social justice and counseling psychology in context, In R. L. Toporek, L. H. Gerstein, N. A. Fouad, G. Roysircar, & T. Israel (Eds.), *The handbook for social justice in counseling psychology: Leadership, vision, and action* (pp. 1–16). Thousand Oaks, CA: SAGE.

Gallardo, M. E., & Ivey, A. (2014). What I see could be me. In M. E. Gallardo (Ed.), *Developing cultural humility* (pp. 223–263). Thousand Oaks, CA: SAGE.

Germer, C. K. (2009). *The mindful path to self-compassion: Freeing yourself from destructive thoughts and emotions.* New York, NY: Guilford Press.

Gordon, L. R. (2004). Critical reflections on three popular tropes in the study of whiteness. In G. Yancy (Ed.), *What white looks like: African-American philosophers on the whiteness question* (pp. 173–194). New York, NY: Routledge.

Gordon, L. R. (2015). White privilege and the problem of affirmative action. In B. Bergo & T. Nicholls (Eds.). *"I don't see color": Personal and critical reflections on white privilege* (pp. 25–38). University Park: Pennsylvania State University Press.

Hays, P. A. (2014). Finding a place in the multicultural revolution. In M. E. Gallardo (Ed.), *Developing cultural humility* (pp. 49–59). Thousand Oaks, CA: SAGE.

Hoggard, L. S., Byrd, C. M., & Sellers, R. M. (2015). The lagged effects of racial discrimination on depressive symptomatology and interactions with racial identity. *Journal of Counseling Psychology, 62,* 216–225. doi:10.1037/cou0000069

Hotchkiss, S. (2003). *Why is it always about you? The seven deadly sins of narcissism.* New York, NY: Free Press.

Hurtado, S., Engberg, M. E., Ponjuan, L., & Landreman, L. (2002). Students' precollege preparation for participation in a diverse democracy. *Research in Higher Education, 43,* 163–186. doi:10.1023/A:1014467607253

Inman, A. G., & Kreider, E. D. (2013). Multicultural competence: Psychotherapy practice and supervision. *Psychotherapy, 50,* 346–350. doi:10.1037/a0032029

Isaacs, W. (1999). *Dialogue and the art of thinking together: A pioneering approach to communicating in business and in life.* New York, NY: Random House.

Johnson, A. G. (2005). *Privilege, power, and difference* (2nd ed.). Boston, MA: McGraw-Hill.

Johnson, W. B., Barnett, J. E., Elman, N. S., Forrest, L., Schwartz-Mette, R., & Kaslow, N. J. (2014). Preparing trainees for lifelong competence: Creating a communitarian training culture. *Training and Education in Professional Psychology, 8*(4), 211–220. doi:http://dx.doi.org/10.1037/tep0000048

Kendall, F. E. (2006). *Understanding White privilege: Creating pathways to authentic relationships across race.* New York, NY: Routledge.

Kivel, P. (2011). *Uprooting racism: How White people can work for racial justice* (3rd ed.). Gabriola Island, BC: New Society Publishers.

Kornfield, J. (2009). *The wise heart: A guide to the universal teachings of Buddhist psychology.* New York, NY: Bantam Books.

Lowe, S. M., Okubo, Y., & Reilly, M. F. (2012). A qualitative inquiry into racism, trauma, and coping: Implications for supporting victims of racism. *Professional Psychology: Research and Practice, 43*(3), 190.

Mahmoud, V. M. (1998). The double binds of racism. In M. McGoldrick (Ed.), *Re-visioning family therapy: Race, culture, and practice* (pp. 255–267). New York, NY: Guilford Press.

McConnell, E. A., & Todd, N. R. (2015). Differences in White privilege attitudes and religious beliefs across racial affect types. *The Counseling Psychologist, 43,* 1135–1161. doi:10.1177/0011000015610436

McIntosh, P. (1989). White privilege: Unpacking the invisible knapsack. *Peace and Freedom,* July/August, 8–10.

McIntosh, P. (2015). Deprivileging philosophy. In B. Bergo & T. Nicholls (Eds.). *"I don't see color": Personal and critical reflections on white privilege* (pp. 13–24). University Park: Pennsylvania State University Press.

Mezirow, J., Taylor, E. W., & Associates. (Eds.). (2009). *Transformative learning in practice: Insights from community, workplace, and higher education.* Hoboken, NJ: John Wiley.

Mio, J. S., & Awakuni, G. I. (2000). *Resistance to multiculturalism: Issues and interventions.* Philadelphia, PA: Brunner/Mazel.

Murray-Garcia, J. L., Harrell, S., Garcia, J. A., Gizzi, E., & Simms-Mackey, P. (2014). Dialogue as skill: Training a health professions workforce that can talk about race and racism. *American Journal of Orthopsychiatry, 84,* 590–596. doi:10.1037/art0000026

Neville, H. A. (2009). Rationalizing the racial order: Racial color-blindness as a legitimizing ideology. In T. Koditschek, S. K. ChaJua, & H. A. Neville (Eds.), *Race struggles* (pp. 115–133). Champaign: University of Illinois Press.

Neville, H. A., Lilly, R., Duran, G., Lee, R., & Browne, L. (2000). Construction and initial validation of the Color-Blindness Racial Attitudes Scale (CoBRAS). *Journal of Counseling Psychology, 47,* 59–70. doi:10.1037/0022-0167.47.1.59

Neville, H. A., Worthington, R. L., Spanierman, L. B. (2001). Race, power, and multicultural counseling psychology. In J. G. Ponterotto, J. M. Casas, L. A. Suzuki, & C. M. Alexander (Eds.), *Handbook of multicultural counseling* (2nd ed., pp. 257–288). Thousand Oaks, CA: SAGE.

Nissim-Sabat, M. (2015). Revisioning "White privilege." In B. Bergo & T. Nicholls (Eds.). *"I don't see color": Personal and critical reflections on white privilege* (pp. 39-49). University Park: Pennsylvania State University Press.

Patterson, K., Grenny, J., McMillan, R., & Switzler, A. (2000). *Better than duct tape: Dialogue tools for getting results and getting along.* Plano, TX: Pritchett, Rummler-Brache.

Pope, R. L., Reynolds, A. L., & Mueller, J. A. (2014). *Creating multicultural change on campus.* San Francisco, CA: Jossey-Bass.

Rogers, C. R. (1957). The necessary and sufficient conditions of therapeutic personality change. *Journal of Consulting Psychology, 21,* 95–103.

Spanierman, L. B., & Heppner, M. J. (2004). Psychosocial Costs of Racism to Whites Scale (PCRW): Construction and initial validation. *Journal of Counseling Psychology, 51,* 249–262. doi:10.1037/0022-0167.51.2.249

Spanierman, L. B., Heppner, M. J., & Neville, H. A. (2002, August). *Psychosocial Costs of Racism to Whites Scale: Measuring the construct.* Poster presented at the annual convention of the American Psychological Association, Chicago, IL.

Spanierman, L. B., & Soble, J. R. (2010). Understanding Whiteness: Previous approaches and possible directions in the study of White racial attitudes and identity. In J. G. Ponterotto, J. M. Casas, L. A. Suzuki, & C. M. Alexander (Eds.), *Handbook of multicultural counseling* (3rd ed., pp. 283–299). Thousand Oaks, CA: SAGE.

Stephan, W. G., & Stephan, C. W. (2001). *Improving intergroup relations.* Thousand Oaks, CA: SAGE.

Stoeber, J., & Otto, K. (2006). Positive conceptions of perfectionism: Approaches, evidence, challenges. *Personality and Social Psychology Review, 10,* 295–319. doi:10.1207/s15327957pspr1004_2

Sue, D. W. (2010). *Microaggressions in everyday life: Race, gender, and sexual orientation.* New York, NY: John Wiley.

Sue, D. W. (2013). Race talk: The psychology of racial dialogues. *American Psychologist, 68,* 663–372. doi:10.1037/a0033681

Sue, D. W. (2015). *Race talk and the conspiracy of silence: Understanding and facilitating difficult dialogues on race.* New York, NY: John Wiley.

Sue, D. W., Rivera, D. P., Watins, N. L., Kim, R. H., Kim, S., & Williams, C. D. (2011). Racial dialogues: Challenges faculty of color face in the classroom. *Cultural Diversity & Ethnic Minority Psychology, 17,* 331–340. doi:10.1037/a0024190

Sue, D. W., & Sue, D. (2016). *Counseling the culturally diverse: Theory to practice* (7th ed.). New York, NY: John Wiley.

Swindler, L. (1983). The dialogue decalogue: Ground rules for interreligious, interideological dialogue. *Journal of Ecumenical Studies, 20,* 1–4.

Takaki, R. (2008). *In a different mirror: A history of multicultural America* (rev. ed.). New York, NY: Back Bay Books/Little Brown.

Talleyrand, R. M., Chung, R. C. C., & Bemak, F. (2006). Incorporating social justice in counselor training programs: A case study example. In R. L. Toporek, L. H. Gernstein, N. A. Fouad, G. Roysircar, & T. Israel (Eds.), *Handbook for social justice in counseling psychology: Leadership, vision, & action* (pp. 44–58). Thousand Oaks, CA: SAGE.

Tatum, B. (2003). *Why are all the Black kids sitting together in the cafeteria? And other conversations about race* (5th anniv. rev. ed.). New York, NY: Basic Books.

Thompson, C. E., & Neville, H. A. (1999). Racism, mental health, and mental health practice. *The Counseling Psychologist, 27,* 155–223.

Todd, N. R., Spanierman, L. B., & Poteat, V. P. (2011). Longitudinal examination of the psychosocial costs of racism to Whites across the college experience. *Journal of Counseling Psychology, 58,* 508–521. doi:10.1037/a0025066

Toporek, R. L., & Williams, R. A. (2006). Ethics and professional issues related to the practice of social justice in counseling psychology. In R. L. Toporek, L. H. Gernstein, N. A. Fouad, G. Roysircar, & T. Israel (Eds.),

Handbook for social justice in counseling psychology: Leadership, vision, & action (pp. 17–34). Thousand Oaks, CA: SAGE.

Toporek, R. L., & Worthington, R. L. (2014). Integrating service learning and difficult dialogues pedagogy to advance social justice training. *The Counseling Psychologist, 42,* 919–945. doi:10.1177/0011000014545090

Trepagnier, B. (2007). *Silent racism: How well-meaning white people perpetuate the racist divide.* New York, NY: Routledge.

Triandis, H. C. (2001). Individualism-collectivism and personality. *Journal of Personality, 69,* 907–924. doi:10.1111/1467-6494.696169

Wah, L. M. (Dir.). (1994). *The color of fear* [video recording]. Available from Stir-Fry Productions, Oakland, CA.

Wang, K. T., Castro, A. J., & Cunningham, Y. L. (2014). Are perfectionism, individualism, and racial color-blindness associated with less cultural sensitivity? Exploring diversity awareness in White prospective teachers. *Journal of Diversity in Higher Education, 3,* 211–225. doi:10.1037/a0037337

Watts-Jones, T. D. (2010). Location of self: Opening the door to dialogue on intersectionality in the therapy process. *Family Process, 49,* 405–406. Retrieved from http://dx.doi.org/10.1111/j.1545-5300.2010.01330.x

Wilcox, D. (2000, February). *Deliberative dialogue: A different kind of talk, another way to act.* Paper presented at the Summit on Blacks in Higher Education, American Association for Higher Education Black Caucus, Savannah State University, Savannah, GA.

Wildman, S. M., & Davis, A. D. (2000). Language and silence: Making systems of privilege visible. In R. Delgado & J. Stefancic (Eds.), *Critical race theory: The cutting edge* (2nd ed., pp. 657–663). Philadelphia, PA: Temple University Press.

Yancy, G. (2015). Whiteness as insidious: On the embedded opaque White racist self. In B. Bergo & T. Nicholls (Eds.), *"I don't see color": Personal and critical reflections on white privilege* (pp. 103–118). University Park: Pennsylvania State University Press.

Zetzer, H. A. (2015). White privilege: The luxury of undivided attention. In B. Bergo & T. Nicholls (Eds.), *"I don't see color": Personal and critical reflections on white privilege* (pp. 119–134). University Park: Pennsylvania State University Press.

Zetzer, H. A., Shockley, M. E., Mar, K., & Betita, J. V. (2000, August). Dismantling resistance with self-disclosure: Dialogue as innovation in multicultural training. Paper presentation. In J. N. Valdez (Chair), *Overcoming resistance, achieving transformation: Innovations in teaching multicultural counseling skills.* Symposium conducted at the annual meeting of the American Psychological Association, Washington, DC.

Correspondence concerning this chapter should be addressed to Heidi A. Zetzer, PhD, Director, Hosford Counseling & Psychological Services Clinic, Department of Counseling, Clinical, & School Psychology, 1151 Education Building, University of California, Santa Barbara, CA 93106-9490. Electronic mail may be sent to hzetzer@education.ucsb.edu

CHAPTER 3

THE CHALLENGE OF ACCEPTING WHITE PRIVILEGE AFTER LIVING A LIFE OF POVERTY

Deborah Megivern Foster

The field of social work has a Code of Ethics that specifies social workers must be educated in dimensions of oppression, privilege, and diversity. They also must be able to utilize their knowledge to work effectively with people of all races, classes, sexual orientations, and disability statuses. But just because something is stipulated in a code of ethics does not mean people automatically adhere to its tenets (Wade, 1993). In addition, social workers can believe they are following the Code of Ethics by practicing cultural competence, but their lack of awareness of their own privilege affects how ethically sensitive they actually are. This lack of awareness can have very negative consequences for the clients whom social workers serve. Clients can feel alienated from or misunderstood by their providers.

That's why, as a social-work diversity educator, I was so invested in helping my students learn about their biases in order to prevent harm to future clients. This process involves asking students to take inventory of the ways in which their identity has given them unearned advantages in life. Being aware of these advantages helps social workers to understand where their clients are coming from when they express pain from oppression. But that still didn't mean that I had overcome all of my own issues. Specifically, I was struggling to acknowledge my own privileges, especially my race privilege.

UNDERSTANDING AND EXPERIENCING WHITE PRIVILEGE: DEBORAH'S STORY

Even after nearly eight years in a graduate social work program—in an environment in which discussion of oppression and privilege occurred frequently, I still had trouble with the idea that I had personally benefitted from any advantages. My challenge was the intersection of being White and growing up poor. I struggled with acknowledging my White privilege when I could not get over feeling deprived by lifelong disadvantages. Educating others around me who just didn't "get" economic or class oppression drew my attention away from my race privilege. It didn't have to be a competition between economic oppression and White privilege, but that's what I made it.

When I became a diversity educator, I saw a strong pattern for White students from low-income backgrounds to do the same thing. They thought their lack of economic privilege meant they didn't have White privilege, just like I did. They were concerned about issues such as how perceived socioeconomic discrimination against low-socioeconomic status (SES) people is a chronic social-environmental stressor. This concern is justified by research showing that health is affected by allostatic load or stress load. In one study, 3% of allostatic load was social class discrimination (Fuller-Rowell, Evans, & Ong, 2012). Another study found 43% of low-SES students reported they had experienced institutional classism at their college (Langhout, Rosselli, & Feinstein, 2007).

The poor and working-class White students I was working with weren't aware of other national research that showed White working-class people actually have a stronger propensity to be racially prejudiced (Carvacho et al., 2013). Evidence for this can be seen in their strong support for the continued use of the Confederate flag in public places, as measured in a randomized survey (73% White working-class versus 45% of White middle/upper-class Americans) and their denial of racial discrimination against people of color (61% White working-class versus 45% for White middle/upper-class Americans) (Jones, Cox, Cooper, & Lienesch, 2015). White working-class students aren't aware that White people have a demonstrated racial bias to believe African Americans *feel less pain and suffering* when they experience injury or illness (Traywalter, Hoffman, & Waytz, 2012).

Jones et al. (2015) found that 87% of African Americans report they experience racism, but only 57% of White Americans acknowledge racism against African Americans. Nearly 60% of White Americans believe the United States has made sufficient changes to make the races equal, while only 12% of African Americans agree with this (Jones et al., 2015).

Reserve discrimination is the belief that minorities are being given preferential treatment, despite the fact that study after study finds employment discrimination is still against people of color, and not White people (Nunley, Pugh, Romero, & Seals, 2015; Pager, Western, & Bonikowski, 2009). Jones et al. (2015) found that, while nearly half of White Americans believe reverse discrimination occurs, only 29% of Latino/a respondents and 25% of African American respondents endorsed reverse discrimination as a problem. Moreover, 60% of poor and working-class Whites believe in reverse discrimination, versus 36% of middle/upper-class White Americans who do.

Again, the research data do not support the White viewpoint on reverse discrimination, and this is true in both employment and other areas of life. Many studies suggest discrimination against people of color is the reality in securing housing (e.g., Turner et al., 2013), obtaining finances for buying a home (e.g., Ross, Turner, Godfrey, & Smith, 2008), and being serviced in public accommodations (e.g., Pager & Shepherd, 2008).

ROOTS OF AN IDENTITY

Although I am a White, heterosexual, young woman, the identity most salient throughout my life has been "poor trash"—a welfare child. Many life experiences reinforced the importance of this identity over the more privileged identities I appreciate. Both of my parents suffered from psychiatric illnesses. My mother received disability payments, and my father was employed as a janitor, which meant minimal income. Economic struggles within my family led to bouts with homelessness, daily reliance on the Salvation Army for meals, and dependence on charity from public and private sources. Lack of food and heat led child protective services to remove my siblings and me from my parents, to be placed in foster care. We were eventually returned to our parents, but the strain of family separation and poverty led my parents to divorce shortly thereafter. My mother became a single parent to six children, while my father moved into a roach-infested, single-room-occupancy hotel.

The neighborhood in which we were being raised was dangerous and dilapidated. Indeed, the rampant negative influences likely contributed significantly to the fact that three of my younger siblings were mandated to services within the juvenile justice system, and two of them became drug dependent. Eventually, one of my brothers committed suicide. I will always be convinced that poverty and our childhood life circumstances played the largest role in his death.

My departure from this life of poverty at the age of 17 was the result of support from family and friends, an extensive series of governmental interventions (ranging from Head Start to Project Upward Bound), and a natural inclination toward academia. As I was driven off to college, I felt relieved to have escaped that life of dispossession. Unfortunately, the feeling was short-lived, for it was during college and graduate school that I discovered the seemingly permanent effects of my economic history. My identity, the essence of who I am, had been shaped by adapting to long-term poverty. The majority of my classmates came from middle-class to upper-middle-class families. There were daily reminders of our differences.

In political science and economics classes, my privileged college classmates degraded welfare recipients. I was too frightened of social exclusion to speak up. Instead, I silently sat in isolation, absorbing the significant social distance between us. Outside of class, many acquaintances were frustrated with my seeming unwillingness to spend more time with them in social activities and less time at work. They did not understand that, for me, work was not a choice.

My full-time work schedule throughout college did not allow much time for socializing. Whether I was serving other students food at the school's cafeteria during the day or taking their orders at the popular local restaurant in the evening, I would overhear college classmates complaining about reductions in their allowances from $500 a month to $250. They did not have to pay for their college expenses; they even got an allowance. They did not need to work. I fantasized about what that would be like. It was hard not to feel bitter as my own course work often got behind in a heavy workweek. Chronic fatigue also made me prone to headaches, stomach pain, and colds.

The burden of poverty lingered tangibly as well during graduate school. Each life step I took continued to be plagued by economic hardship. As a graduate student, I found myself in the role of parent. I obtained custody of my two youngest siblings, accumulating more than $125,000 in student-loan debt while attempting to raise them on a graduate student's stipend and other meager employment. It was under these life circumstances of relative deprivation that I studied oppression and privilege in my graduate classes and learned extensively about White privilege. Certainly, it felt to me as though my entire life had been defined by deprivation. If there were White privileges to be recognized, I could not see them. In my mind, what-on-earth good had it done for me to be White? It had not spared me hunger, frostbite, lice, poor medical care, ridicule, violence, or trauma. This feeling of deprivation was especially true in academia because the vast majority of graduate students, including students of color, had spent their lives in material comfort and security.

THE EMBERS OF TRANSFORMATION

Eventually, I gained an intellectual, if not intuitive, understanding of privilege through my graduate program. Vowing to continue work on my own issues of privilege, I decided to become a cofacilitator with a well-regarded lead instructor, Dr. Michael Spencer, in 1999. Dr. Spencer offered multicultural dialogue groups as a major means for learning about social justice, oppression, and privilege in his Contemporary Cultures in the United States class at the University of Michigan. Though I maintained the goal of focusing on my privileged identities, I often felt ambivalent. On the one hand, I felt guilt and defensiveness at being blamed for my culpability in race oppression, as class members of color described their experiences. On the other hand, I felt envy and bitterness toward those individuals who had been economically privileged throughout their lives. I craved their basic privilege of getting fundamental needs met and the sense of security that elicited.

About midsemester, I was asked by Dr. Spencer to give a presentation on classism and poverty. He knew this was an area I knew a lot about because I sought him out for reassurance when I dealt with classism in the highly upper-class environment of graduate school. As I presented general information to the class, I shared specific details from my personal experiences to give fellow students a sense of how economic labeling and stigmatization make an impact. At one point, I showed the class a Child Protective Services document that declared me guilty of child neglect when I left two of my siblings in the house while I went to rescue another younger brother being beaten by kids at the local park. I was 12 years old at the time. We discussed whether the guilty verdict would have occurred for a middle-class family under the same circumstances, and most class members agreed that it likely would not have.

The presentation stirred a mix of emotions in me. To share the lack of power, the deprivation, and the humiliation of my past was empowering. Nonetheless, the stigma of poverty and child neglect, even though I was only 12 years old when this happened, still stung. I felt I had performed a duty to other poor people by telling our story, but the cost was shame that took weeks to shake off.

At the end of the presentation, an African American graduate student I respected a great deal approached me. She told me honestly, "I feel bad for you; but to be blunt, by the end of your talk, I was still thinking, 'So what? You're still White.' I guess I think that being White makes a big difference." Her words stung; her expression seemed defiant and accusatory.

It felt as though my oppression was deniable, because I was White. The weight of race oppression was her burden. To me, it seemed as if she could not see my burden of class oppression or her own class privilege as long as her awareness stayed entirely within race oppression. Another African American friend from a poverty background pointed out to me, "Listen, I went through most of what you did, *plus* I had to deal with racism on top of that."

Later on when I recollected these exchanges, the importance of accepting my White privilege finally became clear to me on an emotional level. If I was unwilling to move beyond my oppression to also recognize my privilege, how could I expect anyone else to do as much with their privilege? When I started thinking about class as intersecting with race, I saw that everything negative about being poor happened to poor People of Color too, and, as I had been reminded, a great many People of Color had to deal with racism on top of class oppression.

This realization meant I was going to have to really attend to all of the daily instances in which my race advantaged me. If I applied for an apartment, I knew any rejection would be because I didn't have enough credit, and not because I was White. In my community, police officers chronically stopped my neighbors for "driving while Black," while I cruised by without significant worry of harassment. I did not have to question whether my race was a factor if I was stopped. During middle school, my best friend, because of her race, was told by a group of White men to stay on her side of town when we went to McDonald's together. I had never been told I had to leave an area because of my race, even though I grew up in a predominantly African American neighborhood. Growing up, I had personally witnessed millions of examples of White privilege, but I had not focused on these. As I became more willing to explore the totality of my life circumstances, I became more conscious of my privileged identity and not just my oppressed identity.

During this period of awakening and transformation, I was fortunate to have the guidance of authors such as June Jordan (2001), who taught me that oppressed people have to examine their privileges just as often as they grapple with their oppression. Jordan wrote about an African woman and an Irish woman joining in solidarity to solve a problem: "It was not who they both were but what they both know, and what they were both preparing to do about what they know, that was going to make them both free at last" (p. 44). This was the lesson. Without understanding my White privilege—privilege being the constant companion to oppression, I could not know or work against either class or race oppression.

So I planned to appreciate my White privilege, notice it, and then work to extend these privileges to others. For example, in 2003 when I was a new professor, I was riding on a city train. A beautiful African American child, about 4 years old, was smiling and talking to passengers. When this little girl and her mother exited the train, a White man with all of the markers of being from a lower-class background made a derogatory comment about the young girl's hair, which had been combed out to a full Afro. I winced to hear his insensitive and disparaging views. He was part of the system of White oppression, a blatant racist asserting cultural dominance based on skin-color privilege. Only a few moments later, an aging African American male trudged up the aisle of the train carrying a mop and a bucket. He looked weary, confined to cleaning up the mess made by other people on train cars.

This story is relevant in my transformation because my previous instincts would have been to overlook what I had in common with the White man who asserted his white supremacy. Instead, I would have felt united with the poverty of the janitor, feeling connected to him by the fact that I had scrubbed my share of toilets, and because my father has been a janitor most of his life. I would not have focused on what I had in common with the lower-class White person, or how I personally benefitted from systemic oppression based on race.

However, this time, I understood in that moment the privilege of being White, and I reminded myself how my race had almost certainly played a beneficial role in my escape from poverty. How many people had just assumed, in part because I am White, that I was bright and easily educated? How often had my merits been recognized where they may have been overlooked if I had darker skin? Instead of denying what I had in common with the racist White man, I recognized that I was exceptionally blessed to be a college graduate, enjoying my free time, having the funds to pay for leisure, and possessing the capabilities to avoid doing the kind of work that would put that immutable wearied look on my face. This middle-aged African American man was still stuck in poverty, while I was not. That's true on a wider scale too, and I know it. White people are more likely to experience upward mobility (Mazumder, 2014).

More and more, I recognize that I am fortunate to have had experiences with being disadvantaged. The circumstances of my life have allowed me to develop an empathy that has resulted in deeper interpersonal relationships with others. The weight of oppression has alerted me to the need to participate actively in efforts to change societal injustices. I have come to consider much of what is White privilege as a set of basic rights all people should be entitled to. I am working, through social and political action, dialogue in classes, and constant reexamination of my self-awareness, to challenge the oppression-privilege dichotomy. There is a certain gift in feeling as if, just maybe, I might be a part of the solution.

THE REPEATING PROCESS OF SELF-EXAMINATION: CONCLUSIONS

Examining one's own privileged status is a constant process. I have had to continually revisit my status as a member of oppressing groups (e.g., White, heterosexual). Freire (1970) called this repeated process of self-examination "critical consciousness." Specifically, I have to repeatedly remind myself that I cannot expect others to examine their economic privileges if I am not willing to work on owning my White privilege. I knew the vexation that came from waiting for others to accept their class advantages. The fact that economically secure people took for granted their safe neighborhoods, regular meals, and designer clothes always seemed to make poverty worse. Instead of concentrating on my frustrations with those middle- and upper-class people, I needed to regularly acknowledge the advantages White people have over people of color (Carvacho et al., 2013). One of the most important things to do is actively listen when you are an ally. It is what makes me feel validated when it comes to classism, and, from my experience, it is what makes people who have experiences with racism feel validated.

DISCUSSION QUESTIONS

1. How does the complication of overlapping identities affect this author's struggle to identify her race privilege?
2. Describe in your own words the author's new awareness of intersectionality. Then consider your own social identities and try to identify any transformative experiences related to oppression and privilege from your own life.
3. How might someone such as the author interact with a client from a different race now in contrast to before her self-exploration and transformation?
4. The author states that White privilege is mostly a set of basic rights that all people should be entitled to receive. First, give examples of White privilege that go beyond basic rights. How would White individuals relinquish an unearned privilege of this nature?
5. In what ways could you demonstrate the importance of *critical consciousness* and continual self-reflection as a crucial component of cultural competence for mental health practice?
6. The author repeatedly describes feelings of marginalization related to her mixed identity of being both poor and White. She laments the lack of community, based on class, in higher education. In what ways might colleges and universities transform their environments to encourage people to collaborate across nontraditional social identity groups?
7. How might a student from outside the United States view the dynamics of class and race in the United States after reading this author's story?

REFERENCES

Carvacho, H., Zick, A., Haye, A., Gonzalez, R., Manzi, J., Kocik. C., & Bertl, M. (2013). On the relation between social class and prejudice: The roles of education, income and ideological attitudes, *European Journal of Social Psychology, 43*(4), 272–285.

Freire, P. (1970). *Pedagogy of the oppressed.* New York, NY: Continuum.

Fuller-Rowell, T. E., Evans, G. W., & Ong, A. D. (2012). Poverty and health: The mediating role of perceived discrimination, *Psychological Science, 23*(7), 734–739.

Jones, R. P., Cox, D., Cooper, B., & Lienesch, R. (2015). *Anxiety, nostalgia, and mistrust: Findings from the 2015 American Values Survey.* Public Religion Research Institute. Retrieved from http://publicreligion.org/site/wp-content/uploads/2015/11/PRRI-AVS-2015.pdf

Jordan, J. (2001). Report from the Bahamas. In M. Andersen & P. Hill Collins (Eds.), *Race, class, and gender: An anthology* (4th ed., pp. 35–44). Belmont, CA: Wadsworth.

Langhout, R. D., Rosselli, F., & Feinstein, J. (2007). Assessing classism in academic settings. *The Review of Higher Education, 30*(2), 145–184.

Mazumder, B. (2014). Black–White differences in intergenerational economic mobility in the United States. *Economic Perspectives, 38*(1), 1–18.

Nunley, J. M., Pugh, A., Romero, N., & Seals, R. A. (2015). Racial discrimination in the labor market for recent college graduates: Evidence from a field experiment. *The B.E. Journal of Economic Analysis & Policy, 15*(3), 1093–1125.

Pager, D., & Shepherd, H. (2008). The sociology of discrimination: Racial discrimination in employment, housing, credit, and consumer markets. *Annual Review of Sociology, 34*, 181–209.

Pager, D., Western, B., & Bonikowski, B. (2009). Discrimination in a low-wage labor market a field experiment. *American Sociological Review, 74*(5), 777–799.

Ross, S. L., Turner, M. A., Godfrey, E., & Smith, R. R. (2008). Mortgage lending in Chicago and Los Angeles: A paired testing study of the pre-application process. *Journal of Urban Economics, 63*(3), 902–919.

Traywalter, S., Hoffman, K. M., & Waytz, A. (2012). Racial bias in perceptions of others' pain. *PLoS ONE, 11*(3), e48546. Retrieved from http://journals.plos.org/plosone/article?id=10.1371/journal.pone.0048546

Turner, M. A., Santos, R., Levy, D. K., Wissoker, D., Aranda, C., & Pitingolo, R. (2013). *Housing discrimination against racial and ethnic minorities 2012.* Washington, DC: US Department of Housing and Urban Development, Policy Development and Research.

Wade, J. C. (1993). Institutional racism: An analysis of the mental health system, *American Journal of Orthopsychiatry, 63*(4), 536–544.

SECTION 2

STORIES OF ETHNIC COMPLEXITIES, PRIVILEGE, AND INTERSECTIONALITY

"What are you? Do you need an interpreter? What? A light-skinned Latino without an accent? White and poor?" Questions like these and many more form the backdrop for the stories in this section shared by Edward Delgado, Ruth Chao, Dibya Choudhuri, Felice Lichaw, Marya Howell-Carter, Meagan Voulo, Michael Harris, Damian Riggs, and Saliwe Kawewe. Much like the questions shared at the beginning of this narrative, these authors tell their individual and collective story of their intersecting markers of identity along with questions most often asked of them before they have even had a chance to speak. The initial silencing and dismissal of the opportunity for these well-educated individuals to speak for and about themselves is often dismissed by people they encounter who make assumptions about who they are, how they speak, how much money they have, and what they can do. By telling their stories, their voices are being used to inform and educate.

Delgado-Romero shares his narrative titled "*No Parace, pero soy Latino:* The Privilege and Prejudice Inherent in Being A Light-Skinned Latino Without an Accent," in which he addresses the roles of privilege and prejudice in his career as a multicultur-ally committed Latino counseling psychology professor. In his update of his previous chapter (Delgado-Romero, 2004), he continues to examine professional and personal triumphs and challenges related to being a light-skinned Latino without an accent. The narrative is framed by the stories of two parades approximately 20 years apart. The first parade is one of an invalidating cultural experience, and the second parade is one of a celebration of personal and collective cultures. The author describes his multicultural development between these two events.

Chao and Zhang are part of a growing percentage of People of Color working in the field of counseling; yet, literature that offers multicultural competence guidelines for counselors of color are limited. In "Going Through Cultural Barriers in Counseling," Chao shares her story of a difficult cultural clash experienced during her practicum training. Chao and Zhang discuss the role of bicultural competence as a potential guide in resolving cultural conflicts with racially diverse clients. The six dimensions of bicultural competence (knowledge of cultural beliefs and values, positive attitudes toward both groups, bicultural efficacy, communication ability, role repertoire, and social groundedness) serve as guidelines that encourage counselors to mindfully examine both their clients' and their own cultural background and to derive resources from the wisdom of their own cultural heritage to address existing differences and achieve mutual understanding in cross-cultural counseling.

Choudhuri's narrative "Oppression of the Spirit: Complexities in the Counseling Encounter" describes the complexities in counseling when racial, ethnic, and cultural identities of the counselor and client intersect across oppression and privilege. In examining the counseling process between an immigrant South Asian counselor and a Biracial Indigenous-African American client, it becomes clear that good intentions and understanding of cultural identity are insufficient. Effective, competent, and ethical multicultural work demands an awareness of the affective and cognitive implications of intersecting markers of identity. However, beyond such awareness is a requirement for cultural humility and interventions that both acknowledge and address oppression. Developed as a personal narrative, this piece describes the work that occurred and its shortcomings and unpacks the process of conceptualizing and reconceptualizing the multiple ways oppression can manifest.

"Unmasking Within-Group Prejudice, Internalized Oppression, and Privilege: A Case Study" highlights the story of Lichaw, a clinical supervisor and her graduate trainee, Howell-Carter. They share their narrative of an emerging cross-cultural supervisory relationship and the student's developing understanding of within-group prejudice. They describe how good intentions can result in problematic outcomes when clients are treated as members of a group, not individuals, even when that group is the same group to which the clinician belongs. The narrative reveals the importance of recognizing privilege and intersectionality when attempting to understand the needs, challenges, and worldview of clients in therapy. The story of their supervisory relationship highlights the impact of internalized oppression and the revelation of internal attitudes through good supervision. The chapter also highlights changes in multicultural competence guidelines to include social-justice competencies.

In "Exploring the Intersections of Race, Gender, Sexuality, and Class in the Clinical Setting," Riggs draws upon the concepts of cultural capital and intersectionality to elaborate an approach to mental health practice that is mindful of the relationships between race, gender, sexuality, and class in the clinical setting. Riggs shares his own experiences as a psychotherapist and provides three stories or cases, which are considered through the lenses of cultural capital and intersectionality. The chapter concludes by connecting the examples to practice guidelines for inclusion and highlights the importance of clinicians reflecting on the operations of power in their relationships with clients.

Kawewe's personal narrative, "Navigating Oppression, Diversity, Power, and Privilege in Pursuit of Achievement and Success: An International Perspective," utilizes a transformative approach in challenging social workers and other human-helping professionals to recognize the prevalence of multisystemic oppression and privilege in the United States. She recounts the pivotal role that access to education afforded her through her journey from impoverished, colonial, sub-Saharan Africa to her current status as an accomplished academic living in the United States. The author challenges helping professionals to examine the various forms of discrimination that she has encountered, their insidious natures, and the capacity of humans to re-create them in social groups irrespective of history or geography. The narrative provides an example of complications and challenges posed by modern, Western notions of identity and diverse social groups. In upholding values of human dignity, equality, and inclusion social workers ought to have intervention competencies in cultural diversity, human rights, and social justice within American pluralism and globally.

CHAPTER 4

NO PARECE, PERO SOY LATINO

The Privilege and Prejudice Inherent in Being
a Light-Skinned Latino Without an Accent

Edward A. Delgado-Romero

am a cisgender male who is a husband and a father to a blended family of five multiethnic children. As a son of immigrants, I was the first child to navigate life in the United States from birth to adulthood (American Psychological Association, 2012). Racially and ethnically I define myself as a Colombian-American, or simply as a Latino. Regardless of how I see myself, for others, I provide an ambiguous racial ethnic stimulus. As a consequence of my ethnic ambiguity, I slip between inclusion and exclusion, visibility and invisibility, and power and powerlessness. The many aspects of my life revolve around a constantly interacting, dynamic mix of privilege and oppression, and my expertise in multicultural psychology has helped me to make sense of the chaos of life and how to best use my privilege to serve others and fight oppression. Much has changed in my life since the publication of the initial edition of this book (Delgado-Romero, 2004), when I wrote the following:

> I was walking around the streets of downtown South Bend, Indiana, during the international festival, wearing my Colombia T-shirt that symbolized my newfound pride in my heritage. A young Latina woman approached me and asked, "¿Colombiano?" I eagerly answered, "¡Si!" She looked at me, wrinkled her nose, and said, "No parece" (you don't look like it). And then she faded into the crowd, leaving me alone with my shame and anger.

MY PROFESSIONAL CONTEXT

I am a professor at the University of Georgia in the College of Education. My specialty is counseling psychology, and I am also an affiliate faculty with the Latin American and

Caribbean Studies Institute. Upon graduation from my doctorate, I worked at a counseling center for five years and then made a career change to join academia. My first academic position was cursed from the beginning. In order to hire two faculty members for one position, the search committee had to make the case (unbeknownst to me) that I was less qualified than the White male candidate hired with me. In doing so, the faculty could use diversity funds to hire me as a "diversity hire." Although this gamesmanship was a common tactic at this university to increase faculty diversity, that manipulation of the system had consequences for me. For example, the department chair focused on the idea that I was not qualified, and I had to fight him on every evaluation of my work. While I labored under the presumption of incompetence (Gutierrez y Muhs, Flores Niemann, Gonzalez, & Harris, 2012), my White male colleague benefitted from every benefit of the doubt. Thus a program designed to address traditional inequity ended up, ironically, ensuring oppression rather than ending it.

As a diversity hire, I was expected to meet the multicultural demands of the campus in addition to my other job duties. I was quickly overwhelmed with requests for services (e.g., serve on committees, attend diversity events, mentor students of color). A senior (White) professor told me that my issue was that I had "a problem saying 'no'" and that I needed to focus on my research. He told me that if I kept saying "no," then people would stop asking me to help. This comment struck me as perfectly capturing the dilemma of socially active, underrepresented faculty. We were hired to serve the community (collectivism), yet the road to success was on the tenure track, which meant publish or perish (individualism). To the university community, it seemed like a classic bait and switch: Hire minority faculty and then not have access to them. Similarly, for me it was frustrating to be courted by the entire university and then told to shut myself in my office for seven years. The allure of gaining tenure and spending my career in the ivory tower of academia was tempting; but I noticed that, once faculty encased themselves in their offices, they rarely emerged to work with the community.

In telling me to "just say no," my colleague was reducing a systemic problem into a personal one. He viewed multicultural campus needs as a nuisance, and he didn't recognize that I, as a culturally committed faculty of color, might derive some connection or fulfillment out of doing some limited service in the university. He also didn't recognize that perhaps I would find a way to weave my research into my service in a creative way. I realized that the hostile academic atmosphere coupled with the lack of multicultural sensitivity compelled me to move on.

I accepted a position at the University of Georgia in 2005, and my colleagues gave me the freedom to realize my potential in research and professional leadership. My work was valued, and I obtained tenure and promotion to full professor. However, over the years I realized that my experiences at my first university meant that I coped with oppression on campus by connecting with colleagues on the national level. This coping style, while ensuring success, left me feeling disconnected locally.

The privilege of the ivory tower is seductive, and I didn't totally escape its shadow. In my pursuit of tenure and promotion, I lost touch with my practitioner side; and that loss has had a negative effect on me. Being a therapist kept me introspective and aware of my impact on others, and it constantly challenged me on an interpersonal level. Over time, however, the professoriate brought out other aspects of my personality. I became fiercely introverted, outcome focused, competitive, and politically manipulative. It was through the process of my own personal therapy that I was able to overcome a painful divorce and identify aspects of my work that I did not enjoy. I now see clients at a small training clinic for bicultural and bilingual Latinos/as and donate all proceedings to a Latino community clinic. My return to therapy has helped to center me, to not be so microfocused on outcomes, and to stay attuned to process. It is a privilege to give away psychology to those who cannot afford it otherwise, and I find it personally rewarding.

INTERNALIZED NOTIONS OF PRIVILEGE, OPPRESSION, AND IDENTITY

As readers of the first two editions of this book will know, my light skin and lack of an accent has often caused me to feel like an ethnic imposter when I am often able to pass for a White person (Delgado-Romero, 2004). Meeting my half-brother from Colombia for the first time helped me examine further my notions of visible and audible otherness (Comas-Diaz, 2010). Meeting Eduardo was like looking in the mirror, with the exception that he has dark wavy hair and much darker skin, which he described as *trigueño*. We discussed how race and color have certain value in South America and how this emphasis on colorism remains largely unexamined in the United States Latino/a community (Adames, Chavez-Dueñas, & Organista, 2016). I thought of the fact that I had benefitted from being lighter skinned, and how from birth I had thought nothing of racist family nicknames such as *blanco* or *negrito*.

Spending time with Eduardo provided me with some understanding of the many struggles for Latino/a people who have darker skin color and African or indigenous heritage (Adames et al., 2016). Eduardo spoke mostly Spanish, and I noticed the prejudice that speakers of other languages often face, both subtle (people speaking loudly in English as if speaking loudly aids comprehension) and overt (dirty looks and snide comments about foreigners). I also noticed the reluctance of many Latino/a professionals to speak Spanish, even at Latino/a-themed events!

It was not until I experienced the United States through Eduardo's eyes and ears that I was able to gain a deeper understanding about how privilege works even within oppressed communities (Arredono et al., 2014). I decided to take some steps to address these issues. For example, I started a Spanish-language conversation group for my research team so that speaking Spanish would become easier and less pressure and stress filled. I took care to talk about racism within marginalized communities during my lectures and wrote about the intersection of oppression and privilege.

Raising my children and stepchildren has been another experience in which I can challenge internalized notions of privilege, oppression, and identity. My biological children are both Colombian and European, and they have fair skin and blue eyes. I gave them Spanish names (Javier, Isabel, and Guillermo), and it has been interesting to watch them grapple with aspects of their own identity both physically and culturally as they develop into adulthood (Torres & Delgado-Romero, 2008). My oldest son Javier has embraced Latino culture and the Spanish language: He delights in speaking in Spanish, has many Latino/a friends, and studies the language in high school. Isabel just announced that, "of course," she will also study Spanish. Guillermo knows he is Colombian but tends to define that identity solely through his family members. The children attend a multiethnic school system and often talk about their cultural and ethnic differences quite openly, which is in stark contrast to my educational experiences in Catholic school (Delgado-Romero, 2004).

In 2013 I married Angie, who herself is of Greek and Irish background (her father is a Greek immigrant), and my stepchildren Nick and Emma are also half Chinese. As we became a family, my biological children and I converted to the Greek Orthodox Church. The Greek culture was familiar, and our ethnically mixed family fit right in, sometimes too well.

The first time I attended the Greek Orthodox Church with Angie, I was nervous entering an environment that was new religiously and ethnically. I was surprised at the reception I received: Everyone ignored me! I had expected a warm greeting as a new person to the church. When I mentioned this expectation to Angie, she laughed and told me that everyone thought I was Greek and a member of her family that they had already met, so they didn't bother introducing themselves. Ah, my ambiguous ethnicity at work again!

Our family is very diverse and, therefore, we draw a lot of attention when we go out. We are also faced with constant microaggressions (Sue, 2010) when people ask about the children: "Where are they from?" or "Which one of them is adopted?" It's frustrating to hear such rudeness, but the children mostly laugh it off. They seem to feel a great deal of cultural pride and are interested in the cultural differences of other people. Angie says the children view talking about and sharing culture as a way to make friends.

Although having an ambiguous ethnicity has been painful and invalidating in my life, being ambiguous has also been a form of privilege. I can slip in and out of vastly different settings; for example, I can go from a faculty meeting to my work at a Latino/a community center with functionally illiterate clients without arousing much attention in either place. This adaptability is partly cultural humility (Gallardo, 2014) and partly what my mentor Patricia Arredondo calls the immigrant spirit: the ability to blend in and adapt to different settings in the service of others. Again, adaptability is not the same thing as belonging, and I don't often feel like I truly belong anywhere other than with my family.

PRIVILEGE AND OPPRESSION THAT PERMEATE PROFESSIONAL LIFE

Many White faculty members refer to their colleagues as family, and while I would never use this descriptor, I acknowledge that, as students come and go, faculty and colleagues develop relationships that last over decades. These professional relationships are defined and affected by the intersection of privilege and oppression. For those of us who work in professions that aspire toward social justice and equity, these professional relationships can either facilitate or inhibit our work.

My membership in the National Latina/o Psychological Association (NLPA; Chavez-Korrel, Delgado-Romero & Illes, 2012) has clearly facilitated my ethnic identity development and an examination of the many facets of privilege and oppression that permeate professional life. Through NLPA, I have formed supportive and challenging professional relationships over the past 15 years. I was elected president of the organization in 2008. My election as president triggered a personal crisis, with old feelings of being an imposter and fraud intensified. I could hear the critical voices of everyone who had ever questioned my ability to be a faculty member, psychologist, or leader, and those voices were overwhelming. Around the same time that Melba Vasquez was elected as the first Latina president of the American Psychological Association (APA), she came to town to deliver a keynote address and we went out to dinner.

I confessed that I often felt like a fraud, and I couldn't believe I was elected president of NLPA. Melba confided that the imposter syndrome was real and that she often felt it herself. She told me we both deserved to be elected and had to use our position to make needed changes. I felt a sense of relief. After all, if Melba, the president of APA, could feel like an imposter, then it felt more natural that I did too.

In contrast, my experience in APA was markedly different. In 2015, I quit as a member of this organization after having been a member since the early 1990s. I was spectacularly successful in APA as a fellow and won several national awards. However, my election to the Council of Representatives (COA) caused me to question my affiliation with APA. As a member of COA, I was elected to help govern the association, and this position came with considerable privilege, including paid travel, hotel, and generous food allowances. I felt considerable shame for what I perceived as extravagant perks, but most COA members saw these as an entitlement. During my first meeting, despite concerns about APA's collusion with torture (Hoffman, 2015) and the looming expiration of the multicultural guidelines (APA, 2003), COA members spent considerable time debating raising the meal allowance and including both Internet and gym fees in the reimbursement of expenses. I was outraged by the self-serving nature of the group and resigned my position shortly afterward. I quit my membership in APA after I was asked to represent APA at an international psychological conference in Colombia. I realized that I could not represent APA to psychologists in my ancestral homeland, especially with the allegations of collusion with torture tearing the ethical fabric of APA. Colombians were just emerging from four decades of civil war, and I felt a deep obligation to them not to misuse my influence and power as a US psychologist. I plan to work with Colombian psychologists for peace, but not under the banner of APA.

My purpose in relating this struggle is not to advocate one professional organization or another, nor is it to tell other professionals whom they should support. My point is to show that, by virtue of education and prestige, there are those of us who are afforded a great deal of privilege and power in society. We should be very careful about how we collectively exert our influence, expertise, and status because we might misuse that social capital to support people and policies that oppress others. We have every right (and the responsibility) to demand that those organizations that we give our money and time to behave according to the highest ethical standards.

One way that I personally continue to actively work for equity in the face of oppression is through my mentorship of graduate students. With more than 30 doctoral graduates and several master's and undergraduate advisees, my research team !BIEN! is the tangible manifestation of my values as a faculty member. I try to live up to the Latino cultural value of *familismo* (Arredondo, Gallardo-Cooper, Delgado-Romero & Zapata, 2014) that entails a preference for close interpersonal relationships by fostering a sense of community and closeness with my students, while at the same time providing guidance and support. Team members are often around my wife and children, and this offers them a home away from home and models work/life balance that they don't often see. Eighty percent of my students are people of color, most are first-generation college students, and they all are focused on social justice and multiculturalism. We attended the 2016 NLPA conference together. It was amazing to see a large, joyful, and vibrant group of 22 students and alumni who have been part of my research team during my tenure. They are my professional legacy—one I am proud of.

CONCLUSION

This chapter began with the story of the festival that caused me such identity turmoil some 25 years ago. Back then I was seeking external validation, and I was hoping that a Colombian person would recognize me as one of their own. Despite the love and affirmation of my family, I was seeking confirmation from outside myself that I was truly a Latino person despite the doubts caused by many years of acculturative stress and assimilative pressure. However, there was never going to be confirmation from the outside. The Colombian woman who told me I didn't look Colombian couldn't make me feel authentic. My sense of self had to emerge over years of reflection, traveling, love and loss, and participation in minority communities and in my personal psychotherapy. I began to integrate my identity from the inside out.

I now know who I am. I'm not Colombian because I've neither lived there nor grown up around many other Colombians. I am a son of Colombian immigrants, married to the daughter of Greek and Irish immigrants, and we are raising multiethnic (Colombian, Greek, Chinese, Dutch, and Irish) children in the United States. As the Puerto Rican poet Tato Laveria (2003) wrote in his poem "AmeRican," I was "defining my self, my own way, any way, many ways." It was the integration of my identity, specifically the recognition that being a first-generation Latino in the United States was the source of my strength, not a liability to overcome.

I close with the story of another festival that happened last year, 25 years after the festival that opened this chapter: It is the festival of lights, the annual winter holiday parade in Athens, Georgia. I was walking in the parade with Angie and our children on behalf of the local Latino center I work with. It was the first year in Athens that there were multiple Latino floats participating in the parade, and I could sense the pride in the Latino community, mixed with some apprehension. We all wondered what the reception to Latinos/as being in the parade would be, especially in light of recent immigration raids and heated anti-immigrant political rhetoric. As the adults worried, the children played and laughed. When the parade started, my daughter Isabel quickly grabbed the Colombian flag and boldly walked ahead of the float, surrounded by children and flags from all over Latin America. My daughter waved the flag of our ancestors without fear as I beamed with pride. The reaction from the crowd was positive, and we didn't have a single negative interaction all night. As I watched my daughter, I thought back to the festival in South Bend. I don't know whether anyone thought that I looked like a Latino or not, but it no longer mattered to me. I was using my privilege as a tenured faculty member to work on behalf of Latino immigrants and their children. It didn't matter if people thought I was White or Greek. What mattered to me was what I did, and who I was as a person and as professional. I smiled as I waved to the crowd because I knew from within that: *yo soy Latino* (I am Latino)!

DISCUSSION QUESTIONS

1. How can you be a good ally to someone who is struggling with being invalidated ethnically or culturally?
2. You might be more prepared to deal with oppression than privilege; what might be some of the challenges in helping someone deal with privilege (especially if you don't have that privilege yourself)?
3. How might you have difficult dialogues with colleagues about what they really believe about oppressed groups? That is, how can you discuss aversive or covert forms of discrimination?
4. How can you gain cultural and clinical experiences working with cultural and linguistic minority clients? Specifically, Latinos/as?
5. What do you do when you disagree with your professional association?
6. People are rarely one thing or another. How might you explore the concept of intersectionality with your clients as it relates to dimensions of identity?

REFERENCES

Adames, H. Y., Chavez-Dueñas, N. Y., & Organista, K. C. (2016). Skin color matters in Latino/a communities: Identifying, understanding, and addressing Mestizaje racial ideologies in clinical practice. *Professional Psychology: Research and Practice, 47,* 46–55.

American Psychological Association. (2003). Guidelines on multicultural education, training, research, practice, and organizational change for psychologists. *American Psychologist, 58,* 377–402.

American Psychological Association, Presidential Task Force on Immigration. (2012). *Crossroads: The psychology of immigration in the new century.* Retrieved from http://www.apa.org/topics/immigration/report.aspx

Arredondo, P., Gallardo-Cooper, M., Delgado-Romero, E. A., & Zapata, A. (2014). *Culturally responsive counseling with Latinas/os.* Alexandria, VA: American Counseling Association.

Chavez-Korrel, S., Delgado-Romero, E. A., & Illes, R. (2012). The National Latina/o Psychological Association: Like a phoenix rising. *The Counseling Psychologist, 40,* 675–684.

Comas-Diaz, L. (2010). On being a Latina healer: Voice, consciousness, and identity. *Psychotherapy Theory, Research, Practice, and Training, 47*(2), 162–168. doi:10.1037/a0019758

Delgado-Romero, E. A. (2004). *No parece*: The privilege and prejudice inherent in being a light skinned Latino with no accent. In S. K. Anderson & V. A. Middleton (Eds.), *Explorations in oppression, diversity and privilege* (pp. 119–126). Belmont, CA: Brooks/Cole.

Gallardo, M. (2014). *Developing cultural humility: Embracing race, privilege and power.* Thousand Oaks, CA: SAGE.

Gutierrez y Muhs, G., Flores-Niemann, Y., Gonzalez, C. G., & Harris, A. P. (Eds.). (2012). *Presumed incompetent*. Logan: Utah State University Press.

Hoffman, D. H. (2015). Independent review relating to APA ethics guidelines, national security interrogations, and torture. Retrieved from http://apa.org/independent-review/revised-report.pdf

Laveria, T. (2003). *AmerRican* (2nd ed.). Houston, TX: Arte Publico Press.

Sue, D. W. (2010). *Microaggressions in everyday life: Race, gender and sexual orientation*. Hoboken, NJ: John Wiley.

Torres, V., & Delgado-Romero, E. (2008). Defining Latino/a identity through late adolescent development. In K. L. Kraus (Ed.), *Lenses: Applying lifespan development theories in counseling* (pp. 363–388). Boston, MA: Lahaska Press.

CHAPTER 5

GOING THROUGH CULTURAL BARRIERS IN COUNSELING

Ruth Chu-Lien Chao and Ying Shan Doris Zhang

As members of a racial/ethnic minority group[1] in the counseling psychology profession, we have met diverse cultural obstacles in our counseling experiences. Culture and language differences are often interpersonal barriers that we have been challenged to turn into bridges toward learning and growth. Being members of a racial/ethnic minority group (e.g., Asian) means that we confront stereotypes against us daily. Some examples include being asked if we need an interpreter when we see a doctor, even before we have had a chance to speak; being asked how we pronounce specific English words; or being asked to teach people math because Asians are "math geniuses."

In most cross-cultural counseling cases, counselor–counselee dyads are White counselors working with Clients of Color (Chang & Berk, 2009). Yet, the reverse relations—Counselors of Color with White clients—do exist and are on the rise. In 2002, counseling Trainees of Color occupied 30% of the membership in counseling psychology (Alexander, Heineman, Zarin, & Larson, 2002). A more recent report published by the American Psychological Association (APA) (2010a) indicates a growing percentage of ethnic minorities as counselors. For example, in 2008 and 2009, racial-minority doctoral students represent 26% of first-year, full-time students in health service-provider programs such as counseling psychology and 33% of first-year, full-time students in the professional school setting. At the same time, the literature or research is lacking that discusses the Counselor of Color and client who is White. The following story highlights the experience of a White client and a Counselor of Color.

---

1. Being minority persons, the authors identify themselves more with minority people than with the White majority.

RUTH'S STORY

The experience shared in this chapter occurred during my (the first author's) practicum, when I was an international student in a counseling psychology program. As a non-White counselor-trainee, I faced issues of whiteness on a daily basis. For example, the majority of my classmates were White, most of my clients were White, and even most of my neighbors were White. Coming to this country, I noticed that I needed to understand the history of the ideology of race in United States and to learn how the White majority dominates the society and how racial-minority individuals suffer from racism and discrimination. My training program advocated multiculturalism; however, my practicum supervisor was White, as were most of my professors, most of my peers, and most of my clients. Before coming to the United States, I had been studying psychology, which was treated as a product in Western culture. Even in Taiwan, I studied psychology with textbooks in English. Thus when studying for my PhD degree in the United States, I thought I was at home in Western psychology until I met my client Mary (a pseudonym).

Mary, a White, female client, came to me with issues associated with body image and romantic relationships. As Mary looked askance at me, I could tell from her body language that she was taken aback by having me, an Asian female student, assigned to her as her counselor. Sensing Mary's concern, I reassured her that I would be as empathetic as possible in my commitment to understand her presenting problems. Mary affirmed my suspicion by saying, "But I don't think you would understand me. You are an Asian person and I'm not. I'm afraid you would judge me with your Asian, conservative values." I was taken aback by her suspicion about my willingness and ability to help her. I was too surprised to say anything except "I understand, and it is no fun to be judged, especially by your counselor."

In addition to her concerns about my ability to understand her culturally, Mary gave hints of worrying about my language ability. Specifically, Mary kept apologizing for using slang, idioms, and other culture-bound expressions. In response to her apologies, I repeatedly assured Mary that I thoroughly understood her words and their meanings. When those assurances did not seem to resolve her concerns, I asked her if my accent was keeping her from accepting me as her counselor. At that point, Mary expressed her desire for a White, female counselor with values similar to hers.

Initially, I was shocked numb at Mary's stated rejection of me and request for another counselor. I tried to think of a way to respond to her judgment of my cultural background. She had overlooked my qualifications as a doctoral student and solely focused on my non-Whiteness. I struggled to understand Mary's rejection of me based on my cultural background. Several questions came to my mind: "What's wrong with being an Asian female counselor?"; "Are my Asian values bad or even detrimental to my client?"; "Did I say anything wrong in my self-introduction to Mary to suggest I couldn't work with a White person?" Since I could not change my ethnic origin, I was at a loss about knowing what to do with *myself*.

In the moment, I searched in my mind for resources to address this challenge. I ransacked my memory for readings on multicultural counseling. Unfortunately, I could not recall any magic formula to help me, an Asian, female counselor trying to connect with a White, female client. I did recall literature that proposed a counselor's self-awareness of her cultural values and background as an essential component in her multicultural competence (Collins & Arthur, 2010; Goh, Yon, Shimmi, & Hirai, 2014; Perera, 2012).

I began to mentally let go of the issue of whether I could be her counselor. My own Chinese thinking, *wu-wei*, of letting go at this moment, is similar to *wu-wei* in Taoism. In Chinese thinking, *wu-wei* means natural action that does not involve struggle or excessive effort. When I let go of Mary's judgment and rejection of me, I felt relaxed. I suggested that I role-play her to better understand her presenting problems. Mary casually agreed to my suggestion. Perhaps because of the mindset of *wu-wei* and letting go, I successfully role played her presenting problems. She was amazed by my performance and puzzled by how I could display my understanding of her so well in a brief role-play. She decided to stay and work with me as her counselor.

After this session, I absorbed myself in multicultural literature. Since my encounter with Mary was predominantly based on race and culture, I sought out the meaning of *multicultural competence*. I poured over APA's (2003) guideline about culturally skilled counselors. When I searched for guidance on working with a culturally different client, all I could find was how a White counselor works with a minority client. Indeed, even today, most research on multicultural counseling competence has been focused on White counselors' and trainees' growth in multicultural competence training (Goren & Plaut, 2014; Sue, 2013). For example, research on predictors of competency among White clinicians finds that White racial identity stages and color-blind racial attitudes (denying or minimizing racism in society) predict multicultural counseling competence (Neville, Awad, Brooks, Flores, & Bluemel, 2013). Johnson and Jackson Williams (2015) found that, among White doctoral students, aside from factors such as social desirability, demographic variables, and multicultural training, color-blind racial attitudes and White racial-identity stages added significant incremental variance in predicting multicultural counseling knowledge, awareness, and skills. Most scholars and practitioners stress that counseling necessitates that clinicians be culturally competent and self-efficacious to ethically and effectively work with diverse client populations (Barden & Greene, 2015; Ratts, Singh, Nassar-McMillan, Butler, & McCullough, 2016). Racial-minority counselors desperately need information and literature that guide us in our work with White clients. To date, there has been very limited guidance on how racial-minority counselors could counsel a White client in culturally sensitive ways (Chao, Wei, Good, & Flores, 2011). Racial minority counselors often ask questions such as "How do I counsel my White clients?"; "How do I work with my clients whose religion or race/ethnicity are different from mine?"; "How do I apply Sue and Sue's [2012] multicultural counseling competence such as awareness, knowledge, and skills to work with my clients, especially when most of the information on multicultural counseling competence is based on White perspectives?"

Racial-minority counselors may not receive as much guidance as their White peers do (Pope-Davis et al., 2002), or they may receive the same training and guidance as White counselors. Because experiences of the racial/ethnic-minority counselors are rarely mentioned in multicultural literature, their training needs are being ignored. While White counselors reflect on their awareness of White privilege, racial-minority counselors need to examine how *they* work through marginalization or discrimination in their lives (Vinson & Neimeyer, 2003). Moreover, the APA's (2003) *Guidelines on Multicultural Education, Training, Research, Practice, and Organizational Change for Psychologists* indicates that *all* individuals exist in social, political, historical, and economic contexts, and psychologists should understand the influence of these contexts on individuals' behavior. Thus both White counselors and Counselors of Color need to understand their own race/ethnicity and racial/ethnic identity. Importantly, the training resources may include training on how Counselors of Color translate their experiences of being oppressed and marginalized into multicultural counseling competence.

The APA (2003) encourages psychologists and trainees to reflect on the different needs based on people's culture and background. Does this encouragement mean the same thing for Counselors of Color? Should Counselors of Color consider their points of privilege like their White peers do? Or should they focus on their experiences of racism in their personal life? Many details in the guidelines and literature consistently stress how counselors need to work with clients from diverse and marginalized backgrounds, and they expect counselors to have awareness of their majority culture (American Counseling Association, 2014; APA, 2003, 2010a; National Board of Certified Counselors, 2012; Ratts et al., 2016).

My counseling with Mary exposes a critical issue: that Counselors of Color do not have the needed guidance in working with majority clients. When I have encountered White clients such as Mary who rejected and judged me, my struggle has been that there is no guidance for me in how to manage such cultural or racial clash in counseling.

CULTURAL DIFFERENCES IN COUNSELING AND BICULTURAL COMPETENCE

To find a solution to address the cultural differences between Mary and me, I considered the concept of bicultural competence to accommodate for Mary's majority culture while appreciating my own Asian heritage (David, Okazaki, & Saw, 2009; Wei et al., 2010). The concept of *bicultural competence* refers to the knowledge and capability to negotiate two different cultures (e.g., White and Asian). Concretely, bicultural competence suggests the capability of individuals to face and manage daily challenges that result from two sets of cultural norms, practices, identities, and values. Thus when I examined the cultural clash between myself and Mary, I understood that, from Mary's cultural perspective, a typical counselor could mean someone who shares the same cultural background (i.e., White and "accent free") and gender (i.e., female) with her.

After understanding that Mary's expectation in counseling was derived from her majority culture, I also remembered that my Asian culture encouraged me to endure difficulties in work and to appreciate the challenges I encountered (Shaoming, 2008). The moment I understood where Mary's expectations and assumptions came from, I treated my Asian culture as a resource and became confident in managing this relationship dilemma. I was able to reach out to my Asian wisdom and seek solutions using the method of "To know the road ahead, ask those coming back." In other words, instead of feeling helpless and anxious, I felt empowered by my Asian wisdom that has been in my life for decades. Without hesitance, I decided to utilize and incorporate relevant wisdom that was passed on through time in my native culture as a resource to guide me through dilemmas faced in counseling.

Recognizing that perhaps little research has focused on investigating issues in working with clients who express bias and prejudice toward the counselor during counseling (MacLeod, 2013), I turned inward to my own culture and upbringing for wisdom. I sought wisdom from the paradigms of Chinese sages (e.g., Mencius) and other cultural paradigms (Taoism and Buddhism) that inspired psychotherapy (Hayes, 2016). Somewhat intuitively, I fell back on my own culture and the significance of heartfelt concern for others. From Mencius I recalled the "heart that cannot bear others to suffer . . . seeing people hungry, I am hungry; seeing people drowning, I am drowned" (Mencius 1A7, 4B29, as cited in Lau, 1984, p. 171). I also followed what Zen/Taoism says, "Don't push the river" (Chuang Tzu, as cited in Graham, 1981, pp. 19/22–24).

While working with Mary, I did not take Mary's criticism personally. I accepted the rejection as it was—not manipulating her distaste of me into my advantage but following along and wrapping Mary's rejection with empathy. Such empathy is a combination of deep understanding and Chinese wisdom. My reaction toward Mary was rooted in my deep acceptance learned in training and the Chinese value I grew up with. As my Asian culture suggests, "Try our hardest and accept what comes, do not prejudge future consequences." My Asian culture also encourages me to let go of "right" and "should" and to be open and accommodating.

Later when I met with my White supervisor, my supervisor asked me if I was angry with Mary. Surprisingly, I was not angry. My experience with Mary was typical of the interactions I have had with the majority of White people I encounter, clients or not. My supervisor questioned why I was not angry with Mary. My rationale of not getting angry could be traced back to my Chinese culture. In the Chinese culture, if Mary has the courage to question me to my face, her behavior suggests that she might be honest and sincere. She did not pretend to enjoy my counseling but was transparent with her distrust. Although Mary's suspicion and distrust did hurt me, I cared more about attending to her true needs. Consistent with the wisdom of what my culture suggests, I tried hard to let Mary know that she was honest in her reactions toward me, including her distrust. Seemingly touched by my good intentions, Mary decided to stay with me for one more session.

Theoretically, LaFromboise, Coleman, and Gerton (1993), David et al. (2009), and Wei et al. (2010) have conceptualized a model of bicultural competence that is composed of six dimensions: (a) *knowledge of cultural beliefs and values*—the degree to which a person is aware of and knowledgeable about the history, institutions, rituals, and everyday practices of a given culture, (b) *positive attitudes toward both groups*—the degree to which a person regards both cultural groups positively, (c) *bicultural efficacy*—the belief that a person can function effectively within two cultural groups without compromising one's cultural identity, (d) *communication ability*—the person's ability to communicate verbally or nonverbally in both cultural groups, (e) *role repertoire*—the range of culturally appropriate behaviors or roles a person possesses or is willing to learn/perform, and (f) *social groundedness*—the degree to which a person has established social networks in both cultural groups.

Applying these six domains in counseling, counselors learn to recognize the clients' cultural backgrounds while appreciating their own cultural heritage. This approach provides counselors with more resources to manage cultural differences with diverse clients. Specifically, increased knowledge about cultural beliefs and values helps counselors to reach a better understanding of the clients they are working with, such as how historical events may interact with cultural norms and socially acceptable everyday practices to impact clients' worldviews and behaviors. Moreover, the ability to maintain positive regard toward one's own culture and the culture of others helps both counselors and clients to collaborate on working through their existing cultural differences and striving for mutual understanding. Furthermore, bicultural efficacy is an equally important component of bicultural competence because the belief that one can function equally well in two different cultures without compromising one's own cultural views and beliefs can assist counselors in appearing confident and experienced in front of their culturally diverse clients. Such confidence could strengthen counselors' professionalism in their areas of work, which in turn may lessen clients' doubts about counselors' abilities in cross-cultural counseling.

To enhance bicultural competence, counselors also need to have better awareness of their verbal and nonverbal communication skills when working with diverse clients. Almost every cultural group has its own socially acceptable patterns for conveying messages. Therefore, to be knowledgeable with cultures other than one's own also includes demonstrating a reasonable understanding of the meaning of spoken words and also the implied messages conveyed by tone of voice, facial expressions, body gestures, and physical movements. Most importantly, all verbal and nonverbal messages received should be interpreted in the cultural context of the speaker. In addition, sometimes to demonstrate cross-cultural understanding, counselors should have sufficient knowledge and the willingness to learn about acceptable social roles and behaviors in clients' cultures. Last but not least, for one to achieve an enriched understanding of cultures different than one's own, the best option would probably be direct personal exposure to the target culture. In other words, a culture's beliefs, values, and norms can be best learned through personal experience with that particular culture. The six dimensions of bicultural components, as first presented by LaFromboise et al. (1993), serve as tools that can be used to construct a bridge for culturally different individuals to meet one another and embrace each other's world.

When I began to understand Mary's request for a White, female counselor, my attitude of acceptance toward the situation actually surprised Mary. To Mary, this Asian, female, student counselor in front of her eyes appeared relaxed, calm, and even confident. She also noticed that I did not defend my credentials as a counselor; neither did I argue with her. She was also surprised that I did not persuade her to stay in counseling with me. From the role-play, Mary learned that true understanding did not necessarily have to come from a counselor with the same cultural background. Instead, a meaningful understanding about her problem could begin with having someone else (e.g., a counselor from a different background) step into her White culture and learn about her current struggles. From that moment onward, Mary decided that I was the counselor for her.

From the cultural clash to cross-cultural understanding, Mary eventually learned that, by resisting having me as her counselor, she might bind herself to her White majority culture only. As we worked together, she became more open to my Asian culture and gained some understanding of our two cultural identities. She realized that I was trying to support her from a different cultural perspective. This transition from cultural clash to cross-cultural support actually gave Mary resources to manage her own issues. She was able to use such insight to reflect on her relationship conflict with her boyfriend. She later shared that "I could try to understand and respect my boyfriend's perspective while appreciating my own value in this relationship, just like how I was able to turn our cultural differences into mutual understanding."

CONCLUSION

My experience with Mary may reveal several issues. First, it shows that cultural clash in counseling could exist between racial-minority counselors and White clients. In my role as a racial-minority counselor to Mary, my experience is one of many examples of intercultural experiences that have vastly expanded and enriched my professional growth in counseling. Presently, professional standards that guide culturally sensitive services have grown in depth and expanded in extent. Both the APA (2010b) and the American Counseling Association (2014) have indicated in their respective code of ethics/standards of conduct the importance of incorporating cultural knowledge and awareness into multiple aspects of counseling/therapy services, such as conducting assessments and client conceptualization. The National Board of Certified Counselors (2012) also state in its *Code of Ethics* that counselors are to perform services to culturally diverse clients in a nondiscriminant way and also that all techniques and assessments utilized should take clients' cultural identities into consideration to deem the appropriateness.

Second, my experience with Mary demonstrates the lack of training for counselors of Color. Professional standards and guidelines are not enough to cover every cross-cultural conflict that may arise in counseling sessions. In other words, current multicultural guidelines facilitate White counselors in addressing issues of racism and privilege when they are counseling clients of color, such as the importance of having a thorough understanding of how oppression, racism, discrimination, and stereotypes affect their work (Sue & Sue, 2012). However, it is just as critical for counselors of Color to work through their prejudices or their clients' prejudices. Cultural sensitivity and multicultural guidance, needless to say, is equally important for counselors of Color who need to be culturally sensitive as well as their White counterparts. Therefore, when cultural conflicts arise and few professional guidelines exists, counselors are forced to draw upon the wisdom of interpersonal relations from various cultural paradigms to derive new insight toward working through cultural ruptures. Remember: Cultural differences are not hurdles but potential bridges toward mutual understanding.

Third, despite lack of training for me as a racial-minority counselor in solving cultural conflict, I was still very excited about finding solutions workable for my client and myself. Over time, mutual feelings of openness and serenity seeped into the sessions Mary and I shared. My anxiety and nervousness from Mary's critical judgment shifted to calm, genuine acceptance, and I found that my Asian upbringing would not prejudge her or shut her out. Both my White client Mary and I became motivated to build a bridge of growth and understanding between our cultural differences. We both began to *accept* our differences as we learned to understand each other and Mary's initial mistrust. As a counselor of color, I have seen the power of infusing my Asian cultural upbringing into my Western counseling strategies.

It is ironic that, as I fell back on my cultural roots, the very factor of interpersonal obstacles provided an occasion for ubiquitous, compassionate empathy and acceptance of common humanity. Eventually, I was able to make a connection between my Asian sentiments and Western counseling skills of listening, reflecting, accepting, and being client centered. I realized that what was part of my response to accepting my client's reactions was also in line with what Teyber and McClure (2010) pointed out: "[t]he first step in working with all people is to enter their subjective worldview, listen empathetically. . . respect the personal meaning that experiences hold for different people . . . and affirm the client's subjective experience" (p. 65).

Fourth, my story may highlight that bicultural competence could be a solution to manage the cultural difference. My knowledge with the two cultures—U. S. American and Asian—has provided me with some fresh perspectives on cultural differences in counseling. Western insights on counseling today and wisdom of ancient Chinese philosophers *mutually* echo, complement, and validate each other. This discovery of multicultural interenrichment vastly enrich and expand my counseling horizon.

People with bicultural competence do not live challenge-free lives. They encounter as many challenges as others do. The difference is that they are aware of the contrasting cultural values and demands of their heritage culture and the mainstream culture. When interacting with people from other cultures, individuals with bicultural competence learn to navigate successfully the potential conflicts and dissonance produced by such circumstances and to function well in multiple cultural contexts (David et al., 2009).

DISCUSSION QUESTIONS

1. How would you address prejudice or discrimination that was brought against you by your culturally different clients?
2. How do you integrate your cultural backgrounds (e.g., cultural wisdom) with your professional training and practice?
3. What are some new areas you would hope to see on professional standards and guidelines that would make them more helpful and complete?
4. There are at least two types of cultural differences in counselor–client relations: (a) White counselors with clients of Color and (b) counselors of Color with White clients. What are some of the similarities and differences these two types of counseling dyads share with each other?
5. What cultural barriers do you notice when you work with clients? How might you better address these barriers in the future?
6. How do cultural differences influence counseling? Do you think cultural differences enhance or impair the counseling process? How? Why?

REFERENCES

Alexander, C. M., Heineman, C. J., Zarin, M. S., & Larson, L. (2002). Admission criteria to APA-accredited programs in counseling psychology over 10 years: Reflections of the specialty's values. *The Counseling Psychologist, 30,* 135–148.

American Counseling Association. (2014). *ACA code of ethics.* Alexandria, VA: Author.

American Psychological Association. (2003). Guidelines on multicultural education, training, research, practice, and organizational change for psychologists. *American Psychologist, 58*(5), 377–402. doi:10.1037/0003-066X.58.5.377

American Psychological Association. (2010a, January). 2010: Race/ethnicity of doctorate recipients in psychology in the past 10 years. Center for Workforce Studies. Retrieved from http://www.apa.org/workforce/publications/10-race/index.aspx

American Psychological Association. (2010b). Ethical principles of psychologists and code of conduct. Retrieved from http://apa.org/ethics/code/index.aspx

Barden, S. M., & Greene, J. H. (2015). An investigation of multicultural counseling competence and multicultural counseling self-efficacy for counselors-in-training. *International Journal for the Advancement of Counselling, 37*(1), 41–53. doi:10.1007/s10447-014-9224-1

Chang, D. F., & Berk, A. (2009). Making cross-racial therapy work: A phenomenological study of clients' experiences of cross-racial therapy. *Journal of Counseling Psychology, 56*(4), 521–536. Retrieved from http://doi.org/10.1037/a0016905http://doi.org/10.1037/a0016905http://doi.org/10.1037/a0016905

Chao, R. C., Wei, M., Good, G. E., & Flores, L. Y. (2011). Race/ethnicity, color-blind racial attitudes, and multicultural counseling competence: The moderating effects of multicultural counseling training. *Journal of Counseling Psychology, 58*(1), 72–82. doi:10.1037/a0022091

Collins, S., & Arthur, N. (2010). Culture-infused counselling: A model for developing multicultural competence. *Counselling Psychology Quarterly, 23*(2), 217–233. doi:10.1080/09515071003798212

David, E. J. R., Okazaki, S., & Saw, A. (2009). Bicultural self-efficacy among college students: Initial scale development and mental health correlates. *Journal of Counseling Psychology, 56*(2), 211–226. doi:10.1037/a0015419

Goh, M., Yon, K. J., Shimmi, Y., & Hirai, T. (2014). Experiences of Asian psychologists and counselors trained in the USA: An exploratory study. *Asia Pacific Education Review, 15*(4), 593–608. doi:10.1007/s12564-014-9347-4

Goren, M. J., & Plaut, V. C. (2014). Racial identity denial and its discontents: Implications for individuals and organizations. In K. M. Thomas, V. C. Plaut, N. M. Tran, K. M. Thomas, V. C. Plaut, & N. M. Tran (Eds.), *Diversity ideologies in organizations* (pp. 43–66). New York, NY: Routledge.

Graham, A. C. (1981). *Chuang Tzu: The inner chapters.* London, UK: George Allen & Unwin.

Hayes, P. (2016). *Addressing cultural complexities in practice* (3rd ed.). Washington, DC: American Psychological Association.

Johnson, A., & Jackson Williams, D. (2015). White racial identity, color-blind racial attitudes, and multicultural counseling competence. *Cultural Diversity and Ethnic Minority Psychology, 21*(3), 440–449. doi:10.1037/a0037533

LaFromboise, T., Coleman, H. L., & Gerton, J. (1993). Psychological impact of biculturalism: Evidence and theory. *Psychological Bulletin, 114*(3), 395–412. doi:10.1037/0033-2909.114.3.395

Lau, D. C. (1984). *Mencius. Two volumes.* Hong Kong: Chinese University Press.

MacLeod, B. (2013). Application: Theory to culturally competent practice. *Journal of Multicultural Counseling and Development, 41*(1), 169–184.

National Board of Certified Counselors. (2012). *NBCC code of ethics.* Retrieved from http://www.nbcc.org/ethics

Neville, H. A., Awad, G. H., Brooks, J. E., Flores, M. P., & Bluemel, J. (2013). Color-blind racial ideology: Theory, training, and measurement implications in psychology. *American Psychologist, 68*(6), 455–466. doi:10.1037/a0033282

Perera, N. S. (2012). Experimental Analogue Study of White Students' Evaluations of Psychotherapists of Color (Doctoral dissertation, University of Minnesota). https://scholar.google.com/scholar?q=Experime

ntal+analogue+study+of+White+students%E2%80%99+evaluations+of+psychotherapists+of+color.&h
l=en&as_sdt=0&as_vis=1&oi=scholart&sa=X&ved=0ahUKEwj3sbOBwPrTAhUO1WMKHd1SBREQ
gQMIJTAA

Pope-Davis, D. B., Toporek, R. L., Ortega-Villalobos, L., Ligiéro, D. P., Brittan-Powell, C. S., Liu, W. M., ... Liang, C. H. (2002). Client perspectives of multicultural counseling competence: A qualitative examination. *The Counseling Psychologist, 30*(3), 355–393. doi:10.1177/0011000002303001

Ratts, M. J., Singh, A. A., Nassar-McMillan, S., Butler, S. K., & McCullough, J. R. (2016). Multicultural and social justice counseling competencies: Guidelines for the counseling profession. *Journal of Multicultural Counseling and Development, 44*(1), 28–48. doi:10.1002/jmcd.12035

Shaoming, C. (2008). Endurance and non-endurance: From the perspective of virtue ethics. *Frontiers in Philosophy in China, 3*(3), 335–351. doi:10.1007/s11466-008-0022-x

Sue, D. W. (2013). Race talk: The psychology of racial dialogues. *American Psychologist, 68*(8), 663–672. doi:10.1037/a0033681

Sue, D. W., & Sue, D. (2012). *Counseling the culturally diverse: Theory and practice* (6th ed.). New York, NY: John Wiley.

Teyber, E., & McClure F. H. (2010). *Interpersonal process in therapy: An integrative model* (6th ed.). Belmont, CA: Brooks/Cole.

Vinson, T. S., & Neimeyer, G. J. (2003). The relationship between racial identity development and multicultural counseling competency: A second look. *Journal of Multicultural Counseling and Development, 31*(4), 262–278.

Wei, M., Liao, K. Y., Chao, R. C., Mallinckrodt, B., Tsai, P., & Botello-Zamarron, R. (2010). Minority stress, perceived bicultural competence, and depressive symptoms among ethnic minority college students. *Journal of Counseling Psychology, 57*(4), 411–422. doi:10.1037/a0020790

CHAPTER 6

OPPRESSION OF THE SPIRIT

Complexities in the Counseling Encounter

Devika Dibya Choudhuri

SHANIA: INTRODUCING THE CLIENT

Shania sat before me, face turned obstinately away, looking out of the window, her eyes both distant and angry. I leaned forward to make the plea I had made too many times before. "Shania," I said, "I know you can do it. I know how intelligent you are; all you have to do is try, but you're giving up before you even start!" This conversation was part of a familiar dance we would do throughout the academic year. We would have a productive counseling session in which she busily planned out her schedule, organized her time, and made commitments. Then, during the next session, she would disclose that she had not followed through on those promises and would retreat into silence when I pursued her. I felt sure she could succeed; however, she seemed sure she would fail.

Shania was a sophomore in the university, institutionally identified as African American with little option for complexity in self-description. She was a grudging member of the Black Students Association and an enthusiastic but erratic member of the Women of Color group, and she was passionately attached to the Multicultural Center where I worked as a counselor. Academically, she traversed heights and chasms. Each semester she would start out with As and end up with Incompletes from sympathetic professors who wanted to give her a chance but didn't get much work from her. She received failing grades from professors too busy or too disinterested to notice the emotional chaos in which she was enveloped. When Shania was interested, she was dazzling, with great flashing eyes and beaming smiles, her heart on generous display. She was obviously intelligent, with a facility for taking passionate and insightful part in discussions of multiculturalism. Her faculty noted her brilliant contributions to class discussions but bemoaned her lack of follow-through in producing written work. Indeed, upon first acquaintance, Shania seemed an ardent, committed, and intelligent young woman of unlimited potential. When she crashed, as I later discovered, the results were oftentimes late-night phone calls from her, threatening suicide. After her first year, Shania had been put on academic probation and was mandated to see me for counseling. I had recently graduated from my master's counseling program, and Shania was one of my first clients. I desperately wanted to help her live up to the potential she so obviously had.

DIBYA: THE COUNSELOR'S STORY

I am an Asian Indian woman and a first-generation immigrant. I arrived in this country for college at 17 years of age with my family left behind in India, and I was quite happy to make it on my own. I had always been rebellious, fervent in my support of socialist ideals, and encouraged by my family's tolerance of my activism.

When I came out of four years at an Ivy League women's college, I was committed to issues of diversity. There, I had been one of those students who chanted slogans such as "Racism is a disease." We marched and protested to fight for the institution's divestment in South African business and support of apartheid and for increased ethnic minority representation among the faculty and staff of our college. After college, I continued working in an academic setting, administering a community-service program. This employment kept me in touch with human services, and I continued to work with people in homeless shelters and domestic-violence clinics and via suicide hotlines. I decided to go on to graduate work to formalize what I felt was my intrinsic passion to help.

My graduate program in counseling honed my counseling skills and gave me some theories that I alternatively questioned and accepted. For instance, while I loved the empowerment and respect inherent in the person-centered approach, I also felt intuitively that this approach might not work too well with clients who might be in survival modes. I pursued my interest in multicultural counseling with little support or guidance from faculty. I would read widely, following the work of scholars such as Pedersen, Sue, Ivey, and Arredondo, and would often find my faculty unfamiliar or unaware of the issues I then raised in classes. I attended workshops and conferences at which I could receive some of the training, and I used my electives to take classes in women's studies and anthropology. In spite of my efforts, I was woefully unprepared for Shania.

The American Counseling Association's (ACA's) *2014 ACA Code of Ethics* embraces a multicultural approach that acknowledges the social and cultural contexts within which people are embedded, and this value is a theme that runs through the various sections of the ethical code. The gap between striving to understand Shania's diverse cultural background (ACA, 2014) and actually doing so was large, to a great extent because while the literature on multicultural counseling exhorted cultural sensitivity, there was little practical application available at the time. In addition, as a counselor, I am enjoined in section A.7.a to advocate at multiple levels, from individual to societal, to address barriers that inhibit access (ACA, 2014). An issue that also arises when ethics and real-world practice meet is that, although I did the best I could as a new counselor, I am not sure I was practicing within the boundaries of my competence (C.2.a., ACA, 2014).

SHANIA REVISITED: CONCEPTUALIZING THE CLIENT

Theoretically, I framed Shania's issues in a social and familial context (McGoldrick, Giordano, & Pearce, 2005). The narratives we form about the ethnic histories and group identities from which we emerge pattern how we organize to meet the changing contexts of our environment. In a sense, we are lived[1] by the stories of our race and place. Our stories inform us in togetherness and separation. As I reflect now, Shania may have been better suited by a womanist framework (Williams, 2005), which reflected integrated analyses of Shania's race, gender, class, and sexual orientation identities that then allowed our work to be more holistic.

Shania's father was African American, and she identified her mother as Native American, although she did not disclose to me the particular tribal affiliation, which is often critical to establishing identity (Herring, 1999; Sutton & Broken Nose, 2005). The first 10 years of Shania's life were spent on a reservation, but when her mother died, she was moved to a major city and placed with female relatives of her father.[2] Here, she grew up in poverty and was handed from relative to relative. In spite of the obstacles associated with poverty and her unstable living arrangements, Shania was able to attend college on a full academic scholarship. However, this college was a majority-White institution located in a cosmopolitan but small and monocultural town very different in community from both the reservation of her childhood and the urban surroundings of her youth.

Shania had absorbed the attitudes of women from her Native American nation, women whose position was of greater flexibility and power than in dominant society (LaFromboise, Berman, & Sahi, 1994). I believe that culturally Shania often gave the wrong cues and was subtly contradictory—looking African American but acting in ways her African American peers didn't understand. When disturbed, she retreated into cold silence rather than behaving in the expected response of in-your-face confrontation.

Constantly confronted and frustrated by the issues associated with being a woman of color on a predominately White campus, Shania was likely in the throes of reconstructing her racial and ethnic identity. The Racial/Cultural Identity Development Model developed by Sue and Sue (2015) acknowledges similar patterns of adjustment to cultural oppression experienced by many members of minority groups, regardless of specific ethnic identity. In this model, the individual moves through five stages of development as she strives to come to terms both with the demands of the majority culture and the culture of origin and the oppressive relationship between both. The stages delineated are conformity, dissonance, resistance and immersion, introspection, and finally, integrative awareness (Sue & Sue, 2015).

---

1. This is a postmodernist metaphoric phrase implying that, unlike the notion of individuals approaching their lives independently, the social contexts and histories we inherit have far greater agency than we admit—we may not live them so much as they live us.

2. In African American families, often the female kin will be responsible for child-raising rather than the man whose offspring the child is. The father may offer financial support from time to time, but it is the grandmother and often older aunts who take over the day-to-day responsibilities (Crewe & Wilson, 2007). In Shania's case, she never actually spent much time with her father, who migrated frequently all over the country, another aspect of the legacy of slavery.

Shania seemed to be in the resistance and immersion stage with her passionate endorsement of minority-held views and her blanket rejection of dominant society values. Her anger toward White society, her conflicted empathy toward other groups of color, and, most importantly, her reactivity were key identifiers to place her in this stage. One of the significant issues in such a stage is developing identification with and immersion in one's own reference group of origin.

However, Shania's struggles in this stage seemed complicated by the confusion about the reference group available to her. For Native American clients, an understanding of acculturation level in terms of the four positions of bicultural, transitional, assimilated, and marginalized is considered significant to counseling effectiveness (Schol, 2006). In this majority White, monocultural community, Shania's visible appearance identified her as African American, even though her internal ethnic and cultural reference group was Native American. She struggled with her connection to the Black Students' Association and the African American community because she felt like an outsider (Lorde, 2007). However, given her commitment to activism and her upbringing by her father's family, she did not want to be perceived as rejecting the African American community. At the same time, trying to find a reference group that was similar to her inner experience was difficult for her, given how physically distant her original kin were.

Based on messages she had received from her father's family, Shania feared she would also be considered an outsider among Native Americans because of her appearance. Physical appearance has often been a central part of social relationships, and this is particularly true for women. The physical ambiguity of perceived difference in appearance for mixed-race women can be particularly painful as a central part of self-worth (Root, 2004). Confronted by such dilemmas, Shania lashed out at everyone, sabotaging both her academics and her relationships. As Houston (1985, in Root, 1994) framed it in her poem about her own Amerasian mixed identity, Shania had "a soul composed of wars, mixed pride, and agony" (as cited in Root, 1994, p. 455).

THE COUNSELING PROCESS

Shania and I worked together for a year in counseling. I began our work with providing a space in which she could speak (Thomason, 2011). There were many silences, sometimes lasting half the session, but those I could take in stride, given the cultural encounter (Duran, 2006). In my office, I had arranged the chairs so either one of us could look out the window to the trees beyond, and Shania would spend long moments contemplating the vista while I tried to attend without staring intrusively (Sutton & Broken Nose, 2005). When she was particularly upset, she would take a shawl I had hanging and cover herself with it, as if in a cocoon. She would often miss sessions or come late. These times would be followed by the times when she contacted me every day with anguished refrains that evidenced her disintegrating emotional state.

Whenever there were such opportunities, I tried to bring her into contact with some of the local Native adults I knew who played leadership roles in the Native community. Many responded to her with warmth; but here too she alternated between reaching out and withdrawing (Reynolds, Sandro, Ecklund, & Guyker, 2012).

During a particularly harrowing period, when most of our interaction consisted of her either being silent or accusing me of not caring, I tried storytelling (Ricks, Kitchens, Goodrich, & Hancock, 2014). Using the Ericksonian model of storytelling (Wallas, 1985), I carefully constructed for her a fantasy about a school in which a young girl learns to be a puppet master, only to discover to her shock that she and all those around her have strings attached to them. They too are puppets. I detailed the girl's angry, shamed, and destructive responses and then led into her realization that the strings went both ways. She could dance to others' manipulations, or she could use her connectedness to influence in turn and be interdependent. We didn't delve into the story or analyze it, but after that she seemed somewhat more thoughtful and less reactive. In our journey together, however, we seemed as lost as before, finding no answers that worked for her dilemmas.

My work with Shania brought my competence into question. Essentially, no matter how empathic I tried to be with her, I felt personally let down by her because I could not see why she was failing. I knew that she had encounters with racism on this predominantly White campus, but then, so did I. I had been followed and threatened, both verbally and physically. Through our sessions, I learned that Shania had conflicts with many of the other African American students, especially the men. In my mind, I framed the conflicts as her attempt to self-sabotage and alienate her own support group. My internal litany, especially obsessive after our counseling sessions, sounded something like, "Why can't she focus on the good stuff instead of the bad?" or "Why can't she let it go when a certain young black man talks about women derogatorily?" or "Why can't she hear that they aren't targeting her?"

In spite of my apparent lack of success, Shania kept coming to our sessions with a willingness to give our counseling relationship another try. Perhaps she knew that, despite my judgments and critical attitude (relatively visible despite the patina of my person-centered approach), I did care about her and believe in her. Where I failed her was in translating my awareness of the sociocultural conflicts she brought with her into a clinical approach that was effective.

DIBYA REVISITED: REFLEXIVITY

Self-reflexivity is an essential part of the counseling relationship where one examines the circular nature of both oneself as the counselor and the counseling relationship. What I left out of the clinical description of our process was the required exploration of my own privilege and oppression (section A; ACA, 2014), a lens that might have enabled me to perceive Shania's impasse more clearly. Because I used my own identity as a woman of color as the focal point for understanding and interpreting her behavior, I assumed that Shania's emotional issues were based on the day-to-day harassment women of color face. When she related examples of being overlooked in class by the professor or of being asked whether she had really done the assignment by herself, I responded with understanding but also with some underlying impatience. In my thoughts shaped by my own internalized oppression, I asked, "After all, wasn't this par for the course? One simply had to be twice as good to withstand the criticism." In doing this, I failed to notice the profound differences between us, differences my understanding could not encompass. One important difference between Shania and me was that, for the first 17 years of my life, I did not live in a society in which I was the minority. I was raised middle class and came from a caste background that gave me privileged access in my home country to almost everywhere I wanted to go. These differences in historical and lived experience profoundly affected the interactions and understandings that I brought into our counseling sessions.

As an immigrant of color, I understood the impact of racism in the present United States society, but I had little experiential understanding of racism as a generational force that operated to punish and confirm status, and particularly the impact of historical trauma, a construct that reverberates multigenerationally in the lives of Native Americans (Grayshield, Salazar, Rutherford, Mihecoby, & Luna, 2015). India, by its own history, still struggles with the impact of 200 years of colonization by the British and the legacy of internalized oppression that seeks paleness in its women, adeptness at Western cultural norms to denote competence and achievement, and infinite adaptability to oppressive conditions. My own internalized oppression led me to admire White people because my attitude toward them was that they were absent conquerors who had left an admirable heritage. My cultural heritage that valued harmony made me a compliant and successful assimilator, even if I intended subversion. In other words, I might talk about racism, but I did it in a colonized English that was grammatically flawless. I internalized the immigrant's optimism (Fuligni, 2011) and belief that struggle brought reward—the belief that if a person does everything twice as well as another, success cannot be denied by even unfair systems. After all, many others, including myself, have worked hard and become successful. I often wondered why the next person, in this case Shania, couldn't follow suit. My perspective of "I did, so why can't you?" caused me to overlook how messages of success have been defined by White, middle-class society for people of color in the United States. For some people of color, particularly Native Americans, the defined success may require directions that conflict with cultural lifestyle orientations (Tafoya & Vecchio, 2005).

I wanted Shania to succeed because she was a woman of color with whom I felt kinship; I wanted her to overcome obstacles because I cared, and I thought she could do it because I had. I had no emotional understanding of the paralyzing traps she was in, traps in which failure and success were one and the same (Ryback & Decker-Fitts, 2009). Within the academic context, achievement and success were framed as desirable. However, the meaning of such constructs were defined as achievable through using a language, stance, and process infused with White, middle-class values. But if Shania did achieve that success, she faced losing her already fragile membership in the communities of people of color. She had lost so much in her life already—her indigenous community, her mother, her father, her sense of family, and the norms and values she had come to know. No wonder she resisted when I asked her to risk losing what little she had left. It's important to acknowledge that I had none of these insights at the time; and it was only long after, after I had gained much more clinical experience, that I understood better what had been going on here.

RESOLUTION

At the end of her sophomore year, Shania told me that she was dropping out of school and planned to return to New York. I struggled with her decision, for she relayed no sense of future plans or purpose to go along with her decision. I foreshadowed a life of drifting that might end sharply, given my knowledge of her self-destructive attempts. I dreaded that I would someday hear that she had ended up in a series of positions that took no account of her amazing intelligence and generous spirit—or worse, that she had committed suicide. I felt a lack of competence in my abilities and viewed this act as failure for both of us, even though I argued and fought with her and for her, far more attached than I ever had with any other client. Nevertheless, she still left.

Two years after Shania left and at a time when I was leaving my work site to go on to a doctoral program, I received a letter from her. In it, she detailed an incredible journey in which she had returned to the city but then gone on to return to the reservation. She had made contact with some of her mother's relatives and reconfirmed her roots (Reynolds, Sandro, Ecklund, & Guyker, 2012). She also ended up working with a youth-at-risk program. After having those experiences, she believed that she was ready to continue her education. During that time, she had been successfully taking classes at a local college to finish a degree in education, and she intended to get a graduate degree in social work so she could go back and work on the reservation.

In her letter she wrote that many things I had said to her during our counseling sessions were making more sense now, but she had needed to be at home to hear them properly. She did not elaborate with examples, so I can never know which of the many things I said to her stayed and which faded (and I suspect we might each have chosen different examples when pointing to critical moments). She finished with saying that although we had had our "fights," she wanted to let me know what was happening in her life because she knew I had cared. I cried when I read that letter. My tears were for the thankfulness I felt for her triumphs and also for my own sense of relief.

CONCLUSION

It has been many years since the experiences discussed here, but I have never forgotten the lessons. As a counselor-educator who teaches multicultural counseling, I am framed in the role of expert. However, Shania's example reminds me to stay conscious and humble. I realize we have much to learn about the convoluted nature of oppression and the resistance of privilege to self-scrutiny. The generations of learning and misinformation have deep roots, which can bear poisoned fruit that we ingest without ever knowing we are doing so. Knowing the theory of cultural competence is rarely sufficient compared to knowing the practice. Our own perspectives and worldviews, no matter how scrutinized through classes, theory, and academic experiences, still hold potency when we are challenged to reach across and be respectfully present and engaged with another.

In counseling, it is in the spirit that we perceive the impact of oppression: the defeat and the despair, the self-hatred and the sabotage, the disjunction and alienation. In other roles, we can advocate and struggle against systems, but in the counseling relationship itself, I believe it is essential to work with the noxious messages that sicken the spirit. Effective multicultural counseling goes beyond theoretical knowledge of racial identity development and a "culturegram" awareness of cultural customs (CultureGrams, 2010). To infuse one's counseling and truly recognize the multicultural nature of every encounter is to become committed to interrogating the self in multiple contexts and multiple lenses. If we can look at oppression as a powerful systemic force that shapes our worldviews, status, history, and experience, we must acknowledge that it permeates our practice. Every encounter invokes some aspects of oppression. The degree to which we can scrutinize both the client and ourselves and attend to the ways in which each of us brings to the mix our perspective of the world is the degree to which we can perhaps avoid replicating the toxicity of oppression. And because legacies of oppression and privilege are heavy with emotions such as shame, guilt, anger, and resentment, we must be prepared for the emotional upheaval of such scrutiny. Our reward for perseverance is that of the positive impact that uprooting the legacy of privilege and oppression has on both our clients and ourselves.

DISCUSSION QUESTIONS

1. How might you frame Shania's issues developmentally? Can you decipher ways of self-presentation that might be traced to her intersecting cultural constituencies?
2. How might you apply an analysis of historical trauma to Shania's presenting problems?
3. In working with a client such as Shania, what issues of your own oppression and privilege might you need to explore and bracket?
4. What might the counselor have done that could have been more helpful to Shania?
5. As a counselor, how can you manage your frustration and disappointment when a client is not helped?

REFERENCES

American Counseling Association. (2014). *2014 APA code of ethics*. Alexandria, VA: Author.

Crewe, S. E., & Wilson, R. G. (2007). Kinship care: From family tradition to social policy in the African American community. *Journal of Health and Social Policy, 22*(3), 1–7.

CultureGrams. (2010). *Culturegrams: The nations around us, world edition*. Lindon, UT: Ferguson.

Duran, E. (2006). *Healing the soul wound: Counseling with American Indians and other native peoples* (Multicultural Foundations of Psychology and Counseling Series). New York, NY: Teachers College Press.

Fuligni, A. (2011). The intersection of aspirations and resources in the development of children from immigrant families. In C. García Coll & A. Marks (Eds.), *The immigrant paradox in children and adolescents: Is becoming American a developmental risk?* (pp. 299–308). Washington, DC: American Psychological Association.

Grayshield, L., Rutherford, J. J., Salazar, S. B., Mihecoby, A. L., and Luna, L. L. (2015). Understanding and healing historical trauma: The perspectives of Native American elders. *Journal of Mental Health Counseling, 37*(4), 295–307.

Herring, R. (1999). *Counseling with Native Americans and Alaska natives: Strategies for helping professionals* (Multicultural Aspects of Counseling Series 14). Thousand Oaks, CA: SAGE.

LaFromboise, T. D., Berman, J. S., & Sahi, B. K. (1994). American Indian woman. In L. Comas-Diaz & B. Greene (Eds.), *Women of color: Integrating ethnic and gender identities in psychotherapy* (pp. 30–71). New York, NY: Guilford Press.

Lorde, A. (2007). *Sister outsider: Essays and speeches.* Trumansburg, NY: Crossing Press.

McGoldrick, M., Giordano, J., & Pearce, J. K. (2005). *Ethnicity and family therapy* (3rd Ed.). New York, NY: Guilford Press.

Reynolds, A. L., Sandro, M., Ecklund, T. R., & Guyker, W. (2012). Dimensions of acculturation among Native American college students. *Measurement and Evaluation in Counseling & Development, 45*(2), 125–136.

Ricks, L., Kitchens, S., Goodrich, T., & Hancock, E. (2014). My story: The use of narrative therapy in individual and group counseling. *Journal of Creativity in Mental Health, 9*(1), 99–110.

Root, M. P. (1994). Mixed-race women. In L. Comas-Diaz & B. Greene (Eds.), *Women of color: Integrating ethnic and gender identities in psychotherapy* (pp. 455–478). New York, NY: Guilford Press.

Root, M. P. (2004). From exotic to a dime a dozen. In A. Gillem & C. Thompson (Eds.), *Biracial women in therapy: Between the rock of gender and the hard place of race* (pp. 19–31). New York, NY: Haworth Press.

Rybak, C. & Decker-Fitts, A. (2009). Understanding Native American healing practices. *Counselling Psychology Quarterly, 22*(3), 333–342.

Schol, M. B. (2006). Native American identity development and counseling preferences: A study of Lumbee undergraduates. *Journal of College Counseling, 9,* 48–59.

Sue, D. W., & Sue, D. (2015) *Counseling the culturally diverse: Theory and practice* (7th ed.). New York, NY: John Wiley.

Sutton, C. T., & Broken Nose, M. A. (2005). American Indian families: An overview. In M. McGoldrick, J. Giordano, & J. K. Pearce (Eds.), *Ethnicity and family therapy* (3rd ed., pp. 43–54). New York, NY: Guilford Press.

Tafoya, N., & Vecchio, A. D. (2005). Back to the future: An examination of the Native American holocaust experience. In M. McGoldrick, J. Giordano, & J. K. Pearce (Eds.), *Ethnicity and family therapy* (3rd ed., pp. 55–63). New York, NY: Guilford Press.

Thomason, T. (2011). Best practices in counseling Native Americans. *Journal of Indigenous Research, 1,* 1–4.

Wallas, L. (1985). *Stories for the third ear: Using hypnotic fables in psychotherapy.* New York, NY: Norton.

Williams, C. B. (2005). Counseling African American women: Multiple identities—multiple constraints. *Journal of Counseling & Development, 83,* 278–283.

CHAPTER 7

UNMASKING WITHIN-GROUP PREJUDICE, INTERNALIZED OPPRESSION, AND PRIVILEGE

A Case Study

Felice Lichaw, Marya Howell-Carter, Meagan Voulo,
and Michael R. Harris

I n this chapter, two of the authors, Felice Lichaw and Marya Howell-Carter, share their narrative. Felice is a supervisor in a community-based counseling center and Marya is her supervisee. The story of their supervisory relationship highlights the impact of internalized oppression and the revelation of internal attitudes through good supervision.

INTRODUCTION: FELICE

I come from a Jewish, lower-middle-class family. My mother emigrated from Czechoslovakia with her family when she was quite young, and most of my maternal grandmother's family were killed in the Holocaust. My father was a first-generation American (United States) whose father had been persecuted as a Jew in Poland and Russia before World War I. I am the daughter of this union.

Having spent the majority of my 20-year career working with clients whose cultural contexts differed from my own, I was well down the road toward understanding the role of culture in treatment when I met Marya Carter, then a second-year doctoral student. Marya applied for an externship at our agency, a private, not-for-profit, community-based, youth-service agency. The agency serviced a large and diverse area of Chicago, including a historical port of entry for immigrant populations. The students at the high school closest to our location spoke a mix of 102 languages. Our primary population was African American adolescents and their families, and I was looking for a student who would be available to interact within our clients' diverse cultural contexts. Marya was searching for a site at which to complete her externship, and she had an interest in working with youth and families of Color.

In our first interview, Marya presented herself as an open, enthusiastic, and idealistic young woman. She looked fresh. She seemed surprised by some of my questions, but she gamely answered them, particularly the one I asked all students about what brought them to the agency and what they wanted to get out of the experience for themselves. I cannot remember exactly what Marya said about her motivation for working in our agency. It might have been something about fulfilling the need to give back to her community, or wanting to learn more about working with youth and families, but it was sufficiently self-motivated for her to be offered an externship.

INTRODUCTION: MARYA

My father is African American, born in the 1920s of Southern parents who migrated north to find work during the years following World War I. In the late 1960s, he married my mother, the daughter of a Caucasian German farm family in central Michigan. I was born in Detroit, not long after the fires of the 1967 race riots destroyed much of our city. As I grew up, my father from time to time warned me about the legacy he perceived to be mine. "You are a Black woman; you will always be at a disadvantage. To be successful, you have to work harder and be smarter than everyone else." Though he did not have the language for it at the time, my father was acutely aware of *intersectionality*, the "double discrimination" that was his experience of the position of Black women in American society (Cole, 2009; Crenshaw, 1989, p. 149).

I believed my father and identified with his admonitions. That is, Black women must do more and do it better. What my father did not realize was that, because of my biraciality and light-skin privilege (McIntosh, 1998), I was insulated from many of the harshest realities Black women face.

When I decided to enter the field of psychology, I made the commitment to work with People of Color. As the time for choosing training experiences approached, my graduate-school peers chose field placements in the affluent, White, and Jewish communities of Chicago's North Shore. I assumed that, being Black, I would not feel comfortable in those settings and that the people in those settings might not feel comfortable with me. I wanted to gain experience in a community of "my people" a community with real problems, a community that needed someone like me—an educated, socially conscious, Black clinician.

My requirements for choosing a clinical placement were shaped by an additional assumption that I made about myself: that, being African American, I could not exercise prejudice. Although I had been protected from the most blatant expressions of prejudice, I thoroughly understood the history of pain and disenfranchisement that Black people had endured as subjects of one of its forms—racism. I assumed that this awareness would protect me from engaging in any form of prejudice or discrimination.

UNDERSTANDING THE EXPERIENCE OF PRIVILEGE—COMING TO CONSCIOUSNESS: MARYA

When I began my externship, I was totally unaware of the ways in which dominant cultural stereotypes and internalized racism had infiltrated my thinking about myself, African Americans, and other people of color. I am now aware that the American myth of the meritocracy had pervaded my thinking. I had not yet examined how the ideal of the meritocracy had been distorted by racism and other –isms (Knowles & Lowery, 2012).

Moreover, much as Robin Johnson-Ahorlu (2012) has since articulated, I had come to believe an individual-centered deficit perspective rather than a structural one. My formal academic training in psychology taught me that those who are not successful are flawed—flawed by mental illness, a poor work ethic, or a misunderstanding about the requirements for success. Surprisingly, messages from family were not so different. My father frequently talked about ways that Blacks were oppressed, shut out, ignored, and systematically disenfranchised, but he too had taught me that the way to combat this was personal: by being above reproach. Though he witnessed, cheered, and benefitted from the civil rights movement, he had not been *of* that movement. His was not the social-change generation but the generation before. His generation accepted incremental change from within an existing system. For him, success required personal adaptation and eschewed demanding institutional transformation. It was clear that I had adopted the same belief structure. In becoming a therapist, I sought to help my community by helping individuals and families combat their flaws and achieve success.

I began my externship with Felice at Alternatives, Inc. in the fall of my second year of graduate school. During the first weeks there, my work seemed to be going well. I was making efforts to connect with my clients, and it appeared that they were engaging in the therapeutic process. However, as time progressed, clients stopped regularly attending their therapy sessions with me. I became frustrated with their sporadic attendance or nonattendance and started to look for an explanation.

The psychodynamic perspective I had learned at my privileged, White, upper-class university informed me that my clients were being *resistant* to the therapeutic process. They were unconsciously clinging to their current behaviors because the cost of change might be too great. In contrast, during supervision, Felice attempted to normalize my clients' behaviors. We discussed the agency's client population and the factors that make sporadic attendance, nonattendance, and attendance only during acute crisis common and predictable. We also began to explore ways to change client expectations about attendance and counter the resistance associated with nonattendance. Yet I remained unclear about what kept certain clients and not others engaged in the therapeutic process and uncertain whether I was providing an appropriate therapeutic environment.

Looking for role models, I began to examine more closely the attitudes and practices of other therapists working at the agency. I noticed that my colleagues were not all equally skilled. While some were open, conscious, and sensitive in regard to the cultural contexts of their clients of Color, others were ignorant, even offensive. I judged those in the latter group to be poor therapists: people whose upbringing, race, and education limited their world-view and prevented them from connecting with our client population. At the same time, I realized that I shared something with this group. We had the same pattern of no-shows, cancellations, and premature terminations. I began to experience a growing dissonance between how I viewed myself and how my clients might be viewing me. As my recognition of my problem grew, so did my anxiety and confusion.

REFLECTIONS ON CHANGE: MARYA

Like the therapists I was so quick to judge, I realized that I too had failed to engage my clients by not creating a safe space where their experiences, strengths, and culture defined the context in which change occurred. Instead, I was attempting to replicate the values of the world in which I lived—particularly values around promptness, openness, and parenting. Although I listened to their stories, I did not *truly hear* their stories. Critical race theory emphasizes the importance of letting People of Color tell their own narrative and recognizing it as truth (Delgado & Stefancic, 1993). When I listened to my clients, I did not hear their truths. Instead, I listened for the holes—for the places where they could learn to adapt to the dominant cultural narrative and create their own change. Without being fully aware of it, I expected my clients to tune into my values and to adopt those values as their own. I was replicating the experience of invalidation that they faced in their everyday lives.

I was an extremely reluctant supervisee as I struggled to understand why I was not having the success that I had expected. As the hour for weekly supervision with Felice approached, I experienced a pervasive feeling of heaviness accompanied by nausea. I attempted to avoid supervision by being late or seeming to forget, and I gained a temporary reprieve from self-examination by diverting attention to my acting out. The reason for my symptoms was the dissonance I experienced during supervision. Felice was challenging me to see my clients as whole people who were successful and productive in ways that I, as a product of the dominant culture, did not accept. Felice was asking me to view my clients not as the victims I perceived them to be but as people living within a particular set of circumstances to which they responded adaptively. They were doing the best job they knew how to do. I could not yet see my clients' strength, resilience, and integrity, a view that would enable me to more effectively assist them in creating change.

The feeling in the pit of my stomach before every supervision session with Felice also came from the discovery that my cultural assimilation and internalized racism had been so pervasive that I was having difficulty meeting the needs of my clients and the expectations of my supervisor. I had great difficulty acknowledging that privilege—derived from skin color, middle-class status, and education—made me different from the clients with whom I worked and impeded the therapeutic process. I also found it difficult to accept that Felice, a White Jewish woman—both descriptors are important, given the complex shared history of Blacks and Jews in Detroit—had more insight into, and understanding of, the effects of economic deprivation and racism than I had. Fortunately, I was sufficiently engaged in the learning process to continue with supervision even though the dissonance it created was quite uncomfortable. Moreover, Felice was a savvy teacher, compassionate healer, and gifted storyteller. She facilitated my process, solicited narrative, pushed, and supported.

ENGAGING IN THE PROCESS OF CHANGE: FELICE

While Marya was working through this phase in her identity development, I was thinking about how I could help her to understand the context of the clients she was working with. Although it was true that Marya was biracial and had been raised in a predominantly African American community, it is equally true that there is a great amount of variability within African American communities (Ibrahim, 1991; Putnam 2007) and that relative privilege within these communities does exist (Cole, 2009). She seemed to have a background that engendered that relative privilege. I knew she had done her undergraduate work at a prestigious university and had won a fellowship for graduate study there. Knowing these things led me to believe that, in high school, she had achieved a degree of academic success that surpassed most and that she also had managed to sustain her excellence through four years of undergraduate study to win a fellowship. When Marya and I began to work together, I did not yet understand how the dynamic of relative privilege would unfold within the process of her professional development.

It seemed to me that the best way to help Marya understand our clients and explore her own privilege was to acquire information regarding her context. When we began supervision, I attempted to establish a safe relationship in which we could deliberately, carefully, and strategically discuss race, privilege, and culture. This safe environment has been described as the top-rated supervisory behavior in successful multicultural supervision (Dressel, Consoli, Kim & Atkinson, 2007). Establishing a safe relationship with a trainee is much like establishing a safe relationship with clients in therapy. The supervisor is required to maintain an attitude of acceptance and willingness to engage with the trainee's experiences, knowledge, mistakes, and criticism. If the expectation of the supervisor is that trainees will work within the contexts of their clients, the supervisor has to model this by working within the context of the trainee. Establishing a safe relationship also involves both setting norms for what is appropriate for discussion in supervision and having clear role expectations with the accompanying role accountability.

I communicated some important ground rules to Marya at the beginning of the relationship, most of which are consistent with established models for developing multicultural competence (Dressel et al., 2007) and training standards for multicultural counselors (Ratts, Singh, Nassar-McMillan, Butler, & McCullough, 2015; APA, 2002; CACREP, 2016):

1. Cultural identity is a valid and valuable tool for establishing connection with others.
2. It is important to accept and respect both your own culture and others' cultural identities.
3. Discussion of cultural background, differences, and expectations is normal within the context of both the supervisory relationship and the therapeutic relationship.
4. Respect for clients' cultural contexts is an important tool in establishing relationship.

5. Understanding context is an important part of understanding people's culture.
6. All cultures are adaptive in the sense that they are made up of components that help people get the work of living done.
7. Some adaptive cultural components may have outlived their usefulness yet still remain parts of the culture. These parts are usually referred to as dysfunctional.
8. Cultures' dysfunctional components offer valuable information about history and current functioning, and, through implication, possible roads toward change.

Underlying these ground rules was my assumption that Marya came to our agency with her own set of experiences, beliefs, and assumptions about the world around her and the people in her world. These assumptions formed the framework that she would use in creating relationships. I asked Marya countless questions in an attempt to assist her in making her assumptions explicit. Explicit assumptions are more easily clarified and more easily shaped to include novel situations. I set out to assist her in developing an awareness of her own values, beliefs, and assumptions, with the intention of facilitating both the engagement process and her own countertransference issues.

I was aware of the differences in our cultures and was deliberate in my attempts to understand and bridge the gaps in our culturally based understanding. I was curious about Marya, as I am curious about most people, and I let my curiosity guide me in the process of uncovering the gaps and making connection.

I came to supervision aware that there is no single correct way of doing things or of seeing the world and with the hope that I would model a good example within the supervisory relationship for working in treatment. I encouraged Marya to try new things and to make mistakes. I also encouraged confusion—in my experience the precursor to change. My goal was to assist her in ferreting out her truths and to challenge those truths when I saw them interfering with her efficacy in the development of therapeutic relationships. This approach formed the basis of our supervisory process. There is risk involved in this method—the student may be intolerant of dissonance or may not be developmentally or emotionally ready for change. Happily, Marya was ready to engage in this process. The stage had been set for her to begin to explore her identity as a therapist working with poor minority populations.

INTERNALIZATION OF CHANGE: MARYA

Clinical supervision furthered my understanding of my role with clients and my awareness of my own privilege. It helped me to see that I had been using my own cultural experience to infer my clients' cultural context. Although many things about Felice and her personal style spurred this change, the aspect of supervision that had most influenced me was the inquiries she made. She asked *how* questions about my clients, as well as about my own context and racial identity. Felice asked me for information about how my clients experienced the world and how their life experiences had affected them. Quite often, these were questions that I had never considered. I had learned to ask the *what* questions, such as "What were the client's experiences?" Once I knew *what*, I thought that my theory of psychopathology and my own ability to reason would provide me with the answer to *how* events had affected the client. Coming from a doctoral program that rarely addressed multicultural issues, I had not been encouraged to counsel idiographically. According to Ridley (1995), "The idiographic approach underscores the need to understand the personal meaning held by the client as a particular person, not simply as a representative of certain groups" (p. 83). By believing that I knew something about my clients because I was a person of color, I was ignoring individuality and within-group variation. As Ibrahim (1991) pointed out,

> Treating any person as a stereotype of his or her cultural group violates the person's individuality and may lead to premature termination, with minimal therapeutic effectiveness, and possible negative outcomes regarding the client's perceptions of the counseling ... profession. (p. 14)

The early stages of a therapeutic relationship largely consist of information gathering, assessment, and goal setting—what people's experiences have been, what those experiences mean about them, and how the process of treatment will proceed (Hill, 2005). After meeting with clients in these early phases, I would return to my desk, think through the information the client had given me, and connect that information to the problem that had prompted the client to seek therapy.

For example, if an adolescent client reported that his mother was abusing drugs and that many of his friends were in a gang, I made the assumption that these factors were significant in his choice to be gang involved. Gang membership provides adolescents with a substitute family (Maxson, Whitlock, & Klein, 1998). Based on this logical, research-based, well-intentioned understanding, I would create treatment goals and decide on a treatment approach. Before Felice inquired, I did not routinely ask clients how they interpreted life events or how those events had influenced their decision-making. My cultural encapsulation was so powerful, my socialization so great, and my education so narrow that I believed that I already knew the answers.

At the beginning of my externship and supervisory relationship, I was excited about the treatment-planning work that I had done for those clients because I thought I understood them, particularly those African American clients who I perceived were so culturally similar to me. However, as time progressed and attendance waned, so did my excitement. Fortunately, Felice's questioning regarding how life events had shaped my clients, and her insistence that I answer with what *they* said and the meaning *they* made from their own experiences (rather than with assumptions and theories), prompted me out of my role as the expert who knew more about my clients than they knew about themselves. I began to understand why clients had cancelled, failed to attend appointments, or terminated therapy altogether.

My growing insight led to many discussions in supervision about the difficulty I experienced in asking clients the questions that were so critical to forming a complete understanding. As I learned to consciously question, to allow my curiosity to lead me, I had to constantly remind myself that the clients are the experts on their lives and experiences. Moreover, I was learning to "hold the dialectic" famously described by Marsha Linehan (1993). I learned to hold contrasting beliefs: A client behavior could be rational/adaptive *and* problematic simultaneously. Behaviors could both be logical choices that reflected strength and integrity in the context of discriminative systems and still lead to undesirable outcomes.

The Association of Multicultural Counseling and Development, a division of the American Counseling Association, has recently adopted a new set of multicultural competencies for counseling professionals (Ratts et al., 2015). These competencies, the most comprehensive we have seen, provide a framework for integrating multicultural competencies into therapeutic practice. They describe the complex interplay of therapist and client identities, power, privilege, and oppression on the therapeutic relationship and process. Most important, however, these groups are the first to articulate the importance of social justice competencies, in addition to the more traditional multicultural competencies. This socioecological model articulates the three traditional domains of multicultural competence: (a) counselor self-awareness, (b) client worldview, and (c) culturally appropriate interventions. It adds areas of competence related to the counseling relationship (a direct exploration of how the counseling relationship is affected by privileged and marginalized status) and advocacy interventions (i.e., counselors must advocate with and for clients at all appropriate levels). The implication of these social-justice competencies is that therapists are obligated to work toward social justice as an inherent part of any therapeutic relationship—a critical modification of earlier models of multicultural competence. Each of these competencies is designed to reduce stereotyping, reduce the exertion of privilege, eliminate the imposition of majority culture values, increase awareness of systemic discrimination, and impose an obligation to work toward social reform in counseling.

CONCLUSION

During supervision, Felice asked me how my life experiences had shaped who I was. This question led to conversations that made explicit my own strongly held cultural values, beliefs, assumptions, and countertransference issues, and it helped me develop a tolerance for dissonance, ambiguity, and my own mistakes. Our work together helped to reveal internalized oppression, challenged me to confront my belief in the meritocracy, and allowed me to explore my own privilege. Since my work with Felice, I have gone on to teach and train new counselors in multicultural counseling. The experiences that she and I shared in that formative year helped shape the approach I have taken in training students to be culturally competent.

DISCUSSION QUESTIONS

1. How are dominant cultural stereotypes perpetuated by organizational or institutional structures? How might this perpetuation affect an individual's ability to develop awareness about prejudice?
2. What are some of the values that you hold that might limit your ability to make connections with clients who are different from you?

3. When a direct supervisor has difficulty accepting his or her own privilege, how might a supervisee work through his or her own biases? What other resources might students draw from to further their cultural competence?

4. How might universities better integrate issues of multiculturalism, privilege, and racial identity development into both their curricula and training experiences?

5. Should clients who intend to work only within their own racial/ethnic group receive multicultural competence training? Why/Why not? If so, should that training be different than traditional multicultural training? Explain.

6. What are some ways that a young clinician can reconcile psychotherapy theory with the realities of systemic racism and discrimination? If your university does not explicitly attempt to balance theory with modern social reality, how might you do so?

7. Although some people are ready to confront their stereotyped beliefs and prejudices, others are not. What methods, other than direct confrontation, can help people to uncover their prejudices?

8. If you are interested in resources for classroom or supervision use, Breakingprejudice. org is a good site for activities and assignments to encourage self-awareness, other-awareness, confrontation of stereotyping/prejudice, and increased social activism.

REFERENCES

American Psychological Association. (2002). *Guidelines on multicultural education, training, research, practice and organizational change for psychologists*. Retrieved from http://www.apa.org/pi/oema/resources/policy/multicultural-guideline.pdf

Cole, E. R. (2009). Intersectionality and research in psychology. *American Psychologist, 64*(3), 170–180. doi:10.1037/a0014564

Council for Accreditation of Counseling and Related Education Programs. (2016). *2016 CACREP standards for accreditation*. Retrieved from http://www.cacrep.org/wp-content/uploads/2012/10/2016-CACREP-Standards.pdf

Crenshaw, K. W. (1989). Demarginalizing the intersection of race and sex: A black feminist critique of antidiscrimination doctrine, feminist theory and antiracist politics. *University of Chicago Legal Forum, 1*, 139–167. Retrieved from http://chicagounbound.uchicago.edu/cgi/viewcontent.cgi?article=1052&context=uclf

Delgado, R., & Stefancic, J. (1993). Critical race theory: An annotated bibliography. *Virginia Law Review, 79*(2), 461–516. Retrieved from http://www.jstor.org/stable/1073418

Dressel, J. L., Consoli, A. J., Kim, B. K., & Atkinson, D. R. (2007). Successful and unsuccessful multicultural supervisory behaviors: A Delphi poll. *Journal of Multicultural Counseling and Development,* (35)1, 54–64. doi:10.1002/j.2161-1912.2007.tb00049.x

Hill, C. E. (2005). Therapist techniques, client involvement, and the therapeutic relationship: Inextricably intertwined in the therapy process. *Psychotherapy: Theory, Research, Practice, Training, 42*(4), 431–442. doi:10.1037/0033-3204.42.4.431

Ibrahim, F. A. (1991). Contribution of cultural worldview to generic counseling and development. *Journal of Counseling and Development, 70*(1), 13–19. doi:10.1002/j.1556-6676.1991.tb01556.x

Johnson-Ahorlu, R. N. (2012). The academic opportunity gap: How racism and stereotypes disrupt the education of African-American undergraduates. *Race Ethnicity and Education, 15*(5), 1–20. doi:10.1080/13613324.2011.645566

Knowles, E. D., & Lowery, B. S. (2012). Meritocracy, self-concerns, and Whites' denial of racial inequity. *Self & Identity, 11*(2), 202–222.

Linehan, M. M. (1993). *Cognitive behavioral treatment of borderline personality disorder.* New York, NY: Guilford Press.

Maxson, C. L., Whitlock, M. L., & Klein, M. W. (1998). Vulnerability to street gang membership: Implications for practice. *Social Service Review, 72*(1), 70–92.

McIntosh, P. (1998). White privilege: Unpacking the invisible knapsack. In M. McGoldrick (Ed.), *Re-visioning family therapy: Race, culture, and gender in clinical practice* (pp. 147–152). New York, NY: Guilford Press.

Putnam, R. D. (2007). E pluribus unum: Diversity and community in the twenty-first century. The 2006 Johan Skytte Prize lecture. *Scandinavian Political Studies, 30*(2), 137–174. doi:10.1111/j.1467-9477.2007.00176.x

Ratts, M. J., Singh, A. A., Nassar-McMillan, S., Butler, S. K., & McCullough, J. R. (2015). *Multicultural and social justice counseling competencies.* Retrieved from American Counseling Association website: https://www.counseling.org/docs/default-source/competencies/multicultural-and-social-justice-counseling-competencies.pdf?sfvrsn=20

Ridley, C. (1995). *Overcoming unintentional racism in counseling and therapy: A practitioner's guide to intentional intervention.* Thousand Oaks, CA: SAGE.

CHAPTER 8

EXPLORING THE INTERSECTIONS OF RACE, GENDER, SEXUALITY, AND CLASS IN THE CLINICAL SETTING

Damien W. Riggs

Well over a decade ago, when I was in my honors year, I found myself struggling to write a thesis on race and Whiteness in Australia in which I explicitly positioned myself as a White gay man. The data that I examined in the thesis reflected my own experiences of race privilege, yet many of the experiences I drew upon also involved my identity as a gay man and my experiences of marginalization in this regard. In exploring my own experiences of privilege living as a White person in a colonial nation, I was left feeling somewhat uneasy; I had a nagging feeling that, somehow, while this emphasis upon race privilege told the most important story, it didn't tell all of the story: It didn't locate me within a range of identity categories from which I stand both to benefit and potentially to be disadvantaged.

A year later, I was undertaking my PhD research and again struggling to find a way to account for race, sexuality, gender, and class as mutually constituted categories. The idea of cultural capital (see Lamont & Lareau, 1988) certainly gave me some leeway through which to conceptualize Whiteness as differentially distributed, dependent upon any individual's approximation of the norm of White, middle-class, able-bodied heterosexuality (Hage, 1998). The idea of cultural capital was (and still is) very useful in my research, particularly when I have sought to examine some of the reasons for why White nonheterosexual people such as myself may become highly invested in what often appear to be highly normative political agendas (what Duggan [2002] has referred to as *homonormativity*).

My examinations of cultural capital and its deployment by White lesbians and gay men (particularly in relation to calls for marriage rights and claims related to parenting), however, have often gotten me into some hot water. Some activists have accused me of being divisive and of giving those on the political Right yet more material with which to attack nonheterosexual people in Australia. For example, by stating that it was a very privileged way of thinking to use analogies between racial apartheid and the denial of marriage rights to nonheterosexual people to argue for the latter (e.g., Riggs, 2006), some have suggested that doing so minimizes the psychological and social distress caused by the denial of rights.

To clearly locate my arguments within a theoretical framework, I have extensively engaged with theories of both intersectionality (Crenshaw, 1991) and race privilege (Moreton Robinson, 2000). Intersectionality theory provides the scope to move beyond seeing identity categories as "problems of addition," and instead conceptualize identity categories simultaneously. So, for example, I am not sometimes a gay man and sometimes a White man and yet other times a middle-class man. I am always a White, middle-class, able-bodied, gay man living in a society founded through colonization and subsequent illegal possession of land in which the subject position "White, middle-class, abled-bodied heterosexual" is privileged above all others. Understood in this way, my identity becomes less a matter of breaking it down into its constitutive parts and determining which ones add or subtract from my privilege relative to others (Barnard, 2003). Rather, the approach I adopt aims to recognize that, although race is not the sole category of difference I sit in a relation to, my status as a White person in a colonial nation must always be at the forefront of my analysis, as must my identity as a cisgender male, and that these locations fundamentally shape the other identity categories I inhabit.

Considering identities intersectionally has led me to suggest the utility of focusing upon what I have termed the need for a different "yes, but." Typically, the "yes, but" I see circulating within many White nonheterosexual communities is that yes, members of such communities experience privilege as White people, but we nonetheless experience marginalization and discrimination as nonheterosexual people. This type of "yes, but," I would argue, maintains sexuality as the central node of difference and thus allows race privilege to be subsumed under the dominant focus upon sexuality-based discrimination. In this particular "yes, but," sexuality-based discrimination is at times presented as something akin to a surprise to people who otherwise (on the basis of our race) may expect relative security, as James Baldwin (1984, cited in Bĕrubĕ, 2001) stated so well: "I think White gay people feel cheated because they were born, in principle, into a society in which they were supposed to be safe. The anomaly of their sexuality puts them in danger, unexpectedly" (p. 256).

In contrast, the "yes, but" I propose runs more like this: Yes, I experience marginalization as a nonheterosexual person, but I do so as a White person living in a nation founded upon dispossession and genocide where I am accorded considerable privilege by the very fact of being identified as White. Conceptualized in this way, the most salient factor of my identity becomes my privilege, rather than solely the marginalization I may experience. This type of "yes, but" does not ignore discrimination against White nonheterosexual people, but it ensures that such discrimination is always already placed in a social context whereby race privilege for White people always occurs at the expense of marginalization for non-White people (and particularly Indigenous people in Australia).

To return to the topic of marriage rights, arguments for marriage equality in Australia often position the denial of marriage to nonheterosexual people as the last bastion of discrimination left to tackle. Such arguments, however, are primarily made by White, middle-class, cisgender lesbians and gay men. What falls out of the frame in these arguments, then, are the experiences of people who are not located within these privileged categories, such as transgender and indigenous people. Focusing on marriage equality as the final hurdle to overcome is thus, I would suggest, very much an example of focusing on the wrong "yes, but."

Since completing my PhD and subsequent postdoctoral research, I have found myself in another setting where intersections of a range of identity positions play out in my life. As a psychotherapist, I find that much of what I have written here comes to the fore when I work with a range of clients. Obviously, and as has been well documented, counselors and other practitioners in the helping professions sit in a relatively privileged position in comparison to those we work with. Despite our best intentions, we are typically positioned as those who hold the knowledge and skills and whose role it is to fix the problems faced by others. Of course, narrative and other similar therapies have sought to resist this model of the practitioner–client interaction and to recognize that clients bring with them valuable knowledges and skills that can sit alongside those of the practitioner (Denborough, 2002). Nonetheless, the dominant discourse surrounding the helping professions is one in which those who seek services are positioned as in need of help and practitioners are those who can offer it. This duality sets up a particular dynamic into which practitioners are always already invited and in which we hold a particular privileged position. In the remainder of this chapter I engage in an exploration of how privilege plays out in complex ways in the counseling setting, through the elaboration of three case studies from my practice. I conclude the chapter by considering what the cases I present mean for the guidelines and standards of professional organizations in terms of working intersectionally.

PRIVILEGE IN PRACTICE

In this section, I outline three sets of interactions I have had with clients (one adult couple, one family, and one individual adult client). To retain the confidentiality of the clients, I portray their identities in very broad strokes. Although there is a risk that doing this could be seen as drawing upon or reinforcing cultural stereotypes about particular groups of people, my point is to look at the simultaneous identity categories that both my clients and I inhabit. I also consider how the differing identity categories we inhabit produce a dynamic between us in which multiple forms of privilege and marginalization play out and where cultural capital accrues differently to each of us. Importantly, then, my intention is to exemplify as succinctly as possible the complexities of privilege: both to add complexity to the idea that those of us in the helping professions are always or solely in a position of privilege over clients and to develop our understanding of precisely what that privilege looks like in specific interactions (Riggs & das Nair, 2012).

STORY 1

In my clinical practice, I work with people of a diverse range of genders and sexualities. When I initially began working as a psychotherapist, my interest was to work primarily with nonheterosexual clients. Yet despite this interest (and considerable awareness of research published on this topic), in many ways I was quite unprepared for how challenging doing this would be. Part of my interest in working with nonheterosexual clients was that I felt few public mental health services specifically catered to nonheterosexual people in my local area or employed nonheterosexual practitioners to target this population. The second aspect informing my interest in working with nonheterosexual people was more personal: I felt that working as a nonheterosexual person in couples counseling may be more productive if I were working with nonheterosexual couples. In part, this view was the result of my own relative gender nonconformity and the challenges that this could present in my work with heterosexual clients who viewed my self-presentation with suspicion or as a reason to delegitimize my skills as a counselor. And in part this belief about the potential productivity of my working with nonheterosexual couples was that we would have a shared ground upon which to work. My assumption was that, in sharing a similarly culturally marginalized position, my clients and I would understand the role of cultural capital, be attuned to its operations in our lives, and be able to harness our understandings and apply them to therapeutic ends. How wrong I was!

One particular couple who came to see me illustrate well the challenges I have experienced working with non-heterosexual couples, especially relative to privilege. The couple were two White men in their mid-50s who had been living together for a year. Both men had been heterosexually married previously and had children in that context. Both had left their wives a decade ago. One of the men had since enjoyed a very active sex life, primarily focusing his energies upon anonymous sexual encounters at saunas or as a part of group sex activities. He also had a large group of gay male friends. His partner, in contrast, had no gay sexual experience other than with his current partner and had very little in the way of social networks with other gay men except through his partner. Both men depicted themselves as hardworking in relatively unskilled employment with little economic security. Both depicted themselves as having lost a considerable deal of cultural capital upon their coming out; the partner who had few social networks was especially concerned about his lack of ready access to new networks and how this limitation was impacting their relationship.

From very early on in our sessions, it became clear to me that the men had made a range of presumptions about what having a nonheterosexual counselor would mean. Primarily, the men felt a certain liberty to discuss sexual matters that typically were not germane to our sessions (the sessions were not about sexual incompatibilities between the two men per se but rather about relationship difficulties more generally). In many instances, the men referred to their genitalia or those of other men or to their sexual preferences not specifically in a manner that was offensive to me but certainly in a way that was not necessary in the context of the sessions. In most of these instances, the men prefaced their comments with an inclusive "as you would understand," a rhetorical tool that typically rendered me complicit both with their worldview and with their presumption that I would welcome their sharing of this information. Kane (2004) has identified similar dilemmas in practicing as a gay man with gay clients. He has emphasized the need for clear boundaries with clients and the dilemmas of being engaged in multiple roles with clients (e.g., as practitioner/client, in community settings, and potentially through social contacts). Kane has suggested that while all practitioners must recognize issues relating to multiple relationships with clients, such relationships take unique configurations for those of us practicing with members of our own marginalized communities.

In the instances I have described briefly here, I felt very marginalized by the two men. As a relatively young gay man with three children and not much of a social life, not only could I not identify with the sexual narratives they were assuming I would understand (such as sex parties), but I also felt unable to resist these narratives on the very basis that both men repeatedly stated how important it was for them to have a gay practitioner who "got their situation." When they presumed a shared set of experiences, the intersectional differences between our lives, specifically in terms of age, raising children, and interest (or not) in particular modes of sexual engagement, disappeared. At the same time, I felt compelled to let their comments about sexual practices stand, partly in the off chance those practices were relevant to their relationship difficulties and partly to affirm to them that I did indeed welcome them as gay men and respected (rather than pathologized) their sexual practices. However, I felt a growing need to challenge their voicing of these particular narratives, particularly because they were often not central to the matters we were dealing with. Here my role as a practitioner with a particular injunction to be an empathetic listener was placed in direct competition with my own unease about being rendered complicit, not with the particular sexual practices they engaged in but rather with the assumption that all gay men share a similar set of experiences. In attempts to draw attention to the intersectional differences in our experiences, I repeatedly emphasized the different experiences that all gay men have (particularly the different experiences between the two men themselves), but they seemed invested in collapsing those differences by endorsing an understanding of gay sexual practices as uniform.

As I noted previously, I think that many of the issues we were faced with as practitioner and clients related to our age differences. As a younger gay man, my experiences of coming out, or of discrimination, and of being sexually proud in the face of homophobia were likely quite different from those of my clients. In this sense, I was aware of the relative privilege I held as someone who grew up with perhaps fewer experiences of homophobia, in a location in which services were available to provide positive support to me positively as a gay man, and in which there was at least some degree of recognition by others of my relationships. In this sense, then, I held considerable cultural capital in comparison to the lives of older gay men who have historically had much more negative experiences (Morrow, 2001). Yet at the same time, and based upon discussion in supervision and with other gay practitioners, I came to see that perhaps part of the reason the two men placed such emphasis upon discussing sexual practices with me was precisely because there was an age gap between us: Discussing their sexual practices as older gay men in the presence of a younger gay man may have been liberating or enjoyable for them. My point here, of course, is not to pathologize the men's desire to speak of their experiences but rather to elaborate further upon how privilege played out differently between us as gay men in the counseling setting.

The two men and I also differed in terms of our broader politics and socioeconomic positions. In regard to the latter, the men often framed me as a well-paid professional, in contrast to depicting themselves as working men with little understanding of the helping professions. Of course one could suggest that these evocations of differences in cultural capital were aimed at managing the power imbalances that exist between clients and practitioners in a society in which practitioners are in a position of knowing. But this idea tells us only part of the possible story here. Another suggestion would be that there were indeed class differences between us as gay men, and while in some instances the men appeared invested in asserting that we were "all the same" (i.e., in relation to sexual practices), in other instances they were clearly cognizant of our differences. As such, not only was I positioned in a place of authority as a practitioner (thus evoking the well-recognized power differential that this produces), but as an individual I was positioned as a middle-class gay man working with two working-class gay men.

One implication of these differences between us was that my own politics on race (developed through academic engagement) sat a world away from the politics of the two men, who asserted their own as premised upon "real-world experiences." So (and again speaking on matters unrelated to the issue at hand in counseling) the men twice drew upon racialized stereotypes about Indigenous people to construct themselves as deserving of social-security benefits, in contrast to indigenous people who they depicted as undeserving. When I attempted to carefully introduce the history of colonization as a possible explanation for what they were seeing as special rights for indigenous people, both men quickly asserted that I was speaking from an ivory-tower understanding and that, as men in the "real world," they knew better. In this case, they summarily dismissed any cultural capital I might have had as an academic, instead treating "real-world" knowledge as a more privileged form of capital.

My work with this couple highlights the complexities of working with members of one's own community and the complex ways in which privilege plays out. Importantly, it seems apparent that we cannot understand any of our similarities or differences in isolation from one another; rather, we must be understand them intersectionally. The age- or class-based differences between us are so intimately connected to our sexual and racial similarities that it is very difficult (and I would suggest futile) to attempt to draw out their individual effects. For example, the fact that we managed our racial similarity (but differing viewpoints on race politics) through recourse to a discourse of class and education highlights how thoroughly imbricated these identity categories are, just as the fact that we in some way managed our age differences through repeated emphasis upon sexual practices shows how a more simplistic account of privilege (that would place me as always and solely in a position of privilege in the therapeutic space) fails to address the complex ways in which privilege plays out. In the next example, I further demonstrate some of these complexities.

STORY 2

Throughout my time as a practitioner, I have had the privilege of engaging in long-term psychotherapy with a small number of clients whom I have seen for the duration of my work. This context has brought with it many of the challenges that face all practitioners with long-term clients but also many rewards, particularly in a public mental health system that operates primarily within a model of short-term interventions. One particular client has presented me with a range of challenges relating to my understandings of privilege and marginalization. This client is in his mid-40s; he came to counseling to deal with issues related to childhood trauma. He was born in India and in his childhood migrated from there with his family to Australia. He experienced a great deal of racism as a child and also much trauma related to his family. He is currently experiencing long-term unemployment and relies upon social-security payments for his income. He does not have a clear diagnosis but experiences ongoing negative mental health outcomes akin to those arising from complex posttraumatic stress disorder.

In our early sessions, the client was perhaps understandably very reticent to open up to me, both because he had identified me as "a younger man" (more than 15 years his junior) and as someone he verbally identified as "very different to him." His presumptions about the likely cultural capital I held stymied the development of a therapeutic bond between us for many months. To counter this situation, I often stated to my client that I felt a bond could be developed between a client and practitioner that exceeded their differences, which, I suspect in hindsight, simply appeared to my client as a denial of my cultural capital. For many months, the client depicted me as removed from his life (which in many ways I was because of our different circumstances) and as unable to understand his relationships with women (on the basis of his presumption of my nonheterosexuality). At times, although this is not a tool I generally utilize, I felt drawn to disclose details about personal aspects of my life that would validate for the client that I could indeed connect to some of his experiences. In many instances, this sharing of personal experiences did indeed serve to enable him to feel a sense of shared knowledge with me. At other times, however, complex intersections of privilege were occurring between us, during which he often rightly depicted me as privileged (particularly in relation to experiences of racism). This dynamic in effect called me to account for my privilege, despite the fact that I believed it was possible for us to develop a connection across our differences.

Of course any attempt to develop a relationship "across differences" is fraught by the possibility of those of us in positions of power falling into the trap of well-meaning liberalism, which often functions to deny the cultural capital we hold. In other words, the client could easily see my claim that I had the capacity to connect with him as ignoring the significant power differentials between us as client/practitioner and as a long-term unemployed Indian man and a White middle-class man. Furthermore, it was important for me to recognize that, despite my own relational approach to practice, there will indeed be instances in which a relationship cannot be developed and that clients (and, more specifically, marginalized members of a group) have the right to refuse the goodwill of practitioners or dominant members of a group (Ahmed, 2003). As a result, much of my approach to engaging with this client has required me to go beyond simply recognizing and validating his experiences and instead to recognize the broader social contexts in which those experiences have occurred, contexts that serve to disempower my client and with which I am complicit. What this has meant is that, regardless of our individual politics on race, sexuality, or class (for example), it has been important for me to find ways to acknowledge my client's experiences without being yet another example of a well-meaning White person. Accomplishing this has required me to draw upon my knowledge of intersectionality theory, to locate myself in his story as a participant in the broader society that to a large degree produced his experiences of marginalization. Again, I have not done this in a benevolent fashion in which I have martyred myself as a bad White person who caused his experiences of racism. Rather, the process has been about developing a relational framework in which we can foster the connection between us through mutual recognition of the intersections of our privileges and marginalities.

In my work with this client, there continues to be complex interplays of privilege that in places are similar to those that therapists experience with many clients (i.e. challenges in building rapport across differences, challenges resulting from clients' beliefs that may conflict with our own, etc.), but in other instances they are unique to the particular dynamic that exists between him and me. At times I have felt silenced by his normative statements about sexuality and gender, and certainly I haven't always remained silent at those moments. My drawing attention to the cultural capital he holds as a heterosexual man, even if doing so is at times confronting for him, has often ultimately lead to progress in the treatment. Largely, however, I have emphasized an understanding of our differences that requires me to be accountable for my privilege as a White middle-class person. This emphasis also requires me to work with him through some of the issues he has that relate to masculinity and negative judgements made about those of us located outside normative discourses of gender and sexuality. As such, my interest has not been in letting him off the hook under some misguided form of benevolence. Rather, my point has been to position myself in relationship to him in the context of the institutionalized racism, (hetero)sexism, and classism that conjointly shape both of our lives (albeit in different ways).

STORY 3

In this third and final case example, I consider a family who represents what has come to be my primary area of clinical work, namely transgender children and their families. This particular case involves a young transgender girl of African descent and her White birth mother and stepfather as the child's birth father is no longer involved. My work with this family has involved a constellation of intersections in regard to privilege and marginalization.

Although I noted previously that the child is of African descent, most often this identity category has not been salient in the therapeutic space. The child herself has never explicitly referenced it, though her mother has raised it a number of times in sessions on her own. At times, the child's descent has come up when her mother and I have discussed potential discrimination that her daughter may face, specifically in terms of sexism, transphobia, and racism. The mother is well versed in sexism and transphobia; however, the topic of racism often appears to make the mother uncomfortable. Over many sessions, we have unpacked this discomfort and to a large degree have shifted from a place where race was almost a taboo topic to one where we are able to discuss both potential racism her daughter may have experienced and also the considerable cultural capital that we hold as White people and the ways in which that capital benefits us. After many sessions unpacking these intersections, it became apparent to me that, for the mother, a White woman who previously had been in an abusive relationship with a Black man, racism was difficult to articulate. For her to acknowledge race privilege was, it seemed, to condone the abuse. Addressing these concerns has allowed the mother to see the racism that her daughter may face in the future, rather than maintaining a "race blind" approach that denies both race privilege and thus racism (Frankenberg, 1993).

Also of note, and in contrast to the previous two cases, is the phenomenon of deference that often occurs in the counseling space, again particularly with regard to the mother in this case. This is a strong and articulate woman, knowledgeable about both her daughter's life and the experiences of transgender people more broadly. Yet in many of the lengthy conversations we have had, the mother has often deferred to me as an "expert." This is a subject position I always seek to challenge, both as a therapeutic tool (i.e., people are largely experts on their own lives) and also in a broader social context where the binary of lay versus expert knowledge brings with it considerable power differentials that serve only to naturalize cultural capital. To unpack this binary in the therapeutic space, we have spoken about how gender plays a significant role in notions of expertise and how men are all too often accorded with knowledge a priori. Working through these assumptions and questioning what it means to be a subject who knows has been useful in my time with the mother, particularly as it has strengthened the mother's resolve to be a strong advocate for transgender people, and to do so from a place of knowing. In this sense, her accrual of cultural capital within the context of knowledge about transgender people's lives has been an important outcome of our therapeutic work, highlighting the positive ends to which such capital can be put.

CONCLUSION

In this chapter I have explored some of the complexities that arise for those of us working in the helping professions when we engage with our clients across a range of differences. My emphasis has been upon the importance of locating ourselves as practitioners within our own social contexts and identity positions. From there, we can develop an understanding of privilege that moves beyond a simplistic additive model and to instead engage with the intersections of identity categories and their role in producing particular power relations between clients and practitioners that serve to naturalize or reinforce enactments of cultural capital. Such an approach aligns closely with both the competency guidelines of the Association for Lesbian, Gay, Bisexual and Transgender Issues in Counselling (Harper et al., 2013) and the ethical guidelines of the Australian Psychological Society (2010, 2013). Both organizations advise clinicians to be mindful that we all inhabit multiple identity categories, and the Association for Lesbian, Gay, Bisexual and Transgender Issues in Counselling in particular advises us as clinicians to be mindful of their intersections. The fact that both of these organizations encourage a focus on intersectionality when they focus specifically on gender and sexuality provides a clear warrant for the approach that I take in my own practice and suggests that we should consider theorizing about intersectionality and privilege as central to clinical work.

Reflecting upon my own history of coming to understand my experiences of both privilege and marginalization, I can see the considerable changes in my own thinking and the shift I have made from an individualized account to a more relational understanding of identity, one in which an understanding of cultural capital is often at the fore. For me, this shift has been central to applying the different "yes, but" I outlined in the introduction. After many clinical sessions, reflecting on how power dynamics related to age, class, relationship status, race, sexuality, gender, and ability have played out within sessions has been an important aspect of my own growth as a counselor and has provided opportunities for me to continue to develop my understanding of privilege and its operations. Importantly for me, my understandings of privilege always center upon recognition of the fact that social hierarchies, despite their historical contingency, are unlikely to disappear in my lifetime. As a result, my practice is always directed by my desire to identify the role that cultural capital plays in shaping both my life and the lives of my clients and in the interactions between us. Identifying cultural capital allows me to retain a focus on more than just the individual(s) in front of me and instead to locate us all in relationship to networks of power that potentially determine who will have a voice and who will not.

DISCUSSION QUESTIONS

1. How does privilege and marginalization play out in your life? If you have or you have not reflected on this question before share a past or present response to the prompt.
2. Why do you think there might be resistance from those in dominant social locations to acknowledging the operations of privilege? How might you respectfully challenge this in your practice?
3. What are your thoughts on the idea of raising issues of privilege or marginalization when they are not explicitly salient in a clinical session? How might raising these issues reinforce or help to unpack underlying issues?
4. How might an acknowledgment of the intersections of privilege and marginalization benefit you, your clients, your workplace? What challenges do you foresee in implementing such an approach?
5. To what extent might using personal experiences within the therapeutic space hinder or facilitate engagement?
6. In what other ways might you draw upon ideas of cultural capital to render visible any power differentials at play between you and your clients?

ACKNOWLEDGMENTS

I begin by acknowledging the sovereignty of the Kaurna people, upon whose land I live in Adelaide, South Australia. Thanks must go to the clients and colleagues with whom I have discussed these ideas and whose insights have centrally informed my writing in this chapter.

REFERENCES

Ahmed, S. (2003). In the name of love. *borderlands e-journal*, (2)3. Retrieved from http://www.borderlands. net.au/vol2no3_2003/ahmed_love.htm

Australian Psychological Society. (2010). *Guidelines for psychological practice with lesbian, gay, and bisexual clients*. Melbourne: Author.

Australian Psychological Society. (2013). *Guidelines on working with sex and/or gender diverse clients*. Melbourne: Author.

Barnard, I. (2003). *Queer race: Interventions in the racial politics of queer theory*. New York, NY: Peter Lang.

Běrubě, A. (2001). How gay stays White and what kind of White it stays. In B. B. Rasmussen, E. Klinenberg, I. J. Nexica, & M. Wray (Eds.), *The making and unmaking of Whiteness* (pp. 234–265). Durham, NC: Duke University Press.

Crenshaw, K. M. (1991). Mapping the margins: Intersectionality, identity politics, and violence against women of color. *Stanford Law Review, 43,* 1241–1299.

Denborough, D. (Ed.). (2002). *Queer counselling and narrative practice*. Adelaide, Australia: Dulwich Centre.

Duggan, L. (2002) The new homonormativity: The sexual politics of neoliberalism. In R. Castronovo & D. D. Nelson (Eds.), *Materializing democracy: Toward a revitalized cultural politics* (pp. 175–194). Durham, NC: Duke University Press.

Frankenberg, R. (1993). *White women, race matters*. Minneapolis: University of Minnesota Press.

Hage, G. (1998). *White nation: Fantasies of White supremacy in a multicultural nation*. Sydney, Australia: Pluto Press.

Harper, A., Finnerty, P., Martinez, M., Brace, A., Crethar, H., Loos, B., . . . Lambert, S. (2013). Association for Lesbian, Gay, Bisexual, and Transgender Issues in Counseling competencies for counseling with lesbian, gay, bisexual, queer, questioning, intersex, and ally individuals. *Journal of LGBT Issues in Counseling, 7*(1), 2–43.

Kane, G. (2004). "The unintended use of a pronoun": Coming out in the counselling environment. In D. W. Riggs & G. A. Walker (Eds.), *Out in the antipodes: Australian and New Zealand perspectives on gay and lesbian issues in psychology*. Perth, Australia: Brightfire Press.

Lamont, M., & Lareau, A. (1988). Cultural capital: Allusions, gaps and glissandos in recent theoretical developments. *Sociological Theory, 6,* 153–168.

Moreton-Robinson, A. (2000). *Talkin' up to the White woman: Aboriginal women and feminism*. St. Lucia, Australia: University of Queensland Press.

Morrow, D. (2001). Older gays and lesbians: Surviving a generation of hate and violence. *Journal of Gay & Lesbian Social Services, 13,* 151–169.

Riggs, D. W. (2006). *Priscilla, (White) queen of the desert: Queer rights/race privilege*. New York, NY: Peter Lang.

Riggs, D. W., & das Nair, R. (2012). Intersecting identities. In R. das Nair & C. Butler (Eds.), *Intersectionality, sexuality and psychological therapies: Working with lesbian, gay and bisexual diversity* (pp. 9–30). West Sussex, UK: Wiley Blackwell.

CHAPTER 9

NAVIGATING OPPRESSION, DIVERSITY, POWER, AND PRIVILEGE IN PURSUIT OF ACHIEVEMENT AND SUCCESS

An International Perspective

Saliwe M. Kawewe

The growing pluralistic and multicultural society in which we live demands that helping professionals, such as social workers, be on the frontlines. Further, these helping professionals must be the most prepared to provide competent intervention that caters to people of diverse backgrounds to enable them to live connected and healthy lives (National Association of Social Workers, 2015). In this chapter I demonstrate that, despite the fact that the rest of the world is led to conceptualize the United States of America as a land of the free, of equal opportunity, and one where human dignity is upheld, however, a "reality check" tells a different story. The prevalence of multisystemic privilege and oppression, profound inequality, and prejudice between and within (intra) groups based on racial, socioeconomic, migrant, and marital status; age; sexual orientation; gender identity; religion; disability; geographic location; nationality of origin; and so on persist unabated. Racism and a plethora of all forms of discrimination and oppression remain pernicious in the United States, as found in the lasting injustices and human-rights violations that continue to impede social justice and aspirations of US citizens living within the context of a civilized society. Thus the United States continues to be a land of prejudice, racism, ageism, homophobia xenophobia, Muslimophobia, Christianophobia, atheophobia, ableism, and micro- and macroaggressions that include many other forms of discrimination. The persistence of such discrimination and oppression, despite the existence of laws against many of them, tells a true story that thwarts the American dream and my high expectations of an advanced and civilized society.

My main professional organizations, the National Association of Social Workers and the Council on Social Work Education, prepare social workers with values, knowledge, skills, and competencies that enable these professionals to illuminate not only how and where discrimination and prejudice are thriving at all levels of society (a micro/mezzo/macro continuum), but also how to intervene effectively in changing such situations. Such interventions promote cultural diversity, human rights, and social justice competencies (Council on Social Work Education,2015; Morgaine 2014). A passion for pursuing fairness, human rights, and social justice inspired me to travel the journey that led me to this profession and to where I am, as I share in my life story in this chapter.

My experiences of diversity and navigation of oppression, power, and privilege have been shaped by my country of origin, the places I have lived since, my interactions with people in those environments, my educational pursuits, and my own ingenuity. More importantly, the opportunity and privilege to be able to pursue education in various international settings within Africa and the United States have been both rewarding and agonizing. *Intradiscrimination*, which occurs within a particular group, as well as oppression, has far-reaching, devastating consequences similar to all forms of abuse. *Interdiscrimination*, which occurs between two or more groups, entails reducing the other to less than equal status, as clearly explained by cognitive-dissonance theory (Davis, 2016), and *institutionalized discrimination* further hides the problem. We must go beyond what is on the surface and recognize that the United States, being indeed a great country and one of global hope, still has a long way to go to achieve its noble ideals.

WHERE DID I COME FROM?

It is within such a contextual background and understanding that I tell my story, which reflects a woman, Black, migrant, student, scholar, professional, an educator, and naturalized. My story seeks to provide an avenue through which one can effectively comprehend the dynamics of oppression and power and privilege through critical and transformative frameworks rather than isolated categories. Transformative and critical approaches include the intersectionality of categories as discrete categories alone oftentimes become sources of oppression, power, and privilege (Irving & Young, 2004; Jani, Pierce, Ortiz, & Sowbel, 2011; Lee, Brown, & Bertera, 2010; Lee & Greene, 2008; Loya & Cuevas, 2010; Lum, 2011; Ortiz & Jani; 2010; Sisneros, Stakeman, Joyner, & Schmitz, 2008; Snyder, Peeler, & May, 2008).

I was born and raised in Rhodesia (now Zimbabwe), then a British colony. Europeans had divided Africa into colonies in the way that a turkey is carved out during an American Thanksgiving (Kawewe, 2001; Toler, 1998). I was born in a rural area between Gweru and Kwekwe in the Midlands. Europeans had imposed their will on the natives through deceit, misrepresentation, and ultimately through the armed defeat of the Black natives. Colonists, with the help of missionaries, claimed the most fertile land, which was portioned into White-owned commercial farms, mines, cities, game parks, and reserves. The relationship between European colonizers and the indigenous populations was that of rider and horse (Moyo & Kawewe, 2002). The former had the power and privilege to oppress and exploit the latter through the use of force, trickery, and deceit. Many colonial Whites referred to us

Blacks as *kaffirs*, which is similarly as derogatory as the usage of the term *nigger* in the United States. Blacks were designated the semiarid, impoverished, and overcrowded tribal trust or communal lands where my family (grandparents) raised me and my two siblings until we reached school age.

Colonialism created artificial boundaries in Africa and introduced a cash economy through coercion, legislative discrimination that controlled Black movement, residential segregation, and other initiatives aimed at the "domestication" of Africans. Most able-bodied young male members of my extended family were forced to migrate and work in mines, White owned commercial farms or urban areas in order to earn cash to support their rural family members as they could face retribution and imprisonment for failure to pay newly introduced taxes for such things as dogs, huts, cows, and so forth. Consequently, rural areas became mostly inhabited by women, children, individuals with disabilities, and those identified as elderly. My two other siblings and I were such children, being raised by our grandmother on these reservations. Eventually, young women and others such as my mother, who had become a single parent, would migrate to urban areas as well. Urban workers would visit their families during vacations, such as the newly introduced Christmas holidays. This was the time when children such as us would receive new clothes and shoes and eat lavishly. During these celebrations, urban working relatives brought groceries and other Western sweet foods that we rarely ate.

Similar to the rural arrangement, housing in cities was arranged along racial lines. It was general practice that European employers provided accommodations for the Black workers in high-density areas with beer halls in close proximity. When I later migrated to the city, my family lived in such a township. During colonialism, these workers were referred to as *boys* regardless of their age; thus *boy* (*muboyi*) became synonymous with any servant and included women when they eventually joined the workforce to eke out a living. White peoples' residential areas were often low density, located closer to the cities and far away from Black townships. Whites had decent houses, or even mansions, in suburbs, far away from Blacks. White suburbs had detached living quarters that were called *boy's kaya*, meaning "boy's home," regardless of whether the employee was a man or a woman. To the contrary, Black housing started as military-like, open dormitories for men only and, later, one-roomed housing with public toilets and bathrooms. Municipalities would eventually build cheap four-roomed housing for Blacks. Thus, for Blacks, rural reservations, where my family and I lived before migrating to the city, were considered a safety net to fall back on as necessary due to loss of employment or injury. I always had that safety net because my grandparents lived on those reservations.

MY NEW-WORLD ENCOUNTERS

I had neither been to any urban area nor seen a White person until I was about school-going age when my maternal grandmother, the family matriarch, my two brothers, and I traveled to Gweru, a city in the midlands and now the third-largest city in Zimbabwe. This trip signified my emigration from my rural permanent residency to urban living. Each brother and I were a year apart in age, and we looked like triplets. Because there were no schools in our rural area, my grandmother wanted us to go and live with my maternal aunt, who lived with her husband and two children in Gweru, so that we could go to school. However, she also wanted us to pay short visits in route, first to our mother (who worked as a housemaid) and then to our father (who worked as a cook) in two different White suburbs. We would then proceed to our final destination of our aunt's family, who resided in one of the Black townships.

The first time I saw a White man was when we entered the city after hitching a ride and sitting in the back of the White man's truck and then I saw a White woman in high heels. I thought that these Whites (*Varungu*) might be people just like us except for their skin color. However, when I learned that they were "bosses" or viewed as superior to Blacks, I did not question it. I actually envied them and had many questions that were indicative of my ignorance and naivety about them at the time.

We were among the few native children to be exposed to the city and also to have direct contact with a White family. On this only visit to my mother, which lasted about a week, my brothers and I played a lot with a White child of my mother's employers. She was of our age group. I was so happy to have my newly found White friend and playmate that I spent a lot of time with her while my two siblings mostly played with each other.

Once, when we were playing during this visit, I remember crying because I was upset about something; and this White girl started singing, "Cry baby, cry" repeatedly. I neither knew what this meant nor suspected that she was making fun of me but thought she was singing for me to be quiet. After this encounter, I would sing this song whenever another child cried back home. I was proud that I could sing in English. It took three years of elementary school education for me to understand later what that song meant. Until then, I just thought that whatever White people did or said was inherently superior, nice, and kind.

On a few occasions the White employers let their child come to the servants' quarters, where we would share our food with her. She would eat and tell us not to tell her parents because they did not want her to eat native food. Sometimes our White playmate brought treats to the servant's quarters to share with us. Of course, these foods were new to us; we'd never tasted them before. My mother's employers often gave their leftover food to their Black workers. This was food that we gladly accepted, devoured, and enjoyed. It was European food, and we thought it was better than the *sadza* and *vusavi* we were accustomed to in the rural areas. *Vusavi* consisted of cooked, soup-bone stew with green vegetables, or green vegetables with peanut butter or cooking oil. *Sadza* was made out of cornmeal. Because of the struggle of rural life for Blacks, we were often undernourished and we looked small for our ages.

Although colonialism was about segregation between Black and White people in both commercial farm areas and low density White areas, White parents were not effective in preventing their children from playing with the Black children of their domestic servants; and the same was true of Black parents. Even with strict monitoring, enforcement was nearly impossible because children of both races would mutually find secret rendezvous, to play as kids do anywhere else. Servants were generally not allowed to receive visits from their families. However, my mother's White employers were either kind enough to let us stay and play openly or were not bothered by it.

Our next stop on this visit took us to my father in another part of town. He brought us leftover food from his European employers because he also lived in the servants' quarters.

My father's employer was stricter than my mother's; therefore, we only stayed there for two days. We also had to be quiet, which was very difficult and boring.

EDUCATION AND THE AFRICAN GIRL CHILD

We finally reached our destination, my aunt's home, in a high-density Black neighborhood of the city, where my older brother and I would finally end up enrolling in school. Instead of waiting a year, I was able to begin school with him after I "threw a fit" that swayed my grandmother to allow me to enter school at that time. After living with our aunt for about two years, my siblings and I moved in with my mother, who had remarried. She and my stepfather, who was originally from Zambia, lived in a one-room dwelling, though they would buy a four-room house a year later that included a kitchen, living room, dining room, and bedrooms for all of us. My parents slept on the bed, and we slept separately on the floor. An exterior common bathroom was shared by 10 families. We continued to attend the elementary school where my aunt lived; therefore, we had to travel 4 miles to school each morning. My heroic older brother used my mother's bicycle and carried the two of us on its back carrier.

Within the extended family system, I had already been groomed to be a future "good wife and mother" because I was considered the best house cleaner, cook, and babysitter within both the nuclear and extended family systems. Meetings were held to discuss circulating me among my mother's, aunt's, and grandmother's households to help them with chores. The initial plan was that I would spend a month with each one of the three families. Then my mother told them that I was her child; therefore, there was no need for such an arrangement. My grandmother and my aunt complained that they had helped raise me when my mother was working and that it was unfair for my mother to now want me to only help her with housework and so on. The resolution was that I would primarily live with my mother, but my aunt could have me whenever she had to go on cross-border trading trips so that I would take care of her family while she was gone. My grandmother would have me in the rural areas during all school vacations: two three-week breaks and one four-week break during the Christmas holiday.

I was the second born in a family of six siblings, and as a girl, the odds for further education were against me in a patriarchal society that still values males over females. Once I was enrolled in school, I was motivated to learn how to read and write and "know everything." For a long time, I believed that education would allow me to know everything and I chased this dream until I got to college years later, where I realized that I would never be able to know everything. My mother and stepfather, who had three children together, planned to end my education after elementary school (seventh grade, or then, Standard Six) in December 1964, even though I had done exceedingly well and enjoyed learning.

My older brother had lost interest during his fifth year of elementary education and was allowed to quit, but my younger brother was a year behind me. At that time, I was the most educated person in my family. My parents thought that there was no value in educating a female further because I would soon get married and then end up using my education to benefit my future husband's family. My grandmother is the one who vouched for me by telling my parents that, since I was still too young to be married and I was bright, the best option for me was to proceed with my education. My mother insisted that I would be handy to my grandmother in the rural areas and that, since I had reached puberty, I was at high risk of becoming a pregnant and unwed teenager in the city, which would bring shame to the family. These discussions and debates took place while I was on Christmas break with my grandparents.

In our culture, the decision of the oldest family member generally carries the most weight. As such, my parents ultimately yielded to my grandmother's decision. Subsequently, I was able to seek enrollment in high school. By the time everything was resolved, I had missed the registration deadlines and the first three weeks of school, and all of my area schools were full.

This was a time when neighboring Zambia (formerly Northern Rhodesia) had just gained independence, and Zambians, who had sheltered in Southern Rhodesia during their struggle, were returning home. My stepfather, a Zambian immigrant, was making plans for the whole family to relocate back to Zambia within three months. I also had a maternal uncle who had previously immigrated to Lusaka, Zambia, with his employer.

It was then decided that I would proceed to Zambia to enroll in high school there and live with my uncle. Before I left Southern Rhodesia, my elementary school education and the nationalist movements had enabled me to begin becoming politically conscious and aware of the evils of colonialism and the subjugation of Southern Rhodesian Blacks by White colonists from England and Holland and their descendants. These nationalist movements had ultimately coalesced into two political parties that engaged in an armed liberation struggle against the Southern Rhodesian government. Both Black political parties had branches that operated in neighboring countries, which had already achieved liberation. The arrangement for me to go to Zambia would later turn out to be a blessing in disguise because it opened up better opportunities for me.

INTERNATIONAL EXPOSURE IN PURSUIT OF EDUCATION

At 15 years of age, I left Zimbabwe by train and headed for Lusaka, the capital of Zambia. In my possession, in addition to cash, were two pieces of paper, each folded and labeled—one with my uncle's work address and the other with a school's address. My stepfather had written the addresses down and given the papers to me with instructions before I left. Upon arrival in Lusaka, my uncle gave me a warm reception. I told my uncle I had been sent to live with him so that I could go to school. I gave him the piece of paper with the school's address on it and finally read it myself. The name of the school was Regency Correspondence College. *Correspondence* was a big word for my stepfather, who had had about three years of elementary-school education he had acquired as an adult learner through night school. Had he understood its meaning, I might never have left home.

Zambia, having recently become independent from British colonialism, had a very progressive government, with its people excited. I enjoyed living in a free African country.

I quickly adjusted and made friends, which enabled me to learn the local language and culture and also enjoy a variety of foods. My uncle, who was a political activist in the ZANU party, informed me of the possibilities of further education through scholarships sponsored by the African American Institute (AAI), which had offices in Lusaka. ZANU officials (*vadara*) informed us that party followers were sent to Tanzania, while ZAPU members went to a similar school located in Zambia. This separation was to prevent students in opposing political parties from clashing with each other.

After passing the AAI's educational screening test, two other Zimbabwean girls and I became candidates to attend Kurasini International Education Center, a coeducational school in Dar-es-Salaam, Tanzania. My uncle strongly opposed my intention to migrate to Tanzania. He only told me that traveling there was dangerous. I insisted on going to school and he yielded after senior politicians overruled him and supported me. When we were ready for departure, I was pleasantly surprised that my uncle had taken a leave of absence and was one of the three drivers of the truck that took us to Tanzania. I learned later that politicians were notorious for raping young girls on such trips. My trip was safe because my uncle, who may have known about this, also joined us on the journey. Because of cultural taboos surrounding discussing sexual matters, my uncle had not told me the real reason he had initially opposed this trip.

In June 1966, after I had completed my elementary-school education in Zimbabwe and had spent 18 months in Zambia, I arrived in Tanzania. In the middle of the academic year, I enrolled in the first year (Form 1) of high school by passing a midyear preplacement test administered by a White American who was the principal of the high school primarily for African refugees. I was the only one who passed the test and joined that year's cohort of students midstream; my two companions who enrolled would wait until the beginning of 1967, which placed them one grade behind me.

Most of our teachers were either Black or White Americans who were positive role models for me and allowed me to ask many questions in class. Our African American teachers were most inspiring to us refugees during this civil rights movement era in America. They shared information regarding racial discrimination in the United States and the fight of the civil rights movement for human rights and social justice. My education was transformed when I learned for the first time that Europeans had not actually "discovered" Africans or our land. This was an educational awakening, which included us Africans as actors in history.

Kurasini boarded youth and adult student refugees from all southern African countries (Angola, Zaire, Malawi, Mozambique, Namibia, and South Africa). All of these countries, with the exception of Malawi, were still under colonialism. Later, by 1968, a few nonrefugee students from independent Tanzania, Zanzibar, and Kenya were included. This educational experience nourished my value for cultural diversity and exposure as students shared individual and collective experiences of oppression, dispossession, and homesickness due to their isolation or the loss of family linkages. Sometimes we cried, and at other times we debated about staying in school or joining freedom fighters. Some students left for the bush wars, where they perished, but others of us stayed in school. There were also occasions of happiness and entertainment when we held school dances.

Seven of the first high-school graduates from Kurasini were sent to the United States, and we escorted them to the airport to bid them farewell. I asked why they were going to the

United States, and they told us it was for further education since their motherlands were not yet independent. I told them that I would not stop going to school until I knew everything. This goal had become more compelling after I completed grade school and realized I did not know everything, despite my ability to read and write in both English and Shona. I used every chance to read and learn about many topics. Watching the first Kurasini high-school graduates boarding a plane fueled my ambitions and enthusiasm for more education, which meant the possibility of flying and going overseas someday.

I graduated from Kurasini near the top of my class, and this qualified me to enter the University of Zambia in Lusaka. The AAI guaranteed me a full four-year scholarship. I majored in social work and encountered another diverse population of students from all over Africa, including some Americans. The majority of students were Zambians. Some students had never been to a city before, and others had never used a fork and knife. We were supportive of one another whether we knew each other or not.

The most active branch of ZANU, my political party back then, was at the University of Zambia. We often met and discussed strategies for Zimbabwean's liberation. Regularly, freedom fighters would address our gatherings to apprise us of the conditions in Southern Rhodesia and the liberation war. They gave us insights into the atrocities that were being committed by both the Rhodesian government and the resistance. Among the resistance, tribalism, lack of organization, and lack of sufficient oversight led to the murder of innocents, exploitation of women, and infringements on human and civil rights. These aspects of the liberation struggle turned me away from joining politics full-time after graduation. I graduated with my bachelor's in social work (BSW). I was the only person in my class who graduated with a BSW with merit.

Subsequently, I was fortunate enough to be hired by the University of Zambia as an administrative assistant, where I worked for approximately two years. I then applied for graduate sponsorship from the AAI and was awarded a two-year scholarship to pursue a master's in social work in the United States. I also finally had the opportunity to fly in an airplane.

EXCURSION TO AMERICA AS A STUDENT

In 1977, I arrived in St. Louis, Missouri, where I attended George Warren Brown School of Social Work at Washington University. I experienced some culture shock because America was so different from the places where I had lived in Africa. As it is for most immigrants, I had to adjust to the weather, the food, and so on. I had also never lived in an environment in which there were so many White people and so few Black people. Back home in Southern Rhodesia, although White people ran the government and dominated the economy, they comprised approximately 5 percent of the population. There, White and Black people almost never interacted with one another on equal terms. At Washington University, the learning environment was supportive, and Black and White Americans as well as International students interacted well. Because I really had not had much mixing with White people on an equal basis until I came to the United States, I took additional classes on cultural diversity and racial issues. I also had interactions with Black students that enlightened me on the dynamics of racism, power, and oppression in this country. I found many Americans to be polite and curious to learn about other cultures. I also noticed that, when I was walking in the streets, while White strangers would say nothing to me, Black people would say, "Hi!" or "What's up?" This suggested that there was a connection between us even if we were strangers.

The international student office on campus offered various programs and activities to help one learn about American culture, which helped me feel at home. I was assigned a host and a guest family who took me to their homes and their churches and also invited me to their homes during holidays such as Thanksgiving or Christmas. They often picked me up in their cars and we drove on the highway and went to the most gorgeous neighborhoods where they lived in St. Louis. I was not exposed to poor neighborhoods until I chose to do my practicum on community development in a ghetto area. Had I not done this, I might have left the United States thinking there were no such neglected and poor neighborhoods and people.

RETURN TO ZIMBABWE, TRANSITIONS, AND GENDER DISENFRANCHISEMENT

Soon after my I received my master's degree in the summer of 1979, I went back home. There was much jubilation in the country because it had won independence. Blacks anticipated an end to the racial discrimination that had thus far shaped their lives. Many Zimbabweans were also excited to return home because the war had ended. The country was in a transitional period, moving from a colonial government to a nationalist government (Zimbabwe-Rhodesia). The country would soon be known as Zimbabwe. In 1980, the first election, in which all Blacks were allowed to participate freely, was held in Zimbabwe.

I found work in Bulawayo, the country's second largest city, as a social services/probation officer for about two years. Government agencies were still operating on the colonial model based on racial lines. I was initially hired at the White office that provided social services to Whites and Coloreds (offspring of mixed Black and White races who were considered better than Blacks but not equal to Whites). When the Black office was overwhelmed by the returning masses and refugees who had been displaced during the liberation war, I was selected to join the workforce in the Black office in Bulawayo. The official reason given was that I could speak both Shona and Ndebele indigenous languages, and therefore reassigning me to that location would provide efficient services for those clients. I noticed that in the Black office, social workers were given extremely high caseloads yet all of the White social workers remained in the White office with very small workloads. This situation created an inequity of service to the disadvantage of Black clients and Black workers.

The allocation of government resources available to clients in similar circumstances was racially based. The problem was systemic. My nationalist movement experience and my American social work education gave me the courage to challenge these social injustices, and I presented my concerns to the respective Ministry officials. I proposed that White Zimbabweans learn indigenous languages so that they too could function more effectively, just as I and many other Black professionals had to learn English and could serve Whites efficiently. This opportunity allowed me to observe the discrepancy between the promise of equal treatment and the speed at which that promise would be formalized. Though the work was worthwhile, I had to deal with sexism, corruption, and resistance to change. It had never occurred to me that education had instilled some Western, especially American, values in me that would pose a challenge and present a barrier to my effectively fitting back into a country that I had left during colonialism and as a juvenile. I also realized that, even though I was the most educated person in our local offices at the time, there was more that I wanted to learn.

COMING BACK TO AMERICA

In 1981 I returned to the United States to pursue my PhD degree at Saint Louis University. This time, I was working to pay half of my tuition and living expenses. Fortunately, I had managed to develop a network of part-time jobs babysitting, adult sitting, and housekeeping. My life as a student was simple. I also volunteered to travel to elementary and high schools in St. Louis to share the culture of Zimbabwe with American children. I was highly motivated both to study and finish. Among my cohort, I was the first to graduate from the program. While writing my dissertation, I was also a social services worker in St. Louis County, and my workmates were pleasant and encouraging. Ultimately, I decided to enter the academy.

Whereas I had to struggle with sexism and other gender-disempowering cultural traditions in Zimbabwe and to a certain extent in Zambia, I had not come across blatant sexism or racism as a student in the United States. It could have been covert or institutional, but as long as I was viewed as being here temporarily, I encountered few barriers or obstacles. Often, Americans I met expressed interest in Africa and my country. They also often wanted to know when I was going back. According to them, it was a given that I had to take this American education back home to "help my people," as though I could not do so from abroad. There was never any question about whether my people might possibly reject my American education; neither was there any room for my own sense of self-determination to choose where to live or what to do with my education. In the views of these Americans, there was never any room for me to serve here in the United States.

A PART OF THE "DREAM"

In 1985 I worked in the United States and gained some experience within the social system from which I had earned my highest credentials. I applied for academic positions and secured one at a university in Louisiana, where I taught for three and half years. While I was there, a White, male faculty member from the geography program, which was part of the social work and criminal justice departments, told me to go back to Africa. He told me that I did not have much to offer to American students and that I was *supposed* to return to my own country so that I would not take jobs away from Americans. This was the first time that I had experienced overt discrimination in the United States. I was shocked and not prepared for it. I simply told him that I had the credentials to teach, that I had interviewed for the job, and that I had subsequently been selected as the most qualified from a pool of competitive applicants. To diversify my academic experience and optimize advancement opportunities, I have since moved around to three other universities, one in the East and two in the Midwest, before coming to my current institution.

During the time that I have been working in the United States since graduating with my PhD degree, I have personally experienced prejudicial treatment from American society at large on numerous occasions. My experiences range from the various microaggressions that are common to the American Black experience to overt expressions of racism, such as being called the N-word by a White man who did not wish to take *no* for an answer, to more serious incidents, such as the time after I moved into an all-White neighborhood where someone left a pile of feces on my doorstep. Nonetheless, I continued to work hard because that is what I have done my entire life. After 20 years here, I chose to embrace American citizenship.

CONCLUSION

My experience as an international student and my conception of academia led me to believe that university campuses were more open-minded and less conservative than the rest of society. I went to a Jewish university for my master's degree in social work and a Roman Catholic University for my PhD, and I never felt discriminated against by fellow students or the university establishment, including faculty. As an academic, however, I have learned that campuses are not spaces where minorities are spared from discrimination. To some extent, we are primed to expect and protect ourselves from discriminatory practices committed by actors beyond the group from which we identify. However, People of Color sometimes find themselves marginalized by other members of their own group. For example, on my campus, one male African American associate professor with a position in higher administration and a leadership role within the association for Black faculty and staff accused the university of being deceitful and of disenfranchising African American faculty on campus. He asserted that the university's statistics on Blacks are distorted because they include African faculty members and their contributions. The problem, according to him, is that Africans are overrepresented among Blacks on campus in terms of achievement. Thus he believed that the university's classification of Black faculty as all faculty of African descent should be changed and that a distinction should be made between Black faculty who were born in the United States and those who were born abroad. Further, those born abroad should no longer be considered "Black" or "African American" even if they had become naturalized citizens of the United States. Instead, this man said that people like me should be reclassified as "internationals." These "internationals" would no longer qualify for opportunities or recognition intended for "Black" people in the university. When I applied for tenure and then for promotion at my current institution, I received unanimous support each time at every level within this then Carnegie II research university. Currently on this campus, I am the only Black, female, full professor out of roughly 475 tenured professors. Under his system that number would be zero. When a junior faculty member attempted to communicate the promotion of diversity and inclusion, she was quickly silenced by another tenured professor.

Not only do these comments from my colleague reflect ethnocentrism, but they also represent discrimination by nationality of origin. In my case they aim to strip away the sense of identity that has shaped my life since birth and the relevance of my embrace of citizenship and uniquely American ideals. They seek to undermine group solidarity and cohesiveness. They speak to his ignorance of the circumstances from which faculty of African origin have largely emerged. African Americans extended life-changing opportunities to Africans like myself during the 1950s and 1960s because they recognized our willingness to work hard and our common struggles with oppression. Ironically, the reclassifications this Black administrator suggested would stand in direct violation of the Civil Rights Act of 1964, which prohibits discrimination based on national origin. I experienced this act of discrimination as a rejection and betrayal that cut deeper than many discriminatory actions of most Whites in my lifetime.

The American academy has been a source of both strength and strain regarding issues of professional and personal growth, diversity, power, and privilege (Benjamin, 1997; Devore & Schlesinger, 1999; Kawewe 1997a, 1997b). Where do we go from here? Paulo Freire (1970) offers means by which the oppressed can set themselves free and transform their oppressors into allies. Despite the various struggles that I face in the academy, I continue to be inspired by the interactions I have with students, the passion for my research on women and children, and a commitment to cultural diversity, human rights, and social justice, which are also among Council on Social Work Education (2015) educational policy and accreditation standards. The challenge of life in the United States as a nation of immigrants, is in navigating and accepting the increasing complexity and diversity of our identities. We have to find a way to move forward together and learn to accept and honor our plurality.

DISCUSSION QUESTIONS

1. Consider the way the author was received and treated in Tanzania, Zambia, and the United States. In what ways might the author's experiences as a foreigner in these countries affect her views of these nations and their citizens?
2. Why might the author's American hosts have shielded her from society's impoverished or neglected areas?
3. When reading about the author's entrance into the American job market, identify thoughts that came to mind regarding similarities and differences in your known experiences?
4. Explore how shared histories, ethnicities, power, privilege, oppression, and geographies affect how we perceive and treat those whom we deem to be like and unlike us.
5. In looking at contemporary America and global activities related to conflict, war, and peace, identify useful information from this chapter that is helpful in dealing with current issues rooted in diversity, power, and privilege within the United States and beyond.

REFERENCES

Benjamin, L. (1997). *Black women in the academy: Promises and perils*. Gainesville: University Press of Florida.

Council on Social Work Education. (2015). *2015 educational policy and accreditation standards for baccalaureate and master's social work programs*. Washington, DC: Author.

Davis, L. E. (2016). *Why are they angry at us? Essays on race*. Chicago, IL: Lyceum Books.

Devore, W., & Schlesinger, E. G. (1999). *Ethnic-sensitive social work practice* (4th ed.). Boston, MA: Allyn & Bacon.

Freire, P. (1970). *Pedagogy of the oppressed*. New York, NY: Bloomsbury.

Irving, A., & Young, T. (2004). Perpetual liminality: Re-readings of subjectivity and diversity in clinical social work classrooms. *Smith College Studies in Social Work, 72*, 231–227.

Jani, J. S., Pierce, D., Ortiz, L., & Sowbel, L. (2011). Access to intersectionality, content to competence: Deconstructing social work education diversity standards. *Journal of Social Work Education, 47*, 283–299. doi:10.5175/JSWE.2011.200900118

Kawewe, S. M. (2001). The impact of gender disempowerment on the welfare of Zimbabwean women. *International Social Work Journal, 44*(4), 471–485.

Kawewe. S. M. (1997a). Black women faculty: The dynamics of patriarchal meritocracy in the academy. In L. Benjamin (Ed.), *Black women in the academy: Promises and peril* (pp. 246–251). Gainesville: University Press of Florida.

Kawewe, S. M. (1997b). Black women in diverse academic settings: Gender and racial crimes of commission and omission in academia. In L. Benjamin (Ed.), *Black women in the academy: Promises and perils* (pp. 263–269).Gainesville: University Press of Florida.

Lee, E. O., Brown, M., & Bertera, E. M. (2010). The use of an online diversity forum to facilitate social work students' dialogue on sensitive issues: A quasi-experimental design. *Journal of Teaching in Social Work, 30*(3), 272–287. doi:10.1080/08841233.2010.499066

Lee, M. Y., & Greene, G. J. (2008). A teaching framework for transformative multicultural social work education. *Journal of Ethnic & Cultural Diversity in Social Work, 12*(3), 1–28. Retrieved from http://dx.doi.org/10.1300/J051v12n03_016

Loya, M. A., & Cuevas, M. (2010). Teaching racism: Using experiential learning to challenge the status quo. *Journal of Teaching in Social Work, 30*(3), 288–299. doi:10.1080/08841233.2010.497130.

Lum, D. (Ed.). (2011). *Culturally competent practice: A framework for understanding diverse groups and justice issues*. Belmont, CA: Brooks/Cole.

National Association of Social Workers. (2015). *Code of ethics of the National Association of Social Workers*. Washington, DC: NASW Press. Retrieved from https://www.socialworkers.org/pubs/code/code.asp

Morgaine, K. (2014). Conceptualizing social justice in social work: Are social workers "too bogged down in the trees?" *Journal of Social Justice, 4*, 1–18.

Moyo, O., & Kawewe, S. M. (2002).The dynamics of a racialized, gendered, ethnicized and economically stratified society: Understanding the socio-economic status of women in Zimbabwe. *Feminist Economics, 8*(2), 163–181.

Ortiz, L., & Jani, J. (2010). Critical race theory: A transformational model for teaching diversity. *Journal of Social Work Education, 46*, 175–193. doi:10.5175/JSWE.2010.200900070

Sisneros, J., Stakeman, C., Joyner, M. C., & Schmitz, C. L. (2008). *Critical multicultural social work*. Chicago, IL: Lyceum Books.

Snyder, C., Peeler, J., & May, D. (2008). Combining human diversity and social justice education: A conceptual framework. *Journal of Social Work Education, 44*(1), 145–161.

Toler, D. L. (1998). Secrets and lies: Debunking the myths about Africa. *Essence, 28*(12), 74–79.

REFERENCES

SECTION 3

STORIES OF ASSUMED PRIVILEGE

In this section, Allan Edward Barsky and Helen G. Deines each tell their own story of assumed privilege. Assumed privilege is somewhat a by-product of having a visible privileged status as well as an invisible nonprivileged status. If you are born into society such that you are fortunate to benefit from mainstream or majority status, you are less likely to be aware of social privilege than if you come from an oppressed or minority background (Crisp, 2014). These two authors are not telling stories of "passing" because of their assumed privileged status based on the way others perceive them but instead seek to bring to the forefront the complex process of "coming out" as well as the constant push and pull—acceptance and denial of who they are as others project and reflect their own perspectives onto them of who they are or should be.

In "Assumed Privilege: A Double-Edged Sword," Barsky states, "In my situation, I did not know what I had until I slowly came to the realization that I was part of an oppressed minority group." Being gay is not a choice. Being out and letting others know one's sexuality, however, may be a choice. Barsky's chapter explores his coming out process, including the perceived benefits when people assumed he was heterosexual, and the challenges of growing up in a homophobic society. Although attitudes and laws pertaining to sexuality have changed significantly since the modern gay rights movement began in the 1960s, discrimination continues to exist. For gay, lesbian, bisexual, and transgender people, coming out is both a personal and a political process. Each person creates his or her own life path, choosing whether and when to take the risk of being out. As a political choice, the act of coming out is significant because family, friends, community members, and political decision-makers may be moved to change their beliefs about homosexuality when they get to know a gay person on a personal basis.

Deines describes herself as a multiethnic, reluctantly White person in the United States and shares three stories about her journey in " 'Who, Me? White?': The Process of Acknowledging and Challenging Racial Privilege." Deines was raised in a Mexican-Irish family in California and uses Elder's (1985) life course perspective to explore the development of her fluid social identity now recognized as typical of persons with mixed heritage. She states,

> In my circumscribed neighborhood of many languages and colors, everyone knew me as I knew myself—as both Elena (at home, a little Mexicana with braids) and Helen at school and in the world, one of a motley assemblage of children becoming Americans. My first week at college taught me an unexpected fact—I do not look Mexican.

Deines shares the unique experiences of persons who are multiethnic and provides practice recommendations that start from a stance of cultural humility. Mental health professionals are challenged to incorporate strategies in their practice that undo oppressive policies and practices.

CHAPTER 10

ASSUMED PRIVILEGE

A Double-Edged Sword

Allan Edward Barsky

BACKGROUND

According to the cliché, "You don't know what you've got until it's gone." This seems to be true in the case of social privilege. If you are born into society such that you are fortunate to benefit from mainstream or majority status, you are less likely to be aware of social privilege than if you come from an oppressed or minority background (Crisp, 2014). In my situation, I did not know what I had until I slowly came to the realization that I was part of an oppressed minority group. In fact, the oppression was so strong that I hid my minority status for many years, living in fear about what life would be like without privilege. As my story suggests, living a life of assumed privilege is like a double-edged sword—a double-sided life with both positive and negative consequences.

I am 55 years old, White, male, Canadian-born, American-naturalized, able-bodied, well educated, and employed as a social work professor. In other words, I have a background that has afforded me many privileges. I have not had to endure ageism, sexism, racism, ableism, classism, and so on. Educationally and career wise, many doors have been open that I have generally taken for granted. Yet in two areas of my life—my religion and my sexual orientation—perhaps I am not quite so privileged. In these regards, some say I am "twice blessed" (Balka & Rose, 1991).

As a Jew who grew up in a small prairie city with a small Jewish population, I have experienced numerous forms of discrimination throughout my life. I was the only non-Christian in my elementary-school classes. Although I had classmates from Native Canadian, French Canadian, Guyanese, British, Irish, Ukrainian, German, Polish, and other ethnic backgrounds, being Jewish set me apart. I had different holidays, different customs, and different beliefs. Despite knowing that I was Jewish, several teachers expected me to recite Christian prayers and songs, participate in Christmas pageants, and eat food that went against family traditions. Although our family did not keep strict rules of kashrut (religious dietary laws), I still remember a Christmas party at which I bit into something and said it was the strangest beef I ever tasted. My friends laughed at how I did not even know what ham was. I can still feel the blush of embarrassment in my face. There were times when teachers acknowledged my Jewishness, but those experiences were often worse than when they ignored it. Once I was asked to be Jesus in a school play because Jesus was Jewish and so was I. The play stopped short of crucifixion, so it was not as traumatic as I thought it might be. Still, the play suggested that all Jews were morally responsible for Jesus' death, so it was not an entirely positive experience. Another memory that still haunts me is being asked to sing Chanukah songs at the Christmas pageant. I think the teacher meant to be sensitive to my religion, but the experience felt more alienating and embarrassing than affirming. I also remember teachers asking me questions about the Old Testament, assuming I would be an authority on this because I was Jewish. I was tempted to say, "What do you mean, *Old Testament*? There is only one testament." I didn't. It seemed easier to comply rather than to confront, even in jest.

Most of my classmates had little knowledge of Judaism. Usually, their religious insensitivities could be chalked up to ignorance rather than intentional meanness. One classmate told me that I could not be Jewish because I did not have horns. Another told me his parents would not let him come to my house because we were Jewish, although he did not know why they had this rule. Other classmates used the phrase "I got jewed" (meaning cheated) without even knowing this was an anti-Semitic phrase.

Despite these incidents, my overall experience of being Jewish has been quite positive. I have felt strongly supported by my family and by the Jewish communities with which I have been associated. With few exceptions, my opportunities to make friends, to be admitted to educational programs, to participate in cultural events, to purchase a home, and to be hired for jobs have not been limited by my being Jewish. The same could not be said for my parents and grandparents, however, particularly when they were living in eastern Europe in the early 1900s. Though Christian privilege persists within Canadian and American society (Schlosser, 2003), religious pluralism also flourishes in many spheres of daily experience. Still, when presidential nominees equate Muslims with *terrorists* and threaten to ban people from an entire religion from entering the country, I am reminded about the fragility of religious tolerance and acceptance, even in a modern democratic society. And when my tallit (prayer shawl) bag is checked for weapons by a police officer as I enter a synagogue, I am reminded that there are still people who would seek to murder me and my fellow congregants for no other reason than our religious affiliation (Cromidas, 2010).

My other *blessed* experience of being a minority is more complicated. I am gay and believe that being gay is something I have always been. However, being gay is not an aspect of myself that I was always aware of. From my earliest recollections about sexuality in my childhood and until my early adulthood, I assumed I was heterosexual—I lived a heterosexual life, and I benefitted from living with an assumed heterosexual identity. I was free to date women and be seen with them in social situations without fear of being harassed verbally or physically and without fear of losing a job, family, friends, or other support systems. At the time, I was not conscious of the privileges I possessed. As I came to realize my identity as a gay man, however, I knew that all this privilege could quickly evaporate. I had to make difficult decisions about the life I would lead, the risks I would take, and the privileges I would have to leave behind.

THE ASSUMED PRIVILEGE OF THE CLOSET

When people ask about my being in the closet, most assume that this was a dreadful period of my life. In hindsight, parts of this closeted lifestyle were horrible—living in fear about being found out, not wanting to disappoint or embarrass my parents, doubting who I was, living a double life, feeling as if I was living a lie, and wondering whether suicide was the answer. However, for many years, my closet was actually quite a comfortable place to live.

Although I was gay, people assumed I was heterosexual. I clearly benefitted from heterosexual privilege, the "systemic garnering of unearned privileges that are conferred on heterosexual individuals" (Nunn & Bolt, 2015, p. 279). Most of my mannerisms, interests, clothes, and so on were not stereotypically gay. In grade school, I was sometimes teased for not being the most coordinated or athletic kid, particularly during competitive team sports. Still, I was not the last one chosen for the team or the one who was called *fag* or *fairy*. In retrospect, perhaps I should thank a couple of classmates for taking much of this abuse because I could just as easily have been the victim. As someone who generally fit in, I could talk hockey and football, play sports, drink beer, party, and do most of what *ordinary guys* did with their peers. Although I was somewhat shy and awkward with dating, that did not identify me as gay because many young straight men go through a phase of being shy and awkward with women. For the most part, I had no trouble passing as a heterosexual.

I rarely discussed sexuality—homosexual or otherwise—with peers or family. To avoid the embarrassment of having to talk directly about these issues, my parents strategically placed an old edition of the book *Everything You Always Wanted to Know About Sex but Were Afraid to Ask* (Reuben, 1969/2000), on a bookshelf where each of their young sons could read it in case we had questions about this somewhat taboo subject. This was the first professional literature on homosexuality that I had read. Like most pre-1980s psychological literature on homosexuality, this book alluded to homosexuality as an illness. At the time, I did not know it was telling me I was pathologically disordered. In fact, the book seemed somewhat progressive.

My only other familiarity with gays came from Hollywood movies, such as *Dog Day Afternoon* or *Cruising*, in which gays were portrayed as promiscuous, dangerous, and deviant. This was long before much more positive images of gay characters—such as Mitch and Cam on *Modern Family* or Kenny on *The Real O'Neals*—appeared on television and in other popular media. I accepted that there was something wrong with being gay and that being gay required either punishment or curing. It was not until later in my life that I began to understand the oppressiveness of the media and of how traditional mental health views lesbian, gay, bisexual, transgender, and queer (LGBTQ) individuals.

Throughout my adult education, I had very few role models, teachers, or professors who were gay-positive. Although many schools of law and social work are more progressive today, my 1980s courses and textbooks still viewed homosexuality as immoral (crimes to be punished) or pathological (mental illnesses to be treated and cured). The one law professor who everyone *knew* was gay made deprecating remarks about gays, supposedly in jest. These jokes did not bother me. They were not mocking me because I was still not identifying myself as gay. Although some professors spoke of social justice issues for LGBTQ people, the curricula focused on sexism, racism, and cultural discrimination. I bought into the rhetoric and internalized the view that individuals who are LGBTQ choose their social condition and therefore do not fit into the same category as other oppressed groups.

As I began my professional career, still single, the comfort of my closet was starting to break down. I had to make some choices—would I continue to live a life as if I were heterosexual, or would I start to admit to myself and others that I was gay, with all the risks that doing so would entail?

BEGINNING THE PROCESS: COMING OUT TO MYSELF

For myself, as for many other LGBTQs, coming out is a gradual process, including coming out to oneself, to the gay community, to heterosexual colleagues at work, to heterosexual friends, and, finally, to family members (Poirier, Fisher, Hunt, & Bearse, 2014). Each stage of coming out can be filled with fear and anxiety. Although many LGBTQ individuals share common experiences of discrimination and oppression, different LGBTQ individuals have different coming-out narratives and paths, often depending on the levels of support and dissupport of the people and social systems around them (Klein, Holtby, Cook, & Travers, 2015). For heterosexual adolescents and young adults, exploring sexuality can be a scary stage of life, fearing how the other person will respond to them and whether they will be good enough in spite of their inexperience. Yet, as heterosexuals, society sends many positive messages telling them that intimacy with a person of the other sex is good, fun, and even expected. Heterosexuals also have many positive role models, within and outside their families. For gays, many societal messages still tell them that same-sex intimacy is wrong, corrupt, dirty, or sick. When I had my first sexual and intimate encounters with other men, these were the messages I carried with me. Internally, something felt wonderful about this intimacy, but I also experienced an overwhelming sense of shame and guilt. I tried to rationalize, "Yes, I've had sex with men, but I can't be gay. I'm not effeminate like them. I'm just a bit shy with women." I was not aware that I had internalized homophobia from my social environment (Theodore et al., 2013).

One of the interesting aspects of reflecting on my coming-out process is how my understanding of my experiences at the time was so different from my current understanding. Growing up, I was not familiar with terms such as *homophobia, heterosexism,* and *heteronormativity.* Through my social work education, research, and social action, I have learned not only what these terms mean in the abstract but also how they reflect my own personal experiences. *Homophobia* is the irrational fear or antipathy toward LGBTQ individuals (Nunn & Bolt, 2015). It may be manifest through clear expressions of violence and hate, such as teasing, excluding, harassment, and violence toward people perceived to be

LGBTQ. Sometimes, the manifestations of homophobia are more nuanced—for instance, taking a gay child to sexuality conversion therapy "for his own good." I was not familiar with the term *homophobia*, but I was certainly aware that antigay attitudes existed within my peer groups. I also knew it was important to act *normal* to avoid being singled out for verbal and physical abuse.

Although I was surrounded by heterosexism and heteronormativity, I was not aware that these biases had relevance for me. Actually, I wasn't even aware of what these terms meant. I have since learned that *heterosexism* refers to a system of attitudes that favors different-sex sexual orientation and assumes heterosexuality is morally or socially superior to homosexuality (Croteau, Lark, Lidderdale, & Chung, 2005). *Heteronormativity* refers to a belief system that accepts male–female relationships as acceptable or natural, thereby marginalizing all other forms of sexuality (Dwyer, 2015). I was still deep in my closet, so I could easily rationalize that I fit into socially accepted norms of heterosexuality. Even if I was called a *fruit* or mocked for any *swishy* (effeminate) behavior, this teasing did not go to my identity because I still thought of myself as a normal person.

Growing up, I was also not aware that the *Diagnostic and Statistical Manual of Mental Disorders* (*DSM*) defined homosexuality as a mental disorder. According to heteronormativity, heterosexuality is considered *normal*, so homosexuality must therefore be *abnormal*. I did not feel disordered or abnormal, and, because I was in the closet, no one insisted that I receive treatment for my supposed disorder. Although the American Psychiatric Association removed *homosexuality* from the *DSM* in 1973, *sexual orientation disturbance* was still listed as a disorder until 1987. Gender disorders are still included in the current *DSM* (Drescher, 2015).

Although I was not conscious of this at the time, many social forces encouraged me to remain in the closet. As long as people assumed that I was heterosexual, I would continue to be accepted by my family, my friends, my employers, and people who hardly even knew me. In other words, I could access heterosexual privilege, so long as I played the game. I had a close friend whose parents dismissed him from their lives when they discovered he was gay. He was emotionally devastated for many years. This could have been me. Most people from minority backgrounds are a minority within their community but not within their own family. I felt alienated within my own family, afraid to ask for support from those who loved me most, fearing that I could lose them altogether.

Professionally, I had many experiences that challenged the safety of my assumed heterosexuality. Having pursued careers in law and social work, I was supposed to be an advocate for social justice and promote equality for those in vulnerable situations. As Standard 6.04(d) of the National Association of Social Workers (2008) Code of Ethics suggests

> (d) Social workers should act to prevent and eliminate domination of, exploitation of, and discrimination against any person, group, or class on the basis of . . . race, ethnicity, national origin, color, sex, sexual orientation, gender identity or expression.

If I was too scared to advocate for myself, even within my own family, how could I be effective as an agent of social change for others? Further, the Accreditation Standard 3.0 of the Council on Social Work Education (2015) suggests that social work educators should promote a learning environment that affirms diversity, including sexual orientation. If I could not publicly affirm my own sexual orientation, how could I be an effective educator and positive role model for my students?

MAINTAINING PRIVILEGE OR RISKING SELF-DISCLOSURE

In one of my first social work jobs, I worked with street youth, 14- to 24-year-olds who had either run away from home or been forced out of their homes by their families. Many of these clients were LGBTQ. I felt incredibly troubled about working with these populations, still nervous that I was only starting to work through my own issues. I felt hypocritical trying to help LGBTQ clients feel better about themselves while I was still hiding so much about myself. On one hand, if I started to come out to my clients, I risked losing the safe bubble of my assumed heterosexuality. On the other hand, I knew that being authentic is one of the cornerstones of developing positive therapeutic alliances with clients (Rogers, 1957).

Perhaps the most critical incident of my professional career came when a teenaged client presented to me in crisis: crying, perspiring, and trembling. Through a long and confused story, he divulged that he was gay, that he was just outed to friends on the street, and that he would rather die than face them. Although he had slept with a few men, he did not have any gay friends or support systems. Incorporating what I knew from crisis-intervention training, I went through the protocols for suicidal ideation screening and intervention (Substance Abuse and Mental Health Services Association, 2014). He had a specific plan for killing himself—jumping in front of a subway—so I knew the risk level was high. Of Rogers' (1957) three core conditions for effective psychotherapy, I offered the client empathy and unconditional positive regard but not genuineness or authenticity. I felt that the client responded well to the understanding and respect that I demonstrated; however, I also felt that, had I been more authentic with the client (and with myself), I could have offered much more. I wanted to let him know that he was not alone in his pain—that I had also felt the fear of being rejected by family and friends. I wanted to let him know, "Life gets better." Yet how could I tell him this when I was still living in fear and not confronting my own insecurities? I rationalized that I should not use the counseling situation to work through my own issues, so I chose not to disclose. On a deeper level, I knew that I had internalized societal homophobia; I could not risk coming out to the client, even though he was gay and in need.

Although I recognized that coming out would be helpful for me professionally (particularly in my work with clients who were LGBTQ), my main impetus for starting the coming-out process was an internal need to connect with people who were LGBTQ, or at least LGBTQ-positive. I tested the waters of coming out with people who I assumed had no connection with my family, friends, and coworkers. The easiest places to do this were in foreign cities and at gay venues in neighborhoods that were far from where I lived. I could continue to live as a heterosexual and enjoy the privileges doing this entailed while beginning to develop relationships with people in the gay community. As I began to see more and more openly gay people, I eventually began to visualize a future where I was out *and* gay (in the happiest sense of the word). I would often ask gay friends about their coming-out stories, expecting to hear the worst. More often than not, I would hear a narrative of triumph or freedom. My images of gays as being destined to a life of being teased, bashed, rejected, and lonely were being replaced with stories of people who had accepted their destinies as being gay, who had gone through varying experiences of discrimination and rejection, and who ultimately were finding that being out and living without heterosexual privilege was far better than living a lie.

Since coming out to my family, I have tried to look forward and focus on the positive. I know that I cannot change the past. Still, there are times when I look back and wonder about what I could have done differently. I continue to feel a certain level of regret for putting my parents through a period of misery when I came out to them. They also experienced the challenges of coming out to friends and family about having a gay son. When I was in the closet, they did not have to be concerned about people's reactions to their son, whom they saw as a source of pride. Once I came out, that privilege was lost. Who knew how friends and extended family would react to news of having a gay son? They already questioned whether they were to blame. Interestingly, they never questioned whether they were to blame for the fact that their other three sons are heterosexual.

ASSUMED PRIVILEGE NO MORE

I have worked through many of my issues, accepting that each time I come out to someone I am taking a risk that heterosexuals do not experience when they disclose their sexuality. Although many of my experiences have been positive, I have experienced homophobia and heterosexism in many realms of my life. I have had neighbors who would not speak with me because I am gay. I have had friends who cut me off from their lives when they found out I am gay. I have received hate mail and antigay epithets, posted anonymously on the Internet or sent by letter to my house. For many years, my husband and I could not acquire health coverage or other employee benefits that were available to different-sex spouses. I've been publicly questioned about how two gay men can raise a daughter. Certain family members have excluded my husband and me from family gatherings. I have been chased by drunken teens and harassed by police because they assumed I was gay. I have had students accuse me of being *anti-Christian* because I included LGBTQ content in the curriculum. Each of these incidents hurt, making me feel angry and sad at times, but sometimes even more determined to do what I can to make life easier for the next generation LGBTQ individuals.

As a social work professor, I deliberately include LGBTQ content in my courses and textbooks (Barsky, 2010, 2017). Integration of LGBTQ content in the curriculum can be used to reduce homophobic attitudes among social work students (Frederiksen-Goldsen, Woodford, Luke, & Guttierez, 2011). I also include LGBTQ content to prepare students for work with this population, as required by the accreditation standards of the Council on Social Work Education (2015). For instance, I teach students how to use LGBT-inclusive language when interviewing clients. During certain classes, I provide students with examples from my own experiences with doctors, social workers, and other professionals who had no clue I was gay and were therefore unable to help me with issues related to my gayness and the homophobia I was experiencing. Many LGBTQ individuals are afraid to access help for serious concerns, including domestic violence, substance abuse, suicidal ideation, and other mental health issues (Mallon, 1998; Seelman, 2015; Smalley, Warren, & Barefoot, 2015; Substance Abuse and Mental Health Services Association, 2014). For example, as a young adult, I stopped seeing a doctor because his intake questionnaire asked if I was homosexual; I feared how he would react if he found out I was lying, and I wondered what would happen to my health insurance if the provider found out. Using relevant examples from my own life not only demonstrates pride in who I am but also gives LGBTQ students permission to talk about their experiences with homophobia, in class or privately. In addition, I invite students of other diverse backgrounds to relate their experiences with privilege and oppression. Students learn to appreciate one another's experiences with privilege and oppression. I believe that such discussions help everyone to be more empathic, supportive, and genuine when they are working with clients with similar issues. Students also learn about the intersectionality of social identities—for instance, how the confluence of being African American and bisexual, or being Christian and heterosexual, affects each person's awareness and attitudes toward oppression and privilege (Crisp, 2014).

I still catch myself, once in a while, fearing what others will think or do if they suspect I am gay. I know that accepting heterosexual privilege by not revealing myself to others can be a double-edged sword: Included with the benefits are costs, and these costs are simply too high. Therefore, I am no longer willing to deny who I am in order to make others feel comfortable with me. I am no longer willing to avoid associations with LGBT people or causes in order to avoid homophobic responses. And now that I have a wonderful husband, I am no longer willing to deny myself the joys of a truly happy *gay marriage*.

CONCLUSION

It has been 13 years since I wrote the original version of this chapter for the first edition. Much has happened in this time. I have a bright and compassionate daughter who inspired a whole city with her conception of a rainbow bridge to celebrate diversity (Key West, 2013). I have helped my university add sexual orientation, gender identity, and gender expression to its regulations that prohibit harassment and discrimination. Florida courts have overturned the law that banned homosexuals from adopting children. President Barak Obama annulled the "Don't Ask, Don't Tell" policy of the military. The Supreme Court of the United States has ruled not only that laws criminalizing same-sex sexual activity (sodomy) are unconstitutional but also that same-sex marriages must be permitted and recognized (*Obergefell et al. v. Hodges et al.*, 2015).

When I think about the next generation of LGBTQ individuals, and also their families, I am hopeful that their lives will be much easier. Along with legal protections and marriage equality, many more people and organizations have positive attitudes toward the LGBTQ community. Yet the struggle for equality, support, and respect is not over. My daughter often hears "that's so gay" and other antigay slurs in her school. The LGBTQ community still experiences higher prevalence of depression, suicidal ideation, and other mental health issues (Barnes, Hatzenbuehler, Hamilton, & Keyes, 2014). Under the pressures of homophobia, one of my own students committed suicide. Many states still allow employees to be fired simply because of their sexual orientation or gender expression. And while progressive politicians, corporations, religious groups, and countries are supporting equality and respect of LGBTQ individuals, there is a backlash against the LGBTQ community from many politicians, organizations, groups, and countries that are not so progressive. A prominent American pastor, Kevin Swanson, has called for homosexuals to be rounded up and killed (Maddow, 2015). Some American politicians and organizations have pushed for laws stating that doctors, nurses, licensed mental health professionals, caterers, and other businesses have a right to refuse service to LGBTQ individuals, arguing that freedom of religion includes the right to deny service to certain groups (General Assembly of North Carolina, 2016; National Conference of State Legislatures, 2015). In Uganda and many other countries, there are still very harsh penalties for being LGBTQ or even for supporting LGBTQ causes (Kretz, 2013). When traveling in a Muslim country, I warned my daughter to be discreet about our religion and her parents' sexuality—something I had never asked her to do while in Canada and the United States. And closer to home, although it is wonderful that more LGBTQ youth feel comfortable coming out at younger ages, many continue to be rejected, harassed, and victimized by family, classmates, teachers, and others (Kosciw, Palmer, & Kull, 2015).

Expectations have also changed. In the "olden days," I would have been thrilled if people learned to *tolerate* gays enough that they just stopped actively harassing or abusing us. Now, the notion of *queer consciousness* tells me that mere tolerance is insufficient. Tolerance is a minimal level of acceptance, suggesting that people should not hurt others who happen to be different. Queer consciousness suggests that we should work toward a society in which LGBTQ individuals are not only tolerated but fully accepted, valued, embraced, and supported (Martinez, Barsky, & Singleton, 2011). When I was in the closet, I had no idea that same-sex marriage would even be a possibility. Now it seems like an obvious right, symbolic of acceptance, equality, and respect for all people.

Moving forward, I realize that the challenges of acceptance, equality, and respect go beyond legislative advocacy and court actions to recognition of legal rights and protections. LGBTQ individuals and allies must learn to engage with people who still view these groups as immoral, pathological, or deviant. Although terms such as *heterosexism* and *homophobia* help us conceptualize discrimination and the underlying causes of antigay attitudes, we should avoid labeling others as *heterosexists* or *homophobes*. Such terms ascribe negative identities, making it more difficult to speak with the very people that we need to engage (Barsky, 2017). I can be out and proud without being disrespectful. I can speak with people who believe homosexuality is a sin or who wish people like me did not exist. I know there are risks, but I also know that I stand on the shoulders of many others who have taken risks to ensure a kinder, more civil society for future generations of LGBT individuals and communities. As I wrote this chapter, I felt embarrassed, opening up about topics that are not the easiest for me to discuss. As I wrote this chapter, I also hoped that it would help readers become aware of various forms of social privilege and would encourage them to take their own stands against prejudice and discrimination.

ACKNOWLEDGMENTS

This chapter is dedicated to the 49 members of the LGBTQ community who were callously murdered at the Pulse nightclub in Orlando, Florida, in 2016 and calls on all readers to do what they can to promote dignity, respect, and safety for all.

DISCUSSION QUESTIONS

1. What benefits did the author experience early in life from being able to keep his sexual orientation a secret and having people assume he was heterosexual? What were the costs of remaining in the closet?
2. What is the difference between homophobia and heterosexism? Identify examples from the author's experiences that reflect each of these concepts.
3. How do you identify in terms of your religion and ethnicity? How does your religion or ethnicity traditionally view people who do not fit into the norms of heterosexuality? Have these views changed over the past 50 years? If so, how?
4. If a friend or colleague came out to you but asked you not to share this information with others, how would you respond and why? How would you respond to others who later asked you if your friend or colleague is gay? How might your response depend on the motivation of the person asking for this information?
5. Imagine that your professor asked you to wear a sticker with a rainbow flag symbolizing the gay pride movement. How do you think others on campus would react to you? How would you feel about engaging in this experiment? How would your experiences relate to the notions of homophobia, heterosexism, and heteronormativity? How might the reactions be different if the bumper sticker said, "I am transgender"?
6. Identify an incident in which you observed an act of homophobia or heterosexism but did not respond as positively as you might have liked. What challenges held you back from acting more positively? What would you have liked to do differently? What resources or strategies could you use to enhance your moral fortitude and react more positively if a similar incident arose in the future?

REFERENCES

Balka, C., & Rose, A. (Eds.). (1991). *Twice blessed: On being gay or lesbian and Jewish.* Boston, MA: Beacon Press.

Barnes, D., Hatzenbuehler, M., Hamilton, A., & Keyes, K. (2014). Sexual orientation disparities in mental health: The moderating role of educational attainment. *Social Psychiatry & Psychiatric Epidemiology, 49*(9), 1447–1454.

Barsky, A. E. (2010). *Ethics and values in social work.* New York, NY: Oxford University Press.

Barsky, A. E. (2017). *Conflict resolution for the helping professions.* New York, NY: Oxford University Press.

Council on Social Work Education. (2015). *Educational policy and accreditation standards*. Washington, DC: Author. Retrieved from http://www.cswe.org/File.aspx?id=81660

Crisp, C. (2014). White and lesbian: Intersections of privilege and oppression. *Journal of Lesbian Studies, 18*(2), 106–117.

Cromidas, R. (2010, October 31). Jews in Chicago feel safe, but are cautious. *The New York Times*, p. A13.

Croteau, J. M., Lark, J. S., Lidderdale, M. A., & Chung, Y. B. (2005). *Deconstructing heterosexism in the counseling professions: A narrative approach*. Thousand Oaks, CA: SAGE.

Drescher, J. (2015). Queer diagnoses revisited: The past and future of homosexuality and gender diagnoses in DSM and ICD. *International Review of Psychiatry, 27*(5), 386–395.

Dwyer, A. (2015). Teaching young queers a lesson: How police teach lessons about non-heteronormativity in public spaces. *Sexuality & Culture, 19*(3), 493–512.

Frederiksen-Goldsen, K. I., Woodford, M. R., Luke, K. P., & Guttierez, L. (2011). Support of sexual orientation and gender identity content in social work education: Results from national surveys of U.S. and Anglophone Canadian faculty. *Journal of Social Work Education, 47*(1), 19–35.

General Assembly of North Carolina. (2016). *Religious Freedom Restoration Act*. Retrieved from http://www.ncga.state.nc.us/Sessions/2015/Bills/House/PDF/H348v1.pdf

Key West "rainbow pride bridge" proposed by 10-year-old Adelle Barsky-Moore. (2013. August 23). *Huffington Post*. Retrieved from http://www.huffingtonpost.com/2013/08/29/key-west-rainbow-bridge_n_3836486.html

Klein, K., Holtby, A., Cook, K., & Travers, R. (2015). Complicating the coming out narrative: Becoming oneself in a heterosexist and cissexist world. *Journal of Homosexuality, 62*(3), 297–326.

Kosciw, J., Palmer, N., & Kull, R. (2015). Reflecting resiliency: Openness about sexual orientation and/or gender identity and its relationship to well-being and educational outcomes for LGBT students. *American Journal of Community Psychology, 55*(1/2), 167–178.

Kretz, A. J. (2013). From "kill the gays" to "kill the gay rights movement": The future of homosexuality legislation in Africa. *Journal of International Human Rights, 11*(2), 207–244.

Maddow, R. (2015, November 9). *The Rachel Maddow show*. MSNBC. Retrieved from http://www.msnbc.com/rachel-maddow-show/watch/anti-gay-pastor-event-hosts-3-gop-candidates-563178051820

Mallon, G. P. (1998). *We don't exactly get the welcome wagon: The experiences of gay and lesbian adolescents in child welfare systems*. New York, NY: Columbia University Press.

Martinez, P., Barsky, A., & Singleton, S. (2011). Exploring queer consciousness among social workers. *Journal of Gay and Lesbian Social Services, 23*, 296–315.

National Association of Social Workers. (2008). *Code of ethics*. Washington, DC: Author. Retrieved from http://www.socialworkers.org/pubs/code/code.asp

National Conference of State Legislatures. (2015). *2015 State religious freedom restoration legislation*. Retrieved from: http://www.ncsl.org/research/civil-and-criminal-justice/2015-state-rfra-legislation.aspx

Nunn, L. M., & Bolt, S. C. (2015). Wearing a rainbow bumper sticker: Experiential learning on homophobia, heteronormativity, and heterosexual privilege. *Journal of LGBT Youth, 12*(3), 276–301.

Obergefell et al. v. Hodges et al. (2015). 576, S Ct., 14–556. Retrieved from http://www.supremecourt.gov/opinions/14pdf/14-556_3204.pdf

Poirier, J. M., Fisher, S. K., Hunt, R. A., & Bearse, M. (2014). *A guide for understanding, supporting, and affirming LGBTQI2-S children, youth, and families*. Washington, DC: American Institutes for Research.

Reuben, D. (2000). *Everything you always wanted to know about sex, but were afraid to ask*. New York, NY: Bantam. (Original work published 1969)

Rogers, C. (1957). The necessary and sufficient conditions of therapeutic personality change. *Journal of Counseling Psychology, 25*, 91–103.

Schlosser, L. A. (2003). Christian privilege: Breaking a sacred taboo. *Journal of Multicultural Counseling and Development, 31*(1), 44–51.

Seelman, K. L. (2015). Unequal treatment of transgender individuals in domestic violence and rape crisis programs. *Journal of Social Service Research, 41*(3), 307–325.

Smalley, K. B., Warren, J. C., & Barefoot, K. N. (2015). Barriers to care and psychological distress: Differences between bisexual and gay men and women. *Journal of Bisexuality, 15*(2), 230–247.

Substance Abuse and Mental Health Services Association. (2014). *Suicide prevention among LGBT youth: A workshop for professionals who serve youth.* Washington, DC: Author. Retrieved from http://www.sprc.org/webform/suicide-prevention-among-lgbt-youth-workshop-professionals-who-serve-youth

Theodore, J., Shidlo, A., Zemon, V., Foley, F., Dorfman, D., Dahlman, K., & Hamid, S. (2013). Psychometrics of an internalized homophobia instrument for men. *Journal of Homosexuality, 60*(4), 558–574.

CHAPTER 11

"WHO, ME? WHITE?"

The Process of Acknowledging and
Challenging Racial Privilege

Helen G. Deines

UNDERSTANDING AND EXPERIENCING
WHITE PRIVILEGE: MY STORIES

What follows is my story of being a multiethnic, reluctantly White person in the United States. Over the years I have been called Mexican, White, multiracial, multicultural, biracial, racially ambiguous, mixed—the terminology changing depending on who is doing the naming and at what point in history. In the twenty-first century, the multiracial demographic is the fastest-growing segment of the US population, with estimates that one in five Americans will claim that designation by 2050 (Jackson & Samuels, 2011; Shih & Sanchez, 2009). So my experience is an increasingly common story in a nation in which the dominant racial narrative to those who are seen as People of Color is still White advantage and disadvantage.

Because this chapter is grounded in the life course perspective (LCP; Elder, 1985; Giele, 2006), I emphasize the interaction between the psychological and the contextual in identity development. Although we often think of identity development as a consistent human experience, the LCP draws attention to the unique developmental experiences of those who grew up in different generations; consider, for example, those who grew up in the United States during the Great Depression, World War II, or the civil rights movement, in contrast to children of contemporary Syria or revolutionary China in the 1940s. In this chapter, I emphasize themes the LCP recognizes as influential in identity development, including historical and cultural context, life trajectory, transitions, social networks, and significant social events.

Like all of our stories, mine is simultaneously personal and political. I was born in 1942, and my identity developed over my life course within the context of family life, varied scientific understandings, Census Bureau policies, social movements, Supreme Court decisions, and political candidates whose influences leave lasting marks on experiences of race and social identities. My first week at college taught me an unexpected fact: I do not look Mexican.

I grew up in San Francisco, the daughter of a proud Mexican mother whose family roots had been part of California history since the 1800s and my father, an equally proud Irish immigrant-labor organizer. In my circumscribed neighborhood of many languages and colors, everyone knew me as I knew myself—as both Elena (at home, a little Mexicana with braids) and Helen at school and everywhere else, one of a motley assemblage of children becoming Americans.

In this wonderfully diverse neighborhood, where two languages in a household were the norm rather than the exception, people traded tales of their journeys from other lands; such dual identities were familiar, connected with warm memories from faraway places. For example, our household consisted of not just my Irish father and Mexicana mother but also the German Jewish family my parents sheltered in our basement (I was a toddler during World War II). None of the neighbors found that strange. It seemed as if everyone in our neighborhood had people in extra bedrooms who spoke another language. Some were formal relatives; others were family friends from "the old country." I have a vague memory of the German couple just leaving one day after the war was over, and my parents assuring me that that they were safe.

When I moved 30 miles away to attend Stanford University, my social identity changed practically overnight. What a mess! At 18 years old, for the first time in my life, I was identified as *White*. I learned that most people equate fair skin and unaccented English with *White*, and those around me refused to accept what to them were contradictory terms—*Mexican* or even *Mexican American*.

This is not a story about *intentionally passing* (Hobbs, 2014)—in 1960, I didn't even know that term. Devising my own complex process of racial coming out, I tried repeatedly to explain that I was Mexican. Most people, however, discounted my efforts. Over the years, I continued to grapple with expressing a simple, clear description of who I was. Sometimes I claimed my Mexican roots; at other times I simply did not bother challenging others' intractable assumptions about my Whiteness.

However, one person at Stanford did not see me as White—the young, White, male faculty member assigned as my freshman academic advisor. He gruffly introduced himself during orientation. Without any of the usual relationship-building small talk, he signed my blank course-approval form. When I asked anxiously for guidance about what specific courses I should take, he said, "It doesn't matter. Take anything you want." I must have looked confused, although in the back of my mind I naively thought this might have something to do with my being a National Merit Scholar.

Then he said slowly, seeming to enjoy the words, "You were only admitted because you are a 'three-fer'—a girl, a Catholic, and a Mexican. Take anything you want. You will never last here. I won't be seeing you again."[1]

---

1. I ask twenty-first-century readers to remember this narrative's context. This event occurred in 1960, before the days of affirmative action as it is known today. Stanford undergraduate admissions in the 1950s and early 1960s restricted females

I recall standing up without looking at him, picking up my forms, leaving his office, and walking hurriedly, head down, back to the relative safety of my dorm. The descriptors were accurate. Never before had they been used against me as sources of shame.

I told no one about this encounter until many years later. After all, I knew only two other Catholic girls in my class, and both were Anglo and wealthy. I never met another Mexican American student at Stanford.

To telephone my parents and discuss my experience with them would have been uncharted territory. Irish-Mexican families were common in San Francisco's Catholic parishes. We were never treated as "less than." I had neither words nor heart to share this new, alien world with them.

Edwards and Pedrotti (2015) describe my college experiences as typical challenges in the development of multiracial and multiethnic individuals who find the descriptors they use for themselves repeatedly challenged over their lifetimes. Validations or invalidations occur within family, peer groups, or the larger social contexts as life circumstances change. My invalidation experiences, while shocking to me, were relatively minor because they followed 18 years of consistent support. Consider the far more difficult hurdles faced every day by young mixed-race children riding school buses across this country.

Edwards and Pedrotti (2015) continue, recommending mental health interventions to support multicultural persons in coping with similar challenges, including (a) addressing our national social convention of not talking about race, (b) focusing on common values as well as common sources of conflict in mixed race families, and (c) using narrative techniques to "re-story" one's life. Re-storying offers the individual, couple, or family the opportunity to transform the meaning of an invalidation into a source of wisdom or motivation, for example, using my freshman advisor as a role model of how not to function as a privileged White person (Edwards & Pedrotti, 2015, pp. 110–113).

Two episodes later in life pushed me to delve further into how to live satisfactorily as both White and Latina. I begin this portion with Story 2.

STORY 2

I married after graduating from Stanford. My husband and I moved across the country, picking up graduate degrees and building a family. We settled in Louisville, Kentucky, where Latino culture was rarely mentioned. Along the road, I had discovered that the strong math and science foundation Stanford required prepared me in many ways for social work in academic health settings. I began teaching at a graduate school of social work and lecturing at the medical school, focusing my research on the relationships among poverty, race, and health-care delivery. In Louisville, race meant Black and White.

In 1996, I participated in the Lilly Conference on College Teaching at Miami University of Ohio. I walked across campus in a soaking rain to hear Trinity University's Distinguished

to about 25% to 30% of the class. Other selective criteria (e.g., race, ethnicity, religion) were more covertly applied. In other words, the dominant culture of the university at that time was overwhelmingly White, male, and Protestant. For a more thorough discussion of this topic, see, for example, Leifer (1974), Steinberg (2013), and Weschler, (2014).

Professor of Humanities, Arturo Madrid (1996), present a paper on Latino history. I was unsure of my motivation to hear the speech. I just knew it was sufficiently important to justify a thorough drenching.

I listened, for the first time, to my reality being described as an objective academic topic. Madrid used the words I had grown up with and long ago forgotten or suppressed, words that my mother used to establish norms of behavior and appearance for how the family would present itself to the world. These words may be unfamiliar to Anglo readers but are or were common in Chicano culture (Castro, 2001). First, the demeaning *pachuca* (the 1940s' urban street kid), and my mother's favorite insult, as in, "Elena, dress like that and people with think you are a *pachuca*!" Alternatively, the pride in her voice that made me so uncomfortable when she used the less well-known *californios* ("We are descendants of the original settlers, you know!") rather than the more charged *mexicanos* (the more familiar mixture of Spanish and Indian).

Madrid's voice was slow and sad, I thought, when he used the homogenized, meaningless *Hispanic*. None of us, after all, ever came to the United States from a country named Hispania. We who are Latino/a carry the cultures of Puerto Rico, Mexico, Peru, Colombia, the Dominican Republic, Chile, and so many more—each unique and each worth naming to the persons whose life the country shapes. How those with the power to name deny the strengths and pains we each draw from our unique heritages.

Most importantly, Madrid described my interior life—that of a woman who looks White, carries an Anglo name, speaks Spanish like a four-year-old but is nonetheless Latina at the core. He described the lives of people I had never envisioned—people who looked brown and had Spanish surnames but spoke no Spanish and grew up in totally Anglo cultures; nonetheless, they also identified as Latina/os. I wept throughout the talk, realizing for the first time that my own confusion was common in the United States. These were tears of relief. I felt deeply connected in a whole new way to people whom I had never met. Yet I also felt a fleeting sense of shame that I was so self-absorbed that I was blind to the struggles of others.

At that moment I could not articulate in words how my Whiteness had exempted me from recognizing others' realities, how my white skin separated me from those with brown skin. Neither did I realize that the speaker had never used the terms *multicultural, multiethnic, multiracial,* or *mixed* to describe the varied Latino/a experience that was his topic.

At the end of the conference I returned to Louisville committed to finding ways to reclaim my Latina roots. I began by reading Latino/a authors, fiction, nonfiction, growing-up stories, and Latino/a studies. The famous Richard Rodriguez (1982), whose writings explore how his brownness shaped his life, was educated just as I, by the Sisters of Mercy and Stanford. Yet Rodriguez (1982, p. 130) noted that he "was the student at Stanford who remembered to notice the Mexican American janitors and gardeners working on campus." I had not.

Richard Rodriguez evoked memories of days long forgotten. Spanish lessons rebuilt language skills I had long ago put away when my parents required an English-only household ("You need unaccented English to speak to those in power!"). Eventually I organized a border immersion trip for students (and myself) to experience the lives of Mexicans on both sides of the Rio Grande. When I had visited Ireland some years before, the Irish recognized me as "an exile"—one whose family left the country out of necessity and who always yearns for the homeland (Miller, 1988). So it was in Mexico; the poor families living in the desert outside Juarez also recognized my long-ago connection and welcomed me home in just the same way.

Racial identity is based on self-identification and the racial identification of others in one's community. For the monoracial person, this is a relatively straightforward task usually completed in adolescence and young adulthood.

Social work scholars Salett and Koslow (2015, pp. 154–155) highlight the fluidity of identity development for the mixed demographic, continuing throughout one's life course. Although mixed identity is racialized, it is never simply binary and hierarchical but always open to reinterpretation. First, multiracial persons are far more likely than their monoracial peers to understand race as socially constructed. This knowledge serves to protect them from destructive racial stereotypes as determinants of their future achievement. Second, experiences of biracial family members, such as hazing, impact the development of other biracial siblings. Finally, biracial young adults often cope in varied ways, sometimes claiming one identity in public and another in private—for example, African American in public and biracial within the family.

Salett and Koslow (2015, pp. 155–156) note that these adaptations usually result in one of five different identity patterns, which research shows are influenced by gender and social class: (a) *a foot-in-each-camp*, claiming the racial identities of both parents; (b) *situation-determined identification*, making conscious shifts to meet the immediate context; (c) *a multiracial identification* sometimes called "sitting on the border"; (d) *a monoracial identification*; or (e) *a unique racial social identity* (e.g., Cablinasian[2] or Nuyorican[3]). Again, these adaptations are fluid, influenced by both interior and contextual factors over one's life course.

I do not need to be in Mexico to "feel Mexican." Let a politician rant about illegals, someone speak in a derogatory manner about Latino/as in front of me, or a particular holiday remind me of my mother, and I "feel Latina." In contrast, if I am participating in a statewide commission where members know me only in a distant professional relationship, I am who they see unless it becomes important that others recognize my Latina roots.

STORY 3

Only a few months after the Lilly Conference, I was having lunch with an African American colleague. We were bemoaning the disrespect we experienced as "Women of Color." I ached as I heard my colleague's description of being dismissed as "just one of those affirmative-action hires." I was often told the same thing.

She listened quietly as I described my frustration at repeatedly coming out to colleagues and students who most often responded by denying my claim of being Latina or joking about what might be an apt metaphor for a woman who is white on the outside and brown within. My friend was silent for a few seconds, finally saying, "But you always have the choice."

2. Neologism Tiger Woods uses to describe his racial heritage: Caucasian, Black, Asian-Indian.

3. Person from Puerto Rico living in New York City.

My friend's simple observation was what transformative educators identify as a *disorienting experience*, an event that causes a shift in one's most basic paradigms. What was I doing, calling myself a *Woman of Color*? Suddenly I knew that how I named myself was only one facet of my identity because, in reality, the world sees and treats me as White.

Do you hear the privilege talking in my claiming to be a Woman of Color? Goodman (2011, pp. 12–17) talks about how people with privilege sometimes cling to those aspects of their identity whereby they have experienced discrimination (e.g., I am White, but I am also [fill in the blank]: disabled, poor, gay, Jewish, female, and so forth). It is as if these other dimensions of social identity erase the Whiteness. We are all uncomfortable being told that perhaps we are in some way unduly advantaged, that perhaps we have not earned every inch of what we have attained in life.

There is also a misunderstanding that racism is only about individual intentional meanness. It is not. Very few people intend to do anything that is racially offensive. Nonetheless, systemic and cultural racism, written into the policies and practices of our institutions and pervasive in our media, advantage White people as a group and disadvantage People of Color. These advantages are relative because social identity is complicated. Poor White women, especially those with other differences (disabilities, gay, poorly educated) gain very little. Others may gain a great deal. The most important implication is how this racial hierarchy unnecessarily divides us from each other.

THE CHOICE FOR MIXED-HERITAGE PERSONS: CONTEXT IN HISTORY AND POWER IN THE UNITED STATES

The term *choice* sounds as if it is a personal matter. Yet Salett and Koslow (2015) have observed that social identity functions to meet that need experienced by all individuals "to feel that they are part of a greater community, to connect with others in, and recognize a reflection of themselves within, that community" (p. 4).

The dominant racial context for one's identity in the United States is *binary* and *hierarchical*—*binary* in that it focuses on a clear distinction between Black and White, and *hierarchical* in that White is superior and People of Color are considered inherently inferior (Delgado & Stefanic, 1998; Goodman, 2011; Ifekwunigwe, 2004; Salett & Koslow, 2015). Anyone who deviates from this dominant narrative has been considered inherently subversive and marginalized, threatening the Black/White and superior/inferior distinctions. Where and how does the multiracial or multiethnic person fit?

Numerous public policies dating from the very discovery of this country have served to punish, hide, and exclude interracial and interethnic relationships from history. The first Black people came to Virginia in August 1619 not as slaves but as indentured servants, just as their White counterparts did (Allen, 1997). Interracial marriage became so common in the Virginia colony that in 1691 its House of Burgesses (legislature) outlawed Black–White marriage, with the penalty that the couple be forever banned from the colony, such a large area that it was the equivalent of their entire world. The same penalty applied to the clergy persons who married them (Guild, 1995). Similar laws were passed in many other British colonies.

In the French colonies in what is now Louisiana, interracial marriages became so numerous that landowners petitioned King Louis for a similar interracial marriage-banning edict, with particularly onerous penalties imposed on the Catholic priests who presided over these weddings (Hayes & Davis, 1998). Nash's (1995) sweeping history of "mestizo America" paints a powerful picture of a rich tapestry of marriages between western trappers and First Nations' members, establishing early commercial relationships that spread across the North American continent, the cornerstones of prosperity to come.

The simple fact of life is that whenever and wherever new groups of people encounter one other, new families are born. However, this nation's misleading dominant binary racial narrative left mixed-race people hidden, labeled as deficient or pathological, and their history omitted from textbooks. Throughout most of US history, mixed-race people were without role models with whom to connect.

Scholars of multiethnic identity and mixed-race studies identify the contemporary dramatic increase in numbers of people self-identifying as *mixed* with four events, all connected with the culmination of the civil rights movement: (a) the US Supreme Court 1967 *Loving v. Virginia* decision that ruled unconstitutional, on the basis of the due process and equal protection clauses, all state laws banning marriages between Black and White citizens (Roberts, 2014–2015); (b) the Immigration and Nationality Act of 1965 that abolished national origin and race-based immigration quotas, which opened doors to increasing numbers of Asian and Latin American legal immigrants; (c) in response to demands from many mixed-race and -ethnicity citizens, the inclusion of a multiracial category as a self-identification option in the 2000 US census; and (d) the election of President Barack Obama in 2008, a man who openly shared his story as a multiracial citizen and who dealt publicly with the consequences (Goodman, 2011; Salett & Koskow, 2015; Shih & Sanchez, 2009).

Having a choice did not just happen by chance. Each of these four events, described as critical to the increase in interracial marriages and stimulating mixed-race families to come out, is the result of significant social movements. Each of these events contributed to building spaces safe for persons to disclose mixed-race identity, signaling that choice was a reality for vast numbers of US citizens. Whether a person or family chooses to exercise that choice is a complex decision, dependent on multiple factors across systems.

Studies exploring these decisions find that better educated, lighter-skinned mixed persons are more likely to disclose their identity (Davenport, 2016; Townsend, Fryberg, Wilkins, & Markus, 2012). At the same time, Williams et al. (2014) found that both Black and White adolescent males of all income and education levels in one state were significantly more likely to change their identity to mixed after President Obama's election than in the months before.

However, this is most certainly not a postracial society. Hobbs (2014) has pointed out that conservatives championed the cause of mixed-race advocates, arguing that an increased multiracial population suggested a decreasing need for compensatory programs such as affirmative action and collection of data by racial categories. Hobbs reminds readers that mixed-race identities remain racialized identities and that mixed-race people must still negotiate a United States rife with racial advantage to some, disadvantage to others.

Putting the pieces together, I think back to being Elena as a toddler, Helen as I walked into my elementary school. The Sisters of Mercy trained me, along with all the other children of immigrants, to succeed in the United States—a little White Catholic girl who would ultimately go to off to Stanford and build a strong family and career. My Mexican mother's values of family, dignity, personalism, and respect (Edwards, 2015) shape my approach to building relationships. My Irish labor-organizer father's unwavering commitment to social justice shapes my life gyroscope.

Nonetheless, as I look back on the experience of leaving home for college, I realize that I knew I was White long before I acknowledged I was White. Like any 18-year-old going off to college, I worried about many things—that I would not be smart enough, that I would be the poorest person in my class, that I would be the only Catholic in a Protestant world. Yet I have no memory of thinking that I would look or sound different from my classmates. For all my conscious thoughts about being Mexican, I knew in an unspoken, deeply visceral way that I would fit.

That pattern has continued throughout my life. When a police officer stops me while I'm driving on the expressway, I assume I must have been speeding; racial profiling would never occur to me. I enter every professional job interview free to focus solely on my qualifications, never diverted by having to manage ethnoracial differences.

Diane Goodman (2011) has described complexities of privilege and social identity in the United States. In the multiple facets of our identities, we all juggle aspects both advantaged and disadvantaged: Race, gender, religion, sexual orientation, ability status, age, class, and nationality are major dimensions. Privilege is insidious. We need not seek it. It is conferred by others in the numerous ways our society determines its preferred ways of looking and living. Exercising privilege also requires no personal meanness. Both silence and inaction maintain the status quo in which some are always unconsciously ahead of the game.

My stories bear the fingerprints of privilege. Goodman (2011, pp. 22–31) describes three ways of thinking that she finds common among individual members of advantaged groups—lack of awareness of their dominant identity, denial of the existence of oppression, and a sense of entitlement to the advantages they usually experience.

Regardless of how much my father was committed to social justice, he had no qualms about connecting me with a high-paying union job each summer during college. And I never had a qualm about accepting it: I never thought about anyone else who needed the job more to support a family or that it was our White advantage that gained me the position. Then there was the Catholic education my parents provided, the annual cross-country rail trips required for my father's work, my mother's activities as a national volunteer for the Girl Scouts, our house full of political activists, even the bad times that taught me how to cope when my parents' progressive political beliefs were out of fashion and those who were in power attacked with viciousness. Although we often lived on some kind of financial precipice, we always had health insurance, a car, a roof over our heads; more important, I assumed everyone lived in like fashion.

As I moved into doing antiracism work in the early 2000s, I slowly came to recognize the more subtle and seriously disruptive signs of White privilege, a cluster of attitudes and behaviors sometimes called *internalized racial superiority*—or "stinkin' thinkin'" (Golden, 2011). Readers may recognize this characteristic in others: White people who are always right, dominate conversations, know more about People of Color than People of Color know about themselves, frequently interrupt, rarely listen to others for prolonged periods.

As I participated in many different kinds of working groups with large numbers of People of Color, first with Casey Family Programs then with the People's Institute for Survival and Beyond (www.pisab.org) and finally with the Kellogg Foundation's Racial Healing Initiative, I could see these patterns of domination in others and finally in myself. Experientially I learned the value of cultural humility, appreciating that, however much I knew, there was so much more to be learned by asking others to share their stories in depth rather than just respond to a few questions (Ortega & Faller, 2011; Tervalon & Murray-Garcia, 1998). Others became the teachers, and we worked together on actions that were no longer predetermined. The questioning, by the way, is now mutual. Now I more often share experiences about Whiteness than speak about Persons of Color.

PRACTICE IMPLICATIONS

The cultural-humility stance is increasingly recommended across health and mental health professions. Its adaptation in working with multicultural persons seems especially timely, given the increasing visibility of this demographic.

Jackson and Samuels (2011) have thoughtfully applied the National Association of Social Workers' Multicultural Competence Standards (2001) to practice with multiracial and mixed populations. Drawing from resources across disciplines, the authors began from the assumption that multiracial persons, rather than being inherently flawed or deficient, are at increased risk of discrimination in a race-focused society.

Given the paucity of social work literature on practice with mixed-race persons, Jackson and Samuels' work (2011) provides an extensive description of what they have called a "cultural attunement" approach to practice, based on the more well-known *cultural humility* perspective. This cultural attunement approach provides the foundation for the authors' discussion of how social workers meet the National Association of Social Workers standard regarding one's own personal values, beliefs, and attitudes (Jackson & Samuels, 2011, pp. 237–239). The authors have provided challenging, thought-provoking questions from multiple perspectives. For example, they have challenged practitioners to think about their reaction when they see someone of their own skin hue walking down the street holding hands with someone of another color.

Next, the authors have provided a well-organized section on essential knowledge for practice with multiracial persons (Jackson & Samuels, 2011, pp. 239–241). Key themes include the sociopolitical history of multiraciality, various models and theories of multiracial identity development, and typical challenges over the life course. Emphasis is on selecting theories that work with specific clients, in the sense of supporting the clients in challenges they encounter and in opening opportunities to them. Throughout, Jackson and Samuels have applied the cultural-attunement model, in which clinicians adopt a stance of not knowing, encouraging their clients to be the expert teachers who know best their own situations. The authors also have encouraged the use of fluid theories of multiracial identity, recognizing the unforeseeable twists and turns over one's life course that stimulate the person to see oneself in a new light.

Moving to the skills-competence standard, Jackson and Samuels (2011, pp. 241–243) have emphasized that a healthy social identity in terms of race is a protective factor in dealing with all of life's challenges. Hence, although a client may not enter the therapeutic relationship to discuss race, it is always a relevant topic, and readers are referred to key resources that discuss how to raise race as a topic in clinical practice.

Validation is another significant dimension of practice, tied to the practitioner's ability to stay closely attuned to the client's racial and broader social identities. Hearing accurately where clients are in their ties to the community, and also how they are known to family and their sense of interiority, is crucial to successful practice. Further, the authors have stressed the importance of practitioners' knowledge of resources, both local and online, with whom clients can connect for support. Resources might include children's books, videos, and websites (particularly important for those in small towns and rural communities).

These practice recommendations seem deceptively simple. Therapeutic relationships provide accompaniment for the journey, not happy endings. It is reassuring that Shih and Sanchez (2009) found that most mixed-race people report a high level of satisfaction with their lives. As a mixed elder, I am content to say, as does Cherríe Moraga, feminist poet, "I am a White girl brown to the blood color of my mother speaking for her" (Moraga & Anzaldua, 1981, p. 12).

These practice implications must include a caution. Were you taught that it was desirable to be color-blind in practice (e.g., the ideology that it is best to focus on the individual person and his problems, without regard to race)? Although this approach was, at one point, considered good manners, I urge you to consider two realities. The first is that multicultural clients indicate a low level of satisfaction with counselors who ascribe to this type of practice (Miller & Buchanan, 2015). The second consideration is that, by consciously deciding not to explore race, counselors close the door on clients raising concerns around this aspect of their identity and experiences of race-based injustices. Color-blind practice may unintentionally foster internalized racial inferiority in the client, matched by the professional's internalized superiority. Malott and Schaefle (2015) present a useful guide for practice that addresses clients' experiences of racism, including having an essential knowledge base and skills for initiating the conversation, supporting the client's identity, promoting coping strategies, and providing trauma-informed care. Partnership with clients is the essential theme of this guide.

Each practitioner adapts these principles to fit his or her own practice style. My personal journey has shaped my professional practice, causing me to intertwine a cultural humility lens with commitment to antioppressive practice (Dominelli, 2008). This integrated stance applies whether I am working with individuals, groups, organizations, or communities, although its application varies in emphasis depending on the setting.

The first thing I try to do is build a space safe for others to share their stories. Doing this requires an environment respectful of all. Similarly, welcoming rituals, icebreakers, ground rules, neutral language, and such are crafted to invite all to the table. And humor helps. For example, when facilitating large group events, I usually wear socks that say, "Peace on earth." I alert participants at the beginning of the day that, if discussions become too heated, I will lift my leg as a reminder of the desired spirit of the workshop.

The second thing I do is approach people from a cultural-humility perspective, reminding both the individual and others present how much we may learn and grow from reflecting on life's challenges. The curiosity central to cultural humility helps me slow down and stay with shared painful moments. Salett and Koslow (2015, p. 21) describe the conflict experienced by a bicultural man who describes his identity as ABCD: Born in the United States to immigrant parents from India, he is expected to succeed according to US standards at school and career while at home maintaining the traditional customs of his family's country of origin, which is ABCD—American Born Confused Desai (Indian).

This brief story may resonate among others who experience different forms of otherness. Many of us are one person at home and another in the world. My job as a facilitator where people are encouraged to share their story is to move gently, not too far from the specific, waiting until someone identifies the common thread. Never should the particular pain be minimized. My experience is that often participants of Color and those whose families have emigrated from other parts of the world will relate easily to the ABCD story. First-generation college students, members of conservative faith traditions who may feel out of place in some professional schools, persons from minority religions, and rural participants in urban settings may also connect. One story can consume a significant amount of time, but if it establishes the principle that there are commonalities of experience, shared feelings form a basis for an unexpected community.

The third thing I do is allow differences to emerge in these conversations. Forms and dynamics of oppression differ. Goodman (2011, pp. 9–10) highlights some of these differences. In racism and sexism, identity and advantage/disadvantage are fixed. There is potential room for change when one considers classism and ableism. In ageism and sexism, one often sees warm relationships among members of the dominant and subordinate groups (e.g., consider diverse senior center and veterans' groups). Contrast this with the fear and hostility one may see when considering racism and heterosexism. These are only a few examples of conflictual feelings that may arise in courageous conversations about difference with individuals, families, and small and large groups.

Silencing is one clear sign of oppression, and it is not uncommon in these sorts of discussions. Sometimes the phrase "playing the race card" is used as a not-so-subtle method of ending a discussion of painful experiences related to race, structural racism based on policies and practices, and the inequitable outcomes that flow from those policies and practices (Rodriguez & Freeman, 2016). It is helpful to remind the group that we all flee from pain but that working together through the pain is the door to healing. People of color daily manage the challenges of race to survive; people who are White are not required to do so. Race is not on our minds so constantly.

Goodman (2011, pp. 50–83) has described and suggested many alternative strategies to address resistance to addressing advantage and disadvantage. Taking breaks, journaling, and working in small groups are all effective in diffusing discomfort and building positive energy. Moving beyond talking to active exercises often generates excitement and pulls people together. One well-developed example for diverse groups numbering 15 to 30 is Paul Kivel's "Examining Race and Class" exercise (available at http://paulkivel.com/resource/examining-class-and-race/).

Diane Goodman (2011, pp. 111–120) has written eloquently about "the joy of unlearning privilege/oppression." Unchanged, our complementary roles of advantage and disadvantage maintain a status quo of power relationships. Professionals perpetuate oppressive social relationships when they close their eyes to research that documents the damage caused by systemic injustice and, by their silence, perpetuate clients' beliefs that their distress is the result solely of personal inadequacies.

CONCLUSION

This conversation leads to a concluding thought. Adopting a stance of cultural humility in practice removes one's blinders. Listening with openness to others sharing their stories reveals realities previously unknown. Simply recognizing everyday dynamics of privilege for some groups and oppression and discrimination for others confronts mental health practitioners with the necessity of challenging the status quo. To passively tolerate power relationships as they are and counseling clients to accept intolerable conditions lead inevitably to professional burnout (Morse, Salyers, Rollins, Monroe-DeVita, & Pfahler, 2012).

Some practitioners may add community practice to their skill repertoire: advocacy in one of its many forms, community organizing, nonviolent actions from letter-writing to testifying on behalf of justice-focused legislation have all been important in improving the lives of Mixed-Race persons. Others may engage in justice-promoting activities unrelated to their professional employment, thus improving their communities in a broader sense. Even checkbook advocacy is fine if that is all one can do.

It is a cliché that the world is shaped by those who show up, but it is also true. Mental health professionals can use their knowledge at many societal levels to improve environments in which individuals and families grow and develop. Jenkins (2015) raises this question regarding African American identity: "Are [they] to be taught to survive in and adapt to a world of insults or to adopt an attitude that would change such a world?" (p. 32). This question applies equally to all Persons of Color and to those of Mixed heritage. David (2014) frames the issue differently, querying why we spend so much energy researching, "charting and applauding the ability of individuals, families, and groups to successfully sustain societal abuse, hardship, and injustice" (p. 5) rather than focusing on the big picture where we could reduce suffering. The way we answer these questions will be determined largely by the words and actions of White Americans who become willing partners in undoing racism.

DISCUSSION QUESTIONS

1. With friends or classmates, watch the Zora Hudson YouTube video *Biracial Hair*. What appealed to you? What was a challenge? How do you account for the audience reaction? If you had trouble catching all the words, just Google the poet's name and the title.

2. Are all the aspects of your family's heritage open for public discussion? Are there taboo topics? How does this influence your practice?

3. When do you open discussion of race and ethnicity with clients? With all clients or just some? What is your standard opening question? How do you invite clients to further explore critical incidents that helped them further develop their social identity?

4. When do you notice Whiteness? When, if ever, do you explore race with clients who appear to be White? What about those who feel disadvantaged because they are White?

REFERENCES

Allen, T. M. (1997). *The invention of the White race.* Vol. II: *The origin of racial oppression in Anglo-America.* London, UK: Verso.

Castro, R. G. (2001). *Chicano folklore: A guide to the folktales, traditions, rituals and religious practices of Mexican-Americans.* New York, NY: Oxford University Press.

Davenport, L. (2016). The role of gender, class, and religion in biracial Americans' racial labeling decisions. *American Sociological Review, 81*(1), 57–84.

David, L. E. (2014). Have we gone too far with resiliency? *Social Work Research, 38*(1), 5–6.

Delgado, R., & Stefanic, J. (Eds.). (1998). *The Latino/a condition: A critical reader.* New York, NY: New York University Press.

Dominelli, L. (2008). *Anti-racist social work* (3rd ed.). London, UK: Palgrave.

Edwards, L. (2015). Latino adolescents and acculturation. In H. Grey & B. N. Hall-Clark, *Cultural considerations in Latino American mental health* (pp. 32–48). New York, NY: Oxford University Press.

Edwards, L. M., & Pedrotti, J. T. (2015). Multiracial individuals in therapy: Clinical considerations across the lifespan. In H. Grey & B. N. Hall-Clark, *Cultural considerations in Latino American mental health* (pp. 127–154). New York, NY: Oxford University Press.

Elder, G. H. (1985). *Life course dynamics: Trajectories and transitions: 1965–1980.* New York, NY: Cornell University Press.

Giele, J. Z. (2006). Homemaker or career woman: Life course factors and racial factors among middle class Americans. *Journal of Comparative Family Studies, 39*(3), 393–411.

Golden, G. (2011). *White privilege as an addiction.* Worksheet from the Antiracist Alliance. Retrieved from http://www.antiracistalliance.com/WhitePrivilegeAsAddiction.pdf

Goodman, D. J. (2011). *Promoting diversity and social justice: Educating people from privileged groups* (2nd ed.). New York, NY: Routledge.

Guild, J. P. (1995). *Black laws of Virginia.* Afro-American Historical Society of Farquier County, Virginia. Westminster, MD: Heritage Books.

Hayes, D. L., & Davis, C. (1998). *Taking down our harps: Black Catholics in the United States.* Maryknoll, NY: Orbis.

Hobbs, A. (2014). *A chosen exile: A history of racial passing in American life.* Cambridge, MA: Harvard University Press.

Ifekwunigwe, J. O. (2004), *"Mixed race" studies: A reader.* New York, NY: Routledge.

Jackson, K. F., & Samuels, G. A. (2011). Multiracial competence in social work: Recommendations for culturally attuned people work with multiracial people. *Social Work, 56*(3), 235–245.

Jenkins, L. (2015). African-American identity and its social context. In E. P. Salett & D. R. Koslow (Eds.), *Multicultural perspectives on race ethnicity and identity* (pp. 25–62). Washington, DC: National Association of Social Workers.

Leifer, A. D. (1974, April). *When are undergraduate admissions sexist? The case of Stanford University.* Paper presented at the Academic/Professional Women in Communication and Related Fields Symposium, International Communications Society, New Orleans, LA. (ERIC Document 095 740)

Madrid, A. (1996, April). *Juntos y revueltos: The U.S. Latino population at the end of the twentieth century.* Paper presented at the Schomburg Memorial Lecture, Mount Holyoke College, Mount Holyoke, MA. Retrieved from https://www.mtholyoke.edu/acad/spanish/juntosyrevueltos

Malott, K. M., & Schaefle, S. (2015). Addressing clients' experiences of racism: A model for clinical practice. *Journal of Counseling and Development, 93*(3), 361–369.

Miller, K. A. (1988). *Emigrants and exiles: Ireland and the Irish exodus to North America* (rev. ed.). London, UK: Oxford University Press.

Miller, R. L., & Buchanan, N. (2015). Growing up multiracial in the United States. In E. P. Salett & D. R. Koslow (Eds.), *Multicultural perspectives on race ethnicity and identity* (pp. 139–159). Washington, DC: National Association of Social Workers.

Moraga, C., & Anzaldua, G. (1981). *Writings of radical women of color.* Watertown, MA: Persephone Press.

Morse, G., Salyers, M. P., Rollins, A. L., Monroe-DeVita, M., & Pfahler, C. (2012). Burnout in mental health services: A review of the problem and its remediation. *Administrative Policy in Mental Health, 39*(5), 341–352.

Nash, G. B. (1995). The hidden history of mestizo America. *The Journal of American History, 82*(3), 941–964.

National Association of Social Workers. (2001). *Standards for cultural competence in social work practice.* Washington, DC: Author. Retrieved from http://www.socialworkers.org/practice/standards/NASWculturalstandards.pdf

Ortega, R. M., & Faller, K. C. (2011). Training child welfare workers from an intersectional cultural humility perspective: A paradigm shift. *Child Welfare, 90*(5), 27–49.

Roberts, D. E. (2014–2015). *Loving v. Virginia* as a civil rights decision. *New York Law School Review, 59,* 175–209.

Rodriguez, J., & Freeman, K. J. (2016). "Your focus on race is narrow and exclusive": The derailment of anti-racist work through discourses of intersectionality and diversity. *Whiteness and Education, 1*(1), 69–82.

Rodriguez, R. (1982). *Hunger of memory: The education of Richard Rodriguez.* New York, NY: Bantam Books.

Salett, E. P., & Koslow, D. R. (Eds.). (2015). *Multicultural perspectives on race ethnicity and identity.* Washington, DC: National Association of Social Workers.

Shih, M., & Sanchez, D. M. (2009). When race becomes even more complex: Toward understanding the landscape of multiracial identity and experiences. *Journal of Social Issues, 65*(1), 1–11.

Steinberg, S. (1977). *The academic melting pot: Catholics and Jews in American higher education.* Piscataway, NJ: Transaction Press.

Tervalon, M., & Murray-Garcia, J. (1998). Cultural humility versus cultural competence: A critical distinction in defining physician training outcomes in multicultural education. *Journal of Health Care for the Poor and Medically Underserved, 9*(2), 117–125.

Townsend, S. S. M., Fryberg, S. A., Wilkins, C. L., & Markus, H. L. (2012). Being mixed: Who claims a biracial identity? *Cultural Diversity and Ethnic Minority Psychology, 18*(1), 91–96.

Weschler, H. S. (2014). *The qualified student: The history of selective college admissions in America.* Piscataway, NJ: Transaction.

Williams, J., Bolland, K., Hooper, L., Church, W., Tomek, S., & Boland, J. (2014). Say it loud: The Obama effect and racial/ethnic identification of adolescents. *Journal of Human Behavior and the Social Environment, 24*(7), 858–868.

SECTION 4

STORIES OF SOCIOECONOMIC PRIVILEGE AND CLASSISM COMPLEXITIES

Socioeconomic status is a general term used to describe one's economic position in a given society. Colleen Loomis and Kathy M. Davis share experiences, stories, and analysis of how class status plays out for themselves and others with whom they work and interact.

Loomis's chapter, "Experiencing Class Oppression and Privilege in Work, Romance, Psychotherapy, and Education," presents an analysis of how classism oppresses individuals living in lower socioeconomic conditions and simultaneously develops them as oppressors. Loomis shares some of her personal experiences of classism in the public education system, employment, psychotherapy, and intimate relationships. She illustrates how others "put her down" or "pushed her to the side" and how over time she naively began to reinforce and sustain the status quo of classism by placing herself above others based on class markers and symbols such as speech patterns, clothing, and material goods. Loomis also raises questions about the impact of disclosing social class and how it relates to multiple and intersecting social positions (e.g., class, race, gender, religion, sexual orientation). Loomis offers suggestions for raising consciousness about social class and for being reflective about how individual actions can disrupt classism rather than perpetuate it.

Davis advocates for People With Disabilities in her story of assumed privilege titled "A Place on the Ladder: Socioeconomic and Ability Privilege," whether they have an obvious, invisible, or hidden disabilities. Davis addresses the daily rigors of living with a disability, the correlation with disability and poverty, and outcomes for European Americans, African Americans, Latinos, and Native Americans. Davis's narrative describes the author's awareness of socioeconomic privilege and able-bodied privilege in relation to critical events in her personal-professional life. These events include early exposure to disability and illness within her family while growing up on the lower rungs of the socioeconomic ladder and experiencing the negative effects of poverty. Davis bravely notes that her white-skin access to education, along with her able-body, helped her climb the socioeconomic ladder. She also shares her experiences with socioeconomic survivor's guilt and clearly articulates the negative effects of a lower socioeconomic status, especially when it coexists with ethnic minority and/or disability status.

CHAPTER 12

EXPERIENCING CLASS OPPRESSION AND PRIVILEGE IN WORK, ROMANCE, PSYCHOTHERAPY, AND EDUCATION

Colleen Loomis

Sufficient social science research evidence argues the existence of classism (at least in the United States) and that mental health professionals such as counselors, therapists, and psychologists may better serve clients and society by developing cultural competence that includes classism (Cook & Lawson, 2016; Greenleaf, Ratts, & Song, 2016; Smith, 2005). Years of research have shown conclusively that children and adolescents raised in poverty who are socioeconomically disadvantaged are two to three times more likely to have negative mental health outcomes (McLaughlin et al., 2011; Reiss, 2013) and lower levels of intelligence and academic achievement (Heckman & Masterov, 2007). In spite of this evidence, professional counseling and humanistic psychology, in particular, have been criticized for largely ignoring classism, given its importance to economic justice (Greenleaf et al., 2016). The American Psychological Association's (2000) *Resolution on Poverty and Socioeconomic Status* provides evidence for why the organization has resolved to advocate, research, and support efforts to reduce poverty and increase access to resources. I encourage you, the reader, to read this brief resolution. The purpose of this chapter is to bring to life class issues by sharing aspects of my life circumstances that influence my understanding of class privilege.

GROWING UP WITH MORE THAN A FEW AND LESS THAN MOST

My three brothers and I grew up in low-income circumstances in the United States. My father had been a private in the army and when he finished his enlistment period he was unemployed and accepted whatever work he could find, such as bailing hay and delivering a load of lumber. Shelter, clothing, and food were sometimes scarce during our early childhood. For example, our mother speaks about my not having shoes during a New York winter. Moving from Virginia to New York where my father had found work as a truck driver, and later moving to Florida, where extended family helped us, we lived in a variety of housing situations (a few without conventional plumbing).

When I was seven years old, we settled for the next six years into a two-bedroom, 60-foot trailer—one of a few located on a dirt road in a relatively rural area. Although our bathtub fell away from the wall, and the way we bathed was to fill gallon milk cartons with water and pour it over us, we were indoors, not living in a barn as we did in Virginia. I have fond memories of swimming in a nearby lake and riding the bus to school because it was too far to walk. Social welfare assisted with the support of our family by providing food stamps, and a few kind neighbors supported us with offers of food, shoes, and hand-me-down clothes before and after my parents divorced when I was 12. My memory of going with my mother to buy groceries and hearing derogatory remarks about us while we made our purchase with food stamps seems to mark the beginning of my awareness of social class differences at the individual level. (For the group level, see Storck, 2002.)

Where I grew up was not gentrified, and much of it remains the same. Although the dirt road is asphalt, many of the simple housing structures in need of repair remain unchanged, and families are still living in poverty. Where I lived was not a neighborhood, per se; it was a rural region. A couple of miles away, orange groves and woods were replaced with new housing subdivisions that brought middle-class families into closer proximity and the need for a new school to support the additional children. I attended high school with students whose families had much more material and educational wealth than I had ever seen.

My family members are intelligent, but they have varying levels of formal schooling. My mother and father had 11th-grade and 6th-grade educations, respectively. Our family did not have opportunities to socialize across class boundaries, and we did not always have a working television, so my exposure to working- and middle-class culture was limited. Economic class distinctions in the high school were apparent daily. The stigmatization began on Monday morning when I, along with about seven other students of 500, had to stand in line to receive free-lunch tickets for the week. During the week, peers excluded me from their friendship circles, and teachers excluded me from certain preparations for postsecondary education.

Speaking generally from my experience, middle-class families socialized their children to spend time with similar others, and teachers tended to help those students whose families were preparing them for postsecondary education. The way I talked (e.g., "We was goin' to the store and . . .") and where I lived (in a trailer on a dirt road) excluded me from many social and college-preparation activities (the use of *college* refers to bachelor's degree programs offered at public and private colleges and universities). Parents, teachers, and guidance counselors did not advise me to take college-prep courses or to pursue other resources that would prepare me for postsecondary education, although I was an honor student from primary school through secondary school. Instead, they focused on what they viewed as my basic needs, such as food, safety, and completing high school. The school personnel knew that my two older brothers had dropped out of school, were using drugs, and were in trouble with the law. During this period of time, researchers reported a strong direct effect of social class on university access, regardless of race and gender (Lang, 1985; Thomas, Alexander, & Eckland, 1977).

I graduated from high school one year early, not prepared for college. For example, I had not taken the SAT, and I did not understand the process of seeking college admission, yet I enrolled in basic courses at a community college. To support myself, I worked full-time operating a check-sorting machine at a bank from midnight to 8:00 AM. Through meeting other bank employees who had been called in to fix problems, I learned about and was interested in becoming a computer programmer. My interest was mostly in the money and the hours—programmers were well paid, worked "8 to 5," and were on call occasionally. But the only viable option for career development while I was supporting myself was to join the military, or so it seemed at the time. I reasoned that in the US military service, food and shelter would be provided, and I would have work and income and physical exercise (i.e., I would not have to pay member fees to go to a gym). In addition, I could get a college education. TV advertisements often highlighted that joining the military was a way to get a college degree and also to "see the world." After visiting a recruiter and scoring well on exams, I was selected and encouraged to choose between the Navy and the Air Force. I wrote my letter of resignation to the bank and met with my supervisor, who immediately suggested that he tear up my resignation letter and create a position for me as a computer-programmer trainee. I had mixed emotions. Why would he create a position for me if I was going to leave but he had not thought about it before? I was both excited and afraid, and he talked me through my options. We agreed I would think it over and give him a response the next day. I had difficulty comprehending that I had an option. I was 18 years old, and I did not remember previously having the possibility to make a choice about my future; it seemed life was happening to me. I decided to continue working at the bank; soon after, I transferred to the day shift and sporadically attended a few different community colleges part-time. I stopped and started my postsecondary education often.

WORK, ROMANCE, AND PSYCHOTHERAPY

This arrangement at the bank continued for a year. At the end of that time, I moved to a city two hours away to live with a partner and obtained a computer programmer job at another bank. I had become aware of class markers, and I began hiding my inherited class and pursuing middle-class symbols, such as speaking Standard English (see also Dews & Law, 1995), wearing classic clothes, and obtaining a formal education (Granfield, 1991). I operated under the model of assimilation (Berry, Poortinga, Segall, & Dasen, 1992)—that is, the more one looks and acts like a person from the middle class, the more one gains access to it. I enrolled in a two-year college, attended part-time, and over four years I completed an associate's degree in liberal arts. This accomplishment occurred six years after I graduated from high school. Several relocations and romantic relationships later, I was living in a different state working as a contract computer programmer.

Although I felt like I was developing a career, my employment was without benefits or job security. I applied for full-time permanent positions as a programmer but was not hired because I did not have a four-year university degree. With the help of a romantic partner, I became an independent consultant and subcontracted myself out to write computer programs for several of the same companies that did not accept an employment application from me. It was clear to me that there are systems in place to keep those without a formal degree out of full-time employment.

In spite of working on contract and not having employee benefits, I was paid fairly well for a 25-year-old woman, particularly one without a bachelor's degree. Acquaintances occasionally paid me a backhanded compliment with their surprise of my being self-employed without having a university degree. This temporary economic success was the beginning of my informal education about precarious work and vulnerable employees who earned less money than peers for the same work only because they did not negotiate a pay rate and sometimes were subjected to sexual harassment. With the lessons, the temporary income afforded me the opportunity to lease several middle-class markers (home, car) that I carried into my dating life.

In addition to learning about classism in the work setting, I experienced it in the sphere of romance. At first glance, others saw me as a young urban professional (yuppie) and often assumed I had a university degree. I dined with entrepreneurs and nonworking adults who had trust funds. I had never heard of a trust fund before moving in the social circle of my clients in the oil and gas industry. I dated twice within this group of friends, and both men broke off our relationship very soon after learning that I was not "born with a silver spoon in my mouth." Was that a coincidence? A kind friend explained what the phrase *silver spoon* meant because it was the first time I remember hearing that expression. Other men were wiser in protecting their social class privilege and would speak and flirt, learn my background, and not pursue me further. This was not my imagination. Here is how I know that discrimination based on class happened to me, more than once. One potential suitor told his sister it was okay for me to be a friend of the family and perhaps even charitable of them to be kind to me but that he would never date me, given my family background. Some friends said that I was "pretty and smart" and thought I would have many suitors. That turned out not to be the case in the social circle I was in at the time, comprised of university-educated men from middle-upper-class families. Gossip in elite circles confirmed classism in dating on multiple occasions. I began to realize how my past socioeconomic standing limited both my intimate life and my educational, professional, and social life. I felt a need to hide my background to be included or to participate more fully in my current seeming peer group. I have since learned that hiding one's background is common among us folks with a history of lesser economic means (Granfield, 1991). The other option was to date men who were living in lower socioeconomic conditions.

Dating men who did and did not have a university degree or a professional position resulted in my wanting to change my dating behavior, which thankfully led me into psychotherapy.

I felt more comfortable with educated men and a misfit for those who had not attended a university. They equally felt uncomfortable with me, with some saying my vocabulary was too big, I was too sophisticated, I worked too much, and so on. I was not putting on airs. My vocabulary had become part of who I was. I did not even consider disguising my vocabulary and manner of speaking, perhaps because I had worked so hard to achieve it, or it was simply part of who I had become. I decided to analyze my dating history and found that most of my relationships lasted about three months. And with men living in my family's social class, I was the one who ended the relationship, or I did things to push the man away from me so he would break it off. My note to self was "I am not good at romantic relationships." I remember having a couple of marriage proposals from age 16 to 25: One man ran away from me and I ran away from the others. I was determined not to marry young and have children because this path felt unfulfilling and threatened my financial security. I remained single but dated, hoping that would eventually lead to marriage. A coworker, knowing a little about my discontent, suggested I talk to her mother who was a therapist and had raised four girls.

My first contact with a psychotherapist was by telephone. I agreed to have a phone conversation, during which I explained my goal was to break what I identified as a problematic pattern of a three-month dating cycle, and I told her that I was resisting therapy for at least two reasons: "(a) I don't want to be on someone's couch for life, and (b) I don't want to relive my childhood." She briefly explained her approach and responded gently, saying that she could help me with my first concern by engaging in therapy once a week for six weeks (she referred to others' having success with her in this short of a timespan) but that she could not help me with the second one: I would have to talk about the past. If I remember correctly, her rate was $85 an hour; when I expressed concern about not being able to afford it, we negotiated a rate of $65 per hour, which was a financial burden for me. I did not have $260 per month extra. At the time, I was unaware that debt is a privilege of those who are not too poor to be allowed to borrow money but poor enough that taking on debt and paying interest is necessary, in this case to access mental health care services. (Later I took on student-loan debt to pursue postsecondary education.) I reasoned that, because I had debt for clothes and leasing a car, I might as well take on more debt for a good cause: hiring a psychotherapist to facilitate my healing journey.

POSTSECONDARY EDUCATION AND PSYCHOANALYSIS: SIMULTANEOUSLY OPPRESSED AND OPPRESSOR

In spite of having experienced some growth with cognitive behavioral therapy, I seriously wonder whether it would have been possible for me to have completed a doctorate degree if it had not been for psychoanalysis, but I am getting ahead of myself. Let me fill in the gap about how, over 15 years, I went from completing a two-year associate's degree at a community college at age 26, having psychotherapy, applying for and attending a university (while working), and completing graduate school while doing psychoanalysis four days a week for four years, to completing a PhD degree.

Although I had obtained, but not secured, many middle-class markings (including knowing psychotherapy from first-hand experience), I felt a deep emptiness inside whenever someone asked me what university I attended. I wanted a degree to remove stigma, but I also wanted it to participate in conversations about university life and its intrinsic qualities. I longed for a traditional university experience (e.g., living on campus, attending classes, reading, spending endless hours in the library, and, importantly, not having to work). I realized that experience was not possible given my accidents of life history—in this case, age and circumstances (for more information about how contexts shape choices, see Sloan, 1996), so I continued to work full-time and enrolled in a four-year university to complete a bachelor's degree. Sixteen years after graduating from high school, I graduated with a four-year university degree, with a major in psychology and a minor in computer science, having decided that a computer-related degree would not change my income. It was during those final two years of undergraduate work that I learned enough about the system of postsecondary education (e.g., student loans, mentoring, and letters of recommendation) to dream and to pursue the dream of living a scholar's life.

Occasionally, throughout the years, folks questioned me in ways that seemed like tests of my authenticity as a middle-class person. However, the question that most frightened me was the one listed on several graduate-school applications: "Please describe your background and discuss any adversity you have had to overcome." I panicked, but I was cognizant enough to seek advice from an uncommon mentor, Tod S. Sloan, who helped me to see the connection between my personal experiences of oppression and my professional interest in using psychology for liberation. He also provided some of the socialization for postsecondary education (e.g., criteria for selecting graduate programs, how to strengthen an application) and helped me to tell my personal story in a way that would be acceptable to the academic audience and comfortable to me. On graduate-school applications, I made what I recall as my first nonapologetic public disclosure of the circumstances of my childhood. I explained how those experiences contributed to the development of my sensitivity to the issues reflected in my interest in graduate programs in community and social psychology. Working with Tod on my personal statement resulted in his learning more about my family history and also my deeper thinking about how context influences our psychology. During this time, Tod advised me on courses to take to complete undergraduate requirements. I had selected a second-year course, and he challenged me by asking why I was taking it. I told him I had done so because I was working 40 hours a week and needed an easy credit. He convinced me to enroll in a graduate course: I was, after all, applying to graduate school. The course was in psychoanalysis, and my mentor was teaching it. When I was accepted into a graduate program near a psychoanalytic institute, Tod took the time to discuss his own experiences in psychoanalysis and to suggest I explore it as well; I said I would not be able to afford therapy, knowing that I would take on student-loan debt to attend graduate school. He quickly explained the possibility of my doing psychoanalysis on a sliding scale while being a graduate student.

One year later, living near to Washington, DC, and feeling I had maximized the benefits of cognitive-behavioral therapy, I went in search of a psychoanalyst. The cost of psychoanalysis seemed prohibitive, but there was a possibility of finding an analyst in training or one who would consider me as a client on pro bono terms. During an initial interview, the psychoanalyst and I discussed my concern about working with a male rather than a female analyst, and he reasoned that my concern in an initial interview was a sign that I might benefit from analysis with a man; he was right. He did not yet know about my childhood history or my past three-month cycle of relationships with men. We also discussed fees, and he offered me psychoanalysis at $10 an hour. The cost made me worried that I could not afford it, and the analyst explained why psychoanalysis does not work if it is completely free. I signed on to the process and paid $160 per month for approximately 48 months, and I have never regretted this investment in my mental health and well-being.

Through psychoanalysis I learned, among many things, how my feelings about sex and power were related to socioeconomic status. When a male professor was sexually harassing me, the work my analyst and I did in psychoanalysis brought me to the realization that coming from a lower socioeconomic background and having been sexually abused as a child interacted with the current situation. I was dealing with "Should I keep another secret?," this one so I can ensure a paycheck. Through analysis, I was educated about power at play in terms of economics, gender, and hierarchical positions at work. I am glad to say I did not become a victim. I began to realize that my questions about if, when, how, to whom, and why to disclose my class background would continually surface and that the consequences of that disclosure would often be unclear. I also noted that my middle-class peers do not carry this burden. A few scenarios illustrate this point.

During my third year of graduate studies, I worked on a research project, conducting a process evaluation of a local, community-based career and learning resource center. One objective of the center was to facilitate women's work and movement from unemployment and underemployment to living-wage jobs (Loomis et al., 2003). My childhood experiences, my passionate concern and respect for the hardships of poverty, my care surrounding issues of women's poverty, and an opportunity to grow professionally—all had attracted me to the research project.

Our research team leader built a diverse team of women who differed by ethnicity, race, age, religious background, educational background, sexual orientation, and years of study. Obviously, not all these categories are visible, so information about members' identification with one or more groups was not necessarily common knowledge. One afternoon, the team leader talked about her recent recruitment of another research-team member, noting how this new member was similar to an existing member because both had attended prestigious, private high schools that developed intellectual prowess. My jealousy of those who enjoyed the benefits of parochial education and the subsequent favoritism that often followed them into higher education surfaced. In spite of, or perhaps because of, previously being oppressed by the act of "classism favoritism" based on educational privileges, I oppressed another woman on the team on similar grounds by criticizing her writing abilities and implying that she had not overcome her working-class language skills. Retrospectively, I see how my access to at least some language instruction on Standard English, and also my independent study of middle-classness, provided me a level of privilege. Naively, I simultaneously was the oppressed and the privileged oppressor.

On another occasion, while we were discussing research-interview transcripts, one team member made a pejorative, stereotypical remark. She said something like "That's the way poor people think." I was incensed, although unaware of the depth of my anger until I analyzed my desire to get back at her because she was one of "them"—the middle- or upper-middle-class oppressors. First, I felt personally affronted, because in my mind

I often identify with being a poor person—or, more accurately, one who lives in poor circumstances. Second, I thought I was the "classism police" and that a comment like that was cause for citation. I was determined to raise class consciousness among my colleagues at all costs, even at the cost of outing myself as a product of poverty. I said something like "Oh, really?" and asked further questions, in an effort to reveal others' underlying assumptions (e.g., "Poor women have children as a way of generating income," and "Poor women are not smart enough to know . . ."). From this exchange and other similar ones, I was dubbed the *class expert* in particular and the *diversity expert* in general. I proudly wore the badge and enjoyed respect from team members for what seemed like the first time. I felt as though I was finally the one with the privileged knowledge. It is only in retrospect that I see the conundrum of my being the class expert. My placement in a position as expert on classism was an act of classism. That is, team members tended to defer to me because of my class background. My voice became privileged. This dynamic is a problem because the diversity and voices of outgroups is lost when one person appoints another as the voice of those who are Black, gay or lesbian, women, or poor. To counter this problem using standpoint statements may be helpful, but these should be used with attention and care.

Including a standpoint statement in our publications is an attempt to make transparent how researchers are privileged over those with whom research is being conducted (Reay, 1996) and to allow readers to assess how researchers' similarities and differences of social location may have influenced the research process, findings, and interpretations. In my experience, both as a student and as a researcher, asking coresearchers or student researchers for a standpoint statement is a classist act, one that assumes researcher privilege and (perhaps unintentionally) outs individuals marginalized by nonvisible markers such as being a survivor of sexual abuse or representing a particular social class. Simultaneously, we have a responsibility to challenge and confront classism by having or not having information about an individual's socioeconomic class status and by using or not using that information to appropriately circumvent its perpetuation (Cook & Lawson, 2016; Hoyt, 1999). To counter this professional bias, I guide my students through a private reflective experience of writing a standpoint statement and ask them to present to me (and then later the thesis committee) the power at play by including or not including a standpoint statement as it relates to multiple and intersecting social positions (e.g., class, race, gender, religion, sexual orientation).

Similarly, I have been on both sides of privilege and oppression in decisions about selecting graduate and faculty applicants. Class differences have resulted in individuals' varied access to privilege and power in many forms related to grades, writing skill development, and publishing, to mention a few. Some of my colleagues and I have expended significantly more personal and material resources to remediate the education of the oppressed. Mentors did that for me. Other colleagues have denied admission or consideration for hiring two individuals because those applicants were from oppressed groups. They often rationalize these kinds of decisions by the claim that an individual had resources the past few years and still did not catch up to more privileged peers. In these critical conversations, I am faced again with a decision of reinforcing the status quo, accepting privileged applicants and making my job easier, or arguing for applicants in the context of their oppressed backgrounds and experiences.

CONCLUSION

In my narrative I have shared some of my life context and experiences that I attribute, arguably, to class oppression. My examples are at the individual and interpersonal level, and although I have provided comments about the social context, I have not analyzed social systems and structures that perpetuate what I call symptoms of classism. By adulthood, I had learned to hide some of my class markers to avoid being a subject of oppression (similar to Carolyn Leste Law in Dews & Law, 1995). More than 10 years ago when I wrote the first edition of this chapter, I did not include how psychotherapy and psychoanalysis played an important role in my personal growth, development, and attainment of formal education. I have no memory of making a conscious decision to exclude that information. Another aspect of my experiences not included is the structural issue that contributed to my taking on $100,000 of student debt for 10 formal years of postsecondary education (four years undergraduate and six years master's degree and PhD). Before entering graduate studies, I made an active choice to have education debt instead of a mortgage. I do not own a house or a car. Through formal education and therapy, I have learned to question society's lack of affordable public postsecondary education (cf. Switzerland) and access to mental health services. I hope my reflections before and after I completed a PhD in psychology provide fodder for others to consider how their individual actions may perpetuate or disturb classism.

ACKNOWLEDGMENTS

I thank my family for the wealth of experiences that enriched my life, in spite of (and because of) our circumstances. I acknowledge that my debt to Tod S. Sloan for his ongoing contribution to our dialogue on oppression cannot be repaid, but I am grateful. Also, I thank Keith Humphreys and Tod Sloan for their feedback on early drafts of the first edition of this chapter, for which financial support (in terms of my salary) came from the Department of Veterans Affairs Office of Academic Affairs and Health Services Research and Development Service and Stanford University Medical Center. Financial support for this revised edition came from Wilfrid Laurier University, Ontario, Canada via my sabbatical salary in 2016.

DISCUSSION QUESTIONS

1. In what ways are your childhood circumstances similar to and different from the author's?
2. Contrast the author's report of material and educational resources to your own understanding of working-class resources.
3. To broaden the classism framework, consider ways social categories interact. For example, reflect on what you learned about the author. What is her ethnicity? What

is her sexual orientation? Is she faced with disabilities? Which if any of these characteristics did you assume? Were you right? Is an indicator missing?

4. How did the author approach consciousness-raising about social class? How do you do it? What are some other strategies that might be helpful?

5. Consider the roles of oppressed and oppressor. The author tells us about being oppressed in her personal life, particularly as a child and young woman, and being both the oppressed and the oppressor in her professional life. How might she avoid oppressing others (e.g., should she disclose [or not disclose] personal experiences)?

REFERENCES

American Psychological Association. (2000). *Resolution on poverty and socioeconomic status.* Retrieved from http://www.apa.org/about/policy/poverty-resolution.aspx

Berry, J. W., Poortinga, Y. H., Segall, M. H., & Dasen, P. R. (1992). *Cross-cultural psychology: Research and applications.* Cambridge, UK: Cambridge University Press.

Cook, J. M., & Lawson, G. (2016). Counselors' social class and socioeconomic status understanding and awareness, *Journal of Counseling & Development, 94*(4), 442–453.

Dews C. L. B., & Law, C. L. (1995). *This fine place so far from home: Voices of academics from the working class.* Philadelphia, PA: Temple University Press.

Granfield, R. (1991). Making it by faking it: Working-class students in an elite academic environment. In *Special Issue: Stigma and Social Interaction. Journal of Contemporary Ethnography, 20*(3), 331–351.

Greenleaf, A. T., Ratts, M. J., & Song, S. Y. (2016). Rediscovering classism: The humanist vision for economic justice. *Journal of Humanistic Psychology,* 1–19. doi:10.1177/0022167816652525

Heckman, J. J., & Masterov. D. V. (2007). The productivity argument for investing in young children. *Review of Agricultural Economics, 29*(3), 446–493.

Hoyt, S. K. (1999). Mentoring with class: Connections between social class and developmental relationships in the academy. In A. J. Murrell & F. J. Crosby, (Eds.), *Mentoring dilemmas: Developmental relationships within multicultural organizations* (pp. 189–210). Mahwah, NJ: Lawrence Erlbaum.

Lang, D. (1985). Stratification and professional education within the academic hierarchy, *Journal of Research & Development in Education, 19*(1), 10–20.

Loomis, C., Brodsky, A. E., Arteaga, S., Benhorin, R., Rogers-Senuta, K., Marx, C., & McLaughlin, P. (2003). What works in adult educational and employment training? Case study of a community-based program for women, *Journal of Community Practice, 11*, 27–45.

McLaughlin, K. A., Breslau, J., Green, J. G., Lakoma, M. D., Sampson, N. A., Zaslavsky, A. M., & Kessler, R. C. (2011). Childhood socio-economic status and the onset, persistence, and severity of DSM-IV mental disorders in a US national sample, *Social Science & Medicine, 73*(7), 1088–1096.

Reay, D. (1996). Dealing with difficult differences: Reflexivity and social class in feminist research. *Feminism & Psychology, 6*(3), 443–456.

Reiss, F. (2013). Socioeconomic inequalities and mental health problems in children and adolescents: A systematic review. *Social Science & Medicine, 90,* 24–31.

Sloan, T. S. (1996). *Life choices: Understanding dilemmas and decisions.* Boulder, CO: Westview Press.

Smith, L. (2005). Psychotherapy, classism, and the poor: Conspicuous by their absence. *American Psychologist, 60*(7), 687–696. doi:10.1037/0003-066X.60.7.687

Storck (2002). "Reality" or "illusion"?: Five things of interest about social class as a large group. *Group Analysis, 35*(3), 351–366.

Thomas, G. E., Alexander, K. L., & Eckland, B. K. (1977). *Access to higher education: How important are race, sex, social class and academic credentials for college access?* Baltimore, MD: Johns Hopkins University Center for Social Organization of Schools.

CHAPTER 13

A PLACE ON THE LADDER

Socioeconomic and Ability Privilege

Kathleen M. Davis

Privilege extends beyond White privilege. Socioeconomic or wealth privilege and ability privilege can present in macro- and microdiscriminatory ways that include judgment, stereotypes, and prejudice. In contrast to privilege, poverty is more prevalent in the United States for African Americans (26%), Hispanics (24%), and Asians (12%), whereas the poverty rate for Whites is 10% (Poverty Facts, 2014). Additionally, people with disabilities (PWD) are more prone not only to the oppression of disability but also to poverty (Annual Disability Statistics, 2015). Of the aforementioned groups in poverty in the United States, PWD in 2014 comprised 29%, or more than 4 million of those persons living in poverty (Poverty Facts, 2014). Greater numbers of women than men live in poverty, and almost 50% of single-parent households live below the poverty threshold (Patten, 2016; Poverty Facts, 2014). Inexplicably, socioeconomic status (SES) and disability are intertwined, although each merits further attention on its own. In this chapter, I share my experiences with socioeconomic privilege and ability privilege.

RUNGS ON A LADDER: SOCIOECONOMIC STATUS AND PRIVILEGE

Socioeconomic privilege often modifies the influence of race, gender, and disability toward the promise of more access to financial, educational, and social advantages in society (Black & Stone, 2005). Socioeconomic privilege can be defined as providing power, rank, status, and resources to ensure and maintain one's place at the top or middle of social order or class (Black & Stone, 2005). Four standard indicators of SES are one's (a) education, (b) health, (c) labor-market status, and (d) poverty status (World Bank, 2012). If we view SES as a hierarchal structure, people living in poverty would represent those at the lowest rungs of the ladder; the middle class, who have more SES privileges above those living in poverty, would represent those in the middle rungs; and the wealthy and very wealthy would represent those on the higher rungs of the ladder. Wealth brings with it power, freedom, and better access to educational and employment opportunities. Economics within the past decade have resulted in a wealth gap between upper-income and middle-income families and a significant widening of the gap between upper-income and lower-income families (Corporation for Enterprise Development, 2016; Fry & Kochner, 2014). People caught on the lower rungs of the income ladder have less access to education, employment, health care, mental health services, and technology (Araque, 2013; Lemieux & Pratto, 2003). Clearly, a person's place higher on the socioeconomic ladder increases one's access to society and its benefits and, conversely, creates difficulty and decreases access for someone with limited access to such benefits.

SOCIOECONOMIC STATUS: EDUCATION, WORK, AND THE AMERICAN DREAM

People living in poverty often face social stigma and the unwanted label of *poor*. While some such as myself, are lucky enough to climb their way out of poverty, climbing the socioeconomic ladder may also contribute to a lifetime of confusion, guilt, and shame, similar to survivor guilt. White people who are able to move to the middle socioeconomic rungs may experience confusion about race privilege and socioeconomic privilege. Crosley-Corcoran (n.d.) shared her experiences about spending her childhood in rural Illinois in a ramshackle mobile home without heat or running water. At some point, a feminist relayed to Crosley-Corcoran that she had White privilege. Her response was the same as mine the first time someone told me that—*What?!* She and I have the distinction of having lived White poverty in America. My family also lived in substandard housing, and there were times when food was scarce (and, in a rural area, there were not the food banks and resources that exist now). This response is not to diminish the stories of poor White Americans—poverty is demoralizing, there are no two ways about it. It leaves scars. But to better understand poverty, we must place it within a multicultural context because it is a chronic, multigenerational concern nationally and globally. Yes, Crosley-Corcoran and I were raised in poverty-ridden childhoods, *but* we are White. What difference, if any, should that make?

My travels to Brazil and South Africa helped shatter the cognitive dissonance (Festinger, 1957) I experienced in my efforts to relate to my own experiences with poverty and likening them to others. In my travels to Sao Paulo, Brazil, and on my second study-abroad experience, perhaps the most startling part of my journey back from Sao Paulo was upon my arrival to my new home in Los Angeles, where I noticed the large numbers of homeless people who appeared to outnumber the homeless in Brazil. In a country as wealthy as the United States of America, it is shocking to see as many homeless as in a developing country. Crosley-Corcoran (n.d.) and I had been raised in poverty, but we had housing, inferior as it may have been. Lummis (as cited in Moreira, 2003) described four types of poverty: (a) *absolute*—destitution, wherein people lack food, shelter, access to water, and live in poor sanitary conditions (our Sao Paulo and Los Angeles friends), (b) *poverty by others*—being called *poor* by others but not considering oneself poor, (c) *social poverty*—in which the poor are controlled and serve the "economic power of the rich" (p. 73), and (d) *poverty by consumerism*—the sense of poverty associated with the perpetual needs/ wants created by a consumerist society. Of the four types, my family fit into the second and the fourth—growing up, people pitied us and provided my large family with hand-me-down clothing and other cast-offs. We were also poor by consumerism. The real sting of poverty in a materialistic society is in not having the things others have, not being able to afford the things that other people can afford (movies, concerts, vacations, etc.), and so being denied access to the American dream.

My struggle was real, fighting against the oppressive place where poverty exists, but was my experience easier than that of minorities or PWD? Reim (2014) shared what is widely accepted as the key out of poverty—education. Moving up the socioeconomic ladder and into a better life means finding a way to educate oneself. Tim Wise speaks of White privilege in his documentary *White Like Me* (Media Education Foundation, 2013). Many believe affirmative action and scholarships for minorities lead to less opportunity for Whites. In contrast, Wise shares that, for every affirmative-action applicant accepted into a college, two White people were accepted based on a parent's alumni status or other connections to the school. And despite the Americans with Disabilities Act, which assures equal opportunities in employment and education, PWD remain at higher prevalence among the poor and undereducated in the United States (American Psychological Association, 2016).

Despite changes brought forth by the civil rights movement, African Americans have consistently had twice the unemployment rates of Whites for the past six decades (Desilver, 2013). Overall, unemployment for Hispanics and PWD is higher when compared to unemployment for Whites (Persons With a Disability, 2016; Wilson, 2016). Wages continue to reflect the wealth gap because minority men and women (with the exception of Asians) earn significantly less than White men. For Native Americans, it is even worse. American Indian women make 50% less than White males, and unemployment rates for American Indian women are as high as 60% (American Association of University Women, 2016; Peralta, 2014). Finally, PWD work disproportionately in low-wage and part-time occupations, and prevalent stereotypes and prejudice keep employers from hiring PWD (Kirshman & Grandgenett, 1997).

Although education and employment provide opportunities for increasing personal income and wealth, home ownership also is a means of building wealth through equity. Yet Blacks and Latinos face rampant discrimination in mortgage lending (Love, 2016). During the Great Recession that started in 2008, Black and Latino homeowners lost their homes in record numbers, transferring many from the middle-class into the low-income stratum. Additionally, minorities who receive home loans pay a substantially higher interest rate than Whites (White, 2016). As long as minority groups have higher-interest mortgages and less opportunity for education, work, and wealth building, these trends will likely continue for a long time and keep minorities trapped in the lower rung of the SES ladder, with the American Dream just out of reach.

ECONOMIC AND COVERT OPPRESSION: TAKING POWER FROM THE PEOPLE

Economic oppression as defined by Corlett (2010) is the overt or unintentional distribution of economic resources so that they harm specific groups of people. The cycle of oppression continues from one generation to the next because resources are most often available to those with wealth and power and of European descent. In addition to having the distinction of being "heirs of oppression," African Americans and Native Americans are subject to historical trauma from loss of land, forced labor, economic disadvantages, and loss of culture (Nader, Dubrow, & Hudnall-Stamm, 2014). Traditionally, PWD have likewise been oppressed economically and psychologically and shunned by society. Despite passage of laws such as the Americans with Disabilities Act, their limited access to work and education opportunities continues (Mink & O'Conner, 2004; Posarac, 2012). Historically oppressed racial, ethnic, and disabled persons continue to struggle from economic oppression and systemic infrastructures that continue to distribute wealth to middle-class and higher-income people.

COVERT RACISM

Covert racism (CR) is found with those who profess to have open-minded views yet have biases to which they remain unaware. People with covert racist attitudes may make statements such as "I am not a racist" or "There is only one race, the human race" (Smith & Shin, 2008). People with CR may have good intentions, but they have not taken the time to critically assess their own racial biases. Not only do statements of this type ("there is only one race") minimize others, but they also perpetuate continued stereotypes and biases. Those of us who were raised in the United States and tout ourselves as nonracist must admit that there are still ugly biases that seep through from time to time. Most of my White friends or family (especially those living in a homogenous, rural population) will say things like "I met the nicest person today . . .," lower their voice to a whisper and say, "she was *Black*," and then continue in their normal volume, "but she was very nice." Does describing others by racial or ethnic characteristics denote CR?

SOCIOECONOMIC SURVIVOR GUILT

I am ashamed to admit to my struggles with middle-class stature, especially given the inequalities others face. When I was raising my children, my house was the go-to, and my children always had friends over. To help my children be comfortable with diversity, we chose a good inner-city school rather than the majority White schools for them. Many of their friends were from poor families. One night in the kitchen, as I was talking with my daughter and a few of her friends, the conversation became quite uncomfortable as one of her friends, "Jennifer," called me a *yuppie*. I froze, and then scathingly replied, "You don't know anything about me, but I am not a yuppie." This term stung in ways that are difficult to fathom because, most of the time, I feel more connected to people of lower socioeconomic level, and I struggle to fit into the middle class and relate to people within my SES. I felt guilty at Jennifer's remark, knowing that her family struggled financially. For a long time, I was angry at her remark, and I have thought about it quite often. But she was right: There existed a divide between Jennifer and me created by socioeconomic privilege. As guilty and torn as my feelings were, my poverty days were behind me, but hers were not. Jennifer's place on the socioeconomic ladder was very real to her, and it no doubt created the same loathing I had at her age for those considered wealthy. Because life progresses and we lose touch with others, I am uncertain what happened to Jennifer. But she was smart, gregarious, and White—so if she wanted to pull herself up financially, she would likely have had the same opportunities I did. She would not face less access to scholarships, as some of the other children who were briefly part of our lives did. And when she goes to buy her first house, it is more likely her mortgage will be approved, and at a much lower interest rate than minority groups often pay. While I am happy for Jennifer's prospects, it is truly heartbreaking as I think about the other children—Katie, Shania, Jerome, and Jose—and how they may be facing these very real struggles associated with minority status. Socioeconomic privilege provides an avenue to living a better life. Unfortunately, privilege comes at a cost for others: the complete veracity of White and SES privileges.

MY FAMILY WAS SICK: DISABILITY EXPERIENCES

Little research reflects the impact of socioeconomic level and the disabled. Various sectors such as workers' compensation insurance and Social Security Disability Insurance (SSDI) provide their own definitions of disability, based on eligibility criteria. Generally, a person with a disability is defined by the Americans with Disabilities Act as a person who has a physical or mental impairment that substantially limits one or more major life activities such as self-care, sensory activity, manual tasks, and work (Kirshman & Grandgenett, 1997).

For several years, I have worked as a rehabilitation counselor. My exposure to disability started at a young age. Both parents were ill during my childhood, and my dad eventually died of a rare form of leukemia. For most of my childhood, he was unable to work. My mother was also unwell during this time; she had a kidney removed. At some point during these years, she became pregnant with my youngest brother, Thomas. She had complications with the pregnancy—toxemia—and almost died. I was the quasimother in the home. When Thomas was about two, he suffered a traumatic head injury. Flipping Thomas on his side and ensuring his safety became a habit for all of us. There were other momentous events surrounding illness and disability in my childhood, most significantly, the car accident when I was 16 years old, when a friend lost control of the car. The car lacked restraints, and my body was projected toward the dashboard. The injuries I sustained included a broken right femur, broken C1 vertebra, and lacerations. Recovery required a two-month stay in the hospital in traction and two months in a wheelchair. I did not fully recuperate for a year. More recently, my sister had breast cancer, and my stepdad passed away following complications from a right-leg amputation. These experiences no doubt have shaped my resiliency and my acceptance of PWD.

ASCENDING THE SES LADDER: BARRIERS TO PEOPLE WITH DISABILITIES

As someone who advocates for PWD, I find it disheartening to see how persons with obvious disabilities are treated; yet about 10% of PWD have invisible or hidden disabilities (Invisible Disabilities, 2013; Stoddard, 2014) and still face censure. Hidden disabilities may include mental disorders, chronic pain, asthma, diabetes, repetitive stress injuries, cancer, and arthritis, to name a few. I have had clients with severe back injuries who were still able to ambulate for short distances. Their injuries were not discernable to others looking at them until they had a flair-up and would limp or walk bent over. One client told me, "I went to the store and parked in the handicapped parking. When I got out, this lady looked at me and said, 'There is nothing wrong with you; shame on you for parking there!'" These types of stories have been shared over and over, and they reflect how little our society understands disability.

People with disabilities are twice as likely to be poor compared to able-bodied citizens, and less than one in five disabled persons is employed (Fessler, 2015). People might advise someone with a recent disability to apply for SSDI. But this process is long and arduous, and to really maneuver the system, people applying for SSDI must hire an attorney. Even then it will be about two years before a hearing is scheduled, and the attorney will take a chunk of the initial retroactive lump payout. For many minorities with disabilities, access to rehabilitation services may be problematic, and they may face difficulties within the vocational rehabilitation system (Hernandez, 2009). Outcomes for European Americans are more successful than for African Americans and Latinos (Hernandez, 2009). This reality correlates with health-care and mental health services disparities with minorities, wherein the need is largely unmet for African Americans, Latinos, and Asian Americans (Chow, Jaffee, & Snowden, 2003). There are special considerations for Native Americans because they are more than twice as likely as the rest of the American population to live in poverty, have lower life expectancies, and die at significantly higher rates from hidden disabilities such as diabetes and from noticeable conditions such as tuberculosis and alcoholism (American Psychiatric Association, 2010). However, Native Americans are more likely to seek services than the general population *if* traditional healing or 12-step programs are included in the treatment plan (American Psychiatric Association, 2010). Minorities and PWD do not have the same access to services that Caucasians take for granted. We must face our White, socioeconomic, or any other type of privilege we might have and work through what holds us back because such privilege does not simply affect us—it affects those we serve, and it influences others in society.

ABLE-BODIED PRIVILEGE AND BARRIERS TO SERVICES

To show *able-bodied privilege* is to take for granted some type of ableness power over people with limited physical, sensory, or mental ability or disorder, disease, or disfigurement.

Traditionally, models of disability attempted either to explain disability on a continuum from disabled or not or to define disability as abnormal (Hosking, 2008). Differently abled persons may face physical, emotional, attitudinal, and social barriers, and they have been lumped together by many able-bodied others as deficient human beings (Black & Stone, 2005). Covert oppression is often reflected as able-bodied people show excessive sympathy to a PWD or avoid typical social gestures such as eye contact or smiling (Black & Stone, 2005; Smith & Shin, 2008). PWD often view this behavior as offensive, and such behavior perpetuates oppression (Black & Stone, 2005).

Critical disability theory regards disability as a social construct, an intricate interrelationship among a person's response to impairment or injury, the social environment, and the disadvantages PWD experience that stem from social infrastructure (attitudes and physical environment) that fails to meet the needs of PWD who do not meet a social expectation of normal (Hosking, 2008). The *biopsychosocial model* of disability combines interactive effects of the disease, such as psychosocial stressors and environmental and personal factors (Rath & Elliott, 2012).

CASE STUDIES

The following brief case studies focus on two clients with disabilities with whom I have worked. Please note that all identifying information was changed to protect the identity of the clients.

TARA

Tara was an African American woman diagnosed with a mental disorder. During a visit, the usually jovial, friendly Tara was irritable. She snapped at me, "You god damn cracker, you don't understand a damn thing!" Though I found this humorous, I bit my lip to keep from smiling. This response sounds terrible, I know. Thankfully, my professionalism kicked in, and I stopped myself. It will sound even more stupid when I tell you that I thought *cracker* meant White, like saltine. No, it was a reference to slave owners—not so funny. This moment turned into horror for me when I learned more about Tara's past. She had suffered significant racism as a child, and this had profoundly affected her. My moment of stupidity could have caused Tara more pain. Mental disabilities may be more profound than physical disabilities for those persons who experience them, especially when something or someone is there to remind them of past humiliations. I realize that, within the biopsychosocial model, which considers psychosocial factors (Rath & Elliott, 2012), my laughter could have triggered a negative response from Tara. Although I would not have been laughing *at* her, Tara might not have stopped to think about *why* a White person was laughing, and she probably would have thought my response was directed at her. Multicultural counselors must understand the potential manifestation of mental disorders (Sue et al., 1998). I remember Tara well, not only because she was one of my favorite clients but also because she taught me this valuable lesson.

PETER

A White male, Peter was referred to me following a work injury. He was extremely articulate and loved to try to provoke arguments at our sessions.

Right around the time Peter was my client, I was going through this designer-handbag phase. That is to say, I was buying knock-off handbags and accessories. (This phase appeased my poverty by consumerism [Moreira, 2003].) This was my first well-paying job since getting my master's, and it felt good to finally afford nice things and to feel I belonged to something denied in my childhood because of SES, even if it was a fake belonging.

During one meeting with Peter, while we were talking about the difficulties of financially supporting our families, Peter became frustrated. He told me, "What the hell would you understand, with your designer purses and hundred-dollar sunglasses?" This response was sobering. How could I tell him the bags were fake? They looked real. My image, as seen through others' eyes, flashed before me. Though Peter was White, his image of me reflected privilege to him from a socioeconomic standpoint; I was middle class now—no longer the poverty-ridden child.

My ego had gotten the best of me. My style is a bit flamboyant at times, and I acknowledge that. However, I have learned that it is important to know how to dress for the audience because attire can exude SES. Simply put, is privilege denoted by style? Peter taught me that it certainly is an important consideration. Both Peter and I are White, but momentarily I had blinded myself to the key differences between his situation and my own, the *social distance* (Sacks & Lindholm, 2002) between many White Americans. From a critical-disability stance (Hosking, 2008), this scenario asserted a privilege that Peter was being denied because of his disability—the ability to move up the SES ladder. As counselors, we must understand unequal status relations in society (Sue & Sue, 2015) such as socioeconomic level and have an awareness of the social impact on others of these inequalities (Sue et al., 1998).

CONCLUSION

As helping professionals, it is our responsibility to continuously examine our biases, whether we know about them or they are revealed to us from our clients. Referring to the case study of Peter, it becomes quite apparent that SES can lead to misunderstandings and assertion of privilege. In Tara's case, lack of knowledge on current slang almost caused me to break the ethical golden rule—do no harm. We live in a complex, multicultural, and multieconomic society, and awareness brings with it empowerment, not only to help ourselves to become better people and helping professionals but to provide the best service possible. This reality may mean we have the very uncomfortable task of facing biases and our self-perception of *who we think we are* in order to become *who we really want to be* as human beings. Taking this responsibility can be painful and humiliating, but imagine walking in the steps of our oppressed clientele. And how can we really expect our patients to heal if we are unwilling to heal ourselves?

DISCUSSION QUESTIONS

1. As in Tara's case, have you ever thought something a client said or did was funny? If so, how does this reaction relate to privilege?
2. In Peter's case, was SES privilege asserted through perceived wealth? How do you think your image or presentation may affect others?
3. How do you react when someone with a visible disability enters a room? Do you avoid the person? Would you treat the person differently because of the disability?

REFERENCES

American Association of University Women. (2016). *The simple truth about the gender pay gap.* Retrieved from http://www.aauw.org/research/the-simple-truth-about-the-gender-pay-gap/

American Psychiatric Association. (2010). *Mental health disparities: American Indians and Alaskan Natives* [Fact sheet]. Retrieved from http://www.integration.samhsa.gov/workforce/mental_health_disparities_american_indian_and_alaskan_natives.pdf

American Psychological Association. (2016). *Disability and socioeconomic status.* Retrieved from http://www.apa.org/pi/ses/resources/publications/disability.aspx

Annual disability statistics compendium. (2015). Section 3: Poverty. Institute on Disability. Retrieved from http://www.disabilitycompendium.org/statistics/poverty

Araque, J. C. (2013, July). Computer usage and access in low-income urban communities. *Computers in Human Behavior, 29*(4), 1393–1401.

Black, L., & Stone, D. (2005). Expanding the definition of privilege: The concept of social privilege. *Journal of Multicultural Counseling and Development, 33*(4), 243–255.

Chow, J. C., Jaffee, K., & Snowden, L. (2003, May). Racial/ethnic disparities in the use of mental health services in poverty areas. *American Journal of Public Health, 93*(5), 792–797.

Corlett, A. J. (2010). *Heirs of oppression.* Plymouth, UK: Rowman & Littlefield.

Corporation for Enterprise Development. (2016, January). *Financial assets and income* (CFED Assets and Opportunity Scorecard). Retrieved from http://assetsandopportunity.org/assets/pdf/2016_Scorecard_Financial_Assets_Income_Report.pdf

Crosley-Corcoran, G. (n.d.). *Explaining White privilege to a broke White person* [Blog post, Occupy Wall Street]. Retrieved from http://occupywallstreet.net/story/explaining-White-privilege-broke-White-person

Desilver, D. (2013, August 21). *Black unemployment rate is consistently twice that of Whites.* Pew Research Center. Retrieved from http://www.pewresearch.org/fact-tank/2013/08/21/through-good-times-and-bad-black-unemployment-is-consistently-double-that-of-Whites/

Fessler, P. (2015). The Americans With Disabilities Act at 25: Why disability and poverty still go hand in hand 25 years after landmark law. National Public Radio. Retrieved from http://www.npr.org/sections/health-shots/2015/07/23/424990474/why-disability-and-poverty-still-go-hand-in-hand-25-years-after-landmark-law

Festinger, L. (1957). *A theory of cognitive dissonance.* Stanford, CA: Stanford University Press.

Fry, R., & Kochnar, R. (2014, December 17). *America's wealth gap between middle-income and upper-income families is widest on record.* Pew Research Center. Retrieved from http://www.pewresearch.org/fact-tank/2014/12/17/wealth-gap-upper-middle-income/

Hernandez, B. (2009). The disability and employment survey: Assessing employment concerns among people with disabilities and racial/ethnic minorities. *Journal of Applied Rehabilitation Counseling, 40*(1), 4–13.

Hosking, D. L. (2008). *Critical disability theory: A paper presented at the 4th Biennial Disability Studies Conference* [Lecture notes]. Retrieved from http://www.lancaster.ac.uk/fass/events/disabilityconference_archive/2008/papers/hosking2008.pdf

Invisible disabilities: List and information. (2013). *Disabled World* e-newsletter. Retrieved from http://www.disabled-world.com/disability/types/invisible/

Kirshman, N. H., & Grandgenett R. L., II. (1997). ADA: The 10 most common disabilities and how to accommodate, *Legal Brief Law Journal, 2*(3). Retrieved from http://legalbrief.com/kirshman.html

Lemieux, A. F., & Pratto, F. (2003). Poverty and prejudice. In S. C. Carr & T. S. Sloan (Eds.), *Poverty and psychology: From global perspective to local practice* (pp. 141–161). New York, NY: Kluwer Academic/Plenum.

Love, D. (2016, January 16). Study: Racial discrimination in mortgage lending continues to impact African Americans, with a "Black" name lowering one's credit score by 71 points. *Atlantic Black Star.* Retrieved from http://atlantablackstar.com/2016/01/31/study-racial-discrimination-in-mortgage-lending-continues-to-impact-african-americans-with-a-black-name-lowering-ones-credit-score-by-71-points/

Media Education Foundation. (2013, January 1). *White like me: Race, racism, and White privilege in America.* [Video featuring Tim Wise]. Retrieved from http://www.mediaed.org/Whitelikeme/

Mink, G., & O'Conner, A. (2004). Disability. In G. Mink, & A. O'Connor (Eds.), *Poverty in the United States: Vol. 1. A—K* (pp. 231–236). Santa Barbara, CA: ABC-CLIO.

Moreira, V. (2003). Poverty and psychopathology. In S. C. Carr & T. S. Sloan, *Poverty and psychology: From global perspective to local practice* (pp. 69–86). New York, NY: Kluwer Academic/Plenum.

Nader, K., Dubrow, N., & Hudnall-Stamm, B. (2014). *Honoring differences: Cultural issues in the treatment of trauma and loss.* New York, NY: Taylor & Francis.

Patten, E. (2016, July 1). *Racial, gender wage gaps persist in U.S. despite some progress.* Pew Research Center. Retrieved from http://www.pewresearch.org/fact-tank/2016/07/01/racial-gender-wage-gaps-persist-in-u-s-despite-some-progress/

Peralta, K. (2014, November 27). Native Americans left behind in the economic recovery. *U.S. News & World Report.* Retrieved from http://www.usnews.com/news/articles/2014/11/27/native-americans-left-behind-in-the-economic-recovery

Persons With a Disability: Labor Force Characteristics Summary. (2016). Economic News Release. Bureau of Labor Statistics, US Department of Labor. Retrieved from http://www.bls.gov/news.release/disabl.nr0.htm

Posarac, A. (2012, May). *Economic status of persons with disabilities and the cost of disability* (World Bank Inaugural Disability and Development Core Course). Washington, DC: World Bank. Retrieved from http://siteresources.worldbank.org/DISABILITY/Resources/280658-1327953883745/8402175-1337109498381/module2_Posarac.pdf

Poverty facts. (2014). US Census Bureau. Retrieved from http://www.povertyusa.org/the-state-of-poverty/poverty-facts/

Rath, J. F., & Elliott, T. R. (2012). Psychological models in rehabilitation psychology. In P. Kennedy (Ed.), *The Oxford handbook of rehabilitation psychology* (pp. 32–46). New York, NY: Oxford University Press.

Reim, M. C. (2014). *Barriers to high school completion create barriers to economic mobility* (Discussion Paper #17 on Education). Washington, DC: Government Printing Office.

Sacks, M. A., & Lindholm, M. (2002). A room without a view: Social distance and the structuring of privileged identity. In C. Levine-Rasky (Ed.), *Working through Whiteness: International perspectives* (pp. 129–152). New York, NY: State University of New York.

Smith, L. C., & Shin, R. Q. (2008). Social privilege, social justice, and group counseling: An inquiry. *The Journal for Specialists in Group Work, 33*(4), 351–366.

Stoddard, S. (2014). *Disability statistics annual report.* University of New Hampshire Institute on Disability. Retrieved from http://www.disabilitycompendium.org/docs/default-source/2014-compendium/annual-report.pdf

Sue, D. W., Carter, R. T., Casas, J. M., Fouad, N. A., Ivey, A. E., Jensen, M., . . . Vasquez-Nutall, E. (1998). *Multicultural counseling competencies: Individual and organizational development.* Thousand Oaks, CA: SAGE.

Sue, D. W., & Sue, D. (2015). *Counseling the culturally diverse: Theory and practice* (7th ed.). Hoboken, NJ: John Wiley.

White, G. B. (2016, February 25). Why Blacks and Hispanics have such expensive mortgages. *The Atlantic.* Retrieved from http://www.theatlantic.com/business/archive/2016/02/blacks-hispanics-mortgages/471024/

Wilson, V. (2016, February 11). *State unemployment rates by race and ethnicity at the end of 2015 show a plodding recovery.* Economic Policy Institute. Retrieved from http://www.epi.org/publication/state-unemployment-rates-by-race-and-ethnicity-at-the-end-of-2015-show-a-plodding-recovery/

SECTION 5

STORIES OF SEXUAL IDENTITIES, GENDER, AND CISGENDER

INTRODUCTION

Jessica Pettitt, N. Eugene Walls, Kelly Costello, and Joy S. Whitman speak to identities associated with gender(s). As individuals it is appropriate that all are able to identify themselves as they deem appropriate, utilizing varied terminology and varied pronouns. Each of our authors has a story to tell based on how they identify and how they want others to identify them.

Pettitt shares, in "Fierce Dyke Caught Doing Husband's Laundry: Marriage—The New Frontier," the fluidity of identities and that when various identities are connected to relationships, it is important to examine them fully as well as in connection as each is interdependent on the other. Gender roles, identities, and expressions, paired with labels and perceptions of others, create an interesting intersection of self-worth, communication needs, and chores. The legal marriage of a transman and a lesbian woman and the heteronormative privilege of being yet another straight couple pairs oddly with personal comfort in the queer community. Pettitt shares her story of figuring out how to be a wife in her journey through heterophobia and love.

In "'Head Ladies Center for Teacup Chain': Exploring Cisgender Privilege in a (Predominately) Gay Male Context," Walls and Costello explore the experiences of cisgender privilege, defined as the unearned advantages that individuals who identify as the gender they were assigned at birth accrue solely based on their cisgender identity. Because one author identifies as cisgender and the other as transgender, their differing social locations are used to examine their experiences of the traditionally gendered space of square dancing to illustrate how privilege functions to maintain oppression of trans-identified individuals while it reinforces cisgender supremacy.

Whitman begins her chapter "Becoming a Counseling Professional Lesbian: Revisiting Privilege and Challenges" by sharing experiences related to her different identities, her identity as a lesbian being the most salient. She came out to her family in her late teens. Whitman discusses the privileges enjoyed as a counselor educator that can also be negated by being lesbian. Deciding how and when to come out as a lesbian and managing discrimination while advocating for lesbian, gay, bisexual, transgender, and queer people in a career as a counselor educator is an ongoing and dynamic process. She highlights the concepts of stigma management and minority/ marginalized group stress to help readers better understand the navigation of multiple marginalized identities in the academy.

CHAPTER 14

FIERCE DYKE CAUGHT DOING HUSBAND'S LAUNDRY

Marriage—The New Frontier

Jessica Pettitt

am a die-hard, activist dyke. My former students even went so far as to call me a *Fierce Dyke*, a title that I wore with boastful pride in the streets of New York City. It was when I worked professionally as "gay for pay" on a college campus as the point lesbian, gay, bisexual, transgender (LGBT) person for faculty, staff, students, and the surrounding community that I really understood who I am in regard to my sexuality, gender expression, and passion for social justice. Now I bring my Fierce Dyke crown to the stage while doing trainings and speaking engagements that focus on LGBT advocacy and inclusion. Who knew that, from my office swivel chair, I would meet my *husband*? (Boylan, 2009).

I was born and raised in Texas and got out as soon as I could. I didn't understand sex or gender or identity, let alone the social construction of these concepts and how they in themselves uphold heterosexism, sexism, and heterophobia. I did know that gays (now I would say lesbians and gay men) were not treated equally, and I became a loud (and I mean a loud!) ally in middle school and high school. "Why does anyone care what anyone else does romantically or sexually? If consent is given, then it should not be anyone's business," I argued. I continued to question authority on my college campus, an elite, private, liberal arts school in Arkansas.

"I DO"

While attending graduate school in South Carolina, I researched ally identity development (Wall & Evans, 1991, 2000). I came out as a lesbian in my late 20s; no one was shocked except me. I continued doing LGBT service work, which led to a number of stereotypical lesbian relationships—meaning that we met, two women, dove head first into a committed relationship, and tried to figure it out along the way. Like most advocates, I began focusing on the *L* and the *G* of the *LGBT* acronym, but lessons from my students were what really got me advocating for the bisexual and transgender populations. Fluidity of sex and gender as changing social constructions made so much sense to me once I understood the terms and applied them to my own life, relationships, and identities. The more I understood about gender and sexuality, the more freedom I had to express myself. I realized I am attracted to what I like to call *checked masculinity,* and they (I am using *they* as a gender-neutral pronoun in the singular sense) are usually wearing a hoodie, carrying a book, wearing glasses, and walking around lost but enjoying the view. My attraction has nothing to do with hormones one experiences at puberty or later in life or to preexisting genitalia. So one fateful day, before I packed up the office and went home to the stereotypical U-Haul girlfriend at home, my appointment walked into my office and changed everything—including my views on marriage—forever.

Loren told me that he had started transitioning and had been on hormones for a week or so. He was doing fine and wanted suggestions on how to edit his name and gender marker on his faculty and student records. Reading him as male, I assumed he was transitioning from male to female; I am sure he was flattered at this gender validation on my part because the direction of Loren's transition is female to male. He is a *transman*. Many motorcycle rides, Peace Corps stories, home-cooked meals, and long dog walks later, I can confidently say that I married the man of my dreams, dreams I did not know I had or even wanted to have, for that matter.

We got married, legally as a straight couple, in Las Vegas, as the true romantics tend to do. Nevada requires only two legal documents of those of the opposite sex when they are applying for a marriage license. He and I plopped our Arizona-issued driver's licenses on the counter of the courthouse, paid our money, and, without hesitation, reserve, or even a second glance, we got our marriage license. Somewhere between the woman behind the bulletproof glass at the courthouse and Elvis's stand-in at the Chapel (Elvis had the day off), we marched down a white gauzed aisle and unexpectedly grabbed heterosexual privilege with such gusto that watching the wedding video somewhat saddens me. Neither of us wore political T-shirts or interrupted the service demanding equity for all. I just smiled and cried; I said "I do" and we kissed. I instantly became a certificate-carrying member of an institution that is historically based on ownership, sexism, capitalism, dowries, property, enslavement, and other evils that I have spent most of a lifetime fighting against.

IS LANGUAGE AT MY DISPOSAL OR YOURS?

I am troubled now with using the word *partner*. Some LGBT folks feel that when an ally uses the word *partner,* they may be forgetting their heterosexual privilege, or by saying *husband* or *wife*, they are being insensitive and showcasing a socially constructed norm. I find I am stuck in a contradiction, too. What term should I use? I am more comfortable using the word *partner*, but I do not want to out my husband for my own identity's benefit. I also talk about Loren all the time, as someone deeply madly in love tends to do, and then I get my queerness challenged. I am growing accustomed to, if not proud of, the fact that I am his wife. I like that strangers validate my relationship by making comments about my wedding ring. There seems to be a weight given to my relationship that seems to mean I am a success as a woman in my 40s. One issue with my validation theory is that I also get asked about the inclusion of children. This is a topic that I did not get asked about regarding my committed relationships with women. When I choose to say that Loren and I are not going to have children, I feel my success as a woman begin to recede a little in others' eyes.

I find that I am comfortable with the word *husband* since I am more comfortable with that gender role in the context of lesbian relationships. However, like a discount bra, *wife* doesn't seem to fit me. Sometimes it is perfect, and other times it feels constricting, or too loose, or somehow both at once. I associate the word *wife* with my Texas upbringing and the expectations placed on a "good woman" that I rejected long before coming out as a lesbian. I remember quietly asking my dyke friends, the ones I could really trust, if it was bad that I liked to do laundry, keep a clean house, cook meals, and pack a healthy lunch. They would be surprised at my domestication, but then that seemed to be okay because I certainly am still a dyke. I realized that I could still be accepted as a dyke to my close friends because they did not see my husband as a straight man. To our LGBT friends and chosen family, showing up 100% as myself has an inverse effect on Loren getting to show up 100% as himself.

We do not identify as heterosexual but *heteroqueer*. Loren and I first heard this term *heteroqueer* at a Gender Odyssey Conference and haven't ever seen or read it anywhere else. We liked that the term was queer and prefaced with the privileges we also reap. Depending on whom I am talking with and the context, I am fluid with my personal identities, respectful of my partner's preferences, and vary the language I use to describe the multiple areas of outness. (I believe this statement to be truer for me than for Loren. He is male, a man, and occasionally may identify as a transman to bring visibility to that community. I am much more fluid in identifying myself and my partner and labeling my relationship with language based on the context of the conversation.) Because of my attachment to the lesbian and queer community, I find that I am literally heterophobic and have had to really work on the fact that I will be perceived as straight by others. Loren and I find that we are too straight to glide into queer spaces and can even make others uncomfortable with our heterosexual privilege. We also aren't hip enough or genderqueer enough to navigate a lot of spaces that claim to be progressive and inclusive in nature due to age, class, music taste, and preferences. Neither context feels welcoming to both of us. Transmen and women are stuck between full disclosure and guarded privacy, as are their family members, partners, and so on. It seems that when my identity is validated, Loren's isn't. In spaces where we both used to fit in, we now try to navigate; we have had to learn how to be comfortable without a snug fit. Something is always just a little off, silenced, overlooked, invalidated, or assumed. This has become our new normal—a not-so-comfortable zone.

TRANSITIONING AND TRANSITIONS

Upon the announcement of our marriage, or maybe the 48-hour engagement, people were shocked, to say the least. I really thought folks were surprised that we would do something so quickly and spontaneously, but it turns out that their reactions were more about sex and gender politics. Where his friends and family, and to a large degree Loren himself, are dealing with gender validation both legally and socially, I am seen as no longer a part of the lesbian community. Loyalties, respect, friendship, and camaraderie within my lesbian community seem to slip through the hands that at one point were locked with mine in a movement toward equity for all. Luckily, I have my partner's hand as we support each other in our ongoing fight for equity.

Transitioning, much like being lesbian, gay, bisexual, or queer, is not something someone would ordinarily choose in our society. Because of internalized and externalized transphobia, homophobia, biphobia, fear, hate, bias, and other elements instilled in Western culture, both coming out and transitioning are arduous and painstakingly difficult. For some transmen who were once labeled *lesbian*, transitioning and coming out as a man are seen as being a traitor, as being disloyal to their feminist roots. It is important to note that coming out before transition, during transition, and for the rest of one's life as their gender identity as a trans, and as living differently or having a different gendered history, is a forever thing, and that never consistently gets easier. I hear people talk about "when butch is not enough" or even that a transman is "just butch who could not cut it." Shortly after Loren and I were married, I read an article about butch lesbians transitioning and its impact on the lesbian community (Vitello, 2006). Judith Halberstam's *Female Masculinity* (1998) in the chapter "Transgender Butch: Butch/FTM Border Wars and the Masculine Continuum" added to the conversation as well.

Just as transmen are sometimes thought of as traitors to lesbian communities or womanhood, so too is the "traitor" description leveled at a Fierce Dyke who legally marries a man. I am still the Fierce Dyke who marched in New York. I would think it might even be easy for some to justify my legally marrying a transman as a form of activism, given that our union must be recognized in all states—or, better yet, as a political loophole to show how stupid marriage laws are in the first place (Cannon, 2010). However, I am not getting this reaction from others. There is a similar conversation internally too. I find myself financially dependent on a man, compromising, taking his direction, and at times following his lead. This reality is hard too. It challenges me internally by calling into question my dykeness and also my fierceness.

CONCLUSION

After a decade of being together, Loren and I have still had to revisit these complications. Marriage is as complex as it is simple, and I sometimes find myself confused. When I am able to have conversations with other trans partners and heterosexually identified cisgender couples, we are shocked that we experience similarities.

Why did I think Loren and my marriage were so radically different than other marriages? Is it, and I just do not care anymore—or maybe I just do not care as much? Maybe I have gotten comfortable through practice with just leaving the invasive childish questions hanging when I respond with an easy "No" in response. I used to painstakingly educate the person asking ignorant questions or telling me the definition of *lesbian* as if I didn't know. Now, I just allow the complication to sit there in between their rigid definitions and nosy questions and my deep and undeniable love. I still feel good when I am perceived as a lesbian, validated, seen; and I do not know if that is just being an older lesbian who does not get flirted with like I used to or that I am not being perceived as straight. Loren gets credit for being such an LGBT ally, and it reminds me of when my friends, as straight husbands and fathers, get social points when they hold their children at the center of conversations around time, money, and even current events. It is unexpected for a man to have empathy. I think it is easier for others to write a story about straight men being exceptions and getting kudos for kindness, politeness, thoughtfulness than someone writing a story about their complicated socialization history. I also don't think it takes socialization as a woman to counter masculine machismo.

We bought a house and Loren works in the yard while I organize the cabinets. Together, we struggle on communicating clearly with each other; being honest, challenging, and supportive—just like every other couple I know. Making choices about money, spending and holding time sacred for one another, and not taking each other for granted are regular conversations to maintain our marriage and relationship health—just like my other married friends. Body-image issues, sexuality, attraction, desire, and physical changes are commonplace with us and in these other relationships.

As our society becomes more aware, if not accepting of complicated relationships, it is helpful to take a second and determine how one can better advocate in both personal and professional contexts. Perhaps allowing persons to express themselves without having to ask them to limit or adjust their language would be a good first step. Ideally, an environment can be created where everyones' more complicated truths can be shared, expressed, respected, and safely included as part of the fabric of the relationship and organization.

I am happy. I am devoted to a complicated relationship with a person who makes me a better person. Together we are role models for others to engage in challenging relationships and to stick them out, out of respect, joy, and contentment. Identities thrive on validation, and that can come from a few or several others—and until it comes from those who matter and, even more importantly, from yourself, there cannot be strength. I am strong for myself, my partner, and my community. There is nothing more fierce, more radical, or more queer than that.

DISCUSSION QUESTIONS

1. Marriage was previously understood as a union between a man and a woman. Since gay marriage is legalized, how is a *man* or a *woman* defined? Binary gender expression or roles on a masculine and feminine spectrum may not accurately describe a

couple. Why do we, as a culture, rely on these binaries when we know they do not fit everyone all the time? Who else is limited by these definitions outside of the trans community?

2. Each state has its own process (or lack thereof) for transmen and women to change their names and gender markers on Social Security cards, state-issued identification cards, birth certificates, and other documents or forms of identification. Who develops these processes and systems? Who has access to these systematic changes and who does not?

3. When a state accepts a more inclusive process for name and gender change, how can training, education, and implementation be consistent?

4. What responsibility does each person in a relationship have to fully disclose their identity and that of their partner to their family practitioner, real-estate agent, neighbors, coworkers, new friends, and so on?

5. Legislation addressing religious freedom currently exists that protects business owners from being "sustainably burdened," which results in the ability for those owners to deny services to identified or perceived LGBT community members. What happens when someone is denied a service and identifies as heterosexual and/or cisgender? How does this impact a religiously affirmed and practicing LGBT person as a customer? As a business owner?

6. What kind of support can be offered to someone in a relationship in which identities are complicated? What would being an ally look like?

7. As we get more comfortable with gender and sexuality as a complication, are there areas that we are still uncomfortable with? If so, what are those areas and why are we uncomfortable? Following are a few examples of other relationships that are complicated. How can you be a better ally to them?
   (a) A relationship with more than two people in a long-term, committed relationship
   (b) Nonmonogamous relationships
   (c) Two transmen in a committed relationship; one gives birth to their son
   (d) A transman and a transwoman legally marry and together raise the children he birthed.

8. The marriage-equality debate focused on marriage rights for lesbian and gay couples and not on couples with trans members or multiple partners. Why was this the case and how might adding trans members or multiple partners changed the national debate? Take note that trans marriages remain particularly vulnerable to legal challenge and annulment.

REFERENCES

Boylan, J. F. (2009, March 11). Is my marriage gay? *The New York Times.* Retrieved from http://www.nytimes.com/2009/05/12/opinion/12boylan.html?_r=1

Cannon, L. (2010). Trans-marriage and the unacceptability of same-sex marriage restrictions. In J. Rowan (Ed.). *Social philosophy today* (Vol. 25, pp. 75–89). Charlottesville, VA: Philosophy Documentation Center.

Halberstam, J. (1998). *Female masculinity.* Durham, NC: Duke University Press.

Vitello, P. (2006, August 20). The trouble when Jane becomes Jack. *The New York Times.* Retrieved from http://www.nytimes.com/2006/08/20/fashion/20gender.html?_r=1

Wall, V. A., & Evans, N. J. (1991). *Beyond tolerance: Gays, lesbians and bisexuals on campus.* American College Personnel Association. Alexandria, VA: University Press.

Wall, V. A., & Evans, N. J. (2000). *Toward acceptance: Sexual orientation issues on campus.* American College Personnel Association. Alexandria, VA: University Press.

CHAPTER 15

"HEAD LADIES CENTER FOR TEACUP CHAIN"

Exploring Cisgender Privilege in a (Predominantly) Gay Male Context

N. Eugene Walls and Kelly Costello

Marginalized communities and social movements are not without their internal struggles around issues of power, oppression, and privilege (Goodman, 2011; Harnois, 2016; Kendall, 2006). Both the women's (Butler, 2004, Jonsson, 2016) and the lesbian, gay, bisexual, transgender, and queer (LGBTQ) movements, for example, have been critiqued for their privileging of Whiteness, middle- and upper-class values, and cisgender (nontransgender) identities (Ferguson, 2006; Swartz, 2015).

The scholarship on issues of privilege has been expanding (Bennett, 2012; Manglitz, 2003) and this body of work has included examinations of different types of privilege (see, e.g., Pewewardy, 2007; Wolbring, 2014) and different aspects of teaching about privilege (Curry-Stevens, 2007; Davis, Mirick, & McQueen, 2015; Messner, 2011, Walls et al., 2009). At the same time, the academic literature on cisgender privilege across all of these different arenas is almost nonexistent (Nickels & Seelman, 2009; for exceptions, see Johnson, 2013; Levy, 2013). Finally, the literature that does exist has been written primarily by trans-identified activists and published in nonacademic publications (Koyama, 2002; T-Vox, 2009).

We begin this chapter by defining terms and providing a brief discussion of square dancing to acquaint the reader with the context about which we write; we follow this discussion by sharing our individual social locations. Next, we examine our experiences to illustrate how cisgender privilege functions and end with a discussion of what we have learned and the questions we are still exploring.

AN ACKNOWLEDGEMENT

In this chapter, we explore our experiences of cisgender privilege within the context of an organization that primarily serves a marginalized community—a gay and lesbian square-dance club to which we both belonged. Briefly, *cisgender privilege* is defined as the unearned advantages that individuals who identify as the gender they were assigned at birth accrue solely based on their cisgender identity. Because one of us identifies as transgender and the other as cisgender, we use our differing social locations to interrogate our experiences of the traditionally gendered space of square dancing to illustrate how privilege functions to maintain oppression of trans-identified individuals, while it reinforces cisgender supremacy.

Although there is much overlap in the constellation of our identities (male, White, queer/gay), the reality that one of us identifies as transgender and the other as cisgender shaped this interaction from the onset and is important to acknowledge and interrogate. The social and political risks for writing about cisgender privilege and transgender oppression are different for each of us. Individuals from privileged groups can write about, advocate for, and challenge systems of oppression from which they benefit without being seen as self-serving or biased, while individuals who are oppressed in relation to that same system can be demonized for reporting the same information (Goodman, 2011; Levy, 2013). In addition, acknowledging a cisgender identity carries minimal risks because publicly being cisgender identified is not stigmatized; however, making a transgender identity public is a much riskier endeavor (Grossman & D'Augelli, 2006, 2007). Finally, writing about an oppression that one experiences has potential emotional costs as one is once again exposed to the social, political, and emotional violence of that oppression. Prior to the process of writing this chapter, we discussed and acknowledged these differences and revisited this discussion numerous times during the development of the chapter.

VERNACULAR AND CONTEXT

It is only within the past couple of decades that transgender issues and concerns have gained any traction in the academic literature (see, e.g., Cavalcante, 2016; Ender, Rohall, & Matthews, 2016; Goodmark, 2013), and what has traditionally existed has focused on medical and psychological treatment of trans-identified individuals (Factor & Rothblum, 2007).

Trans-identified individuals have, however, been contributing to the knowledge base regarding gender through writing narratives, zines, blogs, and theorizing about their lived experiences for significantly longer (Buchanan, 2009; Shortandqueer, 2008) and there has been a recent rise in public discussion of transgender issues (e.g., Laverne Cox, Caitlyn Jenner, *Transparent*, and transphobic bathroom bills). Because of this invisibility and marginalization of transgender voices in academic writing, many readers may find themselves unfamiliar with a number of terms we use in this chapter.

DEFINITIONS

We use the term *transgender* within this chapter to refer to individuals whose gender identity differs in some way from the one they were assigned at birth. They may identify and feel internally as the opposite sex (a binary understanding of sex and gender that is problematic) or identify as another gender altogether, or they may feel the gender they were assigned at birth is a misleading, incorrect, or incomplete description of themselves (Colorado Anti-Violence Program, 2007), or both. Some of these individuals may choose some combination of hormones, surgery, and legal name change to allow them greater ability to externally express their gender identity. Access to hormones and surgery is, however, class based and rarely covered by insurance; thus only those with wealth privilege are able to access many such options, should they choose.

By *cisgender*, we mean individuals whose experience of gender is such that their internal sense of their gender matches the one they were assigned at birth (e.g., a woman-identified individual who was designated as a female at birth). Cisgender individuals' identities, behaviors, and roles are considered appropriate for their sex within the society in which they live (Crethar & Vargas, 2007).

As defined in this chapter, *cisgender privilege* is the set of unearned advantages that individuals who identify as the gender they were assigned at birth accrue solely as the result of having a cisgender identity. This set of advantages includes material, political, and social advantages. Some material examples include not having to worry about being fired based on hostile reactions to one's gender identity and feeling certain that medical insurance will cover most medical needs. In the political realm, even as there has been more attention to transgender issues, mainstream gay and lesbian organizations are more likely to advocate and prioritize what they deem as civil rights focused on sexual orientation (along with failure to prioritize the needs of LGBTQ People of Color, working-class LGBTQ people, or LGBTQ people with disabilities); in this realm, one can expect government-issued documents to accurately represent who one is. In the social arena of privileges, cisgender individuals don't live with the fear of being targeted for violence, humiliation, and exclusion based on gender identity, nor do they face interrogation about what their bodies look like. (For a more complete list of cisgender privileges, see T-Vox, 2009.)

The term *queer* is often used as an umbrella term to reference the LGBTQ community. Although the term has a pejorative history, it has been reclaimed by many in the LGBTQ community because it allows for an increased fluidity in both sexual orientation and gender identity and is "a simple label to explain a complex set of sexual behaviors and desires" (Colorado Anti-Violence Program, 2007). For example, the term may include attraction to someone who identifies outside of the gender binary. *Queer* can also often connote a more radical political perspective that aligns with progressive social-justice ethics and values.

THE SQUARE-DANCING CONTEXT

By *square dancing* we mean modern Western square dancing (Mayo, n.d.), something many readers who were raised in the context of U.S. public schools may remember from middle-school physical education classes. Most urban areas in the United States have square-dance groups, including at least one LGBTQ club. LGBTQ square-dance clubs emerged in the 1970s and now exist in approximately 60 cities (International Association of Gay Square Dance Clubs, 2015).

Calls in square dancing are grouped in a series of increasingly difficult and complex sets (*mainstream, plus, advanced,* and *challenge*); they were standardized in the 1970s by the International Association of Square Dance Callers (Callerlab, 2008). Part of the title of this chapter, "Head Ladies Center for a Teacup Chain," for example, is a 32-beat plus-level call.

Square dance is a highly gendered activity in which gender is reinforced through the assignment of certain roles to specific genders. For example, in most nongay square dancing clubs, men typically lead and women typically follow. Some of the square-dance calls are such that men's parts are not interchangeable with women's parts. In other words, one may very well know how to *weave the ring* as a man but not be able to dance the same call as a woman. In LGBTQ clubs, individuals often do not follow the gender norms when choosing to lead or follow.

This gender-reinforcing pattern in square dancing can be so institutionalized that callers have noted that some heterosexual square-dance clubs find all-position dancing—an approach that does not follow the strictures of gender-based calling—"undanceable" (Hurst, 2005). The difficulty in dancing all-position style is partly the result of differences in executing the call, as mentioned previously, and is further reinforced by both the gendered language of some calls (e.g., *ladies center, men sashay*) and the square-dance norms that included gendered notation when the dancers are directed to execute a certain call (e.g., *ladies touch a quarter,* when *centers touch a quarter* would result in the same movement). All-position dance calling is much more common in LGBTQ square-dance clubs.

SOCIAL LOCATION AND PERSONAL CONTEXTS

In this section, we identify our identities and share a bit about our personal history. Following that, we briefly note our history with square dancing.

KELLY

I am a 35-year-old, White, queer, transperson on the female-to-male spectrum who was born and raised in Philadelphia, the only child of divorced parents. I came out as queer during my freshman year of college but struggled with finding identity labels that fit comfortably. It took several years for me to find the term *queer,* a word that gave me flexibility and movement in both my sexuality and gender expression. I graduated from American University with a degree in elementary education and a minor in mathematics.

At the age of 23, I came out as transgender, openly identifying as male to my friends, family, and coworkers. At 24, I began taking testosterone, and my physical characteristics began to change such that I am now almost exclusively perceived as male. In 2013, I had chest reconstruction, or top surgery, to make my body align more with my identity.

Since 2004, I have been self-publishing a zine series that often focuses on my experiences regarding sexuality and gender identity. I have rarely found media that reflects my experience as a transperson, so it has been important for me to publicly create a counternarrative that disrupts the binaristic gender narrative and also creates new transnarratives. In line with that, I cofounded the Tranny Roadshow in 2005, a multimedia performance art tour with an all-self-identified transgender cast.

I have been a member of the Denver-based LGBTQ square-dance club since September of 2008. I currently dance at the advanced level of square dancing.

EUGENE

I am a 54-year-old, White, gay man who was born in Conway, Arkansas, and assigned a male gender. I was raised in Arkansas in a working-class, conservative, Southern Baptist family; attended public schools; and came out as a gay man when I was a senior in high school. I graduated with an undergraduate degree in sociology from the University of Arkansas at Little Rock, a master's in social work from the University of Texas at Austin, and master's and doctoral degrees in sociology from the University of Notre Dame.

I practiced as a community-based social worker for approximately eight years after my master's degree and prior to returning to school for my doctorate. During that time, I worked with people with disabilities and homeless men, women, and children; ran a therapeutic foster-care agency; and worked part-time as a therapist with a mostly LGBTQ clientele.

I am currently an associate professor at the Graduate School of Social Work at the University of Denver, where I teach research methods, multicultural social work practice, and a course on privilege. My research is focused on three primary areas: risks and resiliency among queer youth and young adults, modern forms of prejudice, and multicultural education. Like Kelly, I was an advanced-level square dancer, but, unlike Kelly, I no longer square dance and currently spend much of my social time line dancing, a form of dancing that is not gendered in the same way that square dancing is.

CISGENDER PRIVILEGE FROM THE INSIDE

In this section of the chapter, Kelly shares his experiences of cisgender privilege during the time both of us were involved in square dancing. This includes both transgender-related microaggressions and more overt forms of transphobia. He concludes this section by noting his current relationship with square dancing and the square dancing club.

KELLY

In 2008, I was invited to attend the open house of the LGBTQ square-dance club. I showed up with a friend, not really sure what to expect, and was immediately surrounded by lots of people with smiles on their faces; the excitement was contagious. Before the night ended,

I decided that I wanted to begin taking the mainstream class. I had previously wanted to find more settings where I could meet new people and learn new skills. In many ways, at first glance, this seemed like a perfect opportunity.

I showed up, enthusiastic for class every week, but also with some amount of reservation. This was one of the first times I had experienced being surrounded primarily by gay, White men between the ages of 40 and 60. As a transperson, I am very aware of my history of female socialization when I am participating in spaces with gay men. I am still learning the cultural norms that are assumed and expected—some norms that are similar to heterosexual male norms but others that are unique to gay male culture—especially when other people do not know that I've transitioned.

When entering new social spaces, I am conscious of the fact that many people no longer read me as female, genderqueer, or transgender because I am primarily perceived as male. I generally surround myself with queer community that celebrates fluidity in gender and sexuality; however, my experience in gay and lesbian spaces (as opposed to queer spaces) has been much more rigid, and I've often encountered ignorance of transgender issues, or explicit transphobia. For instance, there have been several occasions on which, after I have told gay men that I am transgender, they have responded, "I don't know what that means," indicating ignorance. Or, in an explicit transphobic manner, people *intentionally* have used the wrong pronouns.

In most areas of my life, it has been important to me to stay visible as a transgender person. So it took me by surprise when I realized that I was making a conscious decision not to disclose this part of my identity in the context of square dancing.

I left class each week, energized about using my body and meeting new people but struggling with feeling like I had to check my transgender identity at the door. Most of this fear of losing access to this space was self-imposed because I have had past experiences of dynamics shifting once I came out as transgender. I wasn't prepared to lose what I viewed as an exciting new activity and an expanded community, and therefore I policed my own behavior and identity disclosure (Foucault, 1975). Still, I found myself wondering when I should come out, in what context, or if it was even relevant. I wasn't particularly avoiding the issue; it just never came up. I know that many people feel entitled to this information and are often upset when they find out after knowing me for a while.

I'm not exactly sure how I was eventually outed, but at some point, I was aware that many people knew I was transgender without my ever telling them. On one hand, this was positive reinforcement that there was no discernible shift in relationships based on this knowledge. On the other hand, a few of the people I know and trust let me know that people were approaching them with inappropriate personal questions about my identity and my body.

Square dancing is a physical activity that includes holding hands and holding one's partner. While I haven't had as much experience in heterosexual square-dancing clubs, I am aware that there is more physical contact in the LGBTQ clubs that have different norms around personal space and physicality (International Association of Gay Square Dance Clubs, 2009). Many transgender people have different boundaries around physical contact because our bodies are often sites of victimization and violation. I am constantly aware of the way my body is being perceived, most often visually but sometimes through physical contact. There were many times when I wondered whether my dance partners perceived any incongruence with what they had expected, since I began dancing years before I had top surgery. Only one time have I been asked a direct question about my body after physical contact with a dance partner.

There are times when I'm aware of inconsistencies for what I'm allowed to do or how I'm allowed to behave with the club. For the most part, when others are uncomfortable with how I am behaving or expressing myself, their discomfort is not brought directly to my attention. Instead, I find out later that others have a desire to police these aspects by limiting or changing them to something more familiar and comfortable. Much of the discomfort and resultant desire to police my behavior is rooted in standards of masculinity that are different for me than for cisgender men—even cisgender gay men—with whom I dance. Eugene writes in the following section about his own process around my choice to dance in the follow position, which, as mentioned previously, is typically the woman's role. When we were initially choosing positions to learn, we were told that, if we like to twirl, we should be follows. That was all of the information I needed. I did not realize that in my choice of dance part, my performance of masculinity would be up for questioning—even by colleagues who I consider to be allies.

Another clear inconsistency occurred at the graduation for my mainstream square-dance class. I had sewn a dress from scratch and accessorized with a blue wig, blue eyelashes, and petticoat. I shaved my beard and knew that many people would not recognize me at first glance. As someone who enjoys drag and costumes in general, I was excited to bring this part of myself into this space. I was even more excited to see, for the first time, the presence of the drag contingent of the club. Although I wasn't wearing the club's official drag outfit, I felt more comfortable having other folks join me in drag in the space. After the graduation, one friend in the club shared with me that people who knew that I'm transgender had a "hard time" with my outfit. Why would I want to be feminine if I wanted everyone to perceive me as male? Interestingly, this was not a question posed for any of the cisgender men wearing dresses.

There has been only one major incident with explicit transphobia, in which one club member began a conversation by policing the validity of another transgender person's identity. This conversation, while frustrating at the time, escalated further in follow-up conversations. I found, both for this specific member and the club in general, that, when one is engaging in a process of accountability, there is a general desire to be inclusive but a lack of knowledge about the best way to move forward. The lack of knowledge exists not only about trans-oppression and the lived experience of transpeople but also about how gay and lesbian people embody cisgender privilege and play a role in the marginalization of trans-identified people. This marginalization is further complicated in a recreational setting such as a square-dancing club, where one wonders whether issues of oppression and privilege should be addressed and how one educates others in an effective way. Like many social settings in my life, being a member of the club presents me with complicated relationships in which I am constantly aware of my transgender identity, how my gender influences my interactions, and the ways I call on the allies around me for support.

Now that I've been square dancing for eight years and have met many other dancers from other clubs, most people know that I identify as transgender. While I still experience instances of transphobia within this community, my personal relationships with dancers have deepened, allowing for more appropriate avenues for them to ask questions and opportunities for them to stand up as allies to the transgender community.

CISGENDER PRIVILEGE FROM THE OUTSIDE

In this section, Eugene explores his experience of the experiences Kelly introduced. This includes both his internalization of cisgender privilege as well as bearing witness to behaviors of others in the club. He concludes the section noting his current relationship with the square-dance community.

EUGENE

The first incident in which I found myself consciously face to face with cisgender privilege was not something "out there" in the square-dance club but rather was something inside myself. Such was the case when I found myself surprised that Kelly, upon joining the club, had decided to learn the follow dance position. It took two weeks of me processing my confusion over his decision to follow before it dawned on me that I was clearly speaking from my cisgender privilege. To be more explicit, let me outline the string of thoughts that led me to this place of confusion. First, I clearly knew from my friendship and conversations with Kelly that he was assigned a female gender at birth but now identified as male. Second, although our particular square-dance club does not solely rely on gender-based teaching of square-dance calls, I was clearly conscious that traditionally the lead role is thought of as the man's part and the follow role as the woman's part. I then reasoned that Kelly would want to learn the man's part so that he could *more convincingly perform the masculinity that was associated with his identity as a male.*

Now this string of thoughts may seem very logical, and, of course, at some level it is. However, what makes this line of reasoning problematic is that, in the context of LGBTQ square-dancing clubs, it is not unusual at all for men to dance the follow part or for women to dance the lead part. In fact, I myself began square dancing the follow part. When other cisgender men in our club make that choice, I do not question why they would want to learn the follow part. However, in Kelly's case, I did. Cisgender men choosing so created no cognitive or emotional dissonance for me, but when a transman made that same choice, I found myself suddenly having a reaction. Why was it that I—a cisgender man—could learn to follow without my maleness being suspect but for my friend Kelly this was different? Why did I expect and need him to perform more stringently masculine behaviors? Does his maleness as a transman become somehow suspect?

In this excavation (Kendall, 2006) of my cisgender privilege, there was the expectation that Kelly had to go above and beyond what I expected of cisgender gay men in order to fully claim his maleness. When I first recognized the entitlement that I was carrying about how loose my performance of masculinity could be without my maleness being questioned, I was sickened.

The second incident, or really a string of incidents over a fairly short period of time, came from well-meaning members of the square-dance club. The similarity in the incidents is that they were all based on the notion that cisgender people have the right to ask very personal questions about transfolks' identities and bodies. The fact that I was friends of Kelly and another transman who joined the club and members were asking me questions about the two of them should have been a clue to the members themselves that their questions were problematic. Among other things, I was asked (a) whether Kelly (who is most often read as male rather than as a transman) is transgender, (b) if Kelly was on hormones or had had "the surgery" (as if there were only one surgery or medically related transition process), and (c) at what point Kelly—since he identifies as a gay man—tells potential sexual partners about his anatomy. On repeated occasions I had to correct pronouns, even after the member I was correcting had already been repeatedly corrected. Finally, in a social setting at a local bar, I experienced a member sharing information in a very blasé manner about a surgical procedure that one of the transmen had undergone.

A third incident occurred when the square-dance club officers were confronted with the transphobic event that Kelly mentions previously in his narrative. In the follow-up discussions that ensued, I had to intervene to explain that expecting the transgender members of our club to educate and train our club members on transphobia and cisgender privilege was not appropriate and is a form of cisgender privilege in and of itself. This dynamic of privileged people expecting marginalized people to be responsible for educating them on power, oppression, and privilege is, of course, all too common (Goodman, 2011; Kendall, 2006).

Although I am fairly knowledgeable about transgender issues, both as an academic who is fairly well read and teaches in the area and as a supporter of the local transgender community, I have no illusions that my work on understanding my own embodiment of cisgender privilege is anywhere near complete. No doubt, I probably fail to recognize and acknowledge my cisgender privilege more often than I actually see it.

I am no longer involved in the square-dancing club as I have made the choice to use my free time to focus instead on line dancing. Because line dancing is not a partnered form of dancing, gender roles are not as blatantly reinforced as they are in square dancing. This is not to say, however, that there are not gendered aspects of line dancing but rather that they are somewhat different than those we have explored here.

CONCLUSION

Although it is often mistakenly believed that marginalized communities somehow automatically understand oppressions they do not experience because of an empathy that reaches across experiences of marginalization, this is not the case in our lived experiences of our participation in a LGBTQ square-dance club. In no way do we believe that this organization is more problematic than most organizations or groups in the LGBTQ community or, for that matter, than most organizations or groups in most marginalized communities. In fact, this group's explicitly stated commitment to inclusivity across axes of difference situates the group further along the progressive continuum than many other groups who have yet to publicly communicate such a commitment to inclusivity. However, intention to be inclusive is not enough.

Our experiences in the group demonstrate that the vast majority of problematic interactions are not at the end of the continuum that we would classify as overtly transphobic (although one incident clearly was) but rather fall along the part of the continuum that we would classify as cisgender privilege and microaggressions—those "brief and common-place daily verbal, behavioral and environmental indignities, whether intentional or unintentional, that communicate hostile, derogatory... slights and insults to the target person or group" (Sue et al., 2007, p. 271). These behaviors, regardless of the well-meaning intent of the members who engaged in them, illustrate how members of the LGBQ community often take part in policing gender. By doing so, the system of gender stratification that is oppressive to trans-identified individuals, and ultimately damaging to cisgender people as well, is reinforced (Kendall, 2006).

Within marginalized communities, certain identities continue to be privileged over others, both mirroring and maintaining the hierarchical paradigm that exists outside in the dominant culture. This within-group ranking based on within-group differences illustrates the importance of intersectionality not only to understanding complex social locations but also in illustrating the role that marginalized others play in reinforcing the stratifying ideologies of the dominant culture.

Of course it is not only the identities of the individuals that are important in the interaction but also how those identities are read by others. In one incident, Kelly was being misread as gay while he identifies as queer. Those identity differences are significant and shape experience in fairly significant ways. Likewise, the question arises as to the authenticity of how people are reading Kelly's maleness. When we use male pronouns while still viewing Kelly as female or as an inauthentic male is still problematic because it privileges our own view of Kelly's gender over his ability to self-define. The arrogance of privileging our own definition of marginalized others (persons or communities), rather than trusting that others have more knowledge about their own experience than we do, is of course another hallmark of privilege.

The privileges that we have uncovered are similar to dynamics of privilege as it exists in other communities. These dynamics include the sense of entitlement that privileged people often have with regard to very personal knowledge about marginalized others, having higher expectations regarding standards of behavior for marginalized others than for people in the privileged group, and judging behaviors very differently depending on the privileged or marginalized status of the person engaging in the behavior. We also raise the issue of how our different social locations as coauthors potentially have very different consequences. Cocreating across difference can be a powerful way to explore, deconstruct, and challenge issues of privilege, but failure to attend to the potentially differential consequences in that process can just as easily reinforce the power dynamics the cocreators are trying to explore. The relationship between coauthors, the level of trust, and the writing process must attend to differences in power or be suspect.

Throughout the writing of this chapter, we have continually asked ourselves how the process of our joint exploration of our different experiences of oppression and privilege has impacted our friendship. Has it led us to a deeper and more authentic understanding of one another, or has it created distrust and fear as Kelly has been exposed to Eugene's disclosure of his own struggles with cisgender privilege? Was it even appropriate for this interaction to occur across this axis of difference? How is Eugene's vulnerability about his own struggles different from Kelly's vulnerability at being exposed to a broader understanding of the cisgender privilege that is part of the square-dance club? On an even larger scale, how does reporting our experiences with the square-dance club shape our relationships with the club, both from our own internal perceptions and narratives about our participation in the group and also the group members' reactions to hearing about our experiences? As Kelly has continued to stay engaged in the activity of square dancing, how has the length of time with the club and the changes in membership influenced the culture of the club around inclusivity? Have there been discernible shifts in attitudes and behaviors among the club's members? Has there been an increase in the number of trans-identified members of the club?

In relationships across cultural differences, these questions are likely to emerge. What we do with them—whether we ignore them or grapple with them in an honest, vulnerable way—no doubt depends upon the context and history of the relationship. In some situations, opening them up may be destructive, while in others, the same thing has the potential to lead to deeper and more authentic connections. Regardless of the context and history, however, those questions are still there.

DISCUSSION QUESTIONS

1. What are the myriad ways that cisgender people benefit from cisgender privilege, and how are those benefits related to the costs transgender people pay?
2. How does one bring up issues of power, oppression, and privilege in the context of social and recreational groups whose primary aims are not political or educational?
3. How often does the issue of privilege get raised in communities in which you participate that are organized around some aspect of your identity that is marginalized—both privilege that corresponds to the marginalization the group experiences and privilege that some (many?) in your marginalized community might embody?
4. Who is responsible for ensuring that organizations and communities are inclusive across cultural axes? How do you incorporate marginalized voices into community decision-making without relying on those who are marginalized to educate everyone? What is the role of policy in changing organizational culture?
5. On what cultural axes of differences do people in your marginalized community get unjustly ranked? How do you make those within-group differences and their connected consequences visible?
6. How do you talk about differences with your friends and colleagues who do not share your marginalized or privileged identity? When is it appropriate? When is it not?
7. How has the increase in prevalence of news and media on transgender issues (e.g., Caitlyn Jenner, antitransgender bathroom bills) influenced the openness and willingness of people in your community to discuss and grapple with transphobia and cisgender privilege?

REFERENCES

Bennett, J. (2012). *White privilege: A history of the concept.* (Unpublished master's thesis). Georgia State University, Atlanta.

Buchanan, R. (2009). *Zine narratives: Subjectivities and stories of five influential zine creators.* (Doctoral dissertation). Temple University, Philadelphia, PA.

Butler, J. (2004). *Undoing gender.* New York, NY: Routledge.

Callerlab. (2008). *The history of callerlab.* Topeka, KS: International Association of Square Dance Callers. Retrieved from http://www.callerlab.org/For-The-Public

Cavalcante, A. (2016). "I did it all online:" Transgender identity and the management of everyday life. *Critical Studies in Media Communications, 33,* 109–122.

Colorado Anti-Violence Program. (2007). *Sex, gender, and orientation: Terms and definitions.* Denver, CO: Author.

Crethar, H. C., & Vargas, L. A. (2007). Multicultural intricacies in professional counseling. In J. Gregoire & C. Junger (Eds.), *The counselor's companion: What every beginning counselor needs to know* (pp. 340–359). Mahwah, NJ: Lawrence Erlbaum.

Curry-Stevens, A. (2007). New forms of transformative education: Pedagogy for the privileged. *Journal of Transformative Education, 5,* 33–58.

Davis, A., Mirick, R., & McQueen, B. (2015). Teaching from privilege: Reflections from white female instructors. *Affilia, 30,* 302–313. doi:10.1177/0886109914560742

Ender, M. G., Rohall, D. E., & Matthews, M. D. (2016). Cadet and civilian undergraduate attitudes toward transgender people: A research note. *Armed Forces and Society, 42,* 427–435.

Factor, R. J., & Rothblum, E. D. (2007). A study of transgender adults and their non-transgender siblings on demographic characteristics, social support, and experiences of violence. *Journal of LGBT Health Research, 3,* 11–30.

Ferguson, R. A. (2006). Race-ing homonormativity: Citizenship, sociology, and gay identity. In E. P. Johnson & M. G. Henderson (Eds.), *Black queer studies* (pp. 52–67). Durham, NC: Duke University Press.

Foucault, Michel. (1975). *Discipline and punish: The birth of the prison.* New York, NY: Random House.

Goodman, D. J. (2011). *Promoting diversity and social justice: Educating people from privileged groups* (2nd ed.). New York, NY: Routledge.

Goodmark, L. (2013). Transgender people, intimate partner abuse, and the legal system. *Harvard Civil Rights-Civil Liberties Law Review, 48,* 51–104.

Grossman, A. H., & D'Augelli, A. R. (2006). Transgender youth: Invisible and vulnerable. *Journal of Homosexuality, 51,* 111–128.

Grossman, A. H., & D'Augelli, A. R. (2007). Transgender youth and life-threatening behaviors. *Suicide and Life Threatening Behavior, 37,* 527–537.

Harnois, C. E. (2016). Race, ethnicity, sexuality, and women's political consciousness of gender. *Social Psychology Quarterly, 78,* 365–386.

Hurst, A. (2005). My first Callerlab. *Allan's Square Dance Articles.* Retrieved from http://www.danceinfo.org/uploads/2/4/6/6/24661272/firstcallerlab13a.pdf

International Association of Gay Square Dance Clubs. (2015, May 25). *Minutes of the general membership meeting of IAGSDC.* St. Louis, MO: Author.

Johnson, J. R. (2013). Cisgender privilege, intersectionality, and the criminalization of CeCe McDonald: Why intercultural communication needs transgender studies. *Journal of International and Intercultural Communication, 6,* 135–144. doi:10.1080/17513057.2013.776094

Jonsson, T. (2016). The narrative reproduction of White feminist racism. *Feminist Review, 113,* 50–67.

Kendall, F. E. (2006). *Understanding White privilege: Creating pathways to authentic relationships across race.* New York, NY: Routledge.

Koyama, E. (2002). *Cisexual/cisgender: Decentralizing the dominant group.* Retrieved from http://eminism.org/interchange/2002/20020607-wmstl.html

Levy, D. L. (2013). On the outside looking in? The experience of being a straight, cisgender, qualitative researcher. *Journal of Gay & Lesbian Social Services, 25,* 197–209. doi:10.1080/10538720.2013.782833

Manglitz, E. (2003). Challenging White privilege in adult education: A critical review of the literature. *Adult Education Quarterly, 53,* 119–134.

Mayo, J. (n.d.). *MWSD—The first ten years.* Square Dance History Project. Retrieved from http://squaredance-history.org/items/show/710

Messner, M. A. (2011). The privilege of teaching about privilege. *Sociological Perspectives, 54,* 3–13. doi:10.1525/sop.2011.54.1.3

Nickels, S., & Seelman, K. (2009). Exploring cisgender privilege in social work education: A qualitative approach. (Unpublished manuscript).

Pewewardy, N. (2007). *Challenging White privilege: Critical discourse for social work education.* Washington, DC: Council on Social Work Education.

Shortandqueer, K. (2008). *Trans(in)formation* (2nd ed.) Retrieved from https://shortandqueer.com/?s=Trans%28in%29formation

Sue, D. W., Capodilupo, C. M., Torino, G. C., Bucceri, J. M., Holder, A. M. B., Nadal, K. L., & Esquilin, M. (2007). Racial microaggressions in everyday life: Implications for clinical practice. *American Psychologist, 62,* 271–286.

Swartz, O. (2015). Gay rights/African American rights: A common struggle for social justice. *Socialism and Democracy, 29,* 1–24.

T-Vox. (2009). *Cisgender privilege.* Retrieved from http://t-vox.org/?s=Cisgender+privilege

Walls, N. E., Griffin, R. A., Arnold-Renicker, H., Burson, M., Johnston, L., Moorman, N., . . . Schutte, E. C. (2009). Graduate social work students' learning journey about heterosexual privilege. *Journal of Social Work Education, 44,* 289–307.

Wolbring, G. (2014). Ability privilege: A needed addition to privilege studies. *Journal for Critical Animal Studies, 12,* 118–141.

CHAPTER 16

BECOMING A COUNSELING PROFESSIONAL LESBIAN

Revisiting Privilege and Challenges

Joy S. Whitman

INTRODUCTION TO MY PRIVILEGE

I am a lesbian who is educated, middle-class, White, Jewish, and in midlife. I have a doctorate degree in counseling psychology and practice as a counselor educator, statuses that are respected by my religion and my culture. The privileged identity as a counselor educator and my devalued identity as a lesbian are the identities I am most aware of as I write this chapter. My journey to understanding all of my identities is layered, and though I value each of them, I do so differently. I have listed my identities in order of salience to me around issues of privilege and oppression. Each has allowed me to experience acceptance and rejection in different measure.

I have a history of embodying stigmatized identities. My parents were born into working-class families who emigrated from eastern European countries either as a result of the pogroms in Russia or the threat of annihilation during the Holocaust. It was their heritage to feel persecuted and their goal to ensure their children did not.

We lived comfortably in a predominantly Jewish, middle-class neighborhood in New York until I was 12 years old, when my father relocated our family of six to Mexico to pursue his dream of becoming a doctor. It was in Mexico that I learned what it meant to have privilege in regard to education, race, and socioeconomic status. The privileges I benefitted from while living in New York as an educated, middle-class, White Jew did not protect me from the experiences of being different and seen as suspect in Mexico. I paid attention to how I was watched, followed, and talked about in stores because of my *gringa* status and stigmatized identity. Patrons assumed I did not speak Spanish and therefore talked about me in front of me. Our socioeconomic position changed because we became less financially stable while in Mexico and, consequently, when we returned to the United States. At almost 16 and back in the United States, I learned quickly how to use food stamps and how to navigate the looks from others who eyed my shopping cart at checkout. Trying to fit back into American culture seemed to require many possessions that I could not purchase. It also required me to engage in stigma management around our changed social status and identity, an identity I was not well prepared to manage given my middle-class upbringing.

Prior to leaving New York and moving to Mexico, I was unaware of the unearned privileges my White skin and middle-class status afforded me. It was clear to me that I had taken my various privileges for granted. I never had to wonder about myself other than to know that being Jewish was not the norm in the United States and that the history of persecution my family experienced was part of me. I took for granted my family's financial position, the quality of my education, and the opportunities I had because of it. Living in another country and returning to the United States in a different economic class awakened me to how I had benefitted from my identities and at what cost to others. These were strong lessons at a young age, and I believe I needed to have that level of intensity to get me out of my middle-class, White comfort zone. I was priming myself to learn how to manage identities that society stigmatized.

OH, AND LESBIAN TOO

At the age of 18, I came out to my parents as a lesbian. Unfortunately, their efforts to protect me from the realities of oppression as a Jew would not and did not protect me from the realities of homoprejudice (Logan, 1996) and heterosexism (Morin, 1997). Though my parents could not protect me, my prior experiences of oppression did prepare me to enter into my next position of marginality. During my senior year of high school, the awareness of being different continued to present itself to me. I wrote off the crushes I had on my female best friends as my need to find others with whom I could fit in, but I knew that my attraction to them was more than theirs for me and that my disinterest in boys meant something. The morning I woke up and told myself, "I am lesbian" will be forever memorable to me. I was relieved to finally have the words to describe my feelings. Even though I was aware that this was not a good thing to be in 1979, I was not ashamed. Because of my parents' liberal political and social positions and the education I had been privileged to have, I knew the identity itself was not wrong but that the societal view of it was. Declassification of homosexuality as a mental illness from the *Diagnostic and Statistical Manual* had occurred only six years before my coming out, and it was not until 1987 that the term was removed from the manual as *ego-dystonic*.

My father, who specialized in psychiatry, also knew that homosexuality had been classified as a mental disorder, and he acted both as a disappointed parent and an unenlightened psychiatrist when I came out to him. He requested that I see a psychiatrist to be sure of my proclaimed sexual identity, and though I agreed, I did so primarily to discuss how to manage the homophobia of my father and that of others. I was aware at age 18 that the reaction of others would not always be favorable and that I would need to educate others to make my life safe. Again, I returned to the security of my privileged educated status to help me navigate the oppression I was experiencing and to manage the stigma of a lesbian identity.

COUNSELING PROFESSIONAL LESBIAN

I embarked in college on a trajectory that made being lesbian a profession for me, one I continue today in my clinical work and position as a counselor educator. I was the poster child for coming out, moving from Cass's (1979) stage of identity confusion right to identity pride. I found an outlet for my need to educate through the human sexuality courses offered on campus and volunteered to tell my coming-out story to hundreds of students whenever I could. I did not want anyone else to be asked to see a psychiatrist or to be rejected because of his or her sexual identity. I experienced this type of rejection from a high-school friend after my first semester in college, and though I still was not ashamed of being lesbian, the pain of the rejection fueled my need to educate others. I wanted everyone to know I was lesbian as a way for them to face their own homoprejudice and heterosexism and to explore their reactions based on fear and misinformation. It was at this stage that I began to understand how managing minority stress had the potential to change a stigmatized identity into one of value and power.

After my college years, as I integrated this identity into my others, I moved in and out of the closet by choosing when and where to come out. I had no outlets by which to educate others until I entered my master's counseling program. I learned from another student that one of the professors believed the topic of homosexuality (the terminology was still being used then) was overdone and therefore would not be addressed in his course on multicultural counseling. When I heard that, I knew I had work to do. I ensured I came out to him and used class assignments to write about issues pertinent to counseling lesbian and gay clients. I thought I would educate this professor and others who read my work. This particular professor was a White Jewish male at a Catholic university, and I used my privileged statuses as an educated, White, Jewish female to educate him. I continued to connect my privileged identities to my stigmatized identity of lesbian.

At the time, the American Association for Counseling and Development's (ACA) ethical standards (1988) had not integrated the language of sexual orientation and the importance of valuing varying sexual orientations of trainees in the section on preparation standards. Today, the Code of Ethics (ACA, 2014) emphasizes the organization's commitment to the value it places on the diverse identities of trainees and the active infusion of multicultural counseling competencies into the curriculum and training. Through my interactions with my professor, I was inviting him to act ethically as a counselor educator.

My professional lesbian identity was solidified during my doctoral program. I sought out a practicum site where I knew I would be supervised by a psychologist experienced in providing affirmative counseling to lesbian, gay, and bisexual (LGB) clients. During those training years, working with transgender clients was not yet the clinical focus. Since that time, the field of psychology and counseling has created clear and evidence-based guidelines for affirmative lesbian, gay, bisexual, and transgender (LGBT) psychological practice and counseling (American Psychological Association, 2011; Harper et al., 2013). I was hungry for information about best practices, I continued to write and study about counseling LGB clients, and I chose my dissertation topic to be centered on lesbian identity development. During my last year of education prior to my clinical internship, the director of the counseling psychology program offered me an opportunity that concretized my professional lesbian identity. He asked me to create a master's level counseling course and gave me free reign to create one focused on counseling gay and lesbian clients. He didn't know this, but he helped to heal the wound created in me during my master's program by the professor who did not acknowledge his own homoprejudice and heterosexism. I now began to believe that other counseling professionals were aware of the need to educate counseling students and practitioners about providing affirmative treatment to LGB clients. I was encouraged as well by my dissertation advisor to write an article about the class I created and have it published in a counselor-education journal.

Ultimately, I felt validated as a counseling psychology–professional lesbian and have now made a career of being one. All of these mentors were heterosexual allies; through them, I learned about the privilege of education and the protection the academy could afford me when I was addressing clinical issues for LGB clients and individuals. I was also aware of the opportunities granted to me because I am lesbian and the elevated status I held as a lesbian in a counseling psychology program and then in my internship. This previously classified mental disorder had become not only a key to opportunities that fostered my professional career as a counseling psychologist and counselor educator but also an asset to others who wanted representation in their clinical and educational settings. Only a Jew would ask, "who knew?"

HOMOPREJUDICE AND HETEROSEXISM REVISITED

I have come to understand my identities through the theories of stigma and stigma management (Goffman, 1963) and minority stress (Meyer, 2003, 2013). Goffman's seminal early work on stigma and its meaning for an individual as it relates to identity, social interaction and roles, and negative valuation of the stigmatized attribute or quality has been critical to my understanding of my identities that U.S. society marginalizes. More specifically, stigma theory discusses how societal valuation of personal characteristics or attributes communicates to the individual and others which attributes are positively or negatively valued. As a result, both the individual and those with whom that individual is interacting manage the either positive or negative valuation of those characteristics in social discourse (Meisenbach, 2010).

Stigma management "is the attempt by persons with stigmatized social identities to approach interpersonal interactions in ways aimed at minimizing the social costs of carrying these identities" (O'Brien, 2011, p. 292). The theoretical lens of stigma management provides a social context within which I can more deeply understand how my identities of limited privilege and status, and the consequent behaviors in which I engaged to manage the impression of others in reaction to those identities, impacted my psychological development and career choices.

Relatedly, understanding the theory of minority stress helped me transform those stigma identities into those of power and status (Meyer, 2003, 2013). Briefly, the theory of minority stress postulates that having a stigmatized identity such as *lesbian* can cause stress, anxiety, depression, and other mental health issues as the result of societal discrimination of the identity and the individual's fear of societal discrimination (Fingerhut, Peplau, & Gable, 2010). The stressors can be both distal and proximal. Distal stressors are those that are external to the individual, such as living in a state with antigay legislation and experiencing the legislation as discrimination. Proximal stressors are localized internally to the individual in terms of how the individual perceives the stigmatized identity and discrimination. These stressors can be mediated by a variety of variables, such as level of exposure to discrimination, LGBT community support, a strong LGBT identity, and level of outness of the individual (Meyer, 2003, 2013). I reduced my stress by having a strong lesbian identity and seeking out the LGBT community for support. Doing so provided me the opportunity to buffer against societal discrimination and to perceive my lesbian identity positively.

As a counselor educator, I continued to write and educate others about providing affirmative treatment to LGB clients and began to address treatment for transgender clients as well. I used the growing body of research and affirmative-practice guidelines (American Psychological Association, 2011; Harper et al., 2013) to bolster my teaching and scholarship. I have had little to deter me from continuing my career as a counseling professional lesbian; however, I have had some moments of concern. One moment of doubt about the wisdom of making my professional mark in this area of scholarship and practice occurred during my first academic position while I was attending an ACA conference, when I met with the former professor from my master's program. He wanted to mentor me, one Jew to another, and asked me to reconsider my research because "You do not want to sacrifice your professional advancement or ability to publish by narrowing your focus so early in your career." His homoprejudice and heterosexism were clear to me once again because he had narrowly focused his scholarship and was still respected in the profession. Yet his advice made me pause because he was a seasoned professional who could be in a position to review my work. Did I need to worry about professionals' homoprejudice? I had not given this possibility serious consideration until he questioned me. I hesitated in my zeal for just a moment and wondered how the stigma of my lesbian identity might influence others' opinions of my scholarship.

Another moment of concern occurred during my first position as a counselor educator at a small regional campus in the Midwest. I considered how and when to come out in classes as lesbian and Jewish. Wondering whether I would get favorable evaluations, a crucial component toward obtaining promotion and tenure, I decided not to come out as lesbian until the end of my first-semester course on multicultural counseling when it seemed appropriate to do so. It was a deliberate decision to manage the stigma of *lesbian*, and it was one I felt quite torn about when deciding. Teaching the course was personally challenging for many reasons but predominantly when I read papers by students expressing their negative beliefs about same-sex attractions prior to my coming out to them. Grading them fairly created an internal battle. I wanted them to freely express themselves to learn, and yet they were talking about me. Managing the stigma of a lesbian identity was personally tiring. I was clearly experiencing minority stress during that first semester (Meyer, 2003, 2013).

When I did come out in class, students commented that they thought I was lesbian because of the considerable amount of work my position required and their belief that I had no social life and therefore had time to grade papers. Others thought so because of my shoes! Apparently, big, black, chunky shoes equals lesbian. I wanted to fail them because it appeared they learned nothing from the course. And yet I knew that we all come to awareness in our own time, and that, if nothing else, they could no longer say they did not know a lesbian.

At this same university, I had a colleague who thought it endearing to call me his "favorite lesbian." I believe I was the only lesbian he knew and therefore of course was his favorite, but the ease with which he said it in front of others and with the privilege that came with his being a heterosexual White male always made me uncomfortable. He was also tenured and I was not, and I did not feel safe to tell him how offensive his endearing term was to me. I knew he wanted me to see him as cool and open to my sexual identity, but he never asked my permission to out me in front of others or to reduce my identity to this one qualifier. Only I had the right to name myself.

I want to offer one last incident I experienced years later in another academic position I held. This incident reinforces how far we still need to go in academia regarding issues of sexual identity. The marketing department at the university was updating its information about our school of education and soliciting feedback from faculty about the content. I reviewed the material and found no mention of sexual orientation included in the descriptive list of diverse identities served by our unit. Soon enough, I was invited to the dean's office to meet with someone from public relations to discuss my belief that sexual identity should be included. I was told we could not add these words to the list because a sentence in the material contained the word *children,* and we were at a religious university. Huh? How did any of this justify the omission of sexual identity? I was aware of how the null environment (Fassinger, 1991) impacts invisible identities and thought it my obligation in an institution of higher education to ensure that this invisible identity be made visible. At first I was speechless and unsure how to respond without jeopardizing my tenure prospects or communicating my intolerance for the homoprejudice I was experiencing. At the time, I was president of the LGB counseling division in the ACA and could not violate my sense of integrity to this organization by backing down. It was not until the person from public relations communicated to the dean how we did not want to turn potential students away from our unit by omitting these words from our print material that the dean acquiesced. I was left with the impression that the language would be included not because we valued human rights but because it was financially wise to do so. I felt assaulted and demoralized at having my sexual identity reduced to a financial decision and seeing the lack of awareness of heterosexual privilege in the process of deciding whether sexual identity was of value to the university. This experience was gravely disheartening. The battle was won; I was scared. I was reminded again of the stigma of a marginalized sexual identity.

In spite and because of these experiences, I made a career of being a counseling professional lesbian. True to the theory of minority stress, I transformed the stigmatized identity into one of power and resilience. In my first academic position, I created a mentoring program for LGBT faculty and students on the campus and was even able to teach the course I created on counseling LGB clients. I became nationally involved in the counseling profession's division for LGBT counseling issues and wrote and presented on the subject. Though

I am acutely aware of the privilege academia and my education provided me to do these things, I am also aware that my heterosexual colleagues were not questioned about their narrowly focused scholarship, were not concerned that their high expectations for their students would be attributed to their sexual identity and ostensible abundance of time this identity provided, and were not called pet names ascribed to their sexual identity. They were privileged in their majority sexual identities and free of minority stress as they developed their academic identities.

CONCLUSION

What I hope readers will take away from this chapter are two key issues. First, privilege is elusive and context dependent. All of the identities I spoke of changed when I moved among environments. For example, inside of academia and in my profession of counseling and counseling psychology, my stigmatized identity as a lesbian now has cachet. It opens doors for me professionally, such as giving me the opportunity to write this chapter. Yet outside of higher education and the world of counseling, legislation continues to pass that is discriminatory. For example, I can still be denied counseling services based on the conflict between my lesbian identity and a counselor's religious values. My educated, White, middle-class identities do not offer me protection from oppression when it comes to the most intimate aspects of my relational life. I am acutely aware of this vulnerability and therefore use my status of lesbian in academia to educate others who, hopefully, will change the world outside.

Second, navigating a stigmatized identity can be psychologically taxing. As I have discussed, the literature on minority stress for LGB individuals bears this out to be true; yet the transformation of the oppressed identity into a source of strength and personal power is also possible (Meyer, 2013). A study by Riggle, Whitman, Rostosky, Olson, and Strong (2008) discussed the positive aspects of being lesbian and gay and found that participants "appreciated that their gay and lesbian identities provided them with insight and awareness, key tools for making meaning out of one's life and circumstances" (p. 214). I learned this lesson at 18 when I began to transform the rejection I experienced into a source of pride and power through education.

Coming out never ends. Every time I taught beginning counseling students, we participated in an exercise that asked participants to stand if they had ever been targets of or agents contributing to a continuum of experiences. I always stood when I read aloud the statement, "stand if you have ever been discriminated against because of your sexual orientation." Sometimes I stood alone and sometimes students stood with me. But I always stood and always felt vulnerable when I did. I am aware that the very identity, which opened up doors for me to stand in front of the students, also opens up the possibility that I will be discriminated against by one of them. I have received evaluations, though not many, that I talked too much about LGBT people.

Now as a counselor educator in a doctoral program, I am again aware of the privilege I have in my status as an educator and the stigma of my lesbian identity. I have the opportunity to educate those who will one day teach counselors. This responsibility is one I take seriously as I continue to meet students who grapple with their views of LGBT people. I have bookmarked websites for appropriate terminology and affirmative treatment, and I routinely direct students who use outdated language in their research proposals and clinical practice to these websites. What my former master's and now current doctoral students are not aware of is how their heterosexual privilege permits them to make statements about LGBT people without concern for the impact of those statements. I also have the privilege of integrating my own scholarship into their coursework and standing firmly and compassionately in my lesbian identity as they honestly wrestle with their professional and personal values.

What I have come to learn and experience through my years as a counselor educator is that if more people stand with me, then coming out can be less of an event and less of an opportunity for others to be ignorant of their homoprejudice and heterosexism. For now, however, I am very aware that coming out and labeling myself as *lesbian* gives me power, pride, and relief from the oppression I feel in many aspects of my life. It also makes my life safer through educating others. Education continues to be my best ally.

DISCUSSION QUESTIONS

1. In what way(s) are you privileged by your sexual identity? In what ways are you oppressed? Discuss whether or not a nondominant status can also be a privileged status.

2. What identities do you have that are stigmatized, and how do you manage those identities personally and professionally? How does stigma management affect your belief in yourself and your professional career?

3. How can a stigma identity be transformed through counseling and experience? What does the minority stress theory offer you as a mental health provider in terms of transforming a stigma identity into one of resilience and strength?

4. How are you aware of the impact of your own homoprejudice and heterosexism on others? What might be the significant implications and consequences for colleagues and clients?

5. How can you discuss privilege and stigma with clients and colleagues to deepen their understanding of their own identities? What do you need to learn about yourself and these issues in order to engage in these kinds of conversations?

REFERENCES

American Association for Counseling and Development. (1988). *Ethical standards*. Alexandria, VA: Author.

American Counseling Association. (2014). *American Counseling Association code of ethics*. Alexandria, VA: Author.

American Psychological Association. (2011). Guidelines for psychological practice with lesbian, gay, and bisexual clients. *American Psychologist, 67*(1), 10–42. doi:10.1037/a0024659

Cass, V. (1979). Homosexual identity formation: A theoretical model. *Journal of Homosexuality, 4,* 219–235. doi:10.1300/J082v04n03_01

Fassinger, R. E. (1991). The hidden minority: Issues and challenges in working with lesbian women and gay men. *Counseling Psychologist, 19,* 157–176. doi:10.1177/0011000091192003

Fingerhut, A. W., Peplau, L. A., & Gable, S. L. (2010). Identity, minority stress and psychological well-being among gay men and lesbians. *Psychology & Sexuality, 1*(2), 101–114. doi:10.1080/19419899.2010.484592

Goffman, E. (1963). *Stigma: Notes on the management of spoiled identity.* New York, NY: Simon & Schuster.

Harper, A., Finnerty, P., Martinez, M., Brace, A., Crethar, H. C., Loos, B., . . . Hammer, T. R. (2013). Association for Lesbian, Gay, Bisexual, and Transgender Issues in Counseling competencies for counseling with lesbian, gay, bisexual, queer, questioning, intersex, and ally individuals. *Journal of LGBT Issues in Counseling, 7*(1), 2–43. doi:10.1080/15538605.2013.755444

Logan, C. (1996). Homophobia? No, homoprejudice. *Journal of Homosexuality, 31*(3), 31–53. doi:10.1300/J082v31n03_03

Meisenbach, R. J. (2010). Stigma management communication: A theory and agenda for applied research on how individuals manage moments of stigmatized identity. *Journal of Applied Communication Research, 38*(3), 268–292. doi:10.1080/00909882.2010.490841

Meyer, I. H. (2003). Prejudice, social stress, and mental health in lesbian, gay, and bisexual populations: Conceptual issues and research evidence. *Psychological Bulletin, 129,* 674–697. doi:10.1037/0033-2909.129.5.674

Meyer, I. H. (2013). Prejudice, social stress, and mental health in lesbian, gay, and bisexual populations: Conceptual issues and research evidence. *Psychology of Sexual Orientation and Gender Diversity, 1*(Suppl.), 3–26. doi:10.1037/2329-0382.1.S.3

Morin, S. E. (1997). Heterosexual bias in psychological research on lesbianism and male homosexuality. *American Psychologist, 39,* 247–251. doi.org/10.1037/0003-066X.32.8.629

O'Brien, J. O. (2011). Spoiled group identities and backstage work: A theory of stigma management rehearsals. *Social Psychology Quarterly, 74*(3), 291–309. doi:10.1177/0190272511415389

Riggle, E. D. B., Whitman, J. S., Olson, A., Rostosky, S. S., & Strong, S. (2008). The positive aspects of being a lesbian or gay man. *Professional Psychology: Research and Practice, 39*(2), 210–217. doi:10.1037/0735-7028.39.2.210

SECTION 6

STORIES OF AGEISM, SEXISM, AND HETEROSEXISM

Ageism, sexism, and *heterosexism* are common words used to describe discrimination based on age, gender, and sexual orientation. Jacqueline J. Peila-Shuster and Geri Miller both examine and exemplify the issue of ageism within their respective selections. Carole L. Langer tackles the changing roles of women in post–World War II America and specifically in rural midwestern America. Allison L. Kramer invites us into the story of her first friendship with a lesbian and her subsequent awakening regarding the lack of rights enjoyed by members of the lesbian, gay, bisexual, and transgender (LGBT) community. Heather Trepal ends this section by debunking the myth that men can't be raped.

Peila-Shuster's "The –Ism We May All Face One Day" tells her story of an unfinished journey of self-discovery that required thoughtful exploration and confrontation of youthful privilege and ageist ideology. She includes examples of life circumstances that facilitated greater understanding of, and empathy for, older adults. Peila-Shuster describes ageism as different from other "–isms" in that it is one area that all individuals have the potential to experience and that the twenty-first century will provide further evidence of continued increases in the ageing population.

Miller's "I Almost Quit My Career Today: The Experience of –Isms at Work" complements Peila-Shuster's by providing a focus on the impact of sexism, classism, and ageism in her 40+ year career development history. Miller begins with an exploration of the interaction of oppression and privilege and then elaborates on the three –isms as separate and interacting influential factors on her career development. Throughout the chapter, Miller provides examples of oppression and how she has learned to live with these forces. Her story ends with a description of her unique *privilege package* (White, heterosexual, and able-bodied) and how, as a part of her career, she uses both oppression and privilege to take effective social justice actions.

Langer's "How I Got My Wings: Growing Up Female in the 1950s" speaks to the changing roles of women in post–World War II America and specifically in rural midwestern America. Her narrative describes the struggles of a poor, White female determined "to be who she was and do what she wanted to do." Upon marrying a man at a very young age and raising a family; before becoming a widow and single parent of three and then marrying an abusive husband, Langer fought to free herself from the constraints of the intersectionality of race, sex, and class. Langer asks that contemporary readers ultimately examine their own lives through the lenses of feminist theories to understand that biology need not be the determining factor of one's destiny.

Kramer describes her first friendship with a lesbian and the subsequent awakening she had regarding the lack of rights enjoyed by members of the LGBT community in "Increasing Awareness of Heterosexism and Homophobia: A Personal and Professional Journey." Kramer shares how the friendship was punctuated by the murder of Matthew Shepard in 1998 and how this tragedy enhanced her personal awareness of heterosexist privilege. Kramer uses her awareness of heterosexual privilege and sexism when working with court-ordered domestic violence offenders while drawing upon Scott and Robinson's Key model, based on Helm's White identity model. Her experiences and work with male clients highlight her self-disclosure of heterosexist assumptions and the use of acceptance and humor as therapeutic tools in the exploration of heterosexism and homophobia.

Sexism remains a societal challenge as evidenced by the gender constraints for both men and women and those who identify as neither. In her chapter, " 'Men Can't Be Raped': The Challenge of Sexism in Counseling," Trepal debunks the notion that rape and sexual assault are women's issues; data reports that men are also victims of such events and suffer from the aftermath as well. Her poignant piece looks at the misnomer and also addresses the social construction of gender that includes specific and limiting role expectations. Strategies and considerations for counselors who work with male survivors are provided.

CHAPTER 17

THE–ISM WE MAY ALL FACE ONE DAY

Jacqueline J. Peila-Shuster

BACKGROUND

I am a White, heterosexual, mostly able-bodied, middle-class, middle-aged, Christian female currently serving as a faculty member in higher education. I grew up in a small town along the front range of Colorado where my childhood exposure to diversity consisted primarily of one extended family with Mexican origins. There were also some children with different learning needs and a few with physical disabilities. Certainly there were individuals with varying sexual orientations and gender identities, but at that time and in that place, there was still extreme secrecy surrounding this topic. I thought this was the extent of my exposure to diversity. It turns out that I, like many others, forgot to include the aging population in my consideration of diversity.

My life was fortunate enough to be blessed with grandparents who lived nearby throughout my childhood and adolescence. Along with my parents, these individuals instilled within me countless values and morals. Their strength flows through me to this day. When I was a teen, one of my grandmothers suffered a stroke, which ultimately resulted in her living the remainder of her years in a nursing home. I recall visiting her there and experiencing various fears of, and judgments about, residents and the various disease and disability processes with which they had to cope. My youthful privilege, and lack of understanding and honoring differences, influenced me to decide never to work with "old people in a nursing home."

As it turns out, during my years as an occupational therapist, I found a passion for working with patients who were older adults, and eventually I worked in a nursing home. There I discovered individuals with rich histories and unique lives. I found this to be a very fortunate and enlightening realization—and I also found it sad that I could have ever assumed otherwise. My previous ability to lump "old people" into one categorical stereotype faded.

Throughout my various educational and career transitions, I have been afforded the privilege of continuing to advance my knowledge of aging and my work with individuals as they approach, or are in, retirement. Throughout this time, I have often been pushed into periods of both cognitive and emotional dissonance. The result has been exponential growth in the understanding of my own "age privilege" (Ridgway, 2013). However, I have also come to understand that privilege can often be ellusive, and I am now more willing than ever to admit that, as I learn more, I seem to know less. Thus it is understandable that in the process of writing this chapter, I have continued to find it necessary to confront my privilege and assumptions about aging.

MY STORY

In 2001, I experienced the onset of pain and swelling in both of my feet. Almost two years later, I was diagnosed with rheumatoid arthritis. Although arthritis is the most common chronic condition among older adults, rheumatoid arthritis typically strikes in middle adulthood (National Institute of Arthritis and Musculoskeletal and Skin Diseases, 2016). In my case, it came about in young adulthood.

I have experienced many ups and downs with this disease and have become increasingly aware of what I took for granted in terms of my physical abilities. My choices, independence, and freedom in life are more limited now, a circumstance that often coincides with later adulthood. In fact, while referring to the work of Butler (1969), Gruman (1978) asserted that one of the most significant constraints to come from aging "is the decrease in the range of choice, a loss which results not only from physiological and economic limitations but also from the restrictive norms of a biased culture" (p. 363).

The losses of choice and independence in my life prompted me to reflect back to my previous work as an occupational therapist. There were many times I had suggested to elderly patients that they complete their activities of daily living in a manner that was different than how they had completed them for years. While my intent was to keep patients safe and improve their ability to function independently, I rarely stopped to get their full story before I barged in with my so-called "professional expertise." Rarely did I ever give more than a cursory consideration to the ramifications of taking away their choice in how they completed activities.

Admitting that one cannot do that which one has always done (or in the way one has always done it) is another limitation on independence and freedom of choice. Doing so can also contribute to *stereotype threat*, which is defined as "being at risk of confirming, as self-characteristic, a negative stereotype about one's group" (Steele & Aronson, 1995, p. 797). Stereotype threat occurs when people are in "situations where their performance has the potential to confirm a negative self-relevant stereotype" (Barber & Lee, 2016). Needing assistance or an assistive device to complete an activity is not only a harsh reminder of one's limitations but can also confirm ageist stereotypes about aging. Furthermore, in addition to coping with these stereotypes on a socioemotional level, older adults may also be affected on a performance level. For example, stereotype threat has been found to affect older adults' performance in a variety of areas, including memory (Kang & Chasteen, 2009), subjective ratings of hearing (Barber & Lee, 2016), and performance on simulated driving tasks (Joanisse, Gagnon, & Voloaca, 2013), to name a few.

In trying to help the individuals I worked with move toward their stated goals, I did not take into consideration that the process of getting to those goals was just as important as reaching them. Some of this lack of awareness was because of my privilege of youth and lack of understanding regarding what these individuals were enduring. Obvious to me now is that the process I used needed to include *how* the individual wanted to maintain independence and complete daily living activities; *my* way (based on my age privilege) was not necessarily the *only* way. Integrated into that process should also have been a deeper discussion regarding the various trade-offs relating to independence, personal choice, and safety. Additionally, conversations could have occurred around what it meant to individuals and their sense of identity to lose some of their choices and independence. These discussions could have brought up fears and fallacies surrounding stereotypes that may have then pointed to areas in which individuals might have benefitted from further emotional support.

I was fortunate to work in a facility that understood the necessity of psychoemotional support for older adults. Unfortunately, and too often, if an older adult has an issue of concern, it may be encountered with the belief that it is just what comes with the territory of being old. We can see a tragic example of this with the diagnosis of depression in older adults. According to the National Institute of Mental Health (2003), a contributing factor to the low rates of diagnosis and treatment of depression in older adults is the belief that depression is an acceptable response to other illnesses or hardships that may accompany aging. Unfortunately, too many in our society, including health professionals, do not realize that depression is *not* a normal part of aging. Additionally, according to Levy and Macdonald (2016), ageism and age discrimination continue to be documented elsewhere in regard to the health care of older adults. Levy and Macdonald went on to state that problems that could be treated with medication are instead attributed to natural aging processes, or even ignored, with the belief that older individuals complain more as they age. Thus ageist stereotypes, attitudes, and behaviors affect older adults in numerous respects.

With lessened independence and fewer choices, and constantly coming up against others' assumptions, it would be easy to resign oneself to not mattering anymore. However, that would be a critical loss, not only for the individual but also for all whose lives that person touches and for our society. I was reminded of this when, as a career counselor, I provided a workshop designed to help those entering retirement to identify and promote their strengths. As I discussed the importance of strengths and using them in our lives, I reminded the individuals attending the workshop that we (as in the collective *we* of families, friends, institutions, communities, and the global society) *needed* them. Their work was not done! That moment was palpable; I could actually feel a collective sigh of relief and an emotional connection as the participants realized that I understood their contributions to this world were not completed, and they still mattered. I was also not there to *tell* them what to do but instead to travel alongside them, help them tell their stories, and journey with them to discover their own power to start writing their next life chapter.

In taking my own journey in understanding ageism and in helping others find their paths as they age, I have found that the power of stereotypes is strong. Even in the face of contradicting evidence, some beliefs are so deeply ingrained in the students I teach (and in myself), that, even with new knowledge, it is easy to revert to those beliefs. It is with an eye toward dispelling some of these preconceptions, and misconceptions, that I approached the courses I previously taught on adult development and aging and also the career counseling courses I teach now. Numerous myths and stereotypes of older adults are easily accessed during discussions. Fortunately, subsequent information I have provided regarding the physical, cognitive, and socioemotional development of middle age and aging adults has functioned to reinforce facts and dispel inaccurate beliefs. Over time, I have noted common areas where surprising realities have often caught students off guard. Some of these are the following:

- Alzheimer's is *one* form of dementia and *not* a normative part of aging; it is a disease for which increasing age is the greatest known risk factor (Alzheimer's Association, 2016).
- Older adults do have sex (Lindau et al., 2007).
- While certain aspects of memory, cognition, and learning might diminish, other aspects may hold relatively steady, or even improve, depending on how intelligence constructs are measured and defined (Hoyer & Roodin, 2009; Moody & Sasser, 2012).
- The myth that older adults become grumpy has been debunked. Indeed, the Big Five personality trait of agreeableness may continue to improve through one's 60s (Srivastava, John, Gosling, & Potter, 2003).
- Given the broad and unique range of life experiences each person has, and also differences in genetics, cultures, and contexts, it is important to remember that each individual will experience aging in different ways. However, the stereotypes of older adults do not give voice to this truth.

In spite of the power of stereotypes, there have been many successes in my journey to contest ageism that have left me feeling inspired, hopeful, and motivated. Following are two such examples from former students:

- I started volunteering at the assisted-living facility on which I did [a class assignment]. Yesterday was my first day . . . and what a day it was! . . . One of my main jobs is to talk one-on-one with the residents and get their stories. I get to talk to them about simple things like what their favorite color is or who their favorite person is. But, in those simple questions are pathways to the stories of their lives. Today I talked with a 90-year-old woman who has significant dementia and depression. We talked for an hour in the morning and every time I could get her to smile at an old, happy memory it was like the clouds parted and the sun shone bright and beautiful. (J. Lawrence, former student)
- I went into [my] major wanting to work with kids . . . and taking your class changed my mind. I now want to work with older adults. . . . I think one of the videos you showed toward the beginning of the semester made me definitely change my mind. It had interviews of older adults and one of them said they feel invisible. I think older adults have so much knowledge and so many stories to tell and people in our society really look past that. (E. Knop, former student)

These are just two of many students who shared their stories of honoring older adults, hearing their stories, and *seeing* them rather than letting them remain invisible.

These previous experiences have highlighted some of the processes and encounters that helped unpack my privilege of youth and informed my current professional work as a career counselor and educator. The question remains, though, whether I have personally experienced ageism directed toward myself. The answer is yes. For example, I have engaged in self-directed ageism in which I talk about how "old I am;" in truth, I am classified, chronologically, as middle age. Additionally, I have been faced with the dilemma of stereotype threat in which I sometimes worry about physically performing in ways that will reinforce aging stereotypes (Steele & Aronson, 1995). I have also been met directly with age discrimination in the workplace (see Age Discrimination in Employment Act of 1967). The latter has been couched as, "at *this* point in your career, do you really want to...." Throughout these experiences, I have sought to increase my critical consciousness (Freire, 1970; Martín-Baró, 1994) as I counter the ageist attitudes, beliefs, and practices of myself and others.

THE AGING POPULATION AND AGEISM

My story is that of one person's unfinished journey of self-discovery. Through this journey, I have had to confront myself on numerous occasions about my beliefs and practices. One of the greatest aides in my confrontation of my ageist self has been knowledge. Toward that end, I next provide some information about aging demographics and ageism that may help to provide some impetus and clarity.

AGING DEMOGRAPHICS

The United States, and the world as a whole, is undergoing a tremendous demographic shift. The number of Americans aged 65 and over are projected to represent 20% of the total US population in 2030, compared with 13% in 2010 (Werner, 2011). In 2050, the number of individuals aged 65 and over in the United States is projected to be 83.7 million, which is almost double their 2012 estimated population of 43.1 million (Ortman, Velkoff, & Hogan, 2014). The baby boomers, who began turning 65 in 2011, are primarily responsible for this increase (Ortman et al., 2014).

This demographic shift is not unique to the United States. Indeed, it is one of the major global demographic trends and is driven by a decline in fertility and mortality (United Nations, 2015a). Worldwide, between 2015 and 2030, it is expected that those aged 60 years and over will grow by 56% and will outnumber children ages zero to 9 (United Nations, 2015b). Furthermore, by 2050, people aged 60 and over will outnumber those aged 10 to 24 years. Those at very advanced ages (80 years and over) are also projected to grow worldwide from 125 million in 2015 to 202 million in 2030 and to 434 million in 2050 (United Nations, 2015b).

AGEISM

The introduction of the term *ageism* in 1969 has been attributed to Robert Butler, MD, and is considered to be "a form of systematic stereotyping and discrimination against people simply because they are old" (Butler, 2008, p. 40). He indicated that the consequences of ageism are similar to those of other prejudices in that older people may feel ignored and invisible, may not be taken seriously, and may be patronized. Additionally, they are often the subjects of physical, emotional, social, sexual, and financial abuse (Butler, 2008).

Understanding and addressing ageism is important for reasons that go beyond the practicality of aging demographics. According to Fiske (1998), age is one of the three basic categories of social perception (race and gender are the other two). Furthermore, the category of age is the only one in which all groups of people will join, given an adequate lifespan. Thus ageism is different from other –isms in that all individuals have the potential to experience it. In spite of this, racism and sexism have experienced greater research (North, 2015). For example, when Nelson (2005) completed a PsycINFO database search, he found 3,111 documents for *racism* and 1,385 for *sexism*. The search for *ageism*, though, produced a trivial 294 documents. Today, in my own search of the same database, there were 10,322 results for *racism*, 3,313 for *sexism*, and 1,230 for *ageism*. Although receiving more attention in the literature (Levy & Macdonald, 2016), ageism has generally remained below the radar for a variety of reasons, including a lack of national systematic research initiatives and the possibility that ignoring the study of ageism may be, in and of itself, a bias (North, 2015).

Denouncing negative ageism has also lagged behind (Levy & Macdonald, 2016). Unlike other forms of discrimination, it is extremely commonplace and accepted to see advertisements and greeting cards openly and unabashedly perpetuate ageism. Older individuals are depicted as less able, forgetful, dependent, sexless persons, and, in effect, the message is that aging is to be avoided at all costs. According to Palmore (2001), in many ways, ageism is something people are unaware of because it is a comparatively new and subtle concept. Additionally, North (2015) proposed that ageism may persist because of a variety of factors, including anxiety around death, sociocultural trends that have devalued the roles of societal elders, and generational tensions over distribution of resources.

Not only may one be the target of ageism from others, but it is also likely that one will have internalized negative messages about aging throughout their lives. Levy (2001) defined *implicit ageism* as the thoughts, feelings, and behaviors toward older adults that operate without conscious awareness. He further stated that "every socialized individual who has internalized the age stereotypes of their culture is likely to engage in implicit ageism" (Levy, 2001, p. 578). Indeed, older people may hold negative attitudes about (Nosek, Banaji, & Greenwald, 2002), and "dis-identify" from (Weiss & Lang, 2012), their own chronological age group. Ageism, when self-directed, hinders people from fairly and accurately assessing their own abilities and makes it easy to rationalize unfair assessments that others make (Bodily, 1991).

According to Bodily (1991), the power of ageism comes from how easily we use the concept of age in an unreflective manner. We attribute various limitations, abilities, and characteristics to different chronological ages and then use those collections of information as resources for discriminatory thoughts, behaviors, and practices (Bodily, 1991). How many times have you used your age, or someone else's age, as a descriptor or explanation of various behaviors, without any thought given to whether age is actually a causal, or even correlated, factor?

PROFESSIONAL COUNSELING
GUIDELINES AND STANDARDS

The profession of counseling and counselor education have multiple ethical guidelines and professional standards that address multicultural competence. The American Counseling Association (ACA; 2014) *Code of Ethics* includes core professional values of "enhancing human development *throughout* [emphasis added] the life span" and also "honoring diversity and embracing a multicultural approach, and "promoting social justice" (p. 3). The ethics code goes on to state that "counselors actively attempt to understand the diverse cultural background of the clients they serve. Counselors also explore their own cultural identities and how these affect their values and beliefs about the counseling process" (p. 4).

Promoting client welfare and respecting the dignity of clients are the primary responsibilities of counselors (ACA, 2014). Included in nondiscrimination practices are "age, culture, disability, ethnicity, race, religion/spirituality, gender, gender identity, sexual orientation, marital/partnership status, language preference, socioeconomic status, immigration status, or any basis proscribed by law" (ACA, 2014, p. 9). Counselors need to understand that nondiscrimination also includes not imposing values on clients, and, therefore, they may need to "seek training in areas in which they are at risk of imposing their values onto clients, especially when the counselor's values are inconsistent with the client's goals or are discriminatory in nature" (ACA, 2014, p. 5). In other words, counselors must take care to continue to unpack their privilege and identify how their values and biases may interfere with client welfare and autonomy.

These counseling-profession core values and standards are also addressed in terms of the responsibilities of counselor educators who are called to "infuse material related to multiculturalism/diversity into all courses and workshops" (ACA, 2014, p. 14). Furthermore, counselor educators must "actively infuse multicultural/diversity competency in their training and supervision practices" (ACA, 2014, p. 15).

The ACA *Code of Ethics* is not the only guideline to consult when practicing career counseling and educating or supervising counselors. The National Career Development Association (NCDA; 2015) *Code of Ethics* includes in its professional values the need to support "the worth, dignity, potential, and uniqueness of everyone" as well as the importance of "honoring diversity and promoting social justice" (p. 1). The NCDA ethics code also highlights multicultural and diversity considerations throughout various sections.

Alongside these aforementioned ethics codes, the ACA has endorsed the "Multicultural and Social Justice Counseling Competencies" (Ratts, Singh, Nassar-McMillan, Butler, & McCullough, 2015), and the NCDA (2009) has endorsed the "Minimum Competencies for Multicultural Career Counseling and Development." These competencies promote counselor self-awareness about one's own cultural beliefs, attitudes, assumptions, and points of privilege and oppression. They also endorse an understanding of the client's worldview and cultural context and how the dynamic interaction of the counselor's and the client's cultural contexts impact the relationship. Finally, these competencies address counseling interventions and advocacy through a diversity, equity, and social justice lens.

Unfortunately, I would contend that age may be one area often overlooked in the practice, supervision, and education of multicultural competence. The pervasiveness, general acceptance, and internalization of ageist stereotypes likely contributes to a lack of conscious and deliberate inclusion of age in even the best intended of multicultural and ethical practices.

CONCLUSION

One lesson I have learned (and keep learning) is that admitting I needed help as arthritis changed my life activities was a painful and sometimes embarrassing process. As a result, it is no longer surprising to me when older adults hesitate to ask for assistance or fail to admit that some activities are too much of a struggle. In general, our society does not reward or respect one's needing help or being dependent on others. We focus so much on independence that we ignore, to our detriment, the positive aspects of, and critical need for, interdependence.

I have also realized in my work as a career counselor with clients of a variety of ages that I am not the expert; they are. While trying to be useful to others in working toward their goals, I must consider the process, not just the outcome. I am there to walk alongside them, listen to their stories, and partner with them to help clarify how they want to continue to find their own meaning and mattering in their lives.

Finally, I have also learned that it is easy to buy into the powerful myths and stereotypes around aging. Stereotype threat and negative internalized messages work as oppressive elements. Thus it is important that I work as a catalyst to promote social justice and inclusivity that honors all forms of diversity.

My journey of self-discovery toward ageism, and also other forms of diversity, is ongoing. On numerous occasions I must challenge myself to face my own beliefs, behaviors, and automatic assumptions about people. This, then, allows me to see and hear the individual and honor who that individual is. It is my hope that by reading my story, readers will be encouraged to look within themselves and face their own ageist thoughts, behaviors, and practices. I hope you will learn to question your automatic assumptions and will learn to *see* older adults rather than allow them to remain invisible. It has been my experience that any type of privilege creates abundant blind spots that one must continually seek out, identify, and explore. Reducing ageism is not easy and will take continued effort on personal, community, societal, and global levels.

DISCUSSION QUESTIONS

1. How often do you notice older adults in public? What immediately comes to your mind when you see an older adult? Explain.
2. What do you fear most about aging? Are your fears based on facts or stereotypes? Explain.
3. What will you have to give up if you stop believing _____ [stereotype about aging]? What pressures do you have not to give up this stereotype? How might these pressures be related to oppression?

4. How have you internalized ageist stereotypes and directed them toward yourself and others? How have these stereotypes led to forms of oppression in your life experiences or the life experiences of others?

5. What is one thing you can and will do to move forward in your journey of understanding and contesting ageism?

REFERENCES

Age Discrimination in Employment Act of 1967, 29 U.S.C. § 621–§ 63.

Alzheimer's Association. (2016). What is Alzheimer's? Retrieved from http://www.alz.org/alzheimers_disease_what_is_alzheimers.asp

American Counseling Association. (2014). *2014 ACA code of ethics*. Alexandria, VA: Author.

Barber, S. J., & Lee, S. R. (2016). Stereotype threat lowers older adults' self-reported hearing abilities. *Gerontology, 62*, 81–85. doi:10.1159/000439349

Bodily, C. L. (1991). "I have no opinions. I'm 73 years old!": Rethinking ageism. *Journal of Aging Studies, 5*, 245–264.

Butler, R. (1969). Age-ism: Another form of bigotry. *The Gerontologist, 9*, 243–245.

Butler, R. N. (2008). *The longevity revolution: The benefits and challenges of living a long life*. New York, NY: Public Affairs.

Fiske, S. T. (1998). Stereotyping, prejudice, and discrimination. In D. T. Gilbert, S. T. Fiske, & G. Lindzey (Eds.), *Handbook of social psychology* (4th ed., Vol. 2, pp. 357–411). New York, NY: McGraw-Hill.

Freire, P. (1970). *Pedagogy of the oppressed*. New York, NY: Continuum.

Gruman, G. (1978). Cultural origins of present-day "age-ism": The modernization of the life cycle. In S. F. Spicker, K. M. Woodward, & D. D. Van Tassel (Eds.), *Aging and the elderly: Humanistic perspectives in gerontology* (pp. 359–387). Atlantic Highlands, NJ: Humanities Press.

Hoyer, W. J., & Roodin, P. A. (2009). *Adult development and aging* (6th ed.). New York, NY: McGraw-Hill.

Joanisse, M., Gagnon, S., & Voloaca, M. (2013). The impact of stereotype threat on the simulated driving performance of older drivers. *Accident Analysis and Prevention, 50*, 530–583.

Kang, S. K., & Chasteen, A. L. (2009). The moderating role of age-group identification and perceived threat on stereotype threat among older adults. *The International Journal of Aging and Human Development, 69*, 201–220.

Levy, B. R. (2001). Eradication of ageism requires addressing the enemy within. *The Gerontologist, 41*(5), 578–579.

Levy, S. R., & Macdonald, J. L. (2016). Progress on understanding ageism. *Journal of Social Issues, 72*, 5–25. doi:10.1111/josi.12153

Lindau, S. T., Schumm, L. P., Laumann, E. O., Levinson, W., O'Muircheartaigh, C. A., & Waite, L. J. (2007). A national study of sexuality and health among older adults in the United States. *The New England Journal of Medicine, 357*, 762–774.

Martín-Baró, I. (1994). *Writings for a liberation psychology*. Edited by A. Aron & S. Corne. Cambridge, MA: Harvard University Press.

Moody, H. R., & Sasser, J. R. (2012). *Aging: Concepts and controversies* (7th ed.). Thousand Oaks, CA: SAGE.

National Career Development Association. (2009). *Minimum competencies for multicultural career counseling and development*. Broken Arrow, OK: Author.

National Career Development Association. (2015). *NCDA code of ethics*. Broken Arrow, OK: Author.

National Institute of Arthritis and Musculoskeletal and Skin Diseases. (2016). *Handout on health: Rheumatoid arthritis.* Retrieved from http://www.niams.nih.gov/Health_Info/Rheumatic_Disease/default.asp

National Institute of Mental Health. (2003). *Older adults: Depression and suicide facts* [Fact sheet]. Retrieved from http://www.nimh.nih.gov/health/publications/older-adults-depression-and-suicide-facts-fact-sheet/index.shtml

Nelson, T. D. (2005). Ageism: Prejudice against our feared future self. *Journal of Social Issues, 61,* 207–221.

North, M. S. (2015). Ageism stakes its claim in the social sciences. *Journal of the American Society of Aging, 39*(3), 29–33.

Nosek, B. A., Banaji, M. R., & Greenwald, A. G. (2002). Harvesting implicit group attitudes and beliefs from a demonstration web site. *Group Dynamics: Theory, Research, and Practice, 6,* 101–115.

Ortman, J. M., Velkoff, V. A., & Hogan, H. (2014). *An aging nation: The older population in the United States* (P25-1140). Washington, DC: US Census Bureau. Retrieved from https://www.census.gov/prod/2014pubs/p25-1140.pdf

Palmore, E. (2001). The ageism survey: First findings. *The Gerontologist, 41,* 572–575.

Ratts, M. J., Singh, A. A., Nassar-McMillan, S., Butler, S. K., & McCullough, J. R. (2015). *Multicultural and social justice counseling competencies.* Retrieved from http://www.multiculturalcounseling.org/index.php?option=com_content&view=article&id=205:amcd-endorses-multicultural-and-social-justice-counseling-competencies&catid=1:latest&Itemid=123

Ridgway, S. (2013, January 24). 20+ examples of age privilege. *everyday feminism.* Retrieved from http://everydayfeminism.com/2013/01/20-examples-of-age-privilege

Srivastava, S., John, O. P., Gosling, S. D., & Potter, J. (2003). Development of personality in early and middle adulthood: Set like plaster or persistent change? *Journal of Personality and Social Psychology, 84,* 1041–1053.

Steele, C. M., & Aronson, J. (1995). Stereotype threat and the intellectual test performance of African Americans. *Journal of Personality and Social Psychology, 69,* 797–811.

United Nations, Department of Economic and Social Affairs, Population Division. (2015a). *World population ageing 2015—highlights* (ST/ESA/SER.A/368). Retrieved from http://www.un.org/en/development/desa/population/publications/pdf/ageing/WPA2015_Highlights.pdf

United Nations, Department of Economic and Social Affairs, Population Division. (2015b). *World population prospects: The 2015 revision, key findings and advance tables* (Working Paper No. ESA/P/WP.241). Retrieved from http://esa.un.org/unpd/wpp/publications/files/key_findings_wpp_2015.pdf

Weiss, D., & Lang, F. R. (2012). "They" are old but "I" feel younger: Age-group dissociation as a self-protective strategy in old age. *Psychology and Aging, 27,* 153–163.

Werner, C. A. (2011). *The older population: 2010.* Retrieved from US Census Bureau website https://www.census.gov/prod/cen2010/briefs/c2010br-09.pdf

CHAPTER 18

I ALMOST QUIT MY CAREER TODAY

The Experience of –Isms at Work

Geri Miller

The title of this chapter captures the frustration of living with *sexism* and elucidates how sexism has woven itself throughout the tapestry of my life, picked up the specific strands of oppression of *classism* (as paired with socioeconomic status and level of poverty) and *ageism* as my life has evolved. As a female professional (counselor, professor), I have experienced sexism throughout my career; more recently, as I have aged into my 60s, I have experienced ageism. At times, the sexism has become so draining that I found myself in a place of wanting to quit my career.

One absurd example of my frustration occurred years ago. As I was headed to the campus library, I had decided that if a videotape I needed to check out for a class was not there, I was going to quit my career—I was seriously lost in my frustration as a female professional. Luckily, the videotape was available for checkout and I did not quit. The absolute absurdity of the sexism I was experiencing was expressed in the absurdity of my willingness to let go of my career in such a flippant manner. Yet, at that moment, I felt I simply could not take one more hurdle, frustration, or barrier.

That decision point was not a result of a specific sexist incident; rather, it was the culmination of several years in the academic world where my voice felt repeatedly silenced by the covert, and occasionally overt, actions of others and a system dominated by White, male professionals (Twale & DeLuca, 2008). Though this particular example was extreme, similar decision points have emerged throughout my career during times when I felt I could not take any more and simply would rather leave that career than continue to face such ongoing prejudice.

My experiences are not unique. Women's work experiences are shaped by discrimination and sexism (Grossman & Chester, 2013), and classism and ageism are common in the

United States (Isenberg, 2016; Nelson, 2016). In this chapter, I examine the interaction of sexism, classism, and ageism as they have influenced my career development. The chapter ends with a discussion of privilege. I discuss my privileges because they are and were interwoven with the oppression I have experienced. At times, these privileges have softened or temporarily marginalized the discrimination I have experienced in various circumstances.

As a Native American elder has stated, "Stories teach us how to live" (Miller, 2015). My story is based on my socialization experience as a woman; and as Sue and Sue (2016) report, "Ongoing socialization experiences affect women's self-perceptions" (p. 727). My hope, then, is that my self-perception of my messy, human story as a woman may provide others with ideas about living life fully in the midst of oppression or, at the very least, provide living options readers can choose to embrace, modify, or reject.

OPPRESSION AND PRIVILEGE

My story is a mixed bag of oppression and privilege. I grew up as a White female, the youngest of eight children, in extreme poverty. Again, my experience is not unique. The United States has one of the highest child poverty rates in the developed world (UNICEF, 2012). My father was an alcoholic and died of alcoholism when I was 16; my mother used welfare benefits to support the family beginning when I was about 8 years old. Once again, this experience is not atypical, as women are more likely to live in poverty than men (Sue & Sue, 2016). I attended a Missouri Synod Lutheran parochial school from kindergarten through the eighth grade, transferred to a large junior high school for one year, and then transferred to a large high school for the next three years.

I state all of these facts because, from the beginning of my life, I experienced a mix of oppression and privilege. Regarding oppression, I was poor and female, came from "the wrong side of the tracks," and was viewed as "poor, white trash." *White trash* was a term used in print in 1821 and that became popular in the 1850s with the phrase *poor, white trash* used to describe those individuals who pushed People of Color out of the way of Andrew Jackson's funeral processional (Isenberg, 2016). I was born into the lowest class of the United States class system, a country with class barriers that make the American dream impossible to achieve for those in the lowest class (Isenberg, 2016). Further, there was the additional discrimination associated with my father's alcoholism.

Even with these socioeconomic barriers, however, I was able to achieve the "American dream." But why or how did that happen? In part, the answer to this question is related to privilege. I am Caucasian, heterosexual, and able-bodied. In the next section, I sort out the pieces in this mixed bag of oppression and privilege to elucidate the aspects of each.

OPPRESSION: SEXISM AND CLASSISM

I was born in 1955. Growing up, I had few career options open to me from the beginning; most women of my class and background were waitresses, secretaries, or wives and mothers. However, I was labeled as "bright" and did well in school. My parochial-school classes were small, and my teachers, for the most part, were kind. No matter what they knew of our families or our social class levels, my teachers encouraged each of us to do the best we could and help one another learn—each classroom learned as a community. For example, if one student was good at reading, as I was, I was expected to help another student in the class learn to read, without regard to gender or class. We were taught to play to our strengths scholastically and strengthen our weaknesses through collaboration and support.

Encouragement from teachers took different forms as I entered public schools, but it was always present for me in this small, Midwestern farming/tourist town. For example, my high school chemistry teacher pulled me aside after I took the Scholastic Achievement Test. He told me my scores indicated that I was smart enough to be whatever I wanted to be. That brief conversation has stayed with me to this day.

Most of my teachers taught me that, by working hard and relying on others, I could face barriers that arose on my career development path. A few teachers were not so supportive. From elementary school and beyond, some ridiculed me and sent both direct and indirect messages that I would not prosper in life, that I was a burden on society because I was being raised on welfare and came from poor, white trash. These discouraging, negative, cruel messages were echoed outside the educational settings and in my personal life.

As I became a teenager, the limited career options presented to me (i.e., waitress, secretary, mother) became more clear, and I became worried, knowing I would not be able to keep my mouth shut in any of these roles long enough to survive them. I was never a female who needed to find her voice. Stories (and an audiotape) from my childhood are evidence that I spoke my mind from the moment I could talk. I have been told that, at age 3, a week after I had learned how to open a door by turning the doorknob, I turned to another little girl standing at a door with me and said, "What's the matter? Don't you know how to open a door?"

A limited career view was strongly paralleled in my family. My father had not finished elementary school, and my mother had completed through the eighth grade. Both of my parents came from poverty and were forced to work from young ages. My father was a thwarted country-western musician who supported his family by painting houses. He deserted our family when I was about 8 years old. While my mother valued education, she had mixed reactions to my obtaining the education that she had so desperately wanted for herself. As I understood her story, she had wanted to go to high school, but her parents made her leave home when she was 14, and she became a housekeeper in order to feed and provide for herself. She was proud of my accomplishments, but she also sent discouraging messages to me. My siblings did not complete college: My sisters became secretaries and eventually married, while my brothers became members of the working class—two of them had attended college but both attended for less than one year. Like my mother, my siblings recognized my intelligence—my mother would ask me to spell words for her, and one of my older sisters asked for my help with studying for exams. Even so, they did not see me as having a career beyond those few options available to a female raised in poverty.

Research indicates that a woman develops and has her life experiences within her relationships (Miller, 1986). Consistent with that, it is through my relationships that I surmounted many of the barriers before me. In addition to my academic success, I was adept at observing others, learning and engaging in social behavior. I had a tendency to smile when I met people (and teeth that looked like I had had braces) and an affable personality, along with a desire to learn and a willingness to work hard. These traits invited a significant event that happened to me in the fifth grade. A wealthy (I now know them to be middle-class) family with a daughter my age moved to town and attended my parochial school. Because of my traits, this family essentially adopted me as a playmate for their daughter and also took a personal interest in me. They took me to restaurants and taught me how to eat with the proper silverware, exposed me to waterskiing, and provided various opportunities for me to socialize with middle-class individuals. Furthermore, when I was a fifth-grader, they introduced me to the idea of college. I remember telling them, "I don't have any money to go to college," but they told me there were scholarships and grants available for people like me. I had never heard of such a thing and did not really believe them, but their insistence over the next few years introduced college as a possibility to me, and that possibility stayed with me. I continued to do well in school and graduated eleventh out of my class of several hundred students. I won the small-town scholarship, which was awarded in increasing amounts to one person over four years. These monies, in combination with the funding from a state school, allowed me to go to college and expand my career paths beyond those of secretary, waitress, or mother.

The poverty from which I came was so extreme that the financial-aid officer at my college, upon our first meeting, told me there was no way my family could have lived on the income we had reported. He was convinced my mother and I had lied. I naively and calmly kept stating that we had accurately reported our income until he eventually believed me, and I was awarded the financial-aid package from the school.

The first day of college orientation, the speaker told us to look at who was sitting to our left, then to look at who was sitting at our right. He then told us that, among the three of us, only one would graduate from college. That speech inspired me to be the one of the three who would graduate. In college, I had a great time taking classes of interest to me. But during my sophomore year, three of my female dormitory friends told me I needed to choose a major because eventually the money would run out, and I needed to have a job. With this in mind, my friends helped me search for a major that would accept most of my classes, and we came upon social work. This major seemed to fit me, as well, because I liked working with people and knew from previous job experiences that I needed a job that did not have a time clock. My friends and I were right: I loved my classes and graduated with a degree that helped me obtain a job in social work.

I learned to listen to these positive, encouraging voices. As I moved from my master's program into my doctoral program, my White, male professors told me they did not know what it was like to be a woman getting her doctoral degree. They encouraged me to be aware of sexism and to "get up one more time when you're knocked down." It was this belief in me, from my teachers, that stayed with me through the –isms (i.e., sexism, classism, ageism) I have experienced and continue to experience in my professional career. I had to force myself to ignore the discouraging words, no matter the source, and to hear only the supportive words of my teachers: "You can be whatever you want to be; get up one more time when you're knocked down."

OPPRESSION: SEXISM

Overall, most people viewed my career as being a choice I made until I married and had children—this was openly stated to me many times. That view was followed by the stated, and also the unstated, expectation that once I married I would leave my career and focus on maintaining a marriage and raising children. These socialization pressures resulted from cultural values (Chrisler, 2013). When I did not marry right away, people were confused and thought maybe there was something wrong with me that no one would want to marry me, or maybe there was some reason I had remained single (i.e., I was a closet lesbian).

Sometime during the first five years of my work life, I came to be viewed as a career woman who would never marry or have children. I do not know how, when, or why others' perspective of me shifted, but I noticed subtle changes in the way I was treated; for example, people began to refer to me as "career woman." When I did marry, the perspective shifted back to the expectation that I would now have children and leave my career. Instead, I did marry, continued in my professional career as a mental health professional, obtained degrees (master's and doctorate), and never had children. As I write this, many memories come to mind where, professionally and personally, people tried to peg me into a category, pressure me into certain behavior, and predict my professional development based on my gender and marital status.

Although the profession I had chosen was a female-dominated one, I was exposed to sexism from the beginning of my career. Many of the mental health field administrators I worked for were male, and although some were encouraging to my career development, others were not. My career development was punctuated by both blatant and insidious sexism. One example of the blatant experiences was a handshake I received from a male helping professional visiting our women's inpatient facility (when shaking my hand, he moved his middle finger back and forth in the palm of my hand). When I told the other female counselors how he had shaken my hand upon leaving the facility, they were livid and told me that was a way of saying he wanted to have sex with me. They proceeded to call his agency and demand he receive consequences for his behavior. I was shocked by the sexism I had experienced, and I felt cared for by my senior female professionals who modeled how to handle such behavior.

Those of us who have experienced sexism know it can be difficult to specifically name actions as sexist because of the insidious nature of discrimination. Subtle sexism emerged in my counseling career (which preceded my higher education career) along avenues such as wages. For example, I once asked a counseling director, "Help me understand how I am paid less than my male colleague while I have more degrees." The director paused for an awkward moment and then continued the conversation. I did not lose my job (fortunately), but, unfortunately, he did not give me a pay increase. Although I continued to experience sexism at this agency, I believe I was successful in that I had named and challenged the sexism I was experiencing. I realized then that sexism would be a constant factor in my career and that I needed to learn how to cope without becoming bitter or outraged with frustration to the extent that the sexism impacted the quality of my life and poisoned me as a person. I had to learn how to persevere with my career despite my experiences with sexism and to stay calm in its throes. Over time, I adopted a calmer, quiet, firm response style to hidden sexism.

The opening story of this chapter, wherein my professional career depended on the availability of a library videotape, was the first choice point I remember as a professor where my denial regarding sexism was broken: I had believed that holding a doctorate in a higher education setting would protect me from the sexist experiences I had experienced as a mental health professional with a bachelor's or master's degree. However, sexism continues to emerge on a frequent basis for me, especially in the area of setting boundaries. Women are socialized to take care of others, to be nurturers and caregivers (Sue & Sue, 2016). I believe this socialization naturally results in both the woman and others in her life expecting her to take care of them in both professional and personal contexts. Professors and students have frequently met my setting boundaries with anger and frustration. I also have often been told by faculty and students, "You have good boundaries." The frustration embedded in that comment comes in response to my setting limits in some typical way (e.g., office hours, accessibility by e-mail, phone, appointments). After years of hearing this type of comment, I asked male professionals how often they hear a comment about their boundaries. They responded by saying they never or almost never received such feedback.

Recently a new female professor said, "I want to learn about setting boundaries from you." I said, without hesitation, "I will teach you all I know, but get ready for people to be angry at you." I believe the anger I experience from individuals when I set boundaries is a projection on me as a professional that is based on my gender. As a woman, I am often expected to drop everything and prioritize the needs of others; when I hold other priorities, individuals tend to respond with anger and frustration.

OPPRESSION: SEXISM AND AGEISM

The interaction of sexism and ageism has been described as a double jeopardy for women (Barnett, 2005). Sue and Sue (2016) report that, as women age, they face additional barriers such as age discrimination at work and being made invisible. Overall, however, research shows that older workers can outperform younger workers (or at least show no performance differences), and that hidden workplace ageism can operate in negative attitudes toward older workers, resulting in discrimination (Malinen & Johnston, 2013).

Sexism currently intersects with ageism in my career in two main areas: technology and retirement. Organizations increasingly rely on information technology (Coles & Hodgkinson, 2008). I have found this to be true in my higher education career over the past 26 years (i.e., online syllabi/classes). Also, computer use and comfort have been associated with age, as people from Generation X (i.e., my students) and baby boomers (i.e., me) have experienced different socialization with technology (Elias, Smith, & Barney, 2012). Therefore, it makes sense that because I am female and "old," I find that many individuals, particularly younger faculty and students, believe I do not know much about technology. They are surprised to learn that 13 years ago I began paying a professional computer consultant to give me computer lessons for a minimum of seven hours a week so I could avoid drowning in my technological ignorance. I typically find that individuals assume I do not know much about computers or technology and that if I do not engage in some technological avenue (e.g., correspond with people on Facebook, use a specific technology form in my teaching), it is out of ignorance rather than choice. This is also an area where I find some positive aspects of ageism, especially among young people raised on technology who feel sorry for me. As a result of their assumptions about my technological ignorance and inexperience, they help me solve technology problems I experience in the classroom or in my office in a kind, patient manner.

Dennis and Thomas (2007) described two types of ageism: *personal ageism*, which is based on an individual's biased attitude toward an older person, and *unintentional ageism*, practiced by the perpetrator who does not recognize the bias. I believe these are two forms of ageism I commonly experience in a higher education setting—for example, when individual faculty and students make assumptions about me regarding technology without intending to be biased. Perceived discrimination based on factors such as sex and age can result in withdrawal that is physical (e.g., intention to quit) or psychological (e.g., burnout and lowered engagement; Volpone & Avery, 2013).

Retirement issues are common among older individuals (Sue & Sue, 2016); older professors, such as myself, may sense a pressure from others (e.g., administrators, faculty, students) to retire. I have now aged out of the expectation that I would have children and aged into the expectation that I will soon retire. As with the pressure to have children—a pressure that I felt almost daily, with the suggestion that something was wrong with me for not having children—the pressure has now shifted to an almost daily questioning about when I am going to retire. My husband and I recently chanced upon a professional woman whom I had not seen in a few years. Within the first minute of our conversation, she asked when I was going to retire (she is not of retirement age). I told her my most recent response to such questions, which is, "I like making money, so I have no plans to retire." She did not ask me any more questions or offer unsolicited advice (e.g., "You should retire"; "You should retire because you can"; "You must be tired of working so you should retire"); rather, she told me that my reasons to continue working made sense.

It was the first time my husband had heard me practice my recent response to the seemingly never-ending questions about retirement I have answered for the past five years. He said my response was effective possibly because of the capitalistic society in which we live. The assumption seems to be that, since I am old enough to retire, I should—this is another formula for living, much like the formulas that have been suggested to dictate my career options, the extent of my professional boundaries, and whether I have children. In utter frustration, I recently told a friend that I have never had a break from the criticism of why I work, why I have a career. The criticism has only shifted from being solely due to my gender and is now due to my being both female and "old." Few individuals understand and respect my hope to "die in my chair," just as few understood and respected my choice not to have children. I believe that the lack of understanding and respect is based on sexism and ageism. Both forms of discrimination have silenced the love of my career (counseling, teaching, research/writing).

PRIVILEGE

Regarding privilege, I have created a phrase, *privilege package*. The use of this phrase is meant to encourage each of us to examine whether we have privileges in an area that may help us persevere despite the oppression we experience in other areas. The privileges I have that temper or negate the oppression related to gender, class, and age are to be White, heterosexual, and able-bodied. This privilege package was interwoven with the oppression I had and have in my life. From the beginning, this package of privilege allowed me advantages that to this day I may minimize or miss in terms of its impact on my professional development. In my early childhood, even though I was considered poor, white trash, I was given educational opportunities that may not have been available to me if I had not been heterosexual or White. Oppressive, discriminatory practices would have likely been more extensive in terms of depth and breadth and possibly more blatant. Further, these inherent advantages in the privilege package continue to work in my favor professionally.

It is easier to note the privileges of being heterosexual or White by describing professional experiences that show the absence of the discrimination. Regarding sexuality, when I was interviewed for a university teaching position, I wanted to provide the interviewers with evidence that I could effectively work across differences with others. In the course of describing the different groups I had led during my doctoral internship, I mentioned that in some groups I was considered the minority. For example, on the medical side of the campus, I, a nonmedical professional, had led a communications enhancement group for medical personnel, and in another area of the campus, I, a heterosexual, had led a gay/lesbian support group (note that this was the terminology used at that time). While there was no noticeable reaction to my description of being a leader in the medical group, I felt, and I believe I heard, a sigh of relief that I was not lesbian when I described my leadership of working across differences in the gay/lesbian support group. That reaction surprised and shocked me. All of this exchange was unspoken but palpable.

Another incident regarding White privilege happened when I taught for a short time on a Lakota Sioux reservation. I was traveling alone across the reservation and stopped in a convenience store to buy some items. I was in line behind a number of male and female Lakota Sioux customers. The White clerk did not look up during her exchanges with her customers, except quite briefly at the end of an encounter. She greeted all of the customers in the same flat, nonemotional, unfriendly tone, asking, "Can I help you?" and at the end of the exchange would look at the customer. Before waiting on me, she had turned her back at the end of her exchange with the Lakota Sioux customer. I received the same greeting in the same manner as the previous customers. My dialect was no different than the other customers when I stated what I needed. The change came when she looked at me as she charged me for the item. Suddenly she visibly relaxed, smiled, and added a friendly comment, "Have a nice day." Again, the reason for the shift was unspoken yet palpable. I ascertained that my skin color drew a more respectful, caring manner from her. This message of relief from her that I was White sickened me inside with the awareness that simply my skin color resulted in my receiving better treatment.

Regarding the privilege of being able-bodied, I have not had to compensate my resources in terms of time, energy, or money to help me survive on a daily basis in response to such barriers. A few years ago, when I was almost killed in a car accident and a few weeks later broke my toes, my physical injuries and crutches made me acutely aware of the privilege of being healthy as I walked painfully on crutches across the mountain campus where I teach.

These stories note how the presence of aspects of my privilege package changed the treatment of me and the opportunities I received based on my privileges. These stories say that privilege hinges on both what I am and what I am not and that, like oppression, there is nothing I initially do that determines the treatment I receive. That means there is probably an ocean of opportunities I receive that I am not aware of as a result of the privileges inherent in being viewed as acceptable. Being White, heterosexual, and physically able softened or marginalized the discrimination I have experienced and continue to experience. The absence of these privileges would have increased the amount of discrimination I experienced (experience), and the presence of any additional discriminatory factors would have created even more barriers in my life because they would interact with and intensify the discrimination I experienced regarding gender, class, and age.

SOCIAL JUSTICE ACTIONS

Based on my experiences with oppression and privilege, how can I take effective action in response to social injustice? First, as stated earlier, I can name the wrong out loud. Such action is quite powerful, especially when it is done in a calm, firm manner. Second, I can listen carefully to and believe the stories of individuals as they present their unique expressions of oppression in their lives, and I can provide a safe place where they can process their experiences. Third, I can send a message to oppressed individuals that they can use whatever parts of my privilege package that can be helpful to them. If appropriate, I may say, "Use my _____-ness" (my privilege) in ways that can open doors and confront discrimination directly or indirectly. In doing so, I might serve as a link that breaks the barriers down for that individual. Some examples in my role as professor may assist the reader in understanding this approach. With regard to race, I have told Students of Color, "I can teach you how to present your information in a format that will enhance this specific audience (i.e., White, male) will hear your message clearly." With sexual orientation, I have provided a transgender student the opportunity to present with me on a panel at a national counseling conference on effective counseling practices with this population. With physical abilities, I have an opening class exercise in my multicultural counseling class that requires students on the first day of class to pair up, walk across campus to the nursing department, and choose to be either able-bodied or alternating in the pair who uses the device (i.e., wheelchair, crutches, slings) to return to the classroom and obtain their syllabus. On the return trip, each pair of students needs to use a restroom, buy a beverage, and retrieve an item they imagine they have left on a campus bus.

CONCLUSION

As helping professionals, we need to create opportunities for dialogue and community in our work settings. I have written a more in-depth description of dialogue and community in the helping professionals' workplace (Miller, 2015). I invite this type of community in the state and national trainings I conduct with counselors and also in classroom settings with undergraduate and graduate students. I state openly:

- We are in a democracy, and we can disagree in a civilized manner with one another.
- We need to live in community with one another, and we can achieve this through dialogue that bridges differences that we have. We need to create that community and openness through dialogue in this training/classroom setting.
- We need to remember that, no matter what we are, it means we are not something else; therefore, all of us need to learn how to work across differences. For example, as a woman, I do not know what it is like to be a male.
- Each person's story is unique, no one in a population is just like everyone else in that group, and each of us is a blend of differences.
- Although some individuals are intent on being discriminatory, many of us live in fear of being discriminatory, which means that we may defend the areas in which we have a fear of being labeled an "–ist." However, this fear may cause us to miss the opportunity to learn about ourselves and to stop our unknown involvement of discriminatory practices. We need to learn to name the "wrongness" in ourselves and to change our behavior and also to forgive ourselves.

I believe that each of us can make a difference in the world. Sue and Sue (2016) state that mental health professionals, such as counselors, need to be prepared to take stands on social justice issues. Each of us can find our own way of taking social-justice stands for ourselves and others that promote the health and safety of all human beings with whom we have contact. We can be a part of creating peace within and between ourselves.

DISCUSSION QUESTIONS

1. In your personal and/or professional life (this includes being a student), how have you experienced *oppression*?
2. In your personal and/or professional life (this includes being a student), how have you experienced *privilege*?
3. What components make up your *privilege package* (if you have one)? What actions can you take to be a part of naming social injustices?
4. How can you create safe environments for individuals to talk about privilege, oppression, and discrimination?
5. How can you use your privilege package to assist oppressed individuals?

REFERENCES

Barnett, R. C. (2005). Ageism and sexism in the workplace. *Generations, 29,* 25–30.

Chrisler, J. C. (2013). Womanhood is not as easy as it seems: Femininity requires both achievement and restraint. *Psychology of Men & Masculinity, 14,* 117–120.

Coles, R., & Hodgkinson, G. P. (2008). A psychometric study of information technology risks in the workplace. *Risk Analysis, 28,* 81–93.

Dennis, H., & Thomas, K. (2007). Ageism in the workplace. *Generations, 31,* 84–89.

Elias, S. M., Smith, W. L., & Barney, C. E. (2012). Age as a moderator of attitude toward technology in the workplace: Work motivation and overall job satisfaction. *Behaviour & Information Technology, 31,* 453–467.

Grossman, H. Y., & Chester, N. L. (2013). *The experience and meaning of work in women's lives.* New York, NY: Psychology Press.

Isenberg, N. (2016). *White trash.* New York, NY: Viking.

Malinen, S., & Johnston, L. (2013). Workplace ageism: Discovering hidden bias. *Experimental Aging Research, 39,* 445–465.

Miller, G. (2015). *Learning the language of addiction counseling.* Hoboken, NJ: Wiley.

Miller, J. B. (1986). *Toward a new psychology of women.* Boston, MA: Beacon Press.

Nelson, T. D. (2016). Promoting healthy aging by confronting ageism. *American Psychologist, 71,* 276–282.

Sue, D.W., & Sue, D. (2016). *Counseling the culturally diverse: Theory and practice* (7th ed.). Hoboken, NJ: John Wiley.

Twale, D. J., & DeLuca, B. M. (2008). *Faculty incivility.* Hoboken, NJ: John Wiley.

UNICEF. (2012). Tens of millions of children living in poverty in the world's richest countries. Retrieved from http://www.unicef.org/media/media_62521.html

Volpone, S. D., & Avery, D. R. (2013). It's self-defense: How perceived discrimination promotes employee withdrawal. *Journal of Occupational Health Psychology, 18,* 430–448.

CHAPTER 19

HOW I GOT MY WINGS

Growing Up Female in the 1950s

Carol L. Langer

MY STORY

Post–World War II life was initially a period of peace. Rosie the Riveter had made an impact on the roles available and accepted for women, but the impact was not felt equally across the nation. Housewives on television vacuumed in pearls, dresses, and high heels, kissing their husbands goodbye as they raced off to work in suits and ties, swinging briefcases. In remote and poverty-stricken areas, the traditional roles for men and women (sans pearls and heels) were still the perceived norm. It wasn't too long until the Cold War began, and in addition to the typical responsibilities of approved roles for women, women and girls in those same areas were charged with making sure there were food, water, blankets, a first-aid kit, a transistor radio, and a flashlight in whatever space they used as a bomb shelter. I was born during this period, and my identity today officially includes baby boomer. I was poor, but I did not know it. I knew my roles as a girl were limited, but I did not understand then why. Now I can begin to explain my experiences based on my awareness of intersectionality (Cho, Crenshaw, & McCall, 2013; Ramsay, 2013; Stoetzler, 2016).

I was born and raised on a farm. At age 5, I had the task of gathering eggs; my brother, at 13 years old, was already driving a tractor, helping in the fields, and doing chores such as milking the cows, feeding the pigs, and taking care of the horses. At age 7, I was allowed to cook for the wheat harvest and hay crews. I cooked the one meal I knew how to cook: pork and beans with ground beef in them, canned peas, bread and butter, and a "scratch" German chocolate cake. My other chores included cleaning house, doing the laundry, helping with meal preparations, and babysitting for three neighbor children who were only slightly younger than me. I recall wishing that I could drive a tractor, milk the cows, and take care of the horses because I would much rather have been outside than inside. However, my father refused to teach me how to drive a tractor, saying, "That's man's work." It is true that I never saw a woman driving a tractor during my youth. I believe my father practiced benevolent sexism, which can be defined as unequal treatment based on sex and wherein men tend to be viewed as strong and women as weak (Connelly & Heesacker, 2012). Benevolent sexism is sometimes viewed as providing protection to a woman or girl, shielding her from the harshness of a task. It is not an intentional way of keeping someone down, but it does have real consequences, such as denial of an opportunity to increase certain skills.

In 1967, when I graduated from high school, the career options my parents approved were secretary, nurse, or teacher. I wanted to go to college and eventually become a doctor. I had been visited by a recruiter for a secretarial school when I was going into my junior year in high school. My mother was thrilled that I would have scholarships, and the education/training would have been almost free. I do not know what made me so assertive at that time, but I refused that option. I did not want to be a secretary. I wanted to be a doctor. My mother threw me out of the house when I refused to go to secretarial school. I turned to some distant relatives who had set aside $500 for my college education, which would have paid for a year of my college in 1967. But my relatives also limited my options by refusing to allow me access to the money unless they approved of my major. And becoming a doctor was still not one of the options.

In fact, I graduated in 1971 from the nearby teacher's college with a four-year degree and owed only $900 in student loans. My father had persuaded my mother to allow me to return home. He did not agree with my mother's actions, but he did agree with and reinforce my career options. So, by default, I chose teaching as my occupation. My father's reasoning was that "if the children become sick, you can be with them; and you'll have all summer to spend with them." He and my mother both had eighth-grade educations. My brother, who also received $500 from our relatives to help pay for his degree, had been the first in the family to attend college. He too had gone to the teacher's college that was close to home. I think part of my parents' reasoning was that if that option was good enough for my brother, it should be good enough for me.

My father was the kindest, most compassionate person I've ever met. He was a sensitive male who was attempting to live up to the standards of Jessie Bernard's (1989) "good provider." My father measured his self-worth by his ability to house, feed, and clothe his family. He was a tenant farmer, and the day came when the crops failed. My mother had to get a job outside the home for our needs to be met. My mother became the primary breadwinner, and, as a result, she made most of the decisions that previously would have been either joint decisions or his alone to make. I think my father felt emasculated by this experience. Sexism through stringent sex roles had forced him into a role that didn't fit and had great personal cost for him (Clow & Ricciardelli, 2011; Gaunt, 2013). The change also made me more vulnerable because my father no longer protected me as he once had.

It is ironic that my view of my mother was not that she was a strong or powerful woman. In fact, I viewed her as unyielding, intemperate, and cold, and her job allowed her to remove herself even further from family.

Only with the benefit of hindsight can I recognize the impact being born a female has had on my life: My marital status, career choice, and many life experiences are directly related to being female. Also directly related is my contemporary concern for professional recognition, future financial stability, and gender-related health issues, including the type and kind of medical care I can receive. I cannot address all of these issues in the space allowed, so I talk about sexism and how sexism relates to financial stability, professional recognition, and personal safety. Growing up as a poor, White female has placed me at least somewhat in the matrix of oppression (Collins, 2008). It is difficult to untangle what experiences relate to my being poor and what experiences relate to my being female: They are inseparable.

Sexism has affected me in profound ways. The irony is that I have not always been able to recognize the unequal treatment as sexism. Because I am a product of the society in which I was raised, this nonrecognition was very much a part of the problem. For much of my life, I just accepted things as a matter of course (Hillard, 2013).

MY METAMORPHOSIS IN PERSPECTIVE

The first story that follows is a revelation of what I would call the cocoon phase of my development, the second reflects the larva stage, and the third depicts the full-fledged butterfly phase. These phases are consistent with Erikson's psychosocial developmental phases of adolescence, young adulthood, and middle age (Erikson, 1993). Our tasks to accomplish that help to form our identities include both the personal, such as identity development in adolescence, and the interpersonal, such as partnering (young adulthood) and parenting (middle adulthood; Erikson, 1993), which continue to help define our identity.

THE COCOON STAGE: WAITING FOR LIFE TO HAPPEN

As a 19-year-old junior in college majoring in education, I met, fell in love with, and married David Langer. All of my friends were getting married and, although I was attracted to David, I didn't make a conscious decision to marry based on what I really wanted. I married because it seemed to be what I was supposed to do—that's just what one did. At least that's the message I received from society, my parents, and my peers.

Part of my reason for getting married was related to the wedding event itself: the white dress, the veil, the honeymoon. *Modern Bride* sold romance, and I was definitely in the market for romance. I wanted to be like the brides I saw on the cover, even though I don't think my husband was at all fascinated with looking like a groom.

Within our first year of marriage, I gave birth to our first child. Like getting married, having children was never a conscious choice for me. During the 1960s, it was a matter of course that one had children if one was married. I wasn't a hippie, so I received the message that I was to be responsible, get married, settle down, have a family, and be a productive member of society.

People sometimes cringe when I say I never made a conscious choice to have children. They automatically assume that I wouldn't have had them if I'd had a choice. To the contrary, I just would like to have known that I actually had a choice. In the era in which I was raised, if one was married, one had children or people would whisper, "There must be something wrong with her." Sometimes the gossiper would go so far as to say, "I wonder if the problem is with him or with her?" If I hadn't married, I would have been called an old maid or a spinster. If I hadn't followed the wedding ceremony with a baby shower or two, I would have been labeled selfish or barren. That's the way the world worked in that place at that time. I was 20, a senior in college, and the mother of a four-week-old baby boy.

Within the next five years, we had two more sons. David was light-years ahead of his generation in terms of male roles and behaviors that were acceptable in the 1970s. Males then were supposed to be the primary wage earner, were not supposed to show emotions other than anger, and most definitely did not help with child care or housework, at least not until the child was of school age. David did change diapers and rotate feedings, but he didn't do laundry or housework. I'm positive he did his own laundry before our marriage. I remember the time he asked me to do his laundry for him; this was a huge event in my mind and indicated the depth of our commitment. Ironing his shirts was initially a labor of love. After our marriage, when he no longer did any laundry or his own ironing, the warm glow of ironing with affection wore off. During our nearly 10 years of marriage, I began to understand more about his behavior. He wanted what he perceived to be a traditional marriage, including sex-based division of labor. Conversely, I wanted a marriage based on who had the skills to do what needed to be done (Fetterolf & Rudman, 2014). This disparate perception of marriage never became a bone of contention, however. His job required him to travel a great deal from the time our oldest son was six, so I did everything for the home, including changing the oil in the vehicles, mowing and fertilizing the lawn, painting and cleaning the gutters, and dealing with all the household financial issues. This was good practice for what was to follow—my more androgynous role was required for our survival (Fetterolf & Rudman, 2014). I became more and more aware of the inequities in our incomes and our workloads and began to awaken to a reality that had been present from the moment of my birth.

From 1971 to 1973 when both of us were teaching high school, I was making $6,400 a year in part-time employment. I am not aware of comparable male salaries, but I am aware of the perception that the male was the primary breadwinner and what the female earned was considered fluff, disposable income. The full-time salary scale for someone in my position was $12,000 annually. Teachers' income was based on their hours of education beyond the bachelor's degree and their years of teaching experience, which on the surface sounds equitable. However, if one was expected to do child care and manage all household responsibilities, taking additional college credit courses was more difficult and had to be reserved for summer; then child care was needed because the children were out of school. These factors alone made additional hours prohibitive for women with such responsibilities. Additionally, most male faculty could subsidize their annual income by coaching, an avenue not open to most females. In fact, most female teachers in the school system where I taught from 1971 to 1973 were elementary teachers. Most secondary teachers and all the administrators and board members were male.

In 1976, to increase our opportunities, we moved from the rural area where both of us had been teaching to a midsize Nebraska city of nearly 25,000 residents, where David assumed the position that required extensive travel.

That same year I (college-educated, professionally attired, and articulate) interviewed for a position as a bookkeeper. The questions I was asked included "How many days do you miss a month for, well, you know?" "Do you plan to have more children?" "What kind of birth control are you using?" As I tried to answer these questions, I became increasingly frustrated and uncomfortable. On the one hand, I needed the job to help support my family because we had underestimated our increased cost of living in the new area; so in that sense

I felt vulnerable and trapped. On the other hand, I felt the questions were none of the interviewer's business. I felt humiliated and objectified, and I was intensely angry: If my husband had been the one being interviewed, those questions would never have been asked. I felt violated. I don't even remember being asked about my qualifications for the position. The only comment possibly related to my competence that I remember was something to the effect of "Well, the college degree you have at least lets me know you can learn." I left that interview before its conclusion, thinking I wouldn't work for this man if he did offer me the job. I called the state's Department of Labor and was told there was nothing they could do because it was my word against his. It seemed to me that things were just that way, and I did not know how to further pursue the issue.

I was soon hired as a secretary-receptionist for a family-planning clinic. My husband was traveling, and child care was frequently an issue. I used to take the two youngest sons to work with me and put them in a playpen in the waiting room. Many clients commented about how this was probably the most effective rationale for birth control they had considered. This whole scenario was another example of the impact of sexism on my life. Females largely held the position of secretary-receptionist in 1976, and I'm certain my husband could not have taken the children to work with him, nor could he have taken a day off to care for them. His income was twice as much as mine, so we could not have afforded for him to miss work. Meanwhile, I continued to juggle child care, work demands, and household duties. Some nights I was so exhausted I couldn't even remember going to bed.

David died in 1979 at age 32. I was 29 and a widow with three young sons to raise. It became imperative that I find a better paying position, so I returned to a dream: an advanced degree.

THE LARVA STAGE: BEING AND BECOMING

I went back to college and earned a master's of social work degree. At the same time, I worked part-time as a cost accountant and part-time as a home-based tutor for the public schools. I also cleaned the grill at the local Dairy Queen from 2 AM to 4 AM. I would probably be arrested today for neglect because I left my three sons home alone during the times I cleaned the grill. Cleaning the grill allowed me to avoid free lunches for my school-age son and provided a little fun money for the kids for things such as a weekly McDonald's drive-through.

In 1986, I began teaching part-time at a four-year liberal-arts institution. I also worked full-time as a school social worker and part-time as a medical social worker. My position at the college gradually increased to full-time, tenure track. My starting salary was $18,600 annually. I felt rich compared to all of the time I had earned part-time income, but I was still not being paid the same as my husband had been paid in 1979 without an advanced degree. I worked at this institution for six years before I decided to leave for reasons tied to issues of sexism:

- I was forced by contract to work on my PhD, while a male in the computer-science department had no such restrictions.
- The school hired a male athletic trainer who had just a bachelor's degree, at a salary $6,000 greater than mine was after six years of service (according to the faculty grapevine).

- I served on six committees, I taught four classes per semester, I had four preparations, and I was both a freshman advisor and an academic advisor. I asked to be relieved of some of my committee work because I was driving quite a distance to night classes twice a week; in addition, my mother had a stroke and I was the only surviving child to see to her care. I was told, "You're just the kind of person we want interacting with our students. There are people on this campus who we don't want near our students." Yet my annual review usually included comments such as "Needs to learn how to say no."

Thinking that my experience in higher education was probably universal, I left college teaching in 1992 in search of another career. I moved to a community about an hour away and assumed a managerial position for a weight-loss center.

GETTING WINGS: THE BUTTERFLY STAGE

I connected on a personal level with Bob, a man I'd known in high school. He seemed charming, witty, attentive, and stable. Bob had been my mother's real-estate agent for nearly five years, and we talked frequently over the course of those years. We began our serious relationship in early 1992 and married the following September.

Within the first month of our marriage, Bob held me captive in his home. Basically, I was supposed to stay home, cook and clean, and be ready for his return from a hard day's work. He secretly sold the items I had in storage and did not allow me to have car keys, while two of my sons were teens and both had cars. My oldest son was in college in another city. Since my sons were in school, I tried to find a job. If I had an interview, Bob would call me before and after my scheduled appointment. I found part-time employment as a home-health, quality-assurance technician. The area where we lived was fairly isolated and had a high rate of rural poverty, so jobs were scarce. I could not afford my prescription medications, and Bob would not put me on his insurance. He would not allow me to call my mother unless I paid for the call because it was long distance.

I remember clearly the day that I asked if I could have a can of diet Coke that I had purchased. Something snapped inside me and I began laying the groundwork to leave. I began to save every cent I could, and I investigated the cost of renting a U-Haul truck to move our remaining items. I could not have predicted how soon I would have to use this information though. Before my plan was fully in place, my middle son and I needed to leave for our safety.

My youngest son was in another state at a choir retreat with a school group. My other son and I were home with Bob on a rainy fall evening. Bob had just bought a purebred chocolate lab and was trying to housebreak the puppy. The puppy had just gone outside in the rain, but when Bob brought her back inside, she squatted and urinated on the floor. This infuriated Bob, and he began shaking and hitting the puppy. My son asked him to stop, and Bob aggressively turned on my son, threatening him in no uncertain terms. I intervened, put myself between them, and told my son to go to the car. We left immediately with only the clothes on our backs.

We stayed overnight at a motel in the nearest town and rented a truck the next morning. We didn't know where we were going until we were forced to give a destination to the rental agent. I have no siblings and had no other family nearby. We returned to the place where I had originally taught college courses. We were homeless. We put our items in storage and stayed with friends until we collectively earned enough to rent our own home. The year was 1993. I had stayed with Bob nearly a year.

When I finally stopped asking, "How did I let this happen?," I again began teaching as an adjunct at the same college I had left in 1991. Both sons worked part-time to help with expenses, and both eventually graduated from high school. My oldest and middle sons completed college. I returned to college and completed my PhD in 2000. I was a telemarketer and a college admissions representative to support myself and assist my younger sons as much as I could.

I am now a social-work professor. As a professor who regularly has classes of students in their late teens and early 20s, I find that they think sexism is dead. They truly believe that women are treated equally in the workplace and the home. I teach a survey course in women's studies and appreciate so much the change in students' perspectives from the beginning to the end of the course. At first, they do not believe what they read. Then they become angry at what they read. Then they are empowered and want to create change. When I tell them I never made a conscious choice to marry or to have children, they are unable to fathom what I mean. When I tell them I did not know I had a choice, they are dumbfounded. That is, until they examine their own lives through the lens of feminism. Feminism can be described generally as a belief in equality between the sexes. There are differences in particular kinds of feminism that include a belief in economic equality, social equality, and sexual equality. A feminist is anyone who avows adherence to the belief system of feminism (Fox, 2015). When they look through a lens of feminism, students begin to see their mothers and sisters in unhealthy relationships. They see that their mother with a graduate degree does not make the same salary as a male counterpart. They ask these questions to family and friends: "Have you experienced sexism in your life, and if so, how?" They are amazed at the answers. If students take anything away from this story, I hope it is a recognition that sexism happens, even to those who are highly educated, and that my story is not out of date or unique. I hope students then believe that it is a good thing to stand up to those who perpetuate sexism, and if it is them, that they no longer act on traditions that may be in the way of empowerment and full personhood for everyone in their life.

I have practiced social work in a variety of areas, including individual and family therapy. As a survivor of a lifetime of sexism that impeded my ability to earn a living for my family and as a survivor of a violent marriage, I brought into my social work practice a profound and persistent feminist perspective. My work with systems of all sizes has focused on helping people and groups to find their voices and then to be heard. In social work, we call this *empowerment*. I have adhered to the work of Lorraine Gutiérrez (1990) and others who developed practice models that encourage personal growth. Gutiérrez discussed empowerment as a process that happens at multiple levels. Individuals become aware of their ability to affect others and of increasing their own sense of personal power. Psychological components of the individual empowerment process are

- increasing self-efficacy;
- developing group consciousness;

- reducing self-blame; and
- assuming personal responsibility to change. (Gutiérrez, 1990, p. 150)

My experience as a client overcoming the trauma of violence, and being with my children as they were in therapy for the same reason deepened my ability to understand family violence and to teach about it with a greater level of authenticity. The reality is that I had to work hard in my lifetime to find someone who would listen to me. I had found my voice early in life but had allowed it to be silenced (Hurst & Beesley, 2013). That alone did me no favors, and I refuse to be silent when I see this happening to others. My world now revolves around empowerment. The personal is political to me. In my role as a department chair, I make sure no voice is silenced. We may disagree, but we are heard. I try to focus on empowerment, recognizing and assessing any risk in doing so, even in the most difficult situations. This approach has served me well throughout the past 30 years of my life.

CONCLUSION

It is an undeniable truth that one's sex at birth—biology—begins a process of socialization that results in one's gender—the social role (Liben, 2016), but that process need not result in determinism. Determinism would mean that one's sex at birth determines or controls the choices and outcomes in one's life. In the 1950s, being male or female resulted in clearly defined social roles (Liben, 2016). As a female born during the 1950s, I didn't see very many choices for myself. As a result, I did what I thought I was "supposed to do"—I followed role-appropriate behaviors. Because I was in roles traditionally held by women, and because I was fulfilling the role responsibilities in a standard way, I experienced sexism—unequal treatment because of one's sex. Because of institutionalized sexism, or sexism that is woven into the fabric of society (Liben, 2016), my life story plays out in several important ways. First, my retirement income will not be equivalent to that of a male counterpart because my salary has been less. This smaller nest egg will be reflected in both my personal retirement and Social Security income. I will have to work longer and save more than my male counterparts with equivalent professional training and jobs. Second, my education and training did little to balance my opportunities in the face of institutional inequality. I was powerless as an individual; however, I believe that positive change can happen with organized groups of educated individuals (Manago, Greenfield, Kim, & Ward, 2014).

While I was writing this chapter, a colleague and I had a brief discussion of my use of the term *sex* as opposed to *gender*. He thought that I should be using *gender* because social implications are at issue. The point in my choice of terms is that the human biological level of sex has influenced my destiny. Gender, on the other hand, is what I can make of my life from this point forward (Gardner, 2015). My colleague then questioned my use of the term *female,* saying he thought it was more empowering for women to identify as *woman* than as *female* ("I am woman, hear me roar," Burton & Reddy 1975). My response to him was that I spent most of my life being "just a *woman,*" doing "*woman's* work." Now, I prefer to think of myself as a human who happens to have been born female and all possibilities are open to me as a result. My basic biology is fundamental to my personal empowerment, no longer a limitation. I continue to think about this response. Part of me recognizes that just being born female is not enough to explain all that has happened to me because it is impossible to underestimate the importance and force of socialization. However, being born female no longer limits how I define myself as a woman. I am a woman of integrity and flexibility, and I honestly do not want to be a male. I never have. I am glad to have been born female. What I have fought against is the channeling of that set of sexual plumbing into set social roles. Therefore, I still prefer to think of myself as a human who happens to be born female, and, as a woman, "the world is my oyster."

Biology is not destiny, and we should not be allowed to use biology as destiny to govern our expectations for women or men. My personal and professional growth has taken place across time—recognizing and combating sexism has not been an overnight development for me. Instead, it is a journey I'm still taking.

As for my sons, their life experiences have allowed them to become very supportive and nurturing males, husbands, and fathers. The oldest son now has two children and values very much the time that he spends with them. He remembers times when he and his brothers were ill at the same time, and there was just Mom to tend to their needs. He finds it incredible that one person could do what needs to be done. He cooks, he cleans, he sews on a button—he does whatever needs to be done.

The middle son missed having someone to show him how to throw a football and change the oil (which I no longer did and so never thought about teaching him). Even though I played catch with him, I didn't have the knowledge to throw a perfect spiral. He recently told me that he blamed me for that for a long time. Now that he is married and a first-time homeowner, he realizes that throwing a perfect spiral was not as important as learning how to budget time and money, and hearing, "I love you." He never fails to tell me that his wife is extremely grateful to me for raising a son with no fear of talking about his feelings.

My youngest son is also married. He treasures his life partner, makes a great beef-and-broccoli stir-fry, and openly cries if he feels he needs to. Because my sons experienced first-hand the results of sexism on my life and theirs, they have vowed not to repeat patterns of inequality (Becker, Zawadzki, & Shields, 2014; Drury & Kaiser, 2014).

I do need to make one final comment. In all of this, I still had privilege. I am White. I have a college education. I have an advanced degree. My occupation has prestige and status associated with it. I sometimes get respect simply for my position. I have been homeless and had my life, as well as the lives of my children, threatened. But these were situational and time-limited circumstances because of my privilege. So a final understanding that I hope readers gain is that looking both inward and outward to truly understand our position in the matrix of oppression can unite us with others in similar circumstances instead of dividing and ranking inequities, as some folks try to do. Understanding privilege and the mechanisms of oppression is necessary for empowerment to be both obtained and meaningful.

DISCUSSION QUESTIONS

1. Examine intersectionality in your own life. How have you been shaped or affected by race, class, ethnicity, or gender?

2. What are the reasons that a woman might stay in an abusive relationship? How do these reasons relate to sexism? What are the reasons that a man might stay in an abusive relationship and how does this relate to sexism?
3. Can men be feminists?
4. If women don't recognize that they are victimized by sexism, how might someone point it out to them? Should this be pointed out?
5. What do you think of the discussion about the use of the terms *female* or *woman* to better explain the author's experiences?

REFERENCES

Becker, J. C., Zawadzki, M. J., & Shields, S. A. (2014). Confronting and reducing sexism: A call for research on intervention. *Journal of Social Issues, 70*(4), 603–614. doi:10.1111/josi.12081

Bernard, J. (1989). The good-provider role: Its rise and fall. In A. Skolnick & J. Skolnick (Eds.), *Family in transition: Rethinking marriage, sexuality, child rearing, and family organization* (6th ed.; pp. 143–162). Glenview, IL: Scott, Foresman.

Burton, R., & Reddy, H. (1975). I am woman, hear me roar. Metro Lyrics.

Cho, S., Crenshaw, K. W., & McCall, L. (2013). Toward a field of intersectionality studies: Theory, applications, and praxis. *Signs: Journal of Women in Culture and Society, 38*(4), 785–810.

Clow, K. A., & Ricciardelli, R. (2011). Women and men in conflicting social roles: Implications from social psychological research. *Social Issues and Policy Review, 5*(1), 191–226.

Collins, P. H. (2008). *Black feminist thought: Knowledge, Consciousness, and the Politics of Empowerment.* New York: Routledge.

Connelly, K., & Heesacker, M. (2012). Why is benevolent sexism appealing? Associations with system justification and life satisfaction. *Psychology of Women Quarterly, 36*(4), 432–443.

Drury, B. J., & Kaiser, C. R. (2014). Allies against sexism: The role of men in confronting sexism. *Journal of Social Issues, 70*(4), 637–652. doi:10.1111/josi.12083

Erikson, E. H. (1993). *Childhood and society.* New York, NY: W. W. Norton.

Fetterolf, J. C., & Rudman, L. A. (2014). Gender inequality in the home: The role of relative income, support for traditional gender roles, and perceived entitlement. *Gender Issues, 31*, 219–237. doi:10.1007/s12147-014-9126-x

Fox, B. (2015). Feminism on family sociology: Interpreting trends in family life. *Canadian Review of Sociology, 52*(2), 204–211.

Gardner, S. (2015). Choice theory: Gender roles and identity. *International Journal of Choice Theory and Reality Therapy, 35*(1), 31–36.

Gaunt, R. (2013). Ambivalent sexism and perceptions of men and women who violate gendered family roles. *Community, Work & Family, 16*(4), 401–416. Retrieved from http://dx.doi.org/10.1080/13668803.2013.779231

Gutiérrez, L. (1990). Working with women of color: An empowerment perspective. *Social Work, 35*, 149–153.

Hillard, A. L. (2013). Book review—Understanding inequality: How dichotomies hold past and present women back. *Analyses of Social Issues and Public Policy, 13*(1), 412–414.

Hurst, R. J., & Beesley, D. (2013). Perceived sexism, self-silencing, and psychological distress in college women. *Sex Roles, 68*, 311–320. doi10.1007/s11199-012-0253-0

Liben, L. S. (2016). We've come a long way, baby (but we're not there yet): Gender past, present, and future. *Child Development, 87*(1), 5–28.

Manago, A. M., Greenfield, P. M., Kim, J. L., & Ward, J. M. (2014). Changing cultural pathways through gender role and sexual development: A theoretical framework. *ETHOS, 42*(2), 198–221. doi:10.1111/etho.12048

Ramsay, N. J. (2013). Intersectionality: A model for addressing the complexity of oppression and privilege. *Pastoral Psychology, 63*, 453–469. doi:10.1007/s11089-013-0570-4

Stoetzler, M. (2016). Intersectional individuality: Georg Simmel's concept of "the intersection of social circles" and the emancipation of women. *Sociological Inquiry, 86*(2), 216–240. doi:10.1111/soin.12110

CHAPTER 20

INCREASING AWARENESS OF HETEROSEXISM AND HOMOPHOBIA

A Personal and Professional Journey

Allison L. Kramer

With the exception of my gender and religious affiliation, I am a member of the dominant culture of the United States (Robinson, 1999): I am White, middle-class, able-bodied, and most importantly in this story, heterosexual. While attending graduate school in the late 1990s, I befriended my classmate, Linda (all names in this chapter are pseudonyms), a lesbian, my first close relationship with a person from the lesbian, gay, bisexual, transgendered, queer, intersex, and asexual (LGBTQIA) community. Over the course of the two years Linda and I pursued our respective MEd in Counseling degrees, I also spent quite a bit of time with her partner, Polly, and their young son.

In November 1998, the city in which we lived was to vote on Human Rights Ordinance Number 22, which, if passed, would legally prohibit discrimination against citizens based on their sexual orientation. Although the City Council had approved the original Human Rights Ordinance, including sexual orientation as a basis for discrimination, constituents of our city had successfully petitioned on March 3, 1998, to separate sexual orientation from the other forms of discrimination addressed in the ordinance, including race, color, creed, and gender. Thus failure to pass Ordinance 22 in November would make it possible for citizens to continue to discriminate against other citizens of our city on the basis of their sexual orientation alone. Hoping to educate others about the importance of this vote, Polly and I distributed literature door to door in support of Ordinance 22.

It was during this time that Matthew Shepard, an openly gay man, was brutally beaten, burned, and murdered in Laramie, Wyoming, ostensibly because of his sexual orientation. He died in our city hospital on October 12, 1998 (Brooke, 1998). While attending a memorial ceremony that night surrounded by my friends, classmates, allies, and members of the LGBTQIA community, I heard sadness, outrage, disbelief, and fear expressed at the fact that something this horrendous could happen in our country in the late twentieth century. I will never forget that night, listening to the speeches of faculty, staff, psychologists, and students and marching *en masse* through the town following the memorial service. I was crying, and for the first time in my life, feeling afraid for the lives of my friends, Linda and Polly, and for the lives of nonheterosexual Americans everywhere.

Polly and I were strengthened in our resolve to convince voters to pass Ordinance 22. We spoke to many, left literature for others, made phone call after phone call, and knocked on as many doors as we could. Sadly, despite the public awareness of homophobia and the highly publicized murder of Matthew Shepard, Ordinance 22 did not pass. Linda and Polly told me they feared for their safety and the safety of their son now more than ever and that they intended to leave our city as soon as Linda completed her degree. And that is just what they did.

HOMOPHOBIA

It seems the tide has turned since Matthew Shepard's murder. *Homophobia*, a term first used in 1969 to describe an "irrational fear of, aversion to, or discrimination against homosexuality or homosexuals" (*Merriam-Webster*, 2016), has become a punishable offense not only at the local level, where my friends and I fought a losing battle in 1998, but now also at the federal level. Legal battles for protection against discrimination based on sexual orientation have made it all the way to the U.S. Congress, White House, and Supreme Court. In 2009, President Obama signed into law the Matthew Shepard and James Byrd Jr. Hate Crimes Prevention Act. This law gives the Federal Bureau of Investigation (FBI) authority to investigate violent hate crimes, including violence directed at the LGBT community. This new federal civil rights law criminalizes willfully causing bodily injury (or attempting to do so with fire, a firearm, or other dangerous weapon) when (a) the crime was committed because of the actual or perceived race, color, religion, national origin, of any person, or (b) the crime was committed because of the actual or perceived religion, national origin, gender, sexual orientation, gender identity, or disability of any person, and the crime affected interstate or foreign commerce, or occurred on federal property (FBI, 2014).

Along with the hate crimes law, the Supreme Court in June 2013 ruled that the federal Defense of Marriage Act, which defines marriage as a union between one man and one woman, is unconstitutional. Further, in a separate ruling, it declined to take on the broader issue of gay marriage. The court decided that supporters of Proposition 8, a 2008 ballot measure that had outlawed same-sex marriages in California, "did not have standing to bring the case to the court" (Peralta, 2013, para. 2). These rulings opened the doors for gay couples to legally marry in all states, not just the 37 states that had legalized gay marriage prior to the Supreme Court ruling.

In 1998, Linda and Polly, who were prohibited from legally marrying in Colorado, were constantly debating whether to come out as a couple. Decisions about whom to come out to and in what settings was a constant topic in their relationship. Linda was out to her peers at school; however, Polly, though she desperately wanted to, had not come out at her work, for fear she would, and could, legally be fired from her job on the basis of her sexual orientation. Although they have not entirely been met with open arms, Linda and Polly, who now have a second child, were finally able to legally marry in 2014. They stated that the federal Supreme Court rulings have helped them to feel happier and safer as a family than ever before.

HETEROSEXISM

Heterosexism can be defined as "the societal and institutional reinforcement of heterosexuality as the privileged and the norm; and the assumption that everyone does or should identify as heterosexual" (University of North Carolina, 2012, para. 1). Because heterosexism is subtle and less overt than homophobia, it is less evident to many heterosexuals. Prior to befriending Linda and Polly, I myself was unaware of the privileges afforded me in the United States because I am straight, including being allowed to legally marry and receive the legal benefits of marriage (e.g., Social Security benefits, joint tax-return filing, tax-free inheritance), to adopt children, to express public displays of affection without fear of reprisal, and to receive legal protection from discrimination in employment and housing. When I asked them how to increase awareness of heterosexism in our culture, Linda and Polly suggested I not assume that all new people I meet are straight. I took this suggestion to heart and began to use it, both professionally and personally. With clients, I included a section for sexual orientation on my client-information forms, and I made sure to gently but deliberately discuss it. With friends and acquaintances, I made a conscious effort never to assume they were straight.

PROFESSIONAL CONTEXT

I am a Licensed Professional Counselor, a Certified Addictions Counselor, and an Approved Domestic Violence Offender Treatment Provider in the state of Colorado. For many years, I maintained a private practice in which I predominately worked with nonvoluntary clientele, specifically, clients who were adjudicated and court-ordered for counseling to prevent recidivism (e.g., alcohol education and therapy for DUI offenders and anger management for domestic-violence offenders). The majority of my court-ordered clients viewed the counseling not as a growth opportunity but rather as a form of punishment.

Homophobia was a topic I was legally required to address with court-ordered domestic-violence offenders. Primarily working with White, able-bodied, lower-middle-class, heterosexual males, I was met with constant resistance from clients when I presented this topic in group counseling. To decrease my frustration and increase empathy for my clients, I often revisited my journey to awareness of heterosexist privilege. I decided I needed a model to gauge my clients' movement, if any, toward awareness of privilege, and I found the Key model (Scott & Robinson, 2001).

THE KEY MODEL

Based on Helms's White Racial Identity Development model (1990), Scott and Robinson (2001) developed the White male identity-development Key model, which describes five types of males who typify the dominant culture. Movement from Type 1 toward Type 5 indicates an increased awareness of heterosexist privilege.

TYPE 1: NONCONTACT TYPE

A man of this type supports the status quo, denies privilege, and seeks power. He works on a fairness principle, which implies he is unaware of the need for legal steps to correct discrimination in its myriad forms. Regarding sexual orientation and heterosexism, his assumption that everyone is straight prevails.

TYPE 2: CLAUSTROPHOBIC TYPE

Others are "closing in" this type of man and taking away his power and privilege. He tends to blame members of nondominant cultures (e.g., women, People of Color, nonheterosexuals) for preventing him from being able to live the American Dream. He sees decisions such as the Supreme Court's striking down of the Defense of Marriage Act as threatening to his way of life and beliefs systems.

TYPE 3: CONSCIOUS IDENTITY TYPE

A man of this type experiences dissonance between his existing belief system and reality. Like me, he has had personal experiences causing awareness that things aren't as fair for everyone as he assumes. Perhaps he has a family member who is gay, or he has been bullied by others who called his sexual orientation into question as part of the abuse.

TYPE 4: EMPIRICAL TYPE

A man of this type questions his role in racism and oppression. He "recognizes that his privileged existence-earned through no effort of his own-is at the expense of" others who do not belong to the dominant culture (Scott & Robinson, 2001, p. 420). He knows his daily choices and assumptions as a White male affects other non-Whites. He is willing to explore and own past experiences in which he may have participated in acts of heterosexism (e.g., using the term *gay* to describe undesirable events, situations, and people). Recognizing these behaviors, he intentionally changes them.

TYPE 5: OPTIMAL TYPE

A man of this type understands how his struggle for power and privilege causes oppression. This man understands "that survival is assured not by oppressing others but by living peacefully and harmoniously with self and others" (Scott & Robinson, 2001, p. 420). This man speaks of conscious attempts to even the playing field regarding sexual orientation. In group, these men describe lived examples of acceptance of and kindness toward people they know who have come out as other than heterosexual.

As Scott (2009) noted, "Because of the possibility of never experiencing true dissonance and/or the inability to become aware of one's privilege, many White men may never leave Type 1 or Type 2" (p. 26). Indeed, I found this to be the case for the majority of my clients. My job, however, was to encourage growth, not place judgment. To encourage these men to move toward Type 3 of the Key model and beyond regarding awareness of homophobia and heterosexism, I continually returned to my friends' suggestions about making heterosexist assumptions. Further, I used humor to point out the narcissism inherent in common statements such as, "I don't care if you're gay; just don't come on to me!" by asking clients if they genuinely believed all *women* wanted them to come on to them as well. Jokes about being sex symbols and irresistible often followed from the other men in the group. Finally, I always took time to tell my clients my story of increased awareness of heterosexism through my experiences with Linda and Polly.

CONCLUSION

Many years have passed since Matthew Shepard's death, and I have moved on from private practice to becoming a counselor educator. Now that I am working in a different setting with a different generation, the vast majority of my students are open about their sexual orientations and accepting of others'. Indeed, one of my students, Keisha, regularly brings her wife to meet up with other students following counseling classes, and the couple is warmly regarded in the cohort. Nevertheless, I continue to tell my story, lest this generation of Americans takes for granted the efforts many have made and continue to make to ensure equality and acceptance for the LGBTQIA community. Further, I use my affiliation with the American Counseling Association (ACA) to point out its position on ethical treatment of clients by referring to current events and relevant passages in the *2014 ACA Code of Ethics*, paying special attention to Section C.5. Nondiscrimination, which states,

> Counselors do not condone or engage in discrimination against prospective or current clients, students, employees, supervisees, or research participants based on age, culture, disability, ethnicity, race, religion/spirituality, gender, gender identity, sexual orientation, marital/ partnership status, language preference, socioeconomic status, immigration status, or any basis proscribed by law. (ACA, 2014, p. 9)

It is my hope that readers of this chapter will continue to recognize and utilize personal and professional opportunities to acknowledge heterosexism and combat homophobia in the United States. Using tools such as inclusivity, self-disclosure, identity-development models, ethical codes, unconditional positive regard, empathy, and humor, those of us in the helping professions can continue to influence others to expand their understanding and acceptance of members of the LGBTQIA community and other nondominant cultures in the United States of America.

DISCUSSION QUESTIONS

1. Describe a personal experience that has increased your awareness of dominant culture privilege in the United States.
2. If you experience dominant culture privileges (e.g., Whiteness, able-bodiedness, maleness, youth, heterosexuality, Christian religious affiliation), identify and discuss which ones and how you have taken them for granted in the past.
3. If you typify the dominant culture, discuss which type within the Key model best fits your awareness at this time. If you are a member of nondominant culture(s), describe your experience of coexisting with the dominant culture of the United States.
4. Make a list of tools you can use to increase your and others' personal awareness of heterosexism and homophobia.
5. Describe techniques counselors and other clinicians can use to increase awareness of privilege and oppression with their clients.

REFERENCES

American Counseling Association. (2014). *ACA code of ethics*. Alexandria, VA: Author.

Brooke, J. (1998, October 13). Gay man dies from attack, fanning outrage and debate. *The New York Times*. Retrieved from http://www.nytimes.com

Federal Bureau of Investigation. (2014). *Hate crimes* [Brochure]. Washington, DC: Author.

Helms, J. E. (1990). *Black and White racial identity: Theory, research, and practice*. Santa Barbara, CA: Greenwood Press.

Peralta, E. (2013, June 23). Court overturns DOMA, sidesteps broad gay marriage ruling. National Public Radio. Retrieved from http://www.npr.org/sections/thetwo-way/2013/06/26/195857796/supreme-court-strikes-down-defense-of-marriage-act

Robinson, T. L. (1999). The intersections of dominant discourses across race, gender, and other identities. *Journal of Counseling and Development: JCD, 77*(1), 73.

Scott, D. A. (2009). White male identity development and the world of work: Using the Key model. In G. R. Waltz, J. C. Bleuer, & R. K. Yep (Eds.), *Compelling counseling intervention: VISTAS 2009* (pp. 21–29). Alexandria, VA: American Counseling Association.

Scott, D. A., & Robinson, T. L. (2001). White male identity development: The Key model. *Journal of Counseling and Development 79*(3), 415–421.

University of North Carolina. (2012). *What is heterosexism?* Retrieved from https://www.google.com/webhp?sourceid=chrome-instant&ion=1&espv=2&ie=UTF-8#q=heterosexism+uncu/

CHAPTER 21

"MEN CAN'T BE RAPED"

The Challenge of Sexism in Counseling

Heather Trepal

On the college campus where I previously worked, we had an annual rape-prevention program for all first-year students. A peer theatre troupe performed skits related to different rape scenarios (e.g., date rape, drug-facilitated rape, female victim–male perpetrator rape, male victim–female perpetrator rape), followed by a question-and-answer session with the students. During one of these sessions, several of the students, both male and female, strongly argued that a scene in which a male was the victim and a female was the perpetrator was unrealistic. When asked to defend their position, one student replied, "Everyone knows that men can't be raped." I thought about it for a minute and realized that, on some level, I bought into that statement.

Extreme feelings of embarrassment arose within me. I was honestly struck with the realization that I was being sexist. Although as a counselor I had worked with male clients who were victims of sexual assault, this incident forced me to take a hard look at what I really thought about sexism, men, and the gender dynamics associated with rape. At its most basic form, sexism relates to stereotyping or discrimination based on someone's sex or gender. While sexism is usually thought of in terms of discrimination against women, it can also be enacted with men and people who identify as gender nonbinary. As a woman, I had more often thought of myself as being on the receiving end of sexism, so the idea that I was having sexist thoughts (or enacting a bias against men) was new and problematic for me. I considered myself informed about rape, sexual assault, and rape myth culture, but somehow I didn't realize the potential for my own unconscious beliefs about men and gender roles to be triggered. I was embarrassed for the way I felt about men and my questioning the veracity of their rape or sexual assault.

The statistics on sexual assault are bleak. For example, it has been globally reported that close to one in five women have been victims of sexual abuse or attempted abuse, compared with about one in 15 men (Rape, Abuse & Incest National Network, 2016). However, there are issues with the underreporting of these crimes. In fact, the World Health Organization (2014) "acknowledges the sexual victimization of boys and men, but indicates this remains poorly documented globally" (p. 3). Despite the underestimation of the problem, the potential consequences of sexual violence are equally devastating for both men and women.

It has been suggested that gender is a social construction (Risman, 2004). How we come to view men and women, and how we participate in dialogues about those views, is how others come to construct their ideas of gender. It has also been suggested that gender socialization and sex-role rules have an impact on the issue of rape for both men and women (Grubb & Turner, 2012).

Statements such as "Men can't be raped" are formed by a social construction of gender that includes specific and limiting sex-role expectations for both men and women. These social constructions are cognitive schemas that represent worldviews about gender norms (Risman, 2004). They support specific sex-role expectations for men and women that, at the most basic level, reduce women to passive and emotional beings and men to aggressive roles. When people are reduced to limited acceptable roles, others have a difficult time seeing other possibilities (e.g., women's aggression or men's passivity seen as abnormal or atypical).

Statements such as "Men can't be raped" are also part of a social construction of gender that has an impact on male survivors' experiences of rape and the meaning that is made from those experiences. The silent squeeze of gender role expectations takes place from cradle to grave and influences male survivors' perceptions of traumatic experiences and how they make sense of them in the future. Because of gender socialization, a man might have a difficult time reconciling conflicting emotions experienced during postassault sex if he feels the emotions are inconsistent with messages he has received about male rape (e.g., men should be emotionally unharmed by rape).

GENDER SOCIALIZATION NORMS FOR WOMEN

Different aspects of gender socialization may impact a person's experience and personal interpretation of rape and healing. For example, women are generally accepted if they express their anger, fear, or hurt (to a friend or a counselor). In both the college counseling center and the rape crisis center in which I worked, we saw far more female than male clients, particularly with issues involving rape and sexual assault. Women are also more likely to hear stories about rape that have happened to members of their own sex, in which women are the victims and men are the perpetrators (Peterson, Voller, Polunsky, & Murdoch, 2011). For example, television movies about rape frequently involve some variation of the female/victim–male/perpetrator situation.

Women are also socialized to enjoy both the physical and emotional components of sex. Haines (1999) stated that although many messages about sex are incongruent, women—particularly women survivors—are encouraged to break the myths and restrictions about sexuality.

MEN'S GENDER SOCIALIZATION NORMS

The gender socialization process also impacts men's experiences and personal interpretation of rape and healing. For example, men are generally accepted if they do not express a variety of emotions, seek help, or tell others (such as a friend or counselor) when they are hurting (Peterson et al., 2011). As a colleague of mine said, "Anger is the default emotion for men—the only emotion they are socially allowed to convey." Another colleague also told me that once, when he was doing a presentation on counseling services, men in the group told him that "counseling was for the weak" and that they were afraid that someone might find out if they went to the campus counseling center.

In addition, men do not often hear stories about rape in which members of their own sex are the victim and not the perpetrator (Peterson et al., 2011). For example, sexual-assault presenters inform audiences typically that, although men are also victims/survivors, they will use the pronoun *she* for the sake of ease. By doing this, presenters not only reinforce masculine-sexist stereotypes (e.g., men as perpetrators) but also disqualify the experiences of the male survivors in the audience.

Men are also socialized to avoid things that could be associated with femininity. In his seminal work on gender socialization, Pollack (1998) stated that a code exists for boys, part of which dictates that expressing feelings or emotions and behaviors that could be associated with femininity is "taboo" (p. 24). This situation connects with the previous point: Expressing emotions (e.g., sadness) and the behaviors associated with these emotions (e.g., crying) is socially acceptable for women but not for men. In addition, men are socialized to have fear or hatred toward nonheterosexuals. Pollack (1998) asserted that this attitude comes from a combination of gender socialization and misunderstanding about sexuality in general. Many male survivors question the effect of rape on their sexuality (Lew, 2004). Finally, men are socialized to enjoy nonrelational sex. In his classic book on men recovering from child sexual abuse, Lew (2004) alluded to the fact that men are expected to enjoy sex without the constraints of emotional involvement and to be the aggressors in sexual situations. Sexual healing can be a component of healing from rape. Ideas about sexuality can hinder or help that process. Society suggests to men that they (a) be reluctant to seek help; (b) restrict their emotions; (c) engage in competition and aggressive behavior, among other things; and (d) accept gender-specific roles (Lew, 2004). Thus many of the issues for male survivors of rape may be invisible.

Although this is difficult to admit, in the past I inwardly and unconsciously believed that men can't be raped. Whenever I worked with a male survivor as a client, I looked for a sign to show that he somehow wanted the sexual activity and that he was not raped. I had unwittingly become part of the problem by somehow convincing myself that men always wanted sex, no matter the circumstances of the encounter. If a male client didn't show any emotion or didn't cry when discussing his sexual assault, I had to fight off the thought that he must have enjoyed the sex. Given a display of rage, I might have assumed that somehow the male was less responsible for the assault. By believing that my male clients were any more responsible for their rapes and sexual assaults than my female clients, I was truly practicing sexism. My reactions were consistent with how sexism is translated into the counseling relationship.

MAKING CHANGES

To overcome my struggles with sexism, I decided to start with self-monitoring. I realized that I did not know a lot about men's issues, so I studied the literature on men and sexual assault. I learned that men do not report rape for many different reasons. Some buy into myths such as (a) all men who get raped are gay, (b) men don't get raped—they are the strong ones, and (c) women cannot rape men—rape is a sexually motivated crime (Turchik & Edwards, 2012). In addition to buying into the myths, men are taught by society that they will be made fun of if they report rape (e.g., teasing by male peers, "Hey, I'd like to get *raped* by a woman"). Further, Turchik and Edwards (2012) have stated that men are far less likely to report a rape or sexual assault, or to seek needed medical or mental health treatment, when doing so calls into question their male identity. This reality has implications for both heterosexual and gay men. For example, both heterosexual and gay men might begin to question their sexual orientation. While heterosexual men might wonder why they didn't fight back, gay men might wonder whether they were being punished for their sexual orientation.

My male clients have also taught me a lot. For instance, working in a feminist organization, I always felt free to decorate my office as I chose—with pictures, quotes, and items representing all things feminine and empowering to women. Quite a few men clients informed me that this was not only unsettling to them but also irresponsible. By decorating with feminine-gender objects, I was possibly negating their experiences and not providing empowering models for my male clients. They also suggested incorporating male-centered contexts into our program literature (e.g., brochures, advertising) and using nonsexist language. In reflecting back on these experiences, I was struck with the awareness of my sexist bias in a powerful way. Once I was aware of the potential harm that I was doing my male clients in counseling, I had the responsibility to examine my own knowledge, awareness, attitudes, and skills with men in counseling who had been sexually assaulted.

The American Counseling Association's *2014 ACA Code of Ethics* lists "honoring diversity and embracing a multicultural approach in support of the worth, dignity, potential, and uniqueness of people within their social and cultural context" as one of the core professional values (p. 3). Further, the Code mandates that counselors must display developmental and cultural sensitivity in their practice. Therefore, as a professional counselor, I need to do my own work on sexism and the ways in which it was manifesting in my practice.

Sue and Sue (2016) state that culturally skilled counselors are (a) aware of their own cultural heritage; (b) aware of value differences; (c) aware of biases and values, and the effects they might have on others of a different culture; (d) comfortable with differences; (e) sensitive to circumstances and able to refer clients to counselors of their choice; (f) aware of and acknowledge beliefs, attitudes, and feelings that are prejudiced (e.g., sexist, racist, anti-Semitic, homophobic, ageist); and (g) engaged in the ongoing process of change.

Neill (2001) recommended that counselors ask themselves about their own comfort level when talking to men about their history of sexual assault. He also suggested that counselors take time to reflect on their comfort level around discussing sexuality issues with men (e.g., asking men about their sex lives, sexual orientation, and sexual and reproductive health, including use of correct or slang terminology based on the language they use).

Further, Neill maintained that counselors should explore their gendered ideas about rape and sexual assault, exploring whether they think it must be more difficult physiologically, or physically, for men to be raped than it is for women—or whether they think that it is easier for a guy if a woman instead of a man rapes him. Neill also suggested that counselors explore the complexity of age and gender related to sexual assault. For example, why does the notion of a 30-year-old man having sex with a 15-year-old girl nauseate people, while the idea of a 15-year-old boy having sex with a 30-year-old woman is easier to tolerate? Finally, Neill (2001) also suggested that counselors examine their internal and external reactions when their male clients express strong emotions (e.g., anger, rage, sadness). Counselors should explore things such as their likelihood to challenge or pacify a male client related to emotional expression.

CONCLUSION

By examining my attitudes and beliefs about men, and by working with men, I was able to begin to have a dialogue with myself about my work. I concluded that I needed to actively seek out training on men and their issues, including men with disabilities; men who are transidentified, gay, or bisexual; and men of various racial, ethnic, and religious backgrounds. In addition to training, I took it upon myself to read about men's issues, talk about men's issues, and write about my work so that I could share ideas and educate others.

By first addressing ourselves and examining our own beliefs, values, assumptions, and biases and then addressing differences in these perspectives between ourselves and our clients in therapy sessions, we as counselors are able to work effectively within the *constraints* of a gendered socialization. In addition, by addressing both our own beliefs and those of our clients, we hope to create space for all of our clients to develop broader conceptions of masculinity. As counselors, we can challenge socially and historically constructed views of masculinity and teach our clients to do the same.

DISCUSSION QUESTIONS

1. Have you ever watched a presentation or heard a discussion (such as the one in the introduction) and felt that, even though you were uncomfortable with the idea, you had a bias about men being raped? If *yes*, what was the bias? If not, what are some thoughts you have on men being raped?
2. If you did recognize your own bias, what did you decide to do about it? If you did not recognize any biases, what is your rationale regarding how well you assessed the situation and whether or not there are other steps you need to take to maintain or build on your growth?
3. Explore your biases, assumptions, values, and beliefs around men and masculinity in personal and professional contexts. Examine some of the recommendations from

Neill (2001) about counselor comfort level, acknowledgment of internal and external reactions to male clients, and gendered beliefs about rape and sexual assault. What are some specific ideas that you believe about men and women and rape and sexual assault? Are there certain gendered myths that you buy into (e.g., "men can't be raped," "women ask to be raped by their choice of clothing")? Explain/discuss your responses.

4. If you do acknowledge a gender bias, how do you plan to take action to resolve it and move toward a different view?

REFERENCES

American Counseling Association. (2014). *2014 ACA code of ethics.* Retrieved from http://www.counseling.org/docs/ethics/2014-aca-code-of-ethics.pdf

Grubb, A., & Turner, E. (2012). Attribution of blame in rape cases: A review of the impact of rape myth acceptance, gender role conformity and substance use on victim blaming. *Aggressive and Violent Behavior, 17,* 443–452. doi:10.1016/j.avb.2012.06.002

Haines, S. (1999). *The survivor's guide to sex: How to have an empowered sex life after child sexual abuse.* San Francisco, CA: Cleis Press.

Lew, M. (2004). *Victims no longer: The classic guide for men recovering from sexual child abuse.* New York, NY: Harper-Collins.

Neill, T. (2001, October). *Treating male survivors of sexual assault.* Paper presented at the meeting of the Ohio Coalition on Sexual Assault, Columbus.

Peterson, Z. D., Voller, E. K., Polusny, M. A., & Murdoch, M. (2011). Prevalence and consequences of adult sexual assault of men: Review of empirical findings and state of the literature. *Clinical Psychology Review, 31*(1), 1–24. doi:10.1016/j.cpr.2010.08.006

Pollack, W. (1998). *Real boys: Rescuing our sons from the myths of boyhood.* New York, NY: Henry Holt.

Rape, Abuse & Incest National Network. (2016). Victims of sexual violence: Statistics. Retrieved from https://www.rainn.org/statistics/victims-sexual-violence

Risman, B. J. (2004). Gender as a social structure: Theory wrestling with activism. *Gender & Society, 18*(4), 429–450.

Sue, D. W., & Sue, D. (2016). *Counseling the culturally diverse: Theory and practice* (7th ed.). New York, NY: John Wiley.

Turchik, J. A., & Edwards, K. M. (2012). Myths about male rape: A literature review. *Psychology of Men & Masculinity, 13*(2), 211–226.

World Health Organization. (2014). *Global status report on violence prevention 2014.* Retrieved from http://www.who.int/violence_injury_prevention/violence/status_report/2014/en/

SECTION 7

STORIES OF DIFFERENTLY ABLED AND ABLEISM

Ableism is a network of beliefs and practices upholding a "perfect" and able body as requisite to being fully human. In this section, Jessica Loyd Hazlett describes her experiences with ableism as she cared for her mother who lived with multiple sclerosis, an immune-mediated disease that damages the nervous system. Paul E. Priester and Karla Ivankovich follow with an exploration of Priester's process toward developing critical consciousness of the roles that disability-based oppression and ability-based privilege play in US society. Both physical and attitudinal barriers are examined.

Hazlett, in her story "Diving Greatly: Reflections on Ableism," invites the reader to dive with her into waters coursed by experiences growing up with a differently abled parent. She explores the ways in which systematic oppression, internalized oppression, and discrimination maintain ableism and considers ways in which ableists' frameworks have influenced experiences within her family system, and she shares how she has advanced these privileged frameworks herself. Ideas are offered for how one might work to dismantle ableism through brave conversations, personal reflections, and examination of our own stereotypes, biases, and assumptions about what it means to be fully human.

Priester and Ivankovich explore Priester's process as he develops critical consciousness of the roles that disability-based oppression and ability-based privilege play in US society. Both physical and attitudinal barriers are examined. In "Dirty Secrets, Unholy Unions, and Death Sentences: Disability-Based Oppression and Privilege," Priester and Ivankovich utilize social stigma theory as a theoretical lens through which to understand oppression. The authors encourage the reader to recognize the socialization process and "unlearn" attitudinal oppression towards individuals with disabilities.

CHAPTER 22

DIVING GREATLY

Reflections on Ableism

Jessica Lloyd-Hazlett

PUTTING A TOE IN THE WATER: BACKGROUND AND INTRODUCTIONS

My mom has a smile that lights up a room and an infectious laugh you cannot help but catch. She excitedly chuckles each time she calls me *Dr. Jesser* and tells me how proud she is. She also has a reputation for laughing when she is not supposed to. A favorite story from my mom's childhood is of her hooting at the dinner table. My grandfather would attempt to call his four children to order, commanding, "No more giggling!," and often before bursting into laughter himself. As beautiful as her laugh is, I will admit, when I first think of my mom it is not this joyful expression that comes to mind. I think of her multiple sclerosis (MS), an immune-mediated disease that damages the nervous system, and that she is right now lying in the bed of an assisted-living facility 2,000 miles away from my day-to-day reality.

I am a 33-year-old, able-bodied, Caucasian woman in my third year as a tenure-track assistant professor in counselor education and supervision. When I learned about the opportunity to contribute to this book, I was eager to be involved. Not only would writing this chapter be a coveted publication opportunity, I would also have the chance to be a part of a unique compilation of personal and professional reflections on complex diversity issues. I perused the available topics, intrigued by each. One of my college majors was cultural anthropology; the postmodern notion of addressing dominant discourses, hegemonic structures, and social constructions tickled my intellectualism. And then I saw it: *ableism*. Ableism encompasses

> a network of beliefs, processes, and practices that produces a particular kind of self and body (the corporeal stand) that is projected as the perfect, species-typical and

therefore essential and fully human. Disability is cast as a diminished state of being human. (Campbell, 2001, p. 44, as cited in Campbell, 2008, p. 153)

The opportunity to write about ableism touched not only my brain but also my heart. It made me uncomfortable; I knew it was the subject I needed to write about. Simultaneous to my pressing *send* on the call for contributors, the doubt crept in. Do I have something to say (and is it worth saying)? If I do have something to say, will I be able to say it? Is my story going to be good enough? As an able-bodied person, what legitimacy do I have? Why did I volunteer for this again?!?

These questions running through my head, I was reminded of the privilege I carry as a Caucasian individual. Most often, I am sheltered from the vulnerability of representing or speaking on a behalf of a group. I also reflected on the times I have grown the most as a person and also in my multicultural competence. For me, growth happens when I am not sure of the answers or how to neatly package my perspective. Development transpires when I have the courage to have a conversation that feels uncomfortable, the outcome uncertain.

With my mom's proud smile and my own nervous chuckle, I proceed. My story begins with sharing some of my experiences growing up with a parent who is differently abled. Along the way, I provide a definition of ableism and a discussion of current literature, including highlights of professional guidelines that address multicultural education, training, and practice for helping professionals. Finally, I conclude with reflections on what I have shared and suggest discussion questions that may help facilitate our continued awareness and action around dismantling ableism in society.

TAKING THE PLUNGE: MY STORY

Following a range of tests, my mom was diagnosed with MS in 1993; I was 10. MS misdirects the body's immune system against the central nervous system. Myelin, a protective covering surrounding nerve fibers, is attacked, which in turn inhibits the transmission of signals from the brain and spinal cord. In the kid-friendly terms I was provided, "Mommy's brain can't talk as well to the rest of her body."

MS typically follows one of four disease courses: relapsing-remitting, secondary-progressive, primary-progressive, and progressive-relapsing (National Multiple Sclerosis Society, 2015). My mom's diagnosis falls into the latter category, the rarest and often most severe of the groupings. In the 23 years since her diagnosis, I have watched helplessly as her mobility has shifted from the use of a cane to the use of a walker, to a wheelchair when needed, then a wheelchair consistently, and ultimately, to a surgical procedure that cut major muscles in her legs and enables her to sit more comfortably, permanently.

My mom has always loved the water, be it a long bubble bath or synchronously jumping "UP" or ducking "UNDER" the ocean's waves with her daughters. On the day of this particular story, I was a young teenager accompanying my mom on a swimming trip. Tangential to bouts of inappropriate laughter, a terrible sense of direction also runs in my family. After circling the block where the community center pool was located a regrettable number of times, we decided to park and resume our exploration by foot. Twenty minutes that felt like hours later, we spotted our destination: and a lot of stairs and no automatic doors. By the time we made our way to the locker room, my mom was fatigued, leaning on me a little more each step. Slowly, we changed into our suits and made our way to the pool, to the water she so loves.

Entering into the water, we were free—free of the gravity that makes movement difficult, momentarily weightless in body and spirit. We glided through the water, walking side by side in ways that had been made increasingly difficult with each progression or relapse of her MS. At one point, she cradled me (shortly before dunking me underwater with one of her characteristic outbursts). At another point, I held her in my arms. Looking back, these movements were metaphoric, symbolizing a blurring of the discrete parent–child hierarchy I yearned for growing up.

When the time came to exit the pool, she tried to climb the ladder but could not, her legs tiring more quickly than her bliss. I proceeded to ungracefully push, pull, and shove her until she leveled with the pool deck. Knowing we still needed to make it to the locker room and ultimately our car, I panicked. I am not sure whether others were around, but if they were, they did not make themselves visible. The resourceful youth that I was (aka, I just wanted to get the hell out of Dodge), I looked for alternate modes of assistance. In an auxiliary room of the community center, I found an office chair. I loaded her onto the seat and pushed her back to retrieve our clothes. Rolling into the locker room, mustering energy for my fourth attempt to lift her out of the makeshift wheelchair, I heard her chuckle. The chuckle grew into a giggle, the giggle into a full belly laugh. A smile cracked over my face, my own laughter building and bellowing out. As our laughter grew, our last bits of strength faded. We fell to the floor, laughing at the image of the duo we had become. Laughing not to cry. Laughing to regain the fortitude to carry on. We made it out of the locker room that day, life moving forward even as my mom no longer physically could. This story represents one of many where I knew my narrative was different. There have been other big reminders— the absence of my mom at graduations, at my wedding. Some are smaller, more subtle—the jealously I feel when a friend talks about shopping with her mom over the weekend, the days I long for my mommy despite being in my third decade of life.

When I first thought of writing a chapter on ableism, naively it is only these incidents I thought of. The moments in which the world had "othered" us or had not been accommodating. However, as I reviewed the literature and reflected on my experiences, a growing awareness crept in, resulting in a sudden epiphany: the recognition of how I myself was exhibiting ableism. I often judge my mom against a standard of normal she falls short of. I characterize her not by her laugh, or any of the other many facets to her identity, but with a label of MS. (Nervous chuckle—again, why did I volunteer for this?)

WAVES IN THE WATER: A REVIEW OF CURRENT LITERATURE

Disability is defined by the US Department of Justice, US Equal Employment Opportunity Commission (2009) as comprising one or more of the three following statuses: (a) a physical or mental impairment of an individual that is significantly restricting at least one major life activity, (b) a history of such impairment, or (c) the external perception of such impairment. Disabilities may be more or less visible, spanning physical, sensory, intellectual, and mental domains. Disability is delineated not by the condition itself but rather in relation to an individual's ability to function in his or her environment.

As previously introduced, ableism represents a deeply held set of negative values toward disability. Ableist frameworks encompass certain beliefs about one's body and how this fits (or does not fit) into the larger social fabric. I am abled; my mom is dis-abled. Central to ableism is an assumption that, regardless of type, impairment is a blemish to be cured or eliminated (Campbell, 2008). While the term *ableism* itself is relatively new (Hehir, 2005), the systematic categorization of otherness based on perceived ability deficiencies is enduring.

Wolbring (2012) differentiates *disableism* and *ableism*, positing two sides inherent to every –ism. The former emphasizes the production of disability, entailing assumptions and practices that promulgate differential and unequal treatment based on actual or presumed disabilities (Campbell, 2008). Disableism was represented in my story through the pool's failure to provide accessible entrances to all members of the community it served. In contrast, ableism emphasizes the production of ability, delineating essential abilities requisite to one's recognition as being fully human (Campbell, 2001; Wolbring, 2012). Ableism extends beyond missing ramps or automatic doors. Ableism makes certain my mom knows she is not welcome at society's literal and metaphorical pools.

Ableism is situated within socially constructed beliefs about health, productivity, and beauty (Campbell, 2008). Such understandings are often disguised as truths or scientific facts reinforced by traditional biomedical models of disability. For example, MS has "destroyed" my mom's body. Within these paradigms, disability is regarded as a tragic negative situation wherein treatment or rehabilitation is required to restore, to the degree possible, an individual's normality (Smart & Smart, 2006). According to biomedical models, both the problem and the solution are housed within the individual with the disability, thus relieving society of responsibility and reducing the individual to a role of a passive and compliant patient (Campbell, 2008; Wolbring, 2012). As an example, my mom is expected to display resilience through her diagnosis or, at a minimum, not to burden others with her struggles.

While critics acknowledge the scientific explanatory power of biomedical models, these voices call attention to the frameworks' inherent reductionism and also the relevance of context in defining disability (Smart & Smart, 2006). Interactional models of disability (Richmond-Frank, 2015; Smart & Smart, 2006) are not exclusive of biological factors but more broadly consider the individual and the individual's environment. Such models bring into question functions of the environment that cause, label, contribute to, and exaggerate disability. Society, rather than the individual, is repositioned as the location of the problem and also the solution.

Emergent models of disability also emphasize parallels between the systematic oppression of individuals with disabilities and hegemonic injustices toward Persons of Color, women, and individuals identifying on the lesbian, gay, bisexual, transgender, and queer spectrum. Specifically, sociopolitical models (Smart, 2009) reflect individuals with disabilities' perspectives of themselves as members of a minority group. For example, these models, which would suggest that my mom would not want to swim, serve as a greater barrier to her entering the water than her physical limitations themselves. Proponents of such models indicate that societal prejudice and discrimination function as more of an obstacle than the actual medical impairments or functional limitations themselves (Smart & Smart, 2006).

Contemporary scholarship examines convergences in social constructionist approaches to race and disability, highlighting likenesses and distinctions in ways individuals with disabilities are stigmatized and denied attributes valued in society (Campbell, 2008; Smart, 2009). A common phenomenon of paternalism seems particularly relevant, wherein members of the dominant majority convey a profound sympathy for members of a minority group while at the same time reinforcing a subordinate position for them (Smart, 2009). I admire my mom's laugh, but I keep her and her MS symbolically cradled in my arms.

The initial realization of my own ableism through authoring this chapter was embarrassing and confusing. I felt shame in perpetuating the same discourses that had resulted (and still do result) in my feelings of aloneness, my perceptions of deficiency. However, as I continued to read and reflect, some of my experience became normalized. Specifically, in considering ableism through the lens of critical race theory, Rosenwasser (2000) emphasizes the role of internalized oppression, which she defines as

> an involuntary reaction to the oppression which originates outside one's group and which results in group members loathing themselves, disliking others in their group, and blaming themselves for the oppression—rather than realizing that these beliefs are constructed in them by oppressive socio-economic political systems. (p. 1)

Internalized ableism is maintained through dual-pronged tactics of dispersal, wherein individuals with disabilities are distanced from each other, which confounds recognition of a larger minority group, and of emulation, wherein "passing" is valued and ableist norms thus recycled (Campbell, 2008). Once internalized, ableism requires little external force to maintain its oppression. I label my mom. She labels herself. The label of *(dis)ability*, though one facet of a person's multifaceted identity, subsumes all.

BLOWING THE WHISTLE ON ABLEISM: IMPLICATIONS FOR HELPING PROFESSIONALS AND OTHER "LIFEGUARDS"

The preamble of the American Counseling Association's (2014) *Code of Ethics* describes "honoring diversity and embracing a multicultural approach in support of the worth, dignity, potential, and uniqueness of people within their social and cultural contexts" (p. 3) as a core principle of the profession. Helping professionals are called to be aware of their personal values and also to avoid imposing these values on clients (American Counseling Association, 2014, A.4.b). Despite professional mandates, most preparation programs for helping professionals, aside from rehabilitation counseling, have not included a specific focus on disability issues. Pieterse, Evans, Risner-Butner, Collins, and Mason (2009) analyzed multicultural and diversity course syllabi from 54 accredited counseling and counseling-psychology programs. The researchers found that disability (as a special population) was included in only 12% of assessed courses. Ableism as a form of discrimination and social oppression was addressed in only four (7%) of assessed courses (Pieterse et al., 2009). Rawlings and Longhurst (2016) conducted focus groups with 19 master's-level students to examine perceptions and integration of disability culture in counselor training programs. Many of these student counselors shared that they had not been exposed to disability issues previously in their coursework. Student counselors also reported they were likely to assume a client's disability related to their presenting concern and that all individuals with disabilities wanted cures for their impairments.

Attending to deficits in clinical practice and preparation is imperative. Ableist beliefs and practices negatively impact not only individuals with disabilities but also society as a whole. Further, disability intersects with other social dimensions such as gender, class, race/ethnicity, and sexual orientation (Smith, Foley, & Chaney, 2008). As such, it becomes necessary to dismantle ableism at personal, interpersonal, institutional, and cultural levels (Jun, 2010). Considering guiding principles of the field, helping professionals are uniquely positioned to play a critical role in the deconstruction of ableism. Chief among these principles is helping professionals' recognition of the interchange between personal characteristics and environmental factors in a developmental context (Smart & Smart, 2006). Helping professionals work to consider and empower individual persons in context and also to address broader social inequities.

SUGGESTIONS FOR HELPING PROFESSIONALS

I forward the following suggestions in the interest of blowing the whistle on ableism. At a personal level, we as helping professionals may examine our own stereotypes, biases, and assumptions. Domains of reflection include clarifying distinctions between empathy and sympathy (Richmond & Frank, 2015), prioritizing nonhandicapping language that affirms individuality and personhood, and evaluating the impact of inappropriate dichotomous or hierarchical ableist schemas on assessment and treatment (Smart & Smart, 2006). Helping professionals are benefitted at an interpersonal level by learning to prioritize the conceptualization of disability and impairment from interactional and sociopolitical models over biomedical models (Jun, 2010). Notably, most individuals with disability do not accept the basic tenets of the biomedical model; instead, they consider disability a valued part of their identity and one that commands respect, not sympathy (Smart & Smart, 2006).

Dismantling ableism also requires that we listen attentively and ask nonjudgmental questions to understand the particular experience of an individual with a disability, rather than work from assumptions or an imagined impact (Richmond-Frank, 2015). Clinical practice is further enhanced by recognition of impairment as one part of a multifaceted identity all clients bring to a session; disability is not the "master status" (Smart & Wegner, 2000, as cited in Smart & Smart, 2006).

Most importantly, confronting our own potential contributions to ableism is necessary (Smith et al., 2008). However (and as experienced through my present authorship), examining points of privilege can be uncomfortable and requires both matched challenge and support from others, whether they be educators, supervisors, colleagues, or mentors.

Reflective writing, such as this piece, has been identified as a critical learning tool. Reflective writing provides a safe area to in which to share our thoughts and to accommodate new perspectives as we question previously assumed ideas and beliefs (Lee, Williams, Shaw, & Jie, 2014).

Facilitating and participating in difficult conversations are also essential to enhancing multicultural competence. The scholarship of Watt and colleagues (2009) highlights eight potential domains of reaction we may experience when we encounter perspectives that disrupt our current ways of understanding others, our experiences, or ourselves. These potential domains include denial, deflection, rationalization, intellectualization, principium, false envy, and benevolence. The latter three domains reflect newer contributions to the literature and are sequentially defined as "avoiding exploration on the basis of religious or personal principle" (principium), "displaying an affection for a person or a feature of a person in an effort to deny the complexity of the political or social contexts" (false envy), and "displaying an overly sensitive attitude toward a social and political issue on the basis of a feeling of charity" (benevolence) (Watt et al., 2009, p. 97). Otherwise stated, "I have a disabled parent, I don't need to examine my own ableism"; "Sometimes I wish I had MS so I would have the courage my mom does"; and "My mom is helpless and needs my help." (Ouch—metaphorical self-reflection belly flop!)

CONCLUSION: TRANSFORMING BELLY FLOPS TO SWAN DIVES

I dove into this chapter with excitement and trepidation. I now emerge from the experience with a similar range of emotions. I am excited about the knowledge, skills, and awareness I have gained about ableism and trepidatious about the responsibility these insights carry. I have learned much about myself and my relationships through writing this piece. During the process, I have had numerous conversations with friends, colleagues, and family; we have shared stories, tears, and, of course, laughter. We spoke of the currents that push and pull in each of our lives, renewing commitments to provide refuge to each other through life's inevitable storms.

I mentioned at the start growing most through conversations that felt uncomfortable, their outcome uncertain. I cannot be certain of the outcome of this reflection, but I carry some hopes for the reader. The first is awareness of the power of engaging in self-reflection internally and also with others. A difficult dialogue is defined as "an exchange of ideas or opinions between individuals that centers on an awakening of potentially conflicting views of individual belies or values on social justice issues" (Watt et al., 2009, pp. 86–87). Though the water feels cold at first, I believe it is only through these explorations that we can begin to discharge the sweeping undertow of social constructions such as ableism and consequent internalized oppressions. As we tread choppy waters, our critical consciousness about the circumstances of oppression emerges and spurs action (Freire, 1970).

My second hope for the reader is an understanding that the waters surrounding privilege and power can be murky. Related to ableism, I have occupied the roles of oppressed and oppressor. Often, we are socialized into dominant courses we are not aware of, voicing privilege we did not wish to assert. Through my mom's immobility, I have learned to be more still—to reflect, to take time to laugh, to sit with my own privilege. Concurrently, I have also grown in courage and motivation to move—to engage in dialogue, to disrupt oppressive systems, to dismantle ableism. Brené Brown (2012) describes *daring greatly* as the courage to be vulnerable, to enter the arena without the false protections of certain victory or perfection (in mind, body, or spirit)—to dare to simply enter the arena. I appreciate this opportunity to "dive greatly" and hope you will jump in with me.

DISCUSSION QUESTIONS

1. What have been your experiences learning about, confronting, or navigating ableism to date? How does this compare to other isms you have been exposed to?
2. Consider the information you have previously received about disabilities/impairments. How might this same information be conceptualized similarly and differently from the lenses of biomedical, interactional, and sociopolitical models of disability?
3. Which of the domains of reaction to disruptive dialogues outlined by Watt and colleagues have you experienced? What steps might you take to work through these challenging domains? Have you ever "othered" someone because of that person's disability? Have you ever had the experience of being "othered" yourself based on a perceived disability? How did you feel about this? What is your reflection on the experience(s) now (Jun, 2010)?
4. What belly flops have you experienced in exploring your own points of privilege and oppression? What have you learned from these experiences? What would be your suggestions to others looking to transform self-reflective belly flops to swan dives?

REFERENCES

American Counseling Association. (2014). *Code of ethics*. Alexandria, VA: Author.

Brown, B. (2012). *Daring greatly: How the courage to be vulnerable transforms the way we live, love, parent, and lead.* New York, NY: Penguin.

Campbell, F. (2001). Inciting Legal Fictions: Disability's Date with Ontology and the Ableist Body of the Law. *Griffith Law Review, 10*, 42–62.

Campbell, F. A. K. (2008). Exploring internalized ableism using critical race theory. *Disability & Society, 23*(2), 151–162.

Freire, P. (1970). *Pedagogy of the oppressed*. New York, NY: Bloomsbury.

Hehir, T. (2005). *New directions in special education*. Cambridge, MA: Harvard Education Press.

Jun, H. (2010). *Social justice, multicultural counseling, and practice: Beyond a conventional approach*. Thousand Oaks, CA: SAGE.

Lee, A., Williams, R. D., Shaw, M. A., & Jie, Y. (2014). First year students' perspectives on intercultural learning. *Teaching in Higher Education, 19*(5), 543–554.

National Multiple Sclerosis Society. (2015). *What is MS?* Retrieved from http://www.nationalmssociety.org/What-is-MS

Pieterse, A. L., Evans, S. A., Risner-Butner, A., Collins, N. M., & Mason, L. B. (2009). Multicultural Competence and Social Justice Training in Counseling Psychology and Counselor Education A Review and Analysis of a Sample of Multicultural Course Syllabi. *The Counseling Psychologist, 37*(1), 93–115.

Rawlings, S. A., & Longhurst, T. (2016). Infusing disability culture into multicultural courses in counselor training programs. *Review of Disability Studies, 7*, 1–14.

Richmond-Frank, S. (2015). Because "Mama" said so: A counselor-parent commentary on counseling children with disabilities. *The Professional Counselor, 15*(2), 304–317.

Rosenwasser, P. (2000, June). *Tool for transformation: Co-operative inquiry as a process for healing from internalized oppression.* Paper presented at the Adult Education Research Conference, University of British Columbia. Retrieved from http://newprairiepress.org/cgi/viewcontent.cgi?article=2216&context=aerc

Smart, J. F. (2009). The power of model of disability. *Journal of Rehabilitation, 75*(2), 3–11.

Smart, J. F., & Smart, D. W. (2006). Models of disability: Implications for the counseling profession. *Journal of Counseling & Development, 84*, 29–40.

Smith, L., Foley, P. F., & Chaney, M. P. (2008). Addressing classism, ableism, and heterosexism in counselor education. *Journal of Counseling & Development, 86*, 303–309.

US Department of Justice. (2009). *A guide to disability rights laws.* Washington, DC: US Government Printing Office.

Watt, S. K., Curtis, G. C., Drummond, J., Kellogg, A. H., Lozano, A., Tagliapietra ... Rosas, M. (2009). Privileged identity exploration: Examining counselor trainees' reactions to difficult dialogues. *Counselor Education & Supervision, 49*, 86–105.

Wolbring, G. (2012). Expanding ableism: Taking down the ghettoization of impact of disability studies scholars. *Societies, 2*(3), 75–83.

CHAPTER 23

DIRTY SECRETS, UNHOLY UNIONS, AND DEATH SENTENCES

Disability-Based Oppression and Privilege

Paul E. Priester with Karla Ivankovich

UNDERSTANDING AND EXPERIENCING PRIVILEGE

I, the first author, am a 54-year-old, European American, nonphysically disabled, heterosexual male.[1] My awareness of privilege associated with being nondisabled developed through a friendship with Eric. I met Eric, a fellow counselor, when I was working at a community-based, substance-abuse treatment center. Eric has a spinal cord injury as a result of a tractor accident when he was a child. As a result of this injury, Eric uses a wheelchair for transportation. I had, up to the point at which I met Eric, viewed such individuals as *wheelchair bound*. Eric, however, educated me that this view itself is offensive and pejorative. He views his wheelchair as a source of freedom and mobility, not as a deficit. For example, he says that most people are highly dependent on their automobiles for transportation, yet we do not refer to them as *automobile bound*.

It is well documented within the Federal civil-rights legislation that stigma and prejudice are fundamental forces behind the exclusion of individuals with disabilities

---

1. This chapter is based on the experiences of the first author. As such, any use of the first-person pronoun reflects his personal biography. The second author contributed to the academic and theoretical explorations related to disability-based oppression and privilege.

(US Department of Justice, 2009; World Health Organization, 2001). At the same time, prior to my discussions with Eric, I had never really analyzed how the use of stigmatizing language further oppresses those with, or who are perceived to have, disabling conditions. Intentional or otherwise disabling language is pervasive in our society and is almost entirely pejorative, thus perpetuating stigmatizing and discriminatory views of those with disabilities (National Center on Journalism and Disability, 2016). Eric offered me some of his favorite examples—how the terms *invalid* or *cripple* demonstrate the negative connotations imbedded in our language. These phrases suggest that an individual who uses a wheelchair for transportation purposes is somehow an invalid or is deformed (as *cripple* would suggest). Later in my rehabilitation-counseling education, I would learn that these are excellent examples of the ways in which our society stigmatizes those who are oppressed (Bandura, 1997; Goffman, 1963, Ivankovich, 2016) and participates in the processes of *deification of normality*. That is, a standard is established based on nondisabled norms, and then any individual who does not rise to that standard is seen as deficient, incapable, pathetic, and in need of assistance. This process is similar to the way in which racism and other forms of oppression operate. The beliefs, values, and behavioral practices of the group in power are placed on a pedestal. The beliefs, values, and behavioral practices of the group whose members do not hold the institutional power are then compared to the beliefs, values, and behavioral practices of the sanctified group on the pedestal (DeLoach & Greer, 1981, Dunn & Andrews, 2015). This stigmatization, known as *social stigma theory*, results in social disapproval, including devaluation and exclusion, whereby privilege, intentional or otherwise, is given to individuals of the sanctified group-those in the in-group.

SOCIAL STIGMA THEORY

Social stigma theory has long sought to understand marginalized populations in an effort to combine theoretical orientation with practical application (Gelso, 2006; Goffman, 1963). Goffman's theory of social stigma posits that stigma happens when an individual is devalued or rejected as a result of a particular attribute that is deemed undesirable by others. In Eric's case, what was deemed undesirable was his inability to walk. Goffman first addressed disability stigma by identifying that stigma is based on any of three categories: (a) "abominations of the body—or the various physical deformities"; (b) "blemishes of individual character perceived as weak will, domineering or unnatural passions, treacherous and rigid beliefs and dishonesty"; and (c) "the tribal stigma of race, nation and religion" (Goffman, 1963, p. 14). Goffman believed that the process of stigmatization involved a complete devaluation of an individual simply because that individual possesses a particular deviant trait or attribute—in this situation, a disabling condition that would result in rejection or exclusion from future social interaction. In this view of stigma theory, once a person has been stigmatized, he or she is no longer under the protection of social norms and may be excluded from all participation.

INCREASED AWARENESS OF PRIVILEGE

Before my friendship with Eric, I was naïve about the degree to which our society invalidates and devalues individuals with disabilities. I grew up in an upper-middle-class, White, suburban family in a metropolitan area in Iowa. The invisible veil of ableism that I failed to question is ironic, given that my oldest brother was deaf. Even though I grew up in a family in which one of my siblings was sent off to deaf boarding school and given a second-class status as a member of our society, not once did I question this disability-based ghettoization. In my affluent high school, I recall becoming engaged in a conflict in which I stood up to football players who were bullying a student with developmental disabilities; but even here, I never considered the larger context of how our society views individuals with disabilities. I earned an undergraduate degree in French from the University of Iowa and then went on to paraprofessional training as a substance abuse counselor, but never in my education were these ideas of ableism explored. This scenario reflects the operational definition of privilege: not being required to be aware of or consider the manner in which I benefit from the system of oppression.

As I became closer friends with Eric, we began to socialize together outside of work. As a former restaurant worker, I had strong preferences about my choice of restaurants, which resulted in a pattern in our dining. Typically, I would suggest a restaurant and then Eric would ask, "Is it accessible?" I would ponder the question for a while, running through my head whether I had encountered any obstacles, and then say, "Yes." When we arrived at the restaurant, we would find obstacles, such as three steps leading to the front door. Although there were only three steps, these steps rendered the establishment off limits to a person in a wheelchair. At first, I did not understand Eric's anger and refusal to eat at any of these businesses until he expressed the sentiment that, in his view, having those three steps was equivalent to having a sign hanging outside that said, "African Americans are not allowed to eat here." Eric felt that he was being excluded in a similar way: "People in wheelchairs are not allowed to eat here."

For Eric, the lack of physical access to these restaurants can be paralleled to the continued racial segregation where African Americans were denied access to eat in restaurants, even after the Supreme Court effectively ended segregation in restaurants as mandated by the Civil Rights Act (1964). Passed in 1990, the Americans with Disabilities Act (ADA) covers most issues of accessibility for people with disabilities in the United States. In addition to state and local governmental offices, this law applies to public facilities that are open and available to the general public. Despite the ADA, Eric's access to such facilities remained limited by his inability to ambulate on his own two feet rather than on the wheels that leveled his playing field. Unfortunately, despite legal mandates, continued segregation remains.

Accessibility issues also affected Eric in his role as a talented billiards player, successful in professional tournaments. Eric often participated in tournaments that were not wheelchair accessible. The accommodation for accessibility that these businesses offered was having two or three bulky bouncers lift and carry Eric up the stairs. Eric found this accommodation to be offensive in that it maintained the myth of helplessness and perpetuated dependence on others for participation in daily activities (Block, n.d.). By spending time with Eric, I have become more aware of how I benefit from the privilege bestowed upon me as a man without a physical disability.

Privilege not only allows but encourages a lack of awareness as a means of maintaining a status quo (McIntosh, 1998). Failure to recognize the internalized resistance to engage in awareness and acknowledgment about privilege only further perpetuates the privilege itself (Remley & Herlihy, 2016). One way in which I personally struggle with my awareness of privilege is that I accept the benefits without questioning the need for change. Each time I enter a restaurant with three stairs before the front door, I am made aware that I am entering a space that is explicitly excluding my friend Eric. This is an uncomfortable awareness, yet I do nothing to challenge the restaurant owner to make changes. The analogy that comes closest to portraying the way I feel is when someone tells me a very salacious and inappropriately intimate piece of information about a third person. Afterward, each time I am in the presence of that third person, I am keenly aware of the information and highly uncomfortable that it was disclosed to me—it is the dirty secret. Similarly, my privileged access to a location actively denied to individuals with disabilities is my dirty secret.

I will admit that, at this point, I do not have the energy or enough sense of social justice to demand change in the physical environment to make it accessible to individuals with disabilities. I am presently at a stage at which I continue to learn to challenge my own internal attitudinal barriers. For example, I realize that it is okay for me to feel grateful for my own physical health but not to do so by thinking, "It could be worse; I could be in a wheelchair." To do this is to prop up my sense of self-worth by standing on the backs of individuals with disabilities. Fein and Spencer (1997) empirically demonstrated this phenomenon. Individuals, especially when they were feeling threatened or negatively evaluated, maintained their self-image by means of viewing others in a pejorative, derogatory, or negative manner. I sometimes feel overwhelmed with knowing that I am at a stage at which my energies are spent changing just my own privileged mindset when there is often a greater need for intervention in the surrounding physical world.

Another incident that brought my relative privilege to awareness was when Eric and his fiancée, who were childhood sweethearts, decided to get married. They were both Roman Catholics and began the process of arranging for a wedding within the Church. The priest who was guiding them through this process inquired of Eric specifics relating to his spinal cord injury (i.e., at what vertebrae level the trauma had occurred). In Catholic culture, there is often a contradiction between canonical law and cultural practices. According to Canon Law 1084, the Church will not marry an individual who is incapable of vaginal intercourse (Coriden, Green, & Heintschel, 1985). Although many if not most priests disregard this theologically conservative stance, priests sometimes continue this practice and refuse to marry the couple.

Later, when the couple met with the priest to complete paperwork, the priest informed them that he was not going to allow the marriage process to proceed within the Church. He went on to explain that the sole purpose of marriage was for procreation and that he had contacted medical professionals and determined that, given Eric's spinal-cord injury, whether he would be able to sire offspring was uncertain. This pronouncement caused a fury of outrage from Eric, his fiancé, and their families, but the priest refused to reconsider. The couple was forced to marry outside of the Church, which is highly stigmatizing to traditional Roman Catholics.

Before Eric had shared this experience with me, I had spent considerable time pondering the heterosexual privilege that I have to marry the person of my choice. Until recent welcome changes, it was unfathomable to me that our society denied people the right to marry the person of the same gender whom they love. But I had never thought that this privilege to marry the person of my choice could also be denied to Catholic individuals with disabilities. Many heterosexual and nondisabled individuals take this privilege for granted. Indeed, one of the notions that we hold sacrosanct is that we are free to choose whom we will marry. This incident brought to my attention the injustice that exists in our society regarding this privilege.

LESSONS UNLEARNED: STIGMA, OPPRESSION, AND PRIVILEGE

For decades, Erving Goffman's work on social stigma theory has sought to foster an understanding of marginalized populations (Gelso, 2006; Goffman, 1963, Ivankovich, 2016). Goffman theorized that social stigma theory is defined as a mark of disgrace associated with a particular circumstance, quality, or person, resulting in social disapproval, exclusion, devaluation, or rejection. Similarly, Bandura's (1997) social cognitive theory posits that behaviors such as privilege are learned, or modeled from others, thus perpetuating the cycle of oppression.

Despite significant efforts, prejudice, stigma, and discrimination remain pervasive today (Ivankovich, 2016), so much so that a central focus among educators, in all disciplines, has been to understand how intergroup biases are perpetuated and to determine effective ways to ameliorate issues that have been plaguing society throughout history (Stewart, Latu, Branscombe, Phillips, & Denney, 2012). Similarly, much noise has been made by counseling educators to include issues of disability and marginalization in multicultural counseling training. A content analysis estimated that only 28% of multicultural-counseling course syllabi explicitly address disability as a content area (Priester, 2001). If this consciousness raising is not occurring in the majority of formal multicultural classes, the counseling trainee is compelled to explore these issues independently.

Sadly, attempts to change this broken system through social action are often avoided or fraught with pitfalls because people feel powerless to change, even as it relates to the laws of the land, where privilege is power (Robinson, 2016). Fortunately, the helping attitudes thought to be essential in the counseling field have been found to be crucial in bias-reduction programs that call for social change (Stewart et al., 2012).

So how can we as individuals learn about these issues of privilege and implicit bias on our own? My suggestion is that we explore and challenge our internalized negative stereotypes and then intentionally cultivate personal relationships with individuals with disabilities. It is my opinion that only in the context of an ongoing personal relationship can we learn about how the world is for other people. Specifically, the us versus them mentality, once proven to be the hallmark of stigma and privilege theory, does not bear the strength previously afforded. However, Hewstone, Rubin, and Willis (2002) found that the more favorable individuals' attitudes were relative to their in-group, the more negative their attitudes were toward any out-groups. At the same time, and likely a credit to stigma-reduction efforts, more recent research suggests that although in-group attitudes remain relatively unchanged, out-group attitudes can and have improved (Stewart et al., 2012). As such, it has been only through my personal, intimate relationships with People of Color that I have also come to an awareness of the extent and pervasiveness of racism in our society. Through my relationship with Eric, my eyes were opened to the reality that our society is set up to specifically exclude and devalue individuals with disabilities. The flipside of this awareness is that the world in which I live has specifically been arranged so that I, as a nondisabled individual, am included, invited, and valued at the expense of individuals who are different from me.

I have learned this reality in professional areas of my life as well. When I first discovered that I was going to be working as a therapist for adolescent sex offenders with developmental disabilities, I had considerable trepidation. The *sex offender* label is not what concerned me because I had been working with similar adolescent clients. Rather, the *developmental disability* label is what caused me to question the job assignment. I thought that it would be terribly boring to do clinical work with individuals with mild mental retardation. My assumption was that a high level of intellect in my clients was required to do effective psychotherapy and that such a process with adolescents with mild retardation would be tedious and unrewarding. In this situation, I was basing the value that I held of individuals on their relative intelligence.

Our society makes this same value judgment in many subtle and explicit ways. An example of an explicit devaluing of an individual is the use of in-vitro amniocentesis tests. Amniocentesis is a procedure in which embryonic fluid is assessed for evidence of chromosomal disorders (American College of Obstetricians and Gynecologists Committee on Practice, 2007). The results of this test can suggest whether or not a fetus is likely to have Down syndrome. When my wife was pregnant with our first child, her physician offered this test to us. The physician's suggestion was that, if the fetus had Down syndrome, we might want to reconsider having the baby and choose to abort the pregnancy (Choi, Van Riper & Thoye, 2012). My wife and I declined the test as we would welcome the birth of the child regardless of the Down syndrome status. This is a concrete, explicit example of both able-body privilege (Goodley, 2010) and disablism (Campbell, 2009). If the fetus were given a diagnosis of Down syndrome, a death sentence could have followed. In fact, in the majority of cases, such pregnancies are terminated. According to a review of the research related to this issue, between 61% and 93% of pregnancies in which the fetus is diagnosed with Down syndrome are terminated (Natoli et al., 2012). It is important to note that this is a distinctively different debate than the prolife versus prochoice paradigm. Here, the issue is whether life should be granted or ended based on the inherent worth of the individual as measured by potential cognitive capacities.

I was not even aware that I harbored a similar, albeit subtler, form of the same oppressive attitudes related to one's relative worth based on intellectual ability in general until after I developed relationships with these aforementioned clients with mild intellectual disability. In truth, disablism, conscious or unconscious, still promotes unequal treatment simply because of actual or presumed disabilities (Campbell, 2009). Despite my biases, these individuals soon became my favorite group with which to work. I worked past my personal barriers and realized these were loving, wonderful kids who deserved respect and who had much to offer in a relationship. In this clinical situation, I believe that I changed more than my clients as I *unlearned* the lessons I had been taught in our society about individuals with developmental disabilities. For me, this process of unlearning started with my identification of, and then challenging, the negative stereotypes that I have held of individuals with disabilities. If I am lucky, the unlearning process can continue in a personal relationship with an individual who happens to have a disability.

The unlearning process will continue indefinitely as I come to awareness of new ways in which I benefit from unearned privilege. My journey started with awareness of White privilege (McIntosh, 1998). Then I discovered the privilege from which I benefit by not having a physical disability. I have also learned about the subtle ways in which I stigmatize and oppress individuals with developmental disabilities by devaluing them based on their intellectual abilities. And then, when I had children, I discovered subtle ways in which I benefit from not only those privileges I have listed but also from gender-based privilege as well (i.e., not hearing the baby crying because I know my wife will take care of the problem, or similarly not smelling the dirty diaper; Pease, 2010).

CONCLUSION

As I explore my own participation in the perpetuation of stigma, oppression, and privilege, I am clear that I must continually self-task if I wish to be an agent of change, for myself and for those with whom I come into contact (Pease, 2010). Further expanding the message of optimism, Stewart et al. (2012) reported increased perceptions of efficacy in inequality reduction when those who were socially active advocated for and explained why the chance for successful outcomes were higher when intergroup attitudes about inequality improved.

Where will my unlearning process take me next? I am starting to explore ways in which I depersonalize individuals based on their social class, another form of stigma and oppression. For example, when a busboy clears my table at a restaurant, am I appreciating this individual as a complete human being with a family and dreams? Or am I viewing him in a role: as a servant? Regardless of the answer I have or you might have, I know that not everyone is willing to evaluate the beliefs he or she holds or the privileges he or she keeps. Todd, Spanierman, and Aber (2010) confirmed such by reporting that those who were confronted with the notion of White privilege reacted with strong negative emotional responses. Failure to explore beliefs such as these suggests individuals believe that they do not hold problematic views or that there is no need to change them if they do.

A final story about my own class-based invisibility: During graduate school, I worked as a waiter to support my family and my studies at an upscale, private dining club. One night, I worked a private reception there at the club. I was walking through a room when a wealthy, middle-aged woman in full gown started gesturing at me. As I approached her, she pointed to dirty cocktail glasses on a nearby table and loudly over enunciated, "*Por favor*" (indicating that she would like me to clear the glasses). I should note that at this dining club I was the only White waiter. My colleagues were all Latino or Filipino. My ethnic background is Irish and German. As an individual in this situation, I was invisible to her. She did not see me, the person, but instead saw a worker in a role as a servant. Because she was used to interacting with Latino servants, she had responded in her stereotypic manner—a manner in support of privilege and in support of a more competent in-group.

In the same way, I fail to see the woman checking out my groceries or the janitor in my building. Do I see them as the persons? Or do I see them only in their role, possibly on a lower level of status? An important component of class-based privilege is having the power to decide who is visible and who is playing a depersonalized role. For my unlearning process to continue, I need to be open to the process, challenge myself, and seek out relationships with individuals who differ from me.

DISCUSSION QUESTIONS

1. You or your partner is pregnant. The doctor tells you the results of your amniocentesis test. Your baby will have Down syndrome. What do you do? If you choose to terminate the pregnancy, why? What does this choice say about the relative value that is placed on infants based on their intelligence potential? How do you think about your response related to defining or deifying normalcy?
2. You are entering a nightclub and see a sign posted that says, "No African Americans Allowed in This Establishment." What do you do?
3. You are entering a nightclub with three high steps outside the door. What do you do? Discuss the similarities and differences in your responses to questions 2 and 3.
4. How would you feel if your faith community did not allow you to get married to the person you love? Does this disability-based oppression remind you of any other characteristics that faith communities or states might use to deny individuals the ability to marry the persons they love? Do you think people who identify as gay or lesbian should be allowed to marry? What about individuals with developmental disabilities? How about people with inheritable conditions?
5. The first author suggests that to think, "It could be worse; I could be in a wheelchair" is to build up one's sense of self-worth by standing on the backs of individuals with disabilities. Do you agree? Why or why not?
6. Stigmatizing situations happen daily. Recall a time when you were not sensitive to the needs of those around you (e.g., Parked in a space designated for People with Disabilities? Blocked a ramp or entryway from a person in a wheelchair? Ignored a person who is deaf because you didn't know the language?) Consider whether you are you more likely to be concerned about events such as these only if you get caught? Explain.
7. Given the devastation of social stigma, what psychological implications exist for those who identify as members of more than one marginalized category (e.g., minority, female with a disability)? Discuss.
8. Discuss the types of privilege you have witnessed at varying levels of your life (childhood, young adult, adult, as an aging adult). Discuss how your understanding of privilege (your own or others) has changed through each of these stages.
9. Many individuals are disabled simply by the attitudes of others. Recall and discuss a time in your life when you assumed that you understood what another person was capable of before you got to know the individual.

10. Stigma is deeply engrained into society. These beliefs and accompanying behaviors lead to discrimination and oppression. Discuss the cost that stigma and oppression exact on society.

REFERENCES

American College of Obstetricians and Gynecologists Committee on Practice (2007). ACOG Practice Bulletin No. 77: Screening for fetal chromosomal abnormalities. *Obstetrics and Gynecology, 109,* 217–227. doi:10.1097/00006250-200701000-00054

Bandura, A. (1997). *Self-efficacy: The exercise of control.* New York, NY: W. H. Freeman.

Block, L. (n.d.). *Stereotypes about people with disabilities.* Disability History Museum. Retrieved from http://www.disabilitymuseum.org/dhm/edu/essay.html?id=24

Campbell, F. (2009). *The contours of ableism: The production of disability and abledness.* London, UK: Palgrave Macmillan.

Choi, H., Van Riper, M., & Thoyre, S. (2012). Decision making following a prenatal diagnosis of Down syndrome: An integrative review. *Journal of Midwifery & Women's Health, 57*(2), 156–164. doi:10.1111/j.1542-2011.2011.00109

Coriden, J. A., Green, T. J., & Heintschel, D. E. (Eds.). (1985). *The code of Canon Law: A text and commentary.* Canon Law Society of America & Catholic Church. New York, NY: Paulist Press.

DeLoach, C., & Greer, B. G. (1981). *Adjustment to severe physical disability: A metamorphosis.* McGraw-Hill Companies.

Dunn, D. S., & Andrews, E. E. (2015). Person-first and identity-first language: Developing psychologists' cultural competence using disability language. *American Psychologist, 70*(3), 255–264.

Gelso, C. J. (2006). Applying theories to research: The interplay of theory and research in science. In F. T. Leong & J. T. Austin (Eds.), *The psychology research handbook.* Thousand Oaks, CA: Sage.

Goffman, E. (1963). *Stigma: Notes on the management of spoiled identity.* Englewood Cliffs, NJ: Prentice Hall.

Goodley, D. (2010). *Disability: Psyche, culture and society.* London, UK: SAGE.

Hewstone, M., Rubin, M., & Willis, H. (2002). Intergroup bias. *Annual Review of Psychology, 53,* 575–604. doi:10.1146/annurev.psych.53.100901.135109

Ivankovich, K. (2016). A correlational study of self-esteem and perceived stigmatization in healthcare among obese African American patients. In *National Association of African American Studies & Affiliates: 2015 special events monograph* (pp. 172–200). Scarborough, ME: National Association of African American Studies & Affiliates.

McIntosh, P. (1998). White privilege, color and crime: A personal account. In C. R. Mann & M. S. Zatz (Eds.), *Images of color, images of crime* (pp. 207–216). Los Angeles, CA: Roxbury.

National Center on Journalism and Disability (2016). *Disability language style guide.* Retrieved from http://ncdj.org/style-guide/

Natoli, J. L., Ackerman, D. L., McDermott, S., & Edwards, J. G. (2012). Prenatal diagnosis of Down syndrome: A systematic review of termination rates (1995–2011). *Prenatal Diagnosis, 32*(2), 142–53. doi:10.1002/pd.2910

Pease, B. (2010). *Undoing privilege: Unearned advantage in a divided world.* London, UK: Zed Books.

Priester, P. E. (2001, August). An overview of current cross-cultural counseling training practices. In P. E. Priester (Chair), Current practices and innovative approaches to multicultural counseling training. Symposium conducted at American Psychological Association, San Francisco, CA.

Remley, T. P., & Herligy B. P. (2016). *Ethical, Legal, and Professional Issues in Counseling* (5th ed.). Boston: Pearson.

Robinson, R. K. (2016). Unequal protection. *Stanford Law Review, 68*(1), 151–233.

Stewart, L., Latu, I. M., Branscombe, N. R., Phillips, N. L., & Denney, H. T. (2012, March). White privilege awareness and efficacy to reduce racial inequality improve White Americans' attitudes toward African Americans. *Journal of Social Issues, 68*(1), 11–27.

Todd, N. R., Spanierman, L. B., & Aber, M. S. (2010). White students reflecting on whiteness: Understanding emotional responses. *Journal of Diversity in Higher Education, 3*, 97–110.

US Department of Justice. (2009, July). *A guide to disability rights laws.* Civil Rights Division, Disability Rights Section. Retrieved from https://www.ada.gov/cguide.htm

World Health Organization. (2001). *International classification of functioning, disability and health (ICF).* Retrieved from http://www.who.int/classifications/icf/en/

SECTION 8

STORIES OF GENDER, RACE, AND IDENTITY DEVELOPMENT

In this section, Kianna M. Middleton; Sametra Polkah-Toe with Valerie A. Middleton, and Linda Robinson share a common thread in their stories as Black women—hair, skin tone, and Black identity development. Although each of their stories were written separately, and they each are separated by at least a decade, they share these common experiences that few Black women (if any) will not have included in telling their stories. The section finishes with Daryl H. Thorne sharing her grave concerns about the way the institution of education perpetuates oppression of marginalized people.

Middleton's "Of Paper Plates and Poetic Things: A Black Lesbian Pedagogy on the Horizon" revisits past moments where her body disturbed the primarily White classrooms, from the preschool teacher's forgetting of her non-white skin in a self-making activity to the isolating space of a college classroom in which her classmates were unable to distinguish her poetry from her body. The White, presumably heterosexual classroom had taken issue with accommodating K. Middleton's body; her body as a type of text, had been misread in the classroom. The author posits that her own embodiment, one of Black lesbian identification, connects with other Black queer embodiments in the academy to create classrooms in which their bodies are part of their intellectual work and a voluntary means through which text(s) and theories come to life.

Polkah-Toe and V. Middleton, in "Ethnic Beauty in a Western Society: An Examination of Black Identity Development," examine the effects of minority status on the ethnic identity development of Women of Color in the United States. While the period of identity development can be a confusing time for all young people, young Women of Color, in particular, face a far more difficult task of needing to integrate multiple distinct identities. Polkah-Toe shares her own experiences with learning to accept and be proud of her natural hair—a distinct African American feature—while forming positive ideals and perceptions of Black female beauty within the context of living in a Western society. The authors pay special attention to the ways in which family, peers, and other societal institutions pass on historically racialized-gendered perceptions of Black women's images and suggest the influence of these perceptions serve as tools of oppression.

Robinson's "Skin Color: An Issue of Social Status and Privilege" contributes to the conversation regarding People of Color by noting that that the varied hues of skin tone make a difference in how one is perceived by those both inside and outside the privilege spectrum. Robinson explains that while African Americans have experienced progress in the United States relative to civil rights and social justice, there still exists a tendency for African Americans and White Americans to prefer light-skinned African Americans—resulting in a prejudice called "colorism." This preference for light-skinned African Americans, beginning during the time of the trans-Atlantic slave trade, continues to negatively impact dark-skinned African American's lives in terms of financial earnings, partner choice, and other critical life situations. The author, a dark-skinned African American female, provides an experiential perspective on the issue of colorism and its impact on her life. Issues of colorism and counseling are also addressed.

In "Racism by Way of Education: The Politics of Privilege and Oppression" Thorne speaks to the lived experiences and collection of events that have settled into particular spaces on the privilege–oppression continuum for a "middle-aged" mixed-ancestry Native American woman who has been socialized and politicized as *Black*. Thorne shares her experiences with overt and covert forms of racism, White privilege, as well as access to educational privilege and oppression. Thorne challenges the political use of education as an instrument to maintain the invisibility of White domination of historically oppressed people. The chapter goes on to highlight a restrictive and oppressive continuum, of academic stages, that deliberately leave historically oppressed and marginalized people grossly undereducated with underdeveloped critical thinking and writing skills. Thorne postulates the idea of using academic privilege to engage students to consciously challenge, disrupt, critique, and make problematic the politic of educational racism in the United States.

CHAPTER 24

OF PAPER PLATES AND POETIC THINGS

A Black Lesbian Pedagogy on the Horizon

Kianna M. Middleton

A MOMENT: SERVING RACE ON A PLATTER

Preschool art tables can be a site of unbelonging. In preschool my classmates and I were given an art project, a face-making and not coincidentally a place-making activity. Our stubby untrained hands ran over yellow coils of yarn and faceless, white paper plates. Basic crayons and markers adorned the kidney-shaped table awaiting our wobbly-circled blue and green eyes, red-dotted freckles, and small triangle noses. The white plates would be made up in the reflection of our 3- and 4-year-old faces. As children, we would not want or need more than a plain, white, paper plate and preschool accessories.

Unsurprisingly, this activity posed no racial predicament to the other children or my teachers because white plates, though not objectively the color of anyone's white skin, still presented the assumption of sameness, normalcy, and of the ability of whiteness to take any form of an unmarked medium. Though I have no memory now of my reaction to the mirroring task, it became a teachable moment for my mother as she rightfully refused to let it stand. I believe my mother was aware of this racial erasure-in-progress, meaning that white plates without other plated options stood to metaphorically erase the existence of anything or anyone other than whiteness. Racial erasure, like color-blind racism, is the belief or practice of removing racial difference to forward or prove an egalitarian society or situation (Bonilla-Silva, 2006). To not *see* race or to erase its presence by simply ignoring it or not preparing for it, as evident in my classroom project, is still a type of discrimination and racism. Whiteness is envisioned as the absence of race, and ignoring race often feels like *only* acknowledging Whiteness. Thus, Whiteness, as a social construct and a lived experience, holds to consume and cover other racialized ways of being. Hence, my mother's fear in lack of arts-and-crafts choices was not merely an aesthetic one but one of ensuring my sheer survival.

Perhaps my mother had realized that, for my teachers, who had not encountered much racial or ethnic differences either in their training or in their lives, ignoring the erasure meant that they never had to account for it. This is, they never had to think about anything past cheap yellow and brown yarn, past picture books with more than white faces, or past pool time and unwettable Black-girl hair. White paper plates were a standardized embodiment, and only White kids saw the plates as a tool of self-expression instead of an unreachable, unmakeable project, a Whiteness I could never mark, claim, or meaningfully disrupt. My mother's discussion with my teachers opened up the possibility of more options for whom I could build, what tangible materials I saw myself to be, what Blackness I was able to embody, and more importantly at that developmental stage, what I was able to imagine.

From this moment forward, racial misidentification and erasure taught me something beyond the realm of speech: that my mother's refusal restored racial agency that a bare paper plate and yarn failed to extend to my body. These pedagogical memories, though piercing and painful, make sense of race on a primal scale. The privilege exuded through blissful facemaking finally met the force of racial disruption.

AN INTRODUCTION TO TEACHABLE MOMENTS

In this chapter, I address how I came to understand and formulate an embodied strategy of learning and future teaching. Preschool isolation and, later in the chapter, my story on vulnerability have worked to teach me and hopefully my White educators something about how bodies become texts and tools of education. I regard my humiliations and active embodiments as necessary pieces of my personal Black, lesbian, and feminist pedagogy. I make no grand claims to know *how to properly teach*; instead I wish to *share my work* and my hopes for how I want my body and my experiences to participate in teaching and learning practices.

I utilize the term *teachable moment(s)* on two fronts. First, I define a teachable moment as it would be understood in, perhaps, any teaching context, as a moment that occurs within a learning space that brings forth new knowledge through a tangible encounter. I extend the definition of *teachable moment* to the ontology of Black queer and lesbian pedagogical practices, which pay close attention to how Black lesbian, gay, bisexual, transgender, queer/questioning, intersex, and asexual (LGBTQIA) people, both visibly and not, become "texts" in the classroom and therefore often encounter moments of hostility, confusion, erasure, and wonder (Clarke, 1995; hooks, 1994; Jordan, 1998; Lewis, 2011; Lorde, 2007).

When I articulate *queerness* I mean to invoke antinormative notions of identity, communication, and politics. Likewise, *queer* has been articulated by queer theorist Eve Sedgwick (2012) to mean "the open mesh of possibilities, gaps, overlaps, dissonances and resonances, lapses and excesses of meaning when the constituent elements of anyone's gender, of anyone's sexuality aren't made (or can't be made) to signify monolithically" (p. 338). Queerness can be thought of as the beginning of what cannot be contained within the bounds of heterosexuality, able-bodiedness, and normative gender and race assumptions.

With this being said, it is my contention that forms of Black queer pedagogy make people visible in the academy who do not typically belong or show up in these spaces. This means that unbelievable, marginal subjectivities such as those of Black, female, and queer educators become believable. To focus, then, on these teachable moments is to build a type of Black queer pedagogy that creates active dialogue around the presence of race, sexuality, and gender difference in the classroom in hopes of interrupting racist and heterosexist violence.

My definition of *embodiment* comes from Black feminist and queer theories of the body that center the lived experiences of Black people while asserting that, on the one hand, our intellectual and theoretical work as scholars becomes legible and originates from ourselves, and, on the other hand, embodiment prevents the abstraction of our work and its distance from our bodies (Alexander, 2005; Holland, 2012; hooks, 1988; Johnson, 2003; Lewis, 2011; Richardson, 2003). This means that theory-making is not a simple classroom exercise. The creation and application of theory should not be disconnected from the lived experiences of Black people (Christian, 1987). Instead, embodiment brings theory to life, or, rather, embodiment may be the visual confirmation of the material existence of such theory (Alexander, 2005; Lewis, 2011). I read my preschool moment as one of my first brushes with embodiment. This is to say that my 4-year-old body in a formerly all-White classroom space signaled the tangible lack of race-conscious inclusion in this preschool community. My teachers did not need to think about making the classroom accessible to racial difference until my physical body forced them to see how noninclusive the classroom was. This experience is an example of the (sometimes unintentional) racism Black theorists argue is always present on the micro and macro scale.

ANOTHER MOMENT: THE PRIVILEGE OF FAILURE

My undergraduate capstone course was a poetry workshop, a class of about 15 college seniors sitting together, in a circle, desk to desk, offering up our poems for lambasting. Similar to my preschool days, I was still the only Black person present. Not coincidentally, my preschool was only a drive down the street from the university. I circulated a poem about cutting my hair and letting it grow naturally. The poem also doubled as personal commentary on my transformation from a normative heterosexual-looking woman into the androgynous or ambiguous woman I position myself as now. The day my class was to offer critique of my poem, my professor was away and the graduate teaching assistant moderated the class. The class did a wonderful job of providing feedback for the other students presenting poems the same day. When it was my turn, my classmates shifted in their seats, scribbled aimlessly on their notes, and avoided making eye contact with me. Very few had anything to say aloud about or in their written feedback to me regarding my poem. Most of their comments were along the lines of

- *I don't have much to say.*
- *I cannot understand the topic of your poem but it's good.*
- *Your structure was good; I cannot comment on your content.*

Our teaching assistant meekly offered that she could relate to having "curly-hair issues," though her wavy hair and freckled skin proved to me, and everyone else in the class, that we did not in fact share the same connection she so awkwardly attempted.

Days after class ended, after my body finally stopped feeling hot from embarrassment, I received an e-mail from a White woman in my class. She wrote to tell me that she worked at our LGBTQ resource office and that she felt she needed to say something to me about my poem. She claimed that my poem pointed out that I was having an identity crisis. She theorized that I was probably experiencing some gender confusion and that she was there to offer whatever support I needed to get through the moment. Taken aback, I replied to her that the poem was truly about my hair journey, that I was not having an identity crisis, and that we could discuss any confusion my poem created. She replied with a forceful undoing of my assertion, claiming that she knew better than I did about what I was experiencing and that I indeed was confused. I then scheduled an appointment with my professor to discuss the e-mails and also the isolation and racist passivity I felt had occurred in our classroom the day she was not there. My professor listened intently and said she had no idea how she was supposed to act or react to the situation. She said she was sorry that she had "failed me."

I remember the potted plants she had outside of her window, the circle patterns the sun made inside on the olive-colored carpet. She *had* failed me. Before this point I had not thought of teaching as either a failure or success. I am not even sure that I had trusted my professor not to fail me. But I suppose I had trusted my professor to take my poem as myself and treat me with compassion when it became clear that my classmates were unable to distinguish my poem from me. I had anticipated my professor's compassion and similar rage when my classmate's personal critique and wrongful labeling of me became oppressive. But my university classroom was simply ill-equipped to deal with my multiple intersecting identities that required unique care. And my professor's failure allowed her to walk away without taking measures to ensure a safe, kind, and inclusive classroom for *every* student. This moment of pedagogical failure was irredeemable to my professor, and consequently so was I.

LESBIAN EMBODIMENT AS PEDAGOGICAL STRATEGY

This more recent experience with embodiment activated other identities that I hold. As a somewhat masculine-looking Black lesbian, I have had to conceptualize both my learning and teaching as products of my hinged existence. The vulnerability I felt in my poetry class cannot be traced to only one of my identities but to all I held at that time. My classmates could not understand Black hair without also considering that I was a Black *woman* writing about hair. This is the vulnerability Kimberle Crenshaw (1993) articulated as a systemic and interlocking disadvantage that intersecting identities are caught in. Nevertheless, the recognition of intersectionality carries humanizing potential.

Likewise, my poem made reference to sexuality that may have been similar to other LGBTQIA students in class but was unfamiliar as I expressed myself through a Black positionality instead of a White one. This is not to argue that all Black LGBTQIA experiences—male, female, or nongendered—are necessarily different from White experiences; rather, I argue that racism, heterosexism and homophobia, sexism (and other –isms) pronounce themselves on People of Color in interesting and sometimes devastating and violent manners. And by violent, I mean not only to point out the potential for physical violence but that verbal violence, the violence of being forgotten in a classroom, the violence of being told who you are, the violence of being failed with no hope for accountability—these are all oppressive and emotionally draining experiences marginalized people and students contend with on a daily basis. Ideally, the classroom should not be a place that reproduces this violence.

I argue that Black lesbian embodiment can surface as a pedagogical strategy when the daily repetitions of racism, heterosexism, and homophobia spill over into classroom interaction. I use theories of phenomenology and space to envision the possibilities that come from Black LGBTQIA people in the classroom. For example, in *Queer Phenomenology*, scholar Sara Ahmed (2006) contends that "When bodies take up spaces that they were not intended to inhabit . . . new impressions, new lines emerge, new objects, or even new bodies, gather" (p. 62). Keeping this image as a model of what I see as the daily struggle and possibility for Black LGBTQUIA teachers and students in educational institutions, I argue that these same bodies, especially instructors, pull into their rotation desires that gather at different positions, desires that turn the play of racial and sexual violations, restrictions, and refusals into moments of mutual desire for learning between students and themselves.

Mel Michelle Lewis (2011) presents this desired gathering in "Body of Knowledge: Black Queer Feminist Pedagogy, Praxis, and Embodied Text." Lewis, aware of her pedagogical power and vulnerability as an out, femme, Black lesbian, reflects, "My identity informs and constructs the classroom both in its difference from expected teaching identity, and in its creative pedagogical power. . . . My body's disruptions signal teachable moments" (pp. 50–51). For bodies like hers, and like mine, that inhabit spaces not meant for our inhabitance, the classroom as a site of visual exploration becomes a practical tool for recognition of LGBTQIA People of Color, the work we produce, and the conjoined impact of such recognitions. Lewis asserts, "I create and theorize what I am transparently naming 'Black queer feminist pedagogy,' an ordered and practical teaching method that relies upon the recognition of embodiment, the teaching of intersectional realities, and teaching through interdisciplinary practices" (p. 50). Her pedagogical style is not meant to be a catchall approach to racial, sexual, or gendered theorization; rather, Lewis strategically creates a way of knowing the self, the other, and the text as alive and a critical piece of intellectual development.

Bryant Keith Alexander (2005), in "Embracing the Teachable Moment: The Black Gay Body in the Classroom as Embodied Text," poses a similar strategy when he practices embodiment in the classroom. Alexander presses, "I am interested in constructing the *material fact* of the black gay body as subtext to the *material context* of the classroom" (p. 250). His materialization in the classroom disrupts the inkling that theory is distant from one's corporeal presence and the violence that makes contact with marginalized people. Lewis (2011) herself notes, "The ways in which my students understand my identities becomes part of the project as they sort out the complicated ideas of race, gender, sexuality, and class through the interpretation of course texts, including my own embodied text" (p. 50). Both Alexander and Lewis perform strategies of Black LGBTQIA pedagogical intervention that are based on the daily brush with racial, sexual, and gendered difference and discrimination on the page and in the flesh.

However, these strategies are not without messy slippages. For Lewis, students often confuse her body as merely another textual authority, a static pedagogical rooting, though she urges that their desire for knowledge need not be exploitative, racist, or homophobic. Lewis admits,

> I have recognized instances in which students have imagined me as authentic and authoritative, based at least in part on my identity in relationship to the course material. My body seems to stand in for the text on some occasions; comments prefaced with "no offense to you," or "I'm sorry, I don't mean you," often turn up in classroom discussions and journal assignments. These statements insist that any critique of the argument is not an attack on me as the teacher, though I bear an uncanny resemblance to the text. (pp. 52–53)

Lewis's problem of misidentification is driven by the assumption of Black female theories and epistemologies as anecdotal and blanketing, thus removing lines of difference between Black women from page to classroom position. In my story, my classmates' limited interaction with the subject of my poem brought forth this very issue. Unable to read my poem as anything other than me myself left them with no language with which to make distinguishing or differentiating remarks without being offensive or without making critiques of me as a person. They did not know how to read *me* and therefore could not read my poem without discomfort.

CONCLUSION: FORGETTING AND REMEMBERING

My professor's "I'm sorry I failed you" sentiment, though sincere, presents a problem for the type of pedagogy I aim to develop. Our private conversation did little to alleviate the unfairness of our classroom space. None of the students were challenged to rewrite the feedback to me or to other students whom they may have forgotten and shrugged off through their inability to understand or relate. The woman who e-mailed me, who also probably meant no harm, did not have to own up to her privileged overstepping. Her labeling of my "gender confusion" erased my self-defined identity and also the possibility of such a discussion to occur between us or with the class at large.

The "I'm sorry I failed you" and my discontinuation of an e-mail thread stopped my body dead in its tracks. The conversation of difference, respect, and power was over. What acknowledgement of my Black lesbian body could have provided then is what I am searching for in my research and practices as an educator in the classroom and broader community. Remembering to, metaphorically and literally, provide more than white paper plates may also be the difference between identity erasure and identity discovery. It is through this that I imagine teaching itself as a *practice of remembrance* and not of forgetting.

DISCUSSION QUESTIONS

1. Search your memory for innocuous projects or other situations in your history. Of these moments, what types of identities and people were left out, on display, or even harmed?
2. What identities do you embody, and what does embodiment mean to you? How is embodiment a type of praxis?
3. How did you come to produce your own pedagogical positioning? How does it account for differences based upon different races, gender identifications, and sexualities?
4. Identify teachable moments you can share to enlighten others about your experiences or revelations relative to inclusive practices.
5. What identities do you feel are important to keep in mind in your work and play spaces? What are ways you can incorporate *remembrance practices* into your philosophical underpinnings?

REFERENCES

Ahmed, S. (2006). *Queer phenomenology: Orientations, objects, others*. Durham, NC: Duke University Press.

Alexander, B. K. (2005). Embracing the teachable moment: The Black gay body in the classroom as embodied text. In E. P. Johnson & M. G. Henderson (Eds.), *Black queer studies: A critical anthology* (pp. 249–265). Durham, NC: Duke University Press.

Bonilla-Silva, E. (2006). *Racism without racists: Color-blind racism and the persistence of racial inequality in America*. Lanham, MA: Rowman & Littlefield.

Christian, B. (1987). The race for theory. *Cultural Critique, 6*, 51–63. doi:10.2307/1354255

Clarke, C. (1995). Lesbianism: An act of resistance. In Beverly Guy-Sheftall (Ed.), *Words of fire: An anthology of African-American feminist thought* (pp. 241–252). New York, NY: New Press.

Crenshaw, K. W. (1993). Demarginalizing the intersection of race and sex: A Black feminist critique of antidiscrimination doctrine, feminist theory and antiracist politics. In D. K. Weisberg (Ed.), *Feminist legal theory: Foundations* (pp. 383–395). Philadelphia, PA: Temple University Press.

Holland, S. P. (2012). *The erotic life of racism*. Durham, NC: Duke University Press.

hooks, b. (1988). *Talking back: Thinking feminist, thinking Black*. Boston, MA: South End Press.

Johnson, E. (2003). Performance and/as pedagogy: Performing Blackness in the classroom. *Appropriating Blackness: Performance and the politics of authenticity*. Durham, NC: Duke University Press.

Jordan, J. (1998). *Affirmative acts: Political essays*. New York, NY: Anchor Books.

Lewis, M. M. (2011). Body of knowledge: Black queer feminist pedagogy, praxis, and embodied text. *Journal of Lesbian Studies, 15*(1),3 49–57. 3http://dx.doi.org/10.1080/10894160.2010.508411

Lorde, A. (2007). *Sister outsider*. Berkeley, CA: Crossing Press.

Richardson, M. U. (2003). No more secrets, no more lies: African American history and compulsory heterosexuality. *Journal of Women's History, 15*(3), 63–76. http://dx.doi.org/10.1353/jowh.2003.0080

Sedgwick, E. (2012). Christmas effects. In E. Meiners & T. Quinn (Eds.), *Sexualities in education: A reader* (pp. 336–339). New York, NY: Peter Lang.

CHAPTER 25

ETHNIC BEAUTY IN A WESTERN SOCIETY

An Examination of Black Identity Development

Sametra Polkah-Toe with Valerie A. Middleton

Adolescence is a time when social issues, identity development, and social comparisons are at the forefront of adolescents' thinking. While this is often a difficult time period for many youth, it has been proposed that Children of Color in the United States, in particular, face a far more difficult task than their White counterparts in developing their identity (Boykin & Toms, 1985). With the necessity of having to integrate multiple, yet distinct, identities in deciding "who they are," Children of Color often must navigate a "triple quandary" as they experience life as a mainstream American, a minority, and an ethnic being (Boykin & Toms, 1985). Navigating multiple identities can often be a complex, competing, and contradictory process, which can leave an adolescent in a "stagnant period of psychological growth" prior to "successful integration" (Boykin & Toms, 1985, p. 43).

I am an African American female in my late 20s pursuing an advanced degree in clinical mental health counseling. In thinking about my experiences with diversity and oppression, my racial and gender identities have always been the most salient. Both my father, an African immigrant, and my mother, a citizen of the United States who grew up in the preintegrated South, experienced extreme racial discrimination and hostility throughout their lifetimes; as a result, they always made a point to remind me that "your differences matter" and that "You will always have to work twice as hard as everyone else." Their way of protecting me from "this cruel world" was to prepare me for it. If I wanted to be successful, *like my White counterparts*, I had to be educated like them, talk like them, and even look like them. In an effort to address my look, my mother would either straighten my hair every week or perm my hair every other month because that is what it took to make my hair "behave" so that it would always be "nice and straight." She specifically said that I shouldn't walk around with my hair "nappy" because "it didn't look nice" and that it "wasn't acceptable out there." These words bothered me and stuck with me throughout my developmental years. I liked myself, I liked my ethnic African features, and I did not have a full understanding of my mother's disapproval of it.

To me, my mother had always been the embodiment of the strong Black woman—strong, intelligent, and resilient. Because of the color of her skin, she experienced traumatic events such as daily racist and sexist taunts from White classmates, the legal denial of the right to play at the same playground as her White friends, and even being forced to quit jobs due to threats of harm from members of White supremacist groups. If there was one person whom I expected to understand the importance of embracing a positive Black identity, it was her; but instead, she expected me to conform. These ideas of conformity as a necessity were further reinforced via school, friends, family members, television, advertisements, and corporations.

The psychological impact of being made to feel less worthy than others was devastating to me. All women in general are exposed to oppressive beauty standards, but the added element of race often makes the experience worse for Women of Color who are fed the narrative that the White/Western standard of beauty is the only standard of beauty. Constant exposure to this narrative makes it easy to doubt self-worth, question beauty, and develop a sense of self-hatred, particularly during such formative years as adolescence.

The following narrative examines the effects of minority status on the ethnic identity development of African American girls in the United States. More specifically, the focus is on adolescent ideals and perceptions of female beauty within the context of living within a Western identity.

EXTENT OF THE PROBLEM

African American adolescent girls report overall higher levels of body-image satisfaction, differ in perceptions of the ideal body type, are more likely to be flexible in their concepts of beauty, and are less likely to receive plastic-surgery services or develop eating disorders than their White counterparts. The implicit assumption in these conclusions seems to be a disagreement with the assertion that Black youth have indeed internalized White beauty standards (Molloy & Herzberger, 1999; Parker, Nichter, Ritenbaugh, Sims, & Vukovic, 1997; Twenge & Crocker, 2002). Missing from many of these studies, however, seem to be analyses of nonweight-related features, such as hair and skin color, in the lives of African American adolescents. If we consider that thinness, fair skin, and long hair are typically what most Westerners associate with the ideal beautiful woman (Duke, 2000), these variables are of extreme importance when we are discussing positive self-identity among African American girls, in that (a) they are key distinguishing features and are historically linked with societal degradation of African American women, and (b) it is almost impossible for African American girls to physically conform to these standards without drastic alterations to their bodies.

I remember, just like it was yesterday, the feeling of intense heat as the pressing comb grazed against my forehead and over the top of my head—the smell of burnt hair as my kinky coils began to fall straight against my face, the loud echoes of "sit still," and the dull headaches that came once the pulling and yanking from the comb finally ceased. Indeed, having to sit through the agonizing hours of getting one's hair straightened or permed is quite the common experience for many African American women. In the eyes of our mothers and grandmothers, it is almost a rite of passage showing that we are getting older and must begin to "look acceptable."

I am sure, at this point, some readers may be thinking, *What possible relevance could hair have when discussing issues of privilege and oppression?* The answer is in the implicit messages imbedded in the experience. Consider for a moment the transformative power of this experience. Generally speaking, Black people's hair differs greatly from the hair of other groups in that it is generally much coarser, tighter, and kinkier, which results in shorter lengths and is atypical of the European beauty standards presented by mainstream culture. So when I use the term *natural hair,* I am referring to unprocessed hair that is free from relaxers and other chemical hair treatments. Some natural hair styles that may be easily recognizable are Afros and dreadlocks. In Western society, straight hair tends to enjoy higher prestige and is considered more acceptable in both professional and everyday contexts. Those early experiences of getting our hair done reinforces the message that our natural selves are unacceptable. We were expected to continue the age-old adages held by our parents that *conformity is a necessary evil.* It is well documented in the literature that African American females who wear their hair natural have faced discrimination in the workplace, in the military, and even as young children in elementary school. The basis of this discrimination is often that these hairstyles are considered abnormal. But I'm confused. How is the natural hair texture one was born with abnormal?

As Robinson and Howard-Hamilton noted in their 2000 article, the politics of hair and skin color has been a contentious intraracial issue within the African American community, irrespective of age or social class. This phenomenon stems back to slavery and the practice of miscegenation, when slave masters accorded preferential treatment to their biracial offspring, who usually had lighter skin and straighter hair textures (Okazzawa-Rey, Robinson, & Ward, 1987). Following the demise of slavery, African Americans still continued to assign greater value to individuals who resembled a more White European aesthetic. Even today, many young African Americans who emphasize their natural/naturally African cultural features endure teasing and ridicule because of their appearance. These experiences can erode their feelings of self-worth and personal adequacy (Holcomb-McCoy & Moore-Thomas, 2001).

Prior research seems to indicate that these ideals do become manifested at early ages. In a qualitative study focusing on the intersection of race and gender on adolescent ideal body types, researchers found that the overwhelming majority of their sample (78% of preteen African American girls) indicated *hair* as their most troublesome physical feature (Hesse-Biber, Howling, Leave, & Lovejoy, 2004). Many of the girls' responses also seemed to indicate an implicit correlation between lack of conformity with White European beauty ideals and lower self-esteem. In the article, the researcher poses the question, "What makes you have a high self-esteem and what makes it bad?" A girl responds, "I don't know what makes me have high self-esteem, but I know what makes me have low self-esteem." Researcher: "What's that?" Girl: "People make fun of you." Researcher: "What do they make fun of?" Girl: "My hair."

This same study also briefly examined the issue of colorism among adolescents within the Black community. Prior studies have shown that most African Americans are partial to skin color that lies somewhere in the middle of the light–dark color spectrum (Clark, Hocevar, & Dembo, 1980; Robinson & Ward, 1995). This data becomes particularly relevant for Black women in that often those who have darker skin feel devalued for not living up to the American standard of "light-skin beauty," while those who have a lighter skin tone face ostracization for being too light (i.e., too white). Other studies on the topic have also concluded that skin tone is connected to feelings of self-worth, self-esteem, and attractiveness among African American females (Thompson & Keith, 2001).

FROM THEORY TO PRACTICE

As I entered my college years, the sense of newfound freedom and independence engulfed my spirit and I slowly started letting go of the hair routine my mother had kept up for me for so many years. My interest in African American studies and identity formation grew; as I spent more time researching the topic, I began to associate positive qualities with my differences, such as identifying my hair as unique and the African American experience as resilient. It is from these experiences that my practice as a counselor-in-training has been informed.

Assisting adolescent African American girls and other visible minorities in combating oppressive beauty ideals involves instilling in young girls a sense of self-acceptance, an understanding of the spectrum of beauty, and awareness of the skills needed to develop into confident young women. Strengths-based counseling and positive psychology are the theories that most inform this line of thinking (Ponterotto & Casas, 1991; Smith, 1977, 1989). Though strength-based counseling is not commonly identified in the literature, the major tenets of this approach position it as being potentially very effective when one is working with African American girls. Strengths-based counseling is a discipline of positive psychology and focuses on a client's strengths rather than her societally perceived weaknesses, deficits, and problems. This approach is particularly relevant because it does not insist that the problem (e.g., discrimination, sexism, oppressive beauty standards) doesn't exist or that we can make the problem go away. Rather, it insists that, although the problem may always exist, it is external from us as individuals, and therefore we should use our strengths to cope with living with it. It is also worth noting that strengths-based counseling developed partly out of the efforts of many cross-cultural counseling psychologists who began to note that many assumptions of the dominant cultural approaches contained inherent biases that were inappropriate for ethnic minority groups. These early theorists asserted that many clients had cultural strengths that were infrequently considered and that minimized societal factors such as racism and sexism on an individual's development (Ponterottor & Casas, 1991; Smith, 1977, 1989).

The strengths-based counseling approach suggests that human strengths act as buffers against mental illness when individuals become aware that they have internal resources that will permit them to overcome obstacles. Therefore, the majority of interventions under this approach revolve around client strengths as the basis for change. Though it may vary, the established basic procedural guideline for counselors using this approach is to

1. externalize the problem;
2. assist the client in identifying strengths and resources;
3. assist the client in considering which strengths/resources she can use to cope with a given problem; and
4. build encouragement.

During the first stage, externalizing the problem should not be viewed as something integrated with the person's identity. Using the aforementioned topics as an example in working with a young woman, the counselor should assist the youth in understanding that negative labels associated with Blackness (nappy hair, unattractiveness, underachievement, etc.) are all social creations and are not inherently associated with her individual identity. Sometimes attaching a nondiagnostic label to the problem can help during this process. For example, instead of calling the problem *having low self-esteem*, address the problem as *an individual with a frustrating relationship with her body*. It is also appropriate during this stage to employ the miracle-question technique as a means to have a clear understanding of the client's goal for seeking therapy. The miracle question basically asks clients to make believe, however fantastical it may be in their particular circumstances, that their life has already changed for the better. Familiar examples of employing this technique include "Suppose tonight, while you slept, a miracle occurred. When you awake tomorrow, what would be some of the things you would notice that would tell you life had suddenly gotten better?" or " Suppose I had a magic wand and by waving it I could make this problem disappear; what would be a sign that the magic is working (what would be the changes you're seeing)?" By using this technique, clients are challenged to look past their obstacles and hopelessness and focus on the possibilities.

In the second stage, the focus of the counselor is on helping the client recognize the personal and environmental resources she has used to keep the problem under control in the past. During this process, the client is given the opportunity to tell her life story in her own words, without worry of not having her feelings validated. However, it should be noted that the client may tend to define herself around traumatic events; therefore, reframing can be a useful intervention during this step, in order to help her retell her story in ways that highlight the positives rather than the negatives. Again, using the example of hair, an adolescent African American youth can be taught to redefine her cultural features in such ways as unique, different, kinky, and so on. Counselors should be sure that in the midst of narrating her story, the client is simultaneously uncovering biological, psychological, social, cultural, environmental, economic, and other such strengths.

The third stage involves finding exceptions, which entails encouraging the client to identify those times when she was most in control of her problems. This is a very educational component of the counseling journey because it is during this process where the client is forced to examine what societal factors (family, peers, media, opposite sex, etc.) are influencing the negative perception of self and what factors were at play during times in her young life when she was not as concerned with attaining these standards. The client should also be asked to recall moments when the problem was not dominating her life and what factors were involved in keeping the problem at bay.

Once the client has a general idea of her personal strengths, she enters the fourth stage, where she begins translating these strengths and resources into a means for actually managing the problem. In this final stage, encouragement is the key source the therapist provides to effect change in the client. Through encouragement (the therapist intentionally honoring/complimenting the client for dealing with her struggles), the client becomes further willing to attempt or consider change in behavior and self.

As previously mentioned, institutionalized racism, sexism, and oppression are not issues that can be eradicated overnight. The pressure will likely always exist for Females of Color to conform to Western notions of beauty, but an awareness of their strengths will provide them with additional coping strategies to deal with the issue.

CONCLUSION

In concluding this chapter, it is important to reinforce the notion that some African American adolescents may need reassurance about their appearance, including strategies for coping with their perception of physical attractiveness, skills to resist internalizing negative messages imposed by society, and opportunities to openly process their experiences and reactions about issues of hair and skin color. Though these may be sensitive issues, it is crucial that counselors not avoid these topics because of personal discomfort and that they recognize these issues as part of the culture and the cultural experience many Youth of Color will face.

The strategy introduced here provides some basic tenets to keep in mind when counseling African American adolescent girls who may be struggling with positive identity formation. These strategies integrate some of what is known about the cultural values, social institutions, and racial identity functioning of African Americans.

One further recommendation for future counselors dealing with this issue is that they introduce their adolescent clients to the many civic/social organizations such as the Beautiful Project, Black Girls Rock, the Sisterhood Agenda, the NAACP Youth chapter, and the National Urban League Youth chapter committed to reinforcing Black culture and instilling confidence in Black youth. These organizations not only provide positive peer and adult role models for children, but they also promote civic responsibility and leadership and offer educational advantages such as scholarships and college tours. Their services appear well suited to Black youth of any socioeconomic class who may be socially or geographically disconnected from neighboring Black communities or generally in need of such support.

DISCUSSION QUESTIONS

1. Where are you in your current racial/cultural identity development? Identify the multiple roles and identities in your own personal life. What strategies have proven effective in integrating them?
2. What is your response to the connections the author makes between sexism, privilege, and oppressive beauty standards?

3. What are some of the issues in your own life that you have experienced or noticed in terms of the relationship between beauty and identity formation?
4. What can those in a position of privilege do to honor beauty along a more inclusive spectrum?
5. The author spoke extensively about contemporary struggles over a historical issue in the African American community. How does learning about historical trauma affect the way you think about race, identity, and culture?
6. In the chapter, the author discusses her relationship with her mother and how she became a perpetuator of the same oppressive ideals as mainstream society. In what ways do patterns or rituals born out of historically traumatic experiences continue to play out in families today? How can these patterns or rituals be understood and addressed in sensitive and healing ways?
7. When there is an historically unequal relationship between individuals and groups of people, how might it impact client–professional relationships? How might one address the underlying hurt and pain to break down barriers and improve communication?

REFERENCES

Boykin, A. W., & Toms, F. D. (1985). Black child socialization: A conceptual framework. In H. P. McAdoo & J. L. McAdoo (Eds.), *Black children: Social, educational, and parental environments* (pp. 33–51). Thousand Oaks, CA: SAGE.

Clark, A., Hocevar D., & Dembo, M. H. (1980). The role of cognitive development in children's explanations and preferences for skin color. *Developmental Psychology, 16,* 332–339.

Duke, L. (2000). Black in a blonde world: Race and girls' interpretation of the feminine ideal in teen magazines. *Journalism and Mass Communication Quarterly, 77*(2), 697–392.

Hesse-Biber, S. N., Howling, S. A., Leavy, P., & Lovejoy, M. (2004). Racial identity of body image issues among adolescent girls. *The Qualitative Report, 9*(1), 49–79.

Holcomb-McCoy, C. C., & Moore-Thomas, C. (2001). Empowering African American adolescent females. *Professional School Counseling, 5*(1), 19–27.

Molloy, B. L., & Herzberger, S. D. (1999). Body image and self esteem: A comparison of African American and Caucasian women. *Sex Roles, 38*(7), 631–643.

Okazzawa-Rey, M., Robinson, T., & Ward, J. V. (1987). Black women and the politics of skin color and hair. *Women & Therapy, 6*(1–2), 89–102.

Parker, S., Nichter, M., Ritenbaugh, C., Sims, C., & Vuckovic, N. (1997). Body images and weight concerns among African American and White adolescent females: Differences that make a difference. *Human Organization, 54*(2), 103–114.

Ponterotto, J., & Casas, M. (1991). *Handbook of racial/ethnic minority counseling research.* Springfield, IL: Charles C. Thomas.

Robinson, T., & Howard-Hamilton, M. (2000). *The convergence of race, ethnicity, and gender: Multiple identities in counseling.* Upper Saddle River, NJ: Merrill.

Robinson, T. L., & Ward, J. V. (1995). African American adolescents and skin color. *Journal of Black Psychology, 21*(3), 256–274.

Smith, E. J. (1977). Counseling Black individuals: Some stereotypes. *The Personnel and Guidance Journal, 55,* 390–396.

Smith, E. J. (1989). Black racial identity development: Issues and concerns. *The Counseling Psychologist, 17,* 277–288.

Thompson, M. S., & Keith, V. M. (2001). The blacker the berry: Gender, skin tone, self-esteem, and self-efficacy. *Gender & Society, 15*(3), 336–357.

Twenge, J. M., & Crocker, J. (2002). Race and self-esteem: Meta-analyses comparing Whites, Blacks, Hispanics, Asians, and American Indians. *Psychological Bulletin, 128*(3), 371–408.

CHAPTER 26

SKIN COLOR

An Issue of Social Status and Privilege

Linda Robinson

Colorism, defined as prejudice based on skin color (Turner, 2013), has been an ongoing concern for African Americans since the time of colonialism in America (Jones, 2000). The need for White slave owners to promote and maintain White supremacy resulted in providing the biracial children of African women and White slave owners a depreciated version of White privilege. These light-skinned offspring were assigned easier work duties than those whose skin was darker, along with access to educational opportunities. Colorism is still operational in contemporary times. For example, Hall (2006) discussed the American preference for light skin among People of Color, including African Americans. The results of a study conducted by Hannon (2015) reveal that Whites are more likely to view light-skinned African Americans and Latinos as intelligent people. Goldsmith, Hamilton, and Darity (2007) found that wage differences in America are often determined by skin color. Similarly, Hunter (2002) found that light skin color improves the wages of African American women. Other researchers have emphasized the importance of skin color and its impact on negative stereotypes (Maddox & Gray, 2002), positions of authority (Jones, 2000), perceived life success (Wade & Bielitz, 2005), and perceived parenting skills, (Watson, Thornton, & Engelland, 2010).

My experience with colorism spans several decades. Hence, the purpose of this chapter is to share my experiences regarding the issue of skin color in the African American community.

MY HISTORY

I was born in the 1950s to a dark-skinned African American mother and a light-skinned African American father. My mother's socioeconomic status during that time is best described as poor working class, and, as a result, she experienced few financial privileges. Her socioeconomic status reflected my family's ongoing struggle to overcome financial challenges dating back to America's Great Depression. My father held a managerial position at a dry cleaner's, and I assume that his socioeconomic status was lower middle class, based on what I have heard about him. My mother and father never married, and they separated when I was still an infant. Hence, my father was not a part of my life. I have always wondered if the difference in their skin color contributed to the demise of their relationship. I will probably never know because my mother insists on maintaining her silence on the issue.

All of my immediate maternal family members were dark-skinned people except for one maternal aunt. My maternal great-grandmother, whom I met just prior to her death, was light-skinned and her mother was reported to be a light-skinned woman of mixed heritage. My maternal great-grandmother's father was a dark-skinned freed slave.

The fact that my youngest maternal aunt was very light-skinned was never discussed openly in my household; however; she received accolades almost daily regarding her appearance in the community. I remember, on several occasions when I was about five or six years old, taking walks with her through the business district of our community. The African American men in particular seemed to be overwhelmed by her beauty, and she would frequently receive, in my opinion, exaggerated complements. I remember a man being so impacted by her that he actually took dollar bills out of his pocket and laid them down on the sidewalk before her as she walked. This image still remains vivid in my mind because I never saw my mother, who was indeed a very attractive, dark-skinned woman, receive such a response. I was told by family and community members that dark-skinned people should not wear bright colors because they did not look good on them. Because bright colors, such as yellow and red, tends to accentuate dark brown tones, avoiding these colors was a way to deemphasize the darkness of the skin. Hence, one thing became apparent to me at a very young age: Skin tone mattered.

MEDIA, MAKEUP, AND NYLONS

During my formative years, few African Americans were seen on television. Women were often described as "She's pretty, but she's dark," and very dark African Americans were thought of as evil people, even before one made their acquaintance. However, light-skinned African Americans were viewed as beautiful, and this judgement was often directed more so toward African American women because it appeared that dark skin for African American men was better tolerated by the African American community. Media icons of African American feminine beauty during the 1940s through the 1950s were movie stars such as Lena Horne and Dorothy Dandridge, two African American actresses whose light skin seemed just as important to African Americans as their acting talent. During the same time, however, dark-skinned actors such as Ossie Davis and Sidney Poitier were also revered by African Americans; their dark skin tones seemed not to matter much, a reflection of the level of tolerance for dark-skinned male entertainers in the media (Wade & Bielitz, 2005). For some reason, even as a youth, I was acutely aware of these distinctions and felt troubled by them.

During the first 18 years or so of my life, I also noticed that dark-skinned women seemed to be invisible to the makeup industry. Dark shades of facial makeup were limited to a few manufacturers. As a result, dark-skinned African American women were forced to wear facial powder and foundations with pink tones, which resulted in a gray, pasty appearance. A popular shade of makeup in my household was *nut brown*. Although I cannot recall the manufacturer, I vividly remember that the makeup contained quite a bit of red overtones that in no way matched a dark-brown complexion. As a young child, I use to laugh to myself about the appearance of women who wore this makeup. I felt that they were made up like circus clowns. I did not realize the real dilemma of finding appropriate facial powder for dark complexions until I grew older and began to experiment with makeup.

Dark-skinned women also seemed to be invisible to the nylon-stocking industry. Beige-toned stockings (along with black stockings) dominated the market. Shades for brown legs were difficult to find, albeit a reddish-hued nylon seemed to be the selection of choice. Hence, the well-dressed, dark-skinned African American woman would be adorned in the fashions of the time, but her face and legs reflected how she was really viewed by society. As a young woman, I felt resentful regarding how the makeup and stocking manufacturers ignored me as a consumer. I began to realize how unimportant I was to these industries, to the extent that they did not even see me as a possible source of revenue.

Some African American women decided to resolve the "problem" of their dark skin via the use of bleaching creams. Several bleaching products were available during my childhood and were advertised to make your skin "lighter and brighter." I abhorred the idea of skin bleaching, but I had to hold my silence because my mother applied these creams to her face every night. The skin on her face did lighten over time.

To stay aligned with my developmental stage, I too acquiesced to the clown makeup and the stockings that gave my legs a dusty appearance. Although I despised the way the powder and stockings made me look, I felt the need to look that way to improve my visage in the eyes of others because of my dark skin and did not want my appearance to be more compromised. During the early 1970s, something wonderful happened. The makeup industry began to recognize the need for products for darker skin tones. However, it was the African American makeup companies that made the mark in this regard (Terrell, 1975). I remember receiving the entire Johnson Product makeup line for Christmas from a boyfriend. I recall opening up the compact pressed powder first and saw something I had never seen before. Instead of shades of pink, I beheld a circle of dark brownness. I stared at it for a while in disbelief. Then, I smeared some on my right index finger and rubbed it on the back of my left hand. Suddenly, magic happened. Instead of the gray-like hue I was accustom to seeing, the pressed powder seemed to disappear into my skin, only to enhance the smoothness and glow of my natural skin tone. I said to myself, "Oh, this is what makeup should be like." I suddenly felt acknowledged as an African American woman. For days after, I felt a need to call Mr. Johnson and thank him for producing the makeup. Although I did not know him, the makeup seemed to be more of a gift from him than from my boyfriend. I continued wearing the Johnson line of makeup for many years because I viewed it as a privilege. It also reminded me of how White women have always enjoyed the privilege of compatible makeup and how it had taken many years and the efforts of an African American–owned business to help dark-skinned women experience the same privilege. During that same time, nylon stockings of various brown hues became available for African American women.

PARTIES AND SOCIAL EVENTS

Issues of skin color actually became more problematic for me as I began my teenage years. On the weekends, chaperoned house parties were quite common in my community, and I attended many of them during those times. I generally found these functions to be enjoyable except for the way the girls were asked to dance. It was customary during those days for girls to wait to be asked to dance by the boys because dancing with other girls or by oneself was considered socially unacceptable. However, there seemed to be a method for how the boys would ask the girls to dance, and that method was based on the girls' skin color. Many of the boys, who were either from a professional family, light skinned, or felt that they were more affluent in some way, would ask the light-skinned girls to dance first. Other boys would then select girls based on the lightness of their skin. By the time my turn came (as one of the dark-skinned girls), there were often no boys left to dance with, or the remaining boys refused to dance with dark-skinned girls. It appeared evident that, in my community, skin color impacted romantic coupling, with light-skinned people selecting other light-skinned people, and boys who were considered more affluent selecting light-skinned girls. Homecoming queens were always selected based on skin color, regardless of whether the girl was deemed attractive in other aspects of her appearance and character. It was obvious that skin color was the most important aspect.

WORKING AS A BLACK PERSON

After college, I remember working for a bank as a young adult and observing the skin-color strata relative to position status. The highest-ranking African American I saw was a young man who was in training to be an officer of the bank. He was very light skinned, to the extent that he was almost indistinguishable from his White counterparts. The only other African American I saw in a position of authority was a light-skinned female who worked in the department adjacent to mine. She was also rather indistinguishable from her White coworkers. I often wondered whether they would have been hired in those positions if they had been dark skinned, but I really don't think they would have been. I was one of two African Americans in my department. The majority of the other African Americans worked in the mail room. My position was a bit more elevated because I had a college degree.

A more personal employment-related experience involved a part-time telemarketer's position I secured to supplement my modest bank salary. The company I worked for was small, and the number of employees in the call room was limited to two evening telemarketers and one supervisor. My supervisor was a dark-skinned African American man. About three weeks into my employment, a light-skinned African American woman was hired to work during my shift. I then began to notice a change in my supervisor's behavior in response to her presence. He spent an inordinate amount of time talking to her about personal matters, and sometimes he would say things to her that I felt were sexually seductive. She seemed to respond favorably to his advances. I felt invisible in the call room because he spent no time supervising or supporting me. This situation went on for about a week, until one day my supervisor told me that he did not need my services any longer so there was no need for me to return. I was shocked because he had never voiced any dissatisfaction with my work. Although he did not use the word *fired*, I knew what he meant, so I just said, "Okay." I felt that he fired me so that he would have the opportunity to spend time alone with the light-skinned woman. I was angry because I was treated unfairly, and I needed the extra money. I felt that colorism caused me to lose my job. I thought about my light-skinned aunt and the incident with the man with the dollar bills. However, I made the necessary adjustment to my budget and moved on.

COLORISM AND COUNSELING

Considering all that I have discussed previously, I often wonder about how colorism impacts current counseling/client relationships. In my search for an answer to this question, the work of Tummala-Narra (2007) brought to light several issues that can arise from skin-color differences in the counseling setting, including mistrust and envy. Since research, as indicated earlier, supports the idea of skin-tone preference in American society, I wonder whether the thought of light-skinned African Americans receiving a better quality of counseling services is an absurd ideation.

Institutions that have the responsibility of training new counselors should be more inclusive of specific cultural issues, such as colorism, and infuse this information throughout their curriculum. Current counselors have the responsibility of seeking ongoing training throughout their career (American Counseling Association, 2014). For African American counselors, training should include a better understanding of intracultural biases. All counselors would benefit from reflecting on their feelings regarding skin color and be frank about it.

CONCLUSION

As an African American of humble beginnings, I have done my best to overcome issues of internalized racism, colorism, and other biases that the American society has placed upon me. The middle-class privileges I currently enjoy were acquired on my own with the support of family and friends, in spite of my skin color. However, the African American community remains "color struck," and those who are negatively impacted continue to suffer in silence with little voice in the matter. As Burnett (2015) stated:

> Colorism is a painful and shameful reminder of our tortuous past. While it is far easier to minimize or ignore, this is not the solution. Given the pervasiveness of colorism and the colorism mindset throughout our society and its difficulty to prove with empirical data, a solution seems painfully illusive. (p. 4)

As a dark-skinned African American, I find the opportunity to tell my story to be a privilege because many dark-skinned African Americans never have a chance to express their feelings around this issue. So I now say to myself, "Okay; what's next? What can be done to lessen or, in an ideal world, eliminate colorism from our society?" As a professor in the field of counseling psychology, I have the responsibility to teach my students about colorism and its impact on People of Color. As a clinician, I have the responsibility to provide bias-free services regardless of my clients' skin color. As a member of the African American community, I have the responsibility to share my experiences with other African Americans and to encourage them to share their experiences with colorism as well. As a member of the American society at large, I have the responsibility to be both an educator and a voice against the power of bias and oppression that comes from individual and cultural groups favoring one skin tone over another.

ACKNOWLEDGMENTS

I wish to thank my family, friends, and specific educators who have helped me survive the oppression of colorism. I am also very grateful to the many community organizations that have served to support healthy self-images of African Americans. I also thank Johnson's Products for my first positive experience with facial makeup.

DISCUSSION QUESTIONS

1. Before reading this chapter, what did you know about colorism in the African American community? How has this chapter impacted your knowledge?
2. In viewing African Americans of various skin tones, what is your preference? Why?
3. What are the common views regarding skin color in your community and family? How have these views impacted you and your work with People of Color?
4. What issues could an African American present in counseling that could point to problems regarding colorism?
5. How could an African American client's views about skin color be different based on the client's birth cohort?
6. What type of self-advocacy would you recommend for dark-skinned African Americans? How could you help them have a voice that is actually heard by their community and the American society at large?
7. How can you help to educate your community and others about the issue of colorism?

REFERENCES

American Counseling Association. (2014). *ACA 2014 code of ethics*. Retrieved from https://www.counseling.org/resources/aca-code-of-ethics.pdf

Burnett, N. (2015). Colorism in mental health: Looking the other way. *Journal of Colorism Studies, 1*(1), 1–5.

Goldsmith, A., Hamilton, D., & Darity, W. (2007). From dark to light: Skin color and wages among African Americans. *The Journal of Human Resources, 42*(4), 701–738.

Hall, R. (2006). The bleaching syndrome among people of color: Implications of skin color for human behavior in the social environment. *Journal of Human Behavior in the Social Environment, 13*(3), 19–31.

Hannon, L. (2015). White colorism. *Social Currents, 2*(1), 13–21.

Hunter, M. (2002). "If you're light you're alright": Light skin color as social capital for women of color. *Gender & Society, 16*(2), 175–193.

Jones, T, (2000). Shades of brown: The law of skin color. *Duke Law Journal, 49*, 1487–1557.

Maddox, K., & Gray, S. (2002). Cognitive representations of Black Americans: Reexploring the role of skin tone. *Personality and Social Psychology Bulletin, 28*(2), 250–259.

Terrell, A. (1975). The beauty business is still bullish. *Black Enterprise,* November, 40–5252.

Tummala-Narra, P. (2007). Skin color and the therapeutic relationship. *Psychoanalytic Psychology, 24*(2), 255–270.

Turner, B. (2013). Colorism in Dale Orlandersmith's yellowman: The effect of intraracial racism on Black identity and the concept of Black community. *Southern Quarterly, 50*(3), 32–53.

Wade, T., & Bielitz, S. (2005). The differential effect of skin color on attractiveness, personality evaluations, and perceived life successes of African Americans. *Journal of Black Psychology, 31*(3), 215–236.

Watson, S., Thornton, C., & Engelland, B. (2010). Skin color shades in advertising to ethnic audiences: The case of African Americans. *Journal of Marketing Communications, 16*(4), 185–201.

CHAPTER 27

RACISM BY WAY OF EDUCATION

The Politics of Privilege and Oppression

Daryl H. Thorne

Beneath the surface of my lived experiences lies a collection of events that, over the years, have settled into particular spaces on the privilege–oppression continuum. I am a middle-aged, mixed-ancestry Native American woman who has been socialized and politicized as *Black*. The sociopolitical creation of *race* is important to understand in relation to privilege and oppression. However, instead of providing an operational definition of this particular social construction, I offer Leonardo's (2013) assertion that to see the effects of something seemingly powerful—in this case, race—it is often necessary to view it from the periphery. In other words, to fully appreciate my narrative, one must employ a paradigm shift that allows the filtration of subtle and indirect exposure to see, clearly, what is not readily defined by the status quo as racism, privilege, or oppression. Race has been tied directly to socioeconomic status and one's ability to gain access to even the most basic needs in life—housing, health care, and (quality) education. Social inequities shaped by race, gender, and socioeconomic status do not happen in isolation. Smedley (2012) has reminded us that "Racism, gender and class exploitation, and other forms of oppression do not act independently of each other; rather, they act on multiple and often on simultaneous levels" (p. 934). My personal and professional journeys overlap, and they take place within these contexts.

Committing to writing this contribution requires me to deliberately think about my formative and subsequent life experiences in political context. In fact, the more I constructively critique the most impactful events in my life related to socioeconomic status—the combination of presumed education, occupation, and income—the more I am sure they are of political relevance. Practices of any form of governance—systems, institutions, individuals, or beliefs—are strictly about power. The power politic sets the boundaries of privilege, which are fast and loose. In many respects, my relationship with education has been informed by elements of limited privilege, but more often than not it has been shrouded by the ideology of oppression via assumptions attached to ascribed meanings of Blackness, perceived socioeconomic status, and beliefs about identity. My ever unfolding story is best understood as one that is in constant creation and is (partially) informed by unspoken politics.

MY STORY

I am a complex individual just like all other people, and I refuse to accept the conditions of my existence as established by the status quo. My individual privileges are confined within an oppressive system that reduces all people by method of *class*ification (e.g., race, gender, socioeconomic status, religious/spiritual affiliation). Problems arise when humanity buys into socially constructed beliefs about privilege and oppression. Several authors have researched and documented the lingering differences in the quality of education provided to Students of Color over the past several decades (Boozer, Krueger, & Wolkon, 1992; Darling-Hammond, 2000; Kozol, 1991). This is not new information, but it is becoming increasingly normalized as acceptable, which remains problematic; the problem of normalized inequities in education is political. As connected to capitalism, the ability to think critically and to express oneself through articulate and skillful writing is powerful on many levels, but money (capital) provides choice. It is an unfortunate reality that much of the noise about quality education is situated in the language of political economy instead of humanistic empowerment for all people.

My parents divorced when I was about three or four years old. However, I continue to have relationships with both. I am an only child—neither parent had any more children after the divorce. Both of my parents are well-educated. They earned their undergraduate degrees from Virginia Union University, but both moved on and earned master's degrees from other respected universities—Howard University was my father's pick, while George Washington University was my mother's. This was in the late 1960s and early 1970s, respectively. My mother spent her entire professional career as a science teacher in the District of Columbia public-school system, while my father began his career as a microbiologist and ended it as an educator in the Virginia Department of Correctional Education. My father's mother was an educator in a small rural southern Virginia town in the mid-1900s when one- and two-room schoolhouses were commonplace. Suffice it to say that I come from a line of educators. I never intended to follow the path of education as a profession, but I believe that in life everything happens as it should.

I grew up in the 1970s and into the 1980s in a northern Virginia community just outside of Washington, D.C., demarcated as a working- to lower-middle-class neighborhood. The area was originally part of the main travel route for indigenous trade prior to the development of *White* settlements. This major trade route was eventually taken by the European invaders for capitalistic endeavors. The railroad became the primary source of commerce in the early 1900s, and the area in which I would come to know as home was an all-White railway community from circa 1940 until the late 1960s. By the time my mother and I moved into this suburban community in the early 1970s—my mother was one of the few homeowners of Color—White flight had quickly come and gone. Fantastically, the first African American family to integrate the street on which I lived is still there. And, as continued evidence of the repetition of history and the social construction of power, or, if you like, the power of social construction, gentrification is firmly in place with young, middle-class Whites quickly moving back into this sought-after area.

As of the writing of this chapter, I work as an assistant professor at a small, private university that prides itself for honoring its historic social-justice mission by providing a liberal arts education to many of the city's historically marginalized citizens. Previously, I worked as a secondary school counselor in one of the largest public school systems in the state of Maryland. Although both of my graduate degrees are in counseling, my undergraduate degree is in mass communications. As I stated, my career trajectory was decidedly *not* going to be in education. I was clearly wrong.

FORMATIVE YEARS

I attended elementary school less than a decade after schools were legally integrated. Busing across formerly segregated school boundaries was in full force, but this was not on the minds or even in the periphery of my thoughts or of the thoughts of my classmates. We just went to school. I did notice, as time went on, the elements of separateness, but more in the way of categorizing students based upon "ability" instead of any beliefs shaped by racism or classism; at least this is what I thought back then. However, the true intentions of people or institutions are rarely without some sort of an agenda, so elements of the latter could have been at play. I can recall going to school with children who represented the race, class, and ability continua. One of the first memories that comes to mind is walking home with (or rather bringing home) a kindergartener—I was in first grade—who I thought was a nice boy and who was being teased by some of the other children. My heart went out to him. I was not cognizant of the fact that he had some developmental challenges or would be considered a person with a disability by today's criteria, nor did it matter. I have always considered myself a person of integrity and a champion of the underdog as long as the underdog has integrity (inclusive of people and institutions). My intentions were to "teach" him and to be his friend so that the other children would not pick on him. It did not matter that he was White or a person with a disability; my heart said it was the right thing to do. My mother had no problem with my intentions; however, she did have a problem with me bringing someone else's child home without anyone's permission. As I reflect back, I am certain that the fact he was White was of equal concern to her, but I will never be sure. So I had to return him to where I found him, which was in front of his babysitter's house. I do not recall bringing stray kids home again—at least those who were virtual strangers.

Elementary school ended with sixth grade. I assumed I would be moving on to one of the two public junior-high schools in the city to which the vast majority of my classmates were going. In fact, I remember the excitement of the junior-high school counselors coming to visit and explaining the 7 period class schedule and all that came with transitioning from elementary to junior-high school. This experience was simultaneously exciting and intimidating. Alas, a few days before the start of my seventh-grade year, I found a private-school uniform on my bed.

Although my elementary-school experience was normalized within the context of diversity on multiple levels, my early junior-high school years were not. I was forced to go to a small, private, Lutheran school where the vast majority of the students in the combined seventh- and eighth-grade class grew up together. There were a few notable exceptions to this configuration. The most obvious were the two non-White students, Larry and I, who were new to this tight-knit, religious-school community. Most of the students had attended this same school since kindergarten and were also members of the church to which it was connected. Needless to say, I was very self-conscious and defensive for most of my seventh-grade year. I felt out of place and did not appreciate being part of this dynamic, where I was met with curiosity by some of my White classmates and forced to adapt, but over time I did.

My experiences there brought me face to face with overt and covert forms of racism, white privilege (i.e., conditioned supremacy expressed through ignorance), and access to educational privilege and oppression in one fell swoop. I did not appreciate this fundamental experience until I was well into adulthood. As a 12-year-old, in 1980, walking 2 miles home in a private-school uniform while a school bus filled with my peers passed was humiliating. The uniform represented a privilege few of my peers had access to regardless of perceived race, and it was absolutely connected to perceived socioeconomic status. Ironically, its meaning was steeped in oppression for me. I cannot say with certainty that the academic instruction I received in private school was that much better than what I experienced in public school, but what I can say is that it provided me with a relative insider's view of white privilege (supremacy) at work. For instance, there was a pivotal exchange between me and the director's wife that involved a disagreement about the physical description of Jesus propagated in America as informed by the power construct of whiteness. A few nights before this exchange, I watched the re-aired 1974 episode of *Good Times* called "Black Jesus," and with confidence asserted or rather challenged my religion teacher with the biblical passage that states, "His head and hair were white like white wool, like snow, His eyes like flames of fire, His feet like white-glowing bronze" (Revelations 1:14–16, American translation). My assertion that Jesus was most decidedly *not* the physical manifestation of the blonde, straight-haired, blue-eyed son of God used to indoctrinate would-be followers of the Christian faith created a bit of an uproar in the tiny school. Although, as a scholar and activist in the making, I had used the same highly regarded source of religious documentation to support my argument, this did not go over too well. Using the church's own doctrine to challenge the ingrained rhetoric created a tension that immediately strained the room and poked holes in the fragile construction of that particular narrative. I was taken to the principal's office, who was also my teacher's husband, and sternly spoken to. I do not remember what was said, but I do remember the distinctive shade of pinkish-red in his face and the arrogance in his tone. I now recognize that the courage I displayed by confronting and challenging the structure of white supremacy as interpreted through religious doctrine was an affront to the status quo, and any affront to the status quo by a nonmember is met by an inequitable oppressive reaction. This pattern of behavior repeats throughout history.

Not all of my educational or social experiences at this small private school were bad. Nonetheless, the most distinctive imprints left marks on my psyche that are repressive and disconcerting. While I benefitted in some respects, in other ways I was denied valuable information. The most impressive moment serving as the harbinger of my work with my current students is when my favorite teacher at the Lutheran school looked at a paper I wrote and said in a nonchalant manner, "you write like you speak." And that was that. There was no explanation, constructive feedback, or follow-up. This statement made an indelible mark on me. In fact, the lack of any further engagement about the matter left me unenlightened and feeling vulnerable in that troublesome space of *otherness*. This is the vacuum space (void) where White America places that which it does not understand or cannot quite mold into its imagery. My mother was educated and intelligent, and by extension so was I. She spoke and wrote well *and* had been published in a science educators' journal numerous times. She instilled the value of using standard English—grammar is implied—at home. This singular exchange with my teacher created the opening of liminal space within which I constantly strive to improve. . . . The ellipses are left with intention to hold the space of ambiguity because I am not completely sure what I am striving to improve, or for whom. I believe this is a silent question that internally plagues many marginalized people in one form or another; the question causes a peculiar form of psychological pain that only aches at the slightest hint of belonging in a space designed by the narcissistic ideology of Eurocentrism.

In my later years, Du Bois's (1903/1994) work would etch in me the meaning of *double consciousness* as a concept of sanity for sociopolitical survival. I took it upon myself to see how my classmates wrote relative to how they spoke. Several thoughts reverberated in my mind: What did this White woman see that was so striking in my writing? There is supposed to be some continuity between the spoken and written word, right? What does my writing suggest about me or my intelligence (this was/is the big question)? What I observed was that my classmates' writing was not, grammatically, any different from my writing, but it lacked the personality or idiosyncratic nuances that often accompanied the spoken word. I quickly taught myself to write decidedly different from the way I spoke; however, this was a process.

The two years in private school allowed me to become intimate with false dichotomies: confidence and insecurity, privilege and oppression. What was as offensive then, as it is now, was that the teacher whom I respected and felt accepted by never once took the time to explain to me what she meant by her comment about my writing in relation to my speaking. I walked away from that exchange not knowing if her intent was to insult or merely to share a legitimate observation worth exploring (and worth correcting if needed for my future success). I was now armed with just the right amount of insecurity to propel me forward.

The message that I received on that day was one of being different—set apart from those around me—in a way that was ambiguous. A feeling that I may have stumbled onto something I would not otherwise have been privy to, except for the "luck" of being forced to attend this private school, was too obvious for me to ignore. I still remember the shift in my consciousness as a result of that experience. This shift allowed me a glimpse into what was characterized as a "good" education in a predominantly White world. Those who could afford this type of education also knew it needed to begin almost from birth but certainly by or before kindergarten. Social constructions influence human life, and all people are conditioned by these constructs (i.e., prescribed norms, rules, expectations, and beliefs about people perceived as different). I was functioning in a society (an institutionalized system) with rules that were not in favor of high expectations of people resembling me or variations of my likeness; of course, there were and are always exceptions to socially constructed rules.

I was awakened to the concept of *white privilege* during this time. This was not its name back then; it was simply called *racism*, with all the micro- and macroaggressions articulated by today's language. However, then, just like today, money and perceptions of whiteness provide access to many privileges. It all made complete sense to me because the social constructionists resembled my classmates, not me. Obviously, these are my current thoughts, which are refined semblances of my preteen conceptions of past experiences. For a time, though, I felt incomplete and disconnected. I carried elements of these feelings with me into high school and college—and, I suppose to a much smaller degree, into today. I think this is in part the reason I push myself in the ways in which I do. It is absolutely the reason I engage and challenge my current students.

COLLEGE YEARS

I attended college in the last half of the 1980s. That decade was laden with large-scale political events that sparked an atmosphere ripe for social change. The mass murder of Chinese student protestors at Tiananmen Square and the crumbling of the apartheid system in South Africa—while the world watched—were pivotal events of the time. Rap music was in its infancy but was already the sociopolitical vehicle for many young Black Americans in white America.

During this time, there were several Black Americans in some form of political office (e.g., Colin Powell, David Dinkins, Harold Washington). In January of 1990, I attended the inaugural ball for Governor L. Douglas Wilder, the only Black governor of Virginia. This was, seemingly, a decade of great strides and respect for Black people. While all of this was going on, I was dealing with my own political drama at my university. I attended a small, predominantly White, private Catholic university in the northeastern part of the country. I, along with many other Black students, dealt with overt and covert forms of racism from some members of the White student body in the form of racial slurs and assumptions about affirmative action and admittance. From some White faculty, micro insults were typically in the form of avoidance—a noticeable lack of engagement or expectations of academic ability, in general. I distinctly remember having an unprovoked encounter with an angry, White male who apparently thought it his (white-privileged) right to project his hatred onto me through narrow-minded and ignorant accusations themed in affirmative action and reverse racism. I countered his venomous verbal assaults with stating the fact that many of us were admitted based on the same criteria they were. I earned the right to be there. One battle down, more to come!

As the old saying goes, hindsight is 20/20. I now see that several of my college experiences occurred at the intersection of racism and sexism. In the fall of 1989, I registered for an African history course. This was to fulfill my history requirement. As with many Black students during this decade, I was conditioned to think that knowing African history was of extreme importance since I was labeled as Black. My generation was heavily invested in *Africanness* and self-pride, as taught to us by our 1960s' and 1970s' Black-power predecessors. Adding to this excitement was director Spike Lee and his major cinematic feature film *School Daze,* which he also wrote. This film depicted college life on a historically Black campus. It tackled longstanding themes of divide and conquer using constructs such as colorism and sexism that continue to plague People of Color in all countries. *Colorism* is the practice of favoring lighter-complexioned people within nominal racial groupings (Hochschild & Weaver, 2007), and it positions darker-skinned people as ethnically authentic (Hunter, 2007). These practices still occur across the world, even where the American Black–White binary is nonexistent; the aforementioned authors highlight the psychological impact of racism with its devastating effects within communities and families of color. I bring this up because the movie *School Daze*, released in 1988, was the metaphorical backdrop to my African history experience, showcasing the essence of colorism and internalized racism.

My African history professor was African. He was an older gentleman, slight in stature, thin, and phenotypically West African. I was very much looking forward to having this experience with someone who not only studied the history but also lived aspects of it. I thought that having an African professor teach the country's history would provide a more authentic learning experience for me than having it taught by a White American professor. As it turns out, this semester-long episode proved to be one of the most complex, and paradoxical, examples of education politics I experienced. This incident provided me a front-row view of the devastating psychological power of racism at work, and it brought me face to face with several interwoven concepts I would grow to recognize as transference, self-hate/internalized racism, and colonial brainwashing.

I remember walking into the classroom for the first time and visually taking stock of being the only Student of Color in the course. This was surprising to me only because of the nature of the course. I was later told that this particular professor made it a practice to isolate and mistreat students he perceived to be Black Americans. I found out firsthand.

I was much more introverted and reserved as a young undergraduate. Therefore, I rarely spoke out in class. Class after class during that semester, I, along with the vast majority of my classmates, listened as our professor rambled on, in his thick regional accent, with endless information about the African geographical landscape. There was one particular day on which I raised my hand to ask the professor to repeat the names of the "seven rivers" he had just recited so that I could include them in my notes. Instead of a quick repeat of what was just stated, I received an intense and explosive reaction from him that was all at once unexpected, inappropriate, and unprofessional. It smacked of some deep-seated rage, and that rage was unleashed onto me. He yelled, "I DID NOT SAY SEVEN RIVERS!!" I do not remember the rest of his tirade, but I will never forget the vicious, ill-fitted response to my simple request. The immediate reaction from the students around me was silence. A few moments later, the student sitting directly behind me tapped my shoulder and whispered, "He *did* say seven rivers," My response was, "I know, and why didn't you say something?!" His response was a shoulder shrug and silence. The event, in its entirety, was unsettling, confusing, and hurtful.

The semester progressed, but it did not get better. My grade and overall enthusiasm for the class diminished. I went to the history department chairperson to report the mistreatment I suffered in the class and to challenge my grade. The department chairperson was a Black American male. I erroneously thought the fact that the chair was an American (Black) male would somehow shift the dynamics of the situation that the alliance would be one that ensured I would be heard, understood, and treated fairly. Instead, I was met with males (African and African American/Black) against a Black female. As I entered the office, I was greeted by the two men with laughter as I proceeded to present my "clearly racist and oppressive" experience. I can still conjure up that moment as if it were last year—not as close as yesterday but not far from the forefront of my memory; it was marked by patronizing, condescending, and twisted behavior by men who represented the Black intelligentsia, and who according to mainstream America should have been concerned with my best interest, not only because we were all considered Black in America but also because I was an engaged student—not a slacker.

The example from my undergraduate years connects to the insidious power that racism has on all people. I will never quite know what my professor was thinking about me, himself, the other students, or the subjective context of the situation. What I know for sure is that his internalized issues about the meanings of Blackness, America, education, oppression, and privilege were comingled, transferred, and projected onto me in that fateful moment. From my perspective, I witnessed the sad reality of an oppressed African man who had been conditioned to think of himself superior to Americans who were ascribed the *Black* identifier with all its propagated negative meanings. He fell into the trap of the global white-supremacy message that propagates narratives, or tropes, positioning non-White Americans as unintelligent and unworthy of respect, much less a quality education. By my estimation, his beliefs that prompted his actions were manifestations of centuries of European imperialism and colonization (aka oppression and mental enslavement). Thankfully, the 1980s was the decade of, ironically, the African consciousness movement in which Black voices were heard across college campuses and through various media outlets. Narratives about the power and worth of Black people across the world were shifting in a multitude of positive directions.

CONCLUSION

I observe today, just as Carter G. Woodson did in the 1920s and 1930s, the ease with which Students of Color are conditioned to be recipients of the "master script" (Swartz, 2007) narrative, which propagates themes of inferiority as connected to Black*ness* or any experience other than White*ness* by omission. These narratives are implicit and part of the institutional and systemic nature of racism employed effortlessly through formal education. Students regardless of ethnicity (or race) are conditioned not to challenge constructed narratives that support the superiority of Eurocentrism. This is where my story continues; but it now includes empowering all historically oppressed and marginalized people with whom I work.

Coming to know my points of privilege is in direct relationship with my students and their experiences with "learning." It is in this space that I have become acutely cognizant of how brilliantly our country continues to maintain the guise of liberation for Persons of Color by skillfully addressing ideas of "access" to education without actually providing students with the necessary tools (or information) to nurture their intellect. Ongoing discrepancies in academic "achievement" reinforce the institutionalized social-system that is built on the fundamental principles of colonization, imperialism, and hegemony experienced as systemic racism. My personal politic is consistently being transformed in the liminal spaces where I coconstruct truths and personal power with myself and my students. Challenging the politic of education as has been disseminated is an arduous task because messages of privilege and oppression, in various iterations, are deeply engrained in America's master script. I have come to know the privilege of boldly confronting educational racism as my right and responsibility, as I share with my students our intersections of oppression every semester. This privilege has united me with my students (and, at times clients) serving as a catalyst for liberation.

DISCUSSION QUESTIONS

1. Think about the social construction, and perception, of race in relation to presumptions of entitlement in the United States, as explored in this chapter. How might helping professionals from varying disciplines (i.e., counseling, social work, psychology, and human services) challenge nuances of racism and oppression (the ideology of white supremacy/privilege) at micro and macro levels?

2. As racial diversity continues to be a focus across the United States, how is diversity valued in public school curricula? Do you think academic expectations of non-White students (lower, middle, and upper class) are the same as those of White students regardless of socioeconomic status? As a school counselor, school psychologist, or social worker, how might you interpret lingering educational gaps between Students of Color and White students? How might you advocate for the students with whom you work?

3. In working on this chapter, I realized that I began challenging the legitimacy of the forced dominant narrative early on in my life. These narratives have had an impact on my worldview—they have inspired me to seek and create empowering counter-narratives. Listening to the stories of my clients (and students) allows me to imagine the subconscious ways the "master script" has been influential in their thinking or being. Hearing these narratives also provides an opportunity to facilitate new ways of empowering them. As a helping professional, how might you recognize the master script and the ways in which it might influence your decision-making as a practitioner, educator, or administrator? How might you work differently with your clients, students, or supervisees?

4. What is the purpose of education for People of Color in the United States? What is the purpose of education for White people in the United States? Think about this question in light of historic discrepancies in education rights, purpose, equity, and quality since the colonizing of the Americas. How might your response implicitly or explicitly inform your therapeutic or clinical approach with White clients, clients of Color or graduate students? Consider this question in terms of professional ethics and personal beliefs.

5. I teach my students to consider the question "By whom and for what purpose?" when they are contemplating political themes such as race, religion, documented history, and so on. As a helping professional, how might you assist clients in recognizing when these themes may be contributing to their current or chronic concerns? How comfortable are you with honest self-reflection and reflexivity? How might past experiences influence your current work?

6. Social justice appears to be a major theme in my life. How do you suppose the works of W. E. B. Du Bois (1903/1994), Carter G. Woodson (1933/2010), and Paulo Freire (1970/2000) influence my current work with marginalized and historically oppressed people in the twenty-first century? How might incorporating the ideologies of the previously mentioned authors influence your clinical or professional work with clients or communities? How might this major paradigm shift inform the policies, practices, and standards of your respective professions? Consider the intersections of politics and the social constructions of race, class, and gender, along with domestic and international interpretations of American exceptionalism, in your thought process. Consider how this particular question has implications relevant to the past and the future.

REFERENCES

Boozer, M. A., Krueger, A. B., & Wolkon, S. (1992). Race and school quality since Brown v. Board of Education. *Brookings Papers on Economic Activity, 269–338.*

Darling-Hammond, L. (2000). New standards and old inequalities: School reform and the education of African American students. *The Journal of Negro Education, 69*(4), 263–287.

Du Bois, W. E. B. (1994). *The souls of black folk.* New York, NY: Dover. (Original work published 1903)

Freire, P. (2000). *Pedagogy of the oppressed.* Translated by M. B. Ramos. New York, NY: Continuum. (Original work published 1970)

Hochschild, J. L., & Weaver, V. (2007). The skin color paradox and the American racial order. *Social Forces, 86*(2), 643–670.

Hunter, M. (2007). The persistent problem of colorism: Skin tone, status, and inequality. *Sociology Compass, 1*(1), 237–254.

Kozol, J. (1991). *Savage inequalities: Children in America's schools.* New York, NY: Crown.

Leonardo, Z. (2013). *Race frameworks: A multidimensional theory of racism and education.* New York, NY: Teachers College Press.

Smedley, B. D. (2012). The lived experience of race and its health consequences. *American Journal of Public Health, 102*(5), 933–935. doi:10.2105/AJPH.2011.300643

Swartz, E. (2007). Stepping outside the master script: Re-constructing the history of American education. *The Journal of Negro Education, 76*(2), 173–186.

Woodson, C. G. (2010). *The mis-education of the Negro.* Lexington, KY: Seven Treasures. (Original work published 1933)

SECTION 9

STORIES OF ALLIES, ACTIVISTS, AND PERSONAL COMPASSION

In times of challenge where prejudice, discrimination, and dehumanization occur, some progress has been made; yet social injustices and inequities persist. As a result, there is still much work to be done. The following authors suggest ways in which we can begin to work on moving ourselves and others forward in this quest. Matthew R. Mock encourages readers to recognize differential treatment related to power and privilege by utilizing personal compassion and alliance building to disrupt cycles of discrimination and dehumanization. Barbara Gormley suggests autoethnographic insights and the application of Helm's White Racial Identity Model toward one's journey to becoming a White ally. David MacPhee advocates for social justice and inclusion from the perspective of cognitive dissonance and identity development. This concluding section of the text seeks to engage all of us in the journey to rid our planet of prejudice, discrimination, racism, social injustice, and microaggressions and, as Mock suggests, replace it with personal compassion and alliance building across communities.

In Mock's chapter, "Personal Compassion and Alliance Building: Interrupting Cycles of Discrimination and Relational Dehumanization," readers are inspired to identify acts of personal compassion toward embracing meaningful alliance building. This chapter is ideal for those who want to help others understand the negative effects of discrimination, increase awareness of how prejudging is learned and can be unlearned, and use storytelling to personally and professionally contribute to social justice movements of all kinds.

Gormley draws upon autoethnographic insights while applying Helm's White Racial Identity model to describe her journey as a White ally. In her chapter, "Allies and Activists: Working With White, Male, Heterosexual, Cisgender, or Christian Privilege," Gormley speaks to the divide caused by privilege being bridged by the author learning to see the world and her racial place in it in a different way. Gormley shares personal life stories as a White person, who illuminates each of the identity statuses of Helm's model. As a roadmap for other forms of privilege, Gormley includes a conceptual framework that extends Helms's model to male allies of feminism, straight and cisgender allies of queer rights, and Christian allies of religious pluralism. Gormley finishes the chapter by discussing the value of people who are committed to exploring and confronting privilege coming together for support, making change and taking action. Gormley recommends a support group to build community across differences and reduce divisiveness.

MacPhee's journey to become an advocate for social justice and inclusion are discussed from the perspective of cognitive dissonance and identity development in "Yes, I See You're Committed to the Cause . . . But Where's Your Credibility, and Why That Angst?" MacPhee's process begins with a worldview naïve to diversity, growing up in a rural, patriarchal, all-White, and blue-collar context. MacPhee shares stories that highlight his growing consciousness about privilege and –isms that contribute to angst but also promote insights about how status, oppression, and privilege function. Finally, MacPhee describes how these developmental processes contributed to his commitment to social justice and his enduring involvement in multicultural education, despite some pushback that White males lack the credibility to address social inequalities and prejudice.

CHAPTER 28

PERSONAL COMPASSION AND ALLIANCE BUILDING

Interrupting Cycles of Discrimination and Relational Dehumanization

Matthew R. Mock

"Racism. Getting sick wasn't our fault. But getting well is our responsibility."

—Anonymous

A STORY OF AN INCIDENT I OBSERVED

I am considered by some honored colleagues to be an expert on cultural competence and social justice. I give lectures, trainings, and presentations nationally and even internationally. One day, after providing a highly successful multicultural training, I went to a major department store to do some gift shopping for the holidays. I witnessed an incident that still stands out in my mind today. Although what I observed took just a few minutes, I can replay it frame by frame as though it were occurring in slow motion. Clearly, what I witnessed had a lasting impact.

While perusing items to buy in the various departments, I observed a man in his mid- to late 30s looking in the cases of the jewelry department. Appearing to be Asian American, the man had also caught my attention because few Asian Americans live in the immediate and surrounding areas. Also being Asian, I felt a silent sense of connection. Because it was the winter holidays, the store and jewelry departments were bustling with activity. This man was casually dressed and wore a trench coat because it recently had been raining sporadically. He seemed quite acculturated, perhaps even native born. I overheard his conversation with an Asian American woman and a child (perhaps his wife and daughter) as they agreed to shop separately for a while. As soon as his wife took the escalator upstairs, heading for another department, I observed the man become keenly focused on some earrings in one of the jewelry cases.

The jewelry cases were situated in a rectangle around the service and purchase area. On this particular day, the department-store salesperson was a woman who appeared to be White and in her mid-40s. After careful scrutiny, the Asian American man seemed to make his decision about his purchase of some onyx earrings and waited in what was now a short line that was forming. He checked his watch. I thought perhaps he was making certain that he had time to make his purchase before his wife and child returned to the shopping area.

Two other customers, one a man and the other a woman, who both appeared to be White, individually made their purchases. Now the only one left in line, the Asian American man waited for the saleswoman's attention and his turn to be served. However, instead of assisting this man, the saleswoman left the immediate counter and register, abruptly diverting her forward attention to serve a woman, also White, who had just come to another side of the counter to ask a question. It was as though the saleswoman looked but did not see the man, so she turned away! The saleswoman opened one of the cases at the female customer's request to show her some watches. She then, as she had the previous male and female customers, proceeded to assist this customer in making her department-store credit-card purchase. Afterward, instead of returning to the Asian American man at the register, she answered the questions from a man passing through the department. Again, it was as though the Asian American customer was invisible or nonexistent. Despite the fact that these customers were being given attention and service out of turn, the man waited patiently. His gaze followed her movements. She turned to her left then right to help others at the cost of neglecting him.

Finally, upon returning to assist the Asian American man, this saleswoman made no mention that she had passed him by and put him off. He pointed to the earrings he had carefully selected and indicated that he also wanted to use his store credit card for the purchase. The woman stepped over to the register, swiping the card in the crediting machine, all the while studying the man up and down, carefully scrutinizing his face. After a pause, she came back to the man and requested his signature on the credit-card slip. He routinely complied. She looked at the signature carefully, paused, and then commented, "I'm sorry. Please sign again." He signed once more, only to have her react with an audible sigh and then request, "I must see your driver's license or some other form of identification." In response, the Asian American man looked at her somewhat perplexed but after a brief pause cooperated. After collecting his driver's license, stepping away, and studying it against his store credit-slip signature, the saleswoman returned from the register. By this time, a small line had formed behind the man. The saleswoman said firmly in a lowered voice, drawing the man closer, "Please sign again. Only this time, make an effort to sign it like your license!" Clearly more flustered, the man complied once again but first commented, "I did not see you request this of the prior customers. And is showing a picture identification store policy?" To this, the saleswoman reiterated her stance for a careful signature. Hoping to draw the man closer to her to not be within earshot of others, she spoke as though she were sharing a secret with him. At a near whisper and with annunciated words pausing between each, as though the man might not understand English, she said in a halting, patronizing tone, "Please, sir. This is for your own good! Do you understand me?" Following this brief dialogue, the interaction finally broke off, with the man hurrying away at last with his purchase, concealing his emotions while searching for the time on his watch.

REFLECTIONS AND CONSIDERATIONS

After reading this story, many of you will appropriately express some form of shock or disbelief at the way this man was treated. Others of you will recognize this type of treatment, racial discrimination, as personal to your own experience. Some of you will assume that there must be more to the story than was witnessed and recounted, for such blatant mistreatment does not occur without a reason. Still others of you may not associate this treatment with racial discrimination at all.

Consider *your* response. Also consider the following questions, some of which perhaps you asked yourself after reading this story: *How do you know the salesperson was discriminating against this Asian American man? Was this really a racist interaction? Was it about skin color or appearance, tone of voice, gender, facial expressions, perceived socioeconomic status, or was it something about this man's assumed attitude? Would it have made a difference if there had not been the earlier slights, invisibility, or acts of disrespect, dehumanization, or marginalization? What might be some reasons the salesperson treated him this way?* Finally, consider other questions you had that could be added to this list. Also review the discussion questions at the end of this chapter before reading on.

AN IMPORTANT REVELATION

There is an important sidebar to my story and its concluding events. I was actually not just an idle witness to this event. I did not just observe this from afar. *This was an actual event that happened to me.* I was that Chinese American man in the department store with my family, shopping like other families do. I felt the saleswoman had discriminated against me.

"THE REST OF THE STORY"

There is an addendum to my department-store story. As I left the store and felt the coolness of the outside air, I had a moment of clarity and inner strength. I questioned what had just happened in just a few minutes' time. I paused to think about who I am and what I stand for: I am a professor and somewhat prominent multicultural psychotherapist who advocates for equality and social justice for others. I am a husband and a father. I am teaching my daughter to speak up both for herself and for others. I know all too well the historical legacy of Asian American mistreatment and what things might be done to help stop the cycle of discriminatory interactions. I thought to myself: "For my daughter Rachel, my family, for others, and for myself, I cannot let this incident go by without having my voice heard." Now the coolness of the outside air contrasted with the warmth of my face, adding renewed spirit to the action I would take.

With internal, firm, and grounded feelings hard to put into exact words, I hastened back into the large, bustling department store, past the fancy displays, sparkling boxes of costume jewelry, and holiday-wrapped colognes and perfumes. As I got closer to the jewelry counter, the saleswoman with whom I had interacted had been joined by another saleswoman. The additional representative was helping customers on the opposite side of the counter make their purchases. The saleswoman with whom I had interacted appeared to be counting receipts and perhaps preparing to take a break. As I walked toward her counter, she recognized me immediately and leaned toward me, although somewhat cautiously from a safe distance. Summoning my collected feelings of being more grounded and strong, I assertively and directly said to her, "During our interaction before, you were not respectful to me. First, you passed me by as though I was invisible. Then you treated me differently than you treated other customers. As a professional, I sign many things. I question if you ask all of your customers equally for their signature multiple times, and for their identification or license, and then respond to them as you did to me. You did nothing to explain. I did not appreciate your condescending demeanor. Please think about this." I kept a clear, calm, firm yet steady voice. Her face registered some shock and dismay. If I had to guess, I think her reaction was because I had actually taken time to address her about what happened. I felt satisfied with my verbal assertion.

Upon realizing that I was a bit overdue to meet up with my wife and daughter, I turned from the counter, taking a few quick steps away. Sweeping through the narrow aisle of holiday merchandise, my open trench coat caught some of the neatly displayed and stacked boxes of jewelry pins, tumbling all of them to the floor. Pausing to pick up the mess I had just made in my haste, I half-wondered if the saleswoman in witnessing this would mistake my actions and have her finger on the phone ready to call security. Suddenly, after apparently witnessing much of what had transpired, a White female customer knelt down beside me and helped me pick up the few remaining small boxes. Kneeling side by side, she gently said to me, "I saw what happened to you. I was shopping too and I was a few customers behind you in line. The way she treated you was not fair or right. I am sorry. I will also say something on your behalf." We stood together briefly, sharing small smiles of personal, connected acknowledgement. I simply thanked her and we parted ways.

To this day, when I think about this scenario, I feel warmth at the *personal compassion* of this anonymous woman, her words, and our nonverbal connection. I recognize an ally. We choose our battles, and sometimes we choose who will jointly participate in the struggle. Although I have gone to the store management, written complaints, and spoken up in similar situations, during this one I let go to have someone willingly carry on where I left off. This partial ending brings me hope and renewed energy, even optimism. An act of one is an act for us all.

OUR IDENTITIES AND CONNECTING OUR STORIES OF PERSONAL COMPASSION

It is perhaps not uncommon for people to prejudge. When we approach a yellow light while driving, we prejudge whether a commonly crossed busy intersection is safe to cross. Based on prior learning, we take stock of the speed of other cars, judging whether we have time to cross or to stop. Discriminating one situation versus another based on prior learning helps us make decisions that help us survive and make good judgments. As humans, we discriminate one person from another, acknowledging how they are separate, different. It is when we discriminate or use prejudice negatively against others that is problematic. When someone engages in acts of discrimination to downgrade, treat someone as "less than" and unequal, these actions must be called into question, interrupted. These are acts of injustice. They are acts of relational dehumanization. Interrupting these cycles of discrimination in small, large, and systemic ways is absolutely necessary.

In the vignette, the salesperson initially "invisibilized" me by not giving me the ready, equal attention she had given others. It was as though she did not see me or perhaps did not consider me worthy of attention. She went on to engage in various acts of microaggressions (Sue, 2010). She did not trust or believe that the store credit card was mine. If there had been problems with my card being approved for the transaction, she could have informed me by letting me know respectfully where the problem seemed to exist. By not doing so, she went down the path of asserting her power-over position on me, further engaging in discriminatory, less-than-equal treatment. Her slow, deliberate speech felt microaggressive. By speaking to me, an Asian American customer, in a slow, halting tone as though I would not understand her, she treated me as though I was a perpetual foreigner, even though I am a full, American-born citizen. This type of experience is shared by many new immigrants, including those of Chinese heritage.

As a Person of Color, I continue to experience racial discrimination throughout my life. In this situation, the source of the discrimination very much pointed to racism. It was my physical appearance that she used to prejudge me. I cannot take on every situation with equal indignation, ire, or rage. To continue to live my life, I must also engage in self-care, taking on situations as they happen, as I feel fit, or just to do so. Friends and allies understand the feelings I experience and offer compassion for the range of challenging emotions that arise.

After I knocked over the store items, the woman assisted me with picking up the items. She first engaged in an equal task action with me. Next, she asked me respectfully if she could speak on my behalf. As an ally, she did not speak for me as though I did not have my own voice but from her own place of observing, her own witnessing of indignities. In other words, as an ally, she did not replace or misplace me but instead spoke up with an additional voice, standing up, interrupting the cycle of oppressive acts.

We each have multiple identities, including ethnicity, gender, race, sexual orientation, religion or faith, professional status, abilities, and others. We must constantly be aware of our intersectionality of identities that contributes to our relationships and interactions on a daily basis. Being aware of which of these identities and statuses earns us relative power and influence in different contexts is essential. I share my personal scenario with the saleswoman and end with the female customer who took the time to help me as an ally to emphasize the fact that even small acts of personal compassion have larger meanings in collective efforts to achieve social justice.

FINDING OUR OWN PERSONAL COMPASSION TOWARD ANOTHER

The events of September 11, 2001, had a profound impact on so many people in the United States and abroad and will for generations. Like many people, I cancelled many flight plans right after that date, thinking about the planes that were used as projectiles to bring down the towers of the World Trade Center in New York City and all the people inside. I had been home watching television as that tragedy unfolded. Through my work, I tried to coordinate efforts through my clinic and school programs to help children and families to cope with all the feelings of profound sadness, fear, anger, loss, confusion, and anxiety. I went into a professional trauma-intervention mode.

As weeks passed, I found myself able to take trips once again. On one of these trips for a workshop presentation, I found myself on a full flight of passengers. As we all settled in, I noticed that one of the last individuals to get seated was a Middle Eastern–appearing woman slightly younger than I. She sat two rows in front of me in a window seat. The flight proceeded without anything unusual except midway through, when there was a slight bit of turbulence.

Shortly after this turbulence began, the Middle Eastern woman got up from her window seat as though to go to the restroom at the rear of the plane. She walked briskly, with downcast eyes. I noticed several people around me looking up from their reading or talking, acknowledging her passing. After several minutes, she returned. However, as the flight proceeded, she asked to be excused by her neighboring passengers once again to use the restroom. She had tissues in one hand and appeared to be dabbing at her face. After some moments of seemingly collective silence among those around her, she returned to the restroom once more. The flight proceeded as expected, with the usual courtesies from the flight crew, and as the plane descended toward landing, the warning to be seated and secure seat belts was announced. A short time after the pilot made this announcement, the Middle Eastern woman arose quickly once again, hurrying to the rear cabin restroom, this time carrying a small purse. Heads turned; several passengers seemed to take additional note, as did one flight attendant. After some moments ticked by, the flight attendant went to check on the woman. Finally, the woman emerged, returned to her window seat, and the plane landed with a near-perfect, smooth touchdown.

What had just happened? Why did I, and others, feel perhaps as we did? Were our feelings normal under the circumstances? Was feeling uncomfortable, or at least questioning the woman's behavior, a reflection of fear, mistrust, or need to be protected? How should we have voiced our concerns? What might the woman have been feeling, and was she aware of how others reacted? I silently toiled over some of these and other questions as we got off the plane, walking on to get our baggage.

As we claimed our luggage coming off the turnstile, I noticed the Middle Eastern woman a few passengers away from me. We picked up our bags close to the same time and then proceeded to the passenger pickup area outside. After sitting there side by side for a few awkward minutes, I finally broke the silence to say "Hello" and make small talk. Within a few minutes, we had a readily flowing conversation, first about trivial matters of the day and then eventually national and worldwide events. She told me how she too had been affected by the 9/11 tragedy in New York, by the violence and loss. She had resided in the Bay Area of California all of her life, and her parents had lived there for more than 20 years. Shortly after September 11, she was cautioned by some of her Muslim neighbors about wearing clothes that more readily identified her as Middle Eastern or Muslim. Her elderly mother, shopping one day as she usually did at her neighborhood grocery store, had her cart run into by another woman, supposedly as an accident. Her mother stopped shopping there unless another family member accompanied her. A Muslim neighbor had also had an obscene gesture and verbal taunts made to her by teenagers as she was in her car at a stoplight.

With each of our rides due to arrive shortly, our conversation turned to her behavior on the plane, when she got up several times to go to the bathroom. She explained how she had to get to the bathroom numerous times because of an upset stomach. She had constantly felt the pressure of all eyes focusing on her, especially each time she got up. This was true throughout this flight and other previous ones. In addition, the airport security staff had carefully screened and checked her and her luggage twice before she boarded. She even told me that recently she had had multiple nosebleeds, perhaps caused by increased stress and feeling the silent yet highly palpable tension of those around her.

As we talked and shared each of our stories, I felt a moment of closeness and commonality with this relative stranger. I expressed how badly I felt and how hard it must be for her, especially when others did not take time to acknowledge her or her feelings and experiences. I told her how I was glad that we had made brief contact to introduce ourselves to each other, to share brief snippets of our stories, especially in the context of tense times. What she shared next I will not forget. She expressed thanks for my taking time to speak with her, to check in about her welfare, and to engage her sincerely as a fellow human being with thoughts, feelings, and family history. She felt troubled with the silence of others but validation through our brief yet meaningful engagement. Finally, as my ride arrived, we parted with short acknowledgments, and I headed home.

Later that evening, upon reflection, I felt a mixture of feelings. At first, I felt bad for being one who experienced moments of tension on the flight, making assumptions about this woman based on her appearance and my own faulty presumptions. I also felt good for having taken the risk to engage this woman, which allowed us to get to know each other briefly and for me to share my feelings of personal compassion toward her and her family's experiences. Last, perhaps most importantly for me, I was reminded how being an ally or successfully engaging with another person, even for a few precious moments, means taking risks, breaking from anonymity, finding and giving humanity, being aware of cultural humility, and discovering commonality across differences. That night, in the warmth of my home, talking with my daughter late into the night about my own learning, I felt hopeful about what our conversation might teach her.

CONCLUSION

One of my core values is teaching and learning about compassion and empathy toward others. It is critical for individuals to begin exercising personal compassion, getting them to understand at a deep, personal level what it means to be treated differently, to understand how differential treatment is related to power and privilege (McIntosh, 1988; Pinderhughes, 1989) and to the conscious or unconscious perpetuation of acts of racism, discrimination, and oppression. We have to consider strategies to constructively address negative acts of others. For me, empowering people with a sense of hope and the ability to take personal action are the true meanings of what it means to be PC—*not* to be *politically correct* but instead to be *personally compassionate* (Mock, 1999, 2003). It is with small acts of one individual and the combined personal acts of hundreds that we can construct lasting alliances toward change. We must practice and embody "cultural humility" (Tervalon & Murray-Garcia, 1998) toward one another.

Knowing and telling personal stories past and present and creating future possibilities are extremely important (Godsil & Goodale, 2013; Mock, 2008). I try to impart some of these powerful narratives as inspirations for my workshop attendees, graduate students, and audiences small or very large.

No matter how many times I present the material or how large the audiences to whom I give workshops on diversity and social justice, I often encounter forms of the same three questions. The first question is "Is fighting racism and oppression for equality primarily the work of People of Color or of White people?" Another often-asked question is "The history of discrimination and oppression in the United States is so long and hard, and I am just one person. What can I do to make a difference?" One other common question might be "What does someone need to do to make a difference when racist acts are still prevalent, covert and overt, and at so many levels of our society?" Although these questions are common, moving toward answers is a continuous challenge.

In the story I shared about my experience in the jewelry store, the source of the discrimination very much pointed to racism. It was my physical appearance that the salesperson used to prejudge me. Given other variables, one might consider other contributory factors. For example, if the salesperson were male and the shopper female, gender might play a role in how the salesperson might try to put the shopper in her place. Gender dominance or sexism might be put into play. And acknowledgement of gender fluidity will lead to future social complexities (Mock, 2011). If as the shopper I had appeared by my manner of dress, use of language, or physical appearance as though I could not afford to make the purchase, or that I would not be a desired shopper to retain in the future because of perceived education or income, the salesperson might have discriminated against me based on my social class or standing. There are times when one or more of these differences played out as isms might be operating simultaneously. Sometimes the source of one's being treated unequally may not be absolutely clear. The multiplicity of an individual's diverse identities and intersectionalities of identities should be considered (Hays, 2008; Mock, 2008; Watts-Jones, 2010). Nonetheless, we must make efforts to interrupt the cycle of oppression, to challenge unequal treatment by taking a stand as an ally for others. Not to take a stand is to remain complicit to the inherited cycles of oppression and inequalities. Taking action, both small and large, is deeply meaningful. Taking responsibility for oneself as well as others contributes to the greater good for equality and justice. Our life and the lives of others should not be anything less.

Similar to what occurs in my classes, I hope I have articulated the following teaching points in this chapter. First, racism and discrimination have an impact on all people, no matter how much individuals seemingly have attained professionally. Second, fighting racism, discrimination, and oppression for social equality are battles for all of us, not for just one person or one group. Third, we all need allies in this hard, ongoing struggle. Finally, I am committed to take the daily position that linking arms strengthens stances against social injustices. I feel that not only should we take such a stand, but we must do so for our survival. We must move beyond simple political correctness to deep personal compassion that leads to a better world for all present and future humanity.

DISCUSSION QUESTIONS

1. Discuss what you look to in order to decide whether or not someone's actions are discriminatory. At what point might you have determined that the saleswoman's behaviors were discriminatory toward the man? How much does the man's perception of the events matter in your decision?

2. Discuss the Asian American man's going back into the store. Do you feel he did enough to address the issue? What might he have done differently? If you were the man, what would you have done? Would you have done more (i.e., go to management directly)? If not, why not?

3. Discuss the interchange from the perspective of the saleswoman and the man. What do think each person was experiencing individually? What were they sharing relationally?

4. For the woman who was identified as an ally, what would you have wanted her to say to the store manager? What elements of her comments would be respectful of the man and be the most beneficial?

5. What do you imagine might have been some of the thoughts or experiences of the saleswoman to cause her to act the way that she did?

6. For the people who were targets of mistreatment in the scenarios, what kind of conversations would you have with them?

7. Think of a time when you observed someone being the recipient of mistreatment or unequal treatment. What happened? What did you do? There may be clear, rational reasons for why you did not intercede. Under ideal circumstances, what would you have wanted to do?

8. Think of a time when you were mistreated or treated unequally or unfairly. What happened? What do you imagine someone bearing witness might have done to interrupt the injustice and to restore humanity and dignity to the interchange?

REFERENCES

Godsil, R. D., & Goodale, B. (2013). *Telling our own story: The role of narrative in racial healing*. New York, NY: America Healing, American Values Institute, and W. K. Kellogg Foundation.

Hays, P. (2008). *Addressing cultural complexities in practice*. Washington, DC: American Psychological Association.

McIntosh, P. (1988). *White privilege and male privilege: A personal account of coming to see correspondences through work in women's studies* (Working paper no. 189). Wellesley, MA: Wellesley College Center for Research on Women.

Mock, M. (1999). Cultural competency: Acts of justice in community mental health. *The Community Psychologist, 32*(1), 38–40.

Mock, M. (2003). Cultural sensitivity, relevance, and competence in school mental health. In M. Weist, S. Evans & N. Lever (Eds.), *Handbook of school mental health: Advancing practice and research* (pp. 349–362). New York, NY: Kluwer Academic/Plenum.

Mock, M. (2008). Visioning social justice: Narratives of diversity, social location, and personal compassion. In M. McGoldrick & K.V. Hardy (Eds.), *Re-visioning family therapy: Race, culture and gender in clinical practice* (pp. 425–441). New York, NY: Guilford Press.

Mock, M. (2011). Men and the life cycle: Diversity and complexity. In M. McGoldrick, B. Carter & N. Garcia-Preto (Eds.), *The expanded family life cycle: Individual, family, and social perspectives* (4th ed.; pp. 59–74). Boston, MA: Allyn & Bacon.

Pinderhughes, E. (1989). *Understanding race, ethnicity and power: The key to efficacy in clinical practice.* New York, NY: Free Press.

Sue, D. (2010). *Microaggressions in everyday life: Race, gender, and sexual orientation.* Hoboken, NJ: John Wiley.

Tervalon, M., & Murray-Garcia, J. (1998). Cultural humility versus cultural competence: A critical distinction in defining physician training outcomes in multicultural education. *Journal of Health Care for the Poor and Underserved, 9*(2), 117–125.

Watts-Jones, T. D. (2010). Location of self: Opening the door to dialogue on intersectionality in the therapy process. *Family Process, 49*(3), 405–420.

CHAPTER 29

ALLIES AND ACTIVISTS

Working With White, Male, Heterosexual, Cisgender, or Christian Privilege

Barbara Gormley

INTRODUCTION

The first time I reached out to someone across the divide caused by my racial privilege, I was in the second or third grade. I noticed that no one in my all-White neighborhood welcomed the first Chinese American family who moved in, so I went over to their house and introduced myself to the girl my age. I grew up in metropolitan Detroit in the 1960s and 1970s, near Irish American grandparents who taught me that prejudice is wrong. They told me stories about the prejudice that they and my great-grandparents had endured, including as immigrants (Ignatiev, 1995/2009). They expected the 1960 election of the first Irish Catholic president, John F. Kennedy, to change this country so that they would be included as equals.

My father and grandfather called themselves feminists and demonstrated that they were male allies by helping promote their secretaries into some of the first executive positions held by women at General Motors. It is part of my family's cultural heritage to use privilege to advocate for those with less power. There was one notable exception, however. I remember the 1967 race riots in Detroit. My other grandfather's response was to take the entire family to stay in a rural area for a month or two, because he was afraid that we might get hurt. Leaving the city was safer only for White families, however, which was evidence of our privilege.

After that incident, my parents helped campaign to defeat busing initiatives that might have equalized educational opportunities by racially integrating schools. For a long time, I struggled to understand how my parents could suddenly become prejudiced. When I learned about a White racial identity status called *reintegration* (Helms, 1990, 1995), it helped me understand how internal conflicts may have led them to suddenly reverse their beliefs. When people are conflicted between fighting for racial equality and maintaining personal safety, fear can influence their choice. Believing that they were entitled to White privilege may have felt safer to my parents than supporting Black rights. Helms (1990, 1995) suggested that anxiety over this choice can lead to defensive blame of the oppressed group for their circumstances.

My parents supported political campaigns in the 1970s that claimed that, if African Americans could not afford better schools for their children, it was their own fault. This claim failed to incorporate the cultural context of that time or to analyze the many economic and political influences on the metropolitan Detroit educational system. As an adolescent, I watched family members give up their social justice beliefs to fit into mainstream American culture, and I thought that what they were doing was wrong. While I tried to think through these issues, what helped me the most was learning how to conduct a power analysis. A power analysis clarifies which groups have political power (Morrow & Hawxhurst, 2013), whether in a country or a school district. Considering the cultural background of those in positions of power helps us identify systemic influences that otherwise go unnoticed.

For example, I learned how to notice that the clear majority of top lawmakers throughout US history have been White, male, Christian, heterosexual, well educated, wealthy, and so on. The cultural values of this small, homogenous group of decision-makers are probably infused in every institution (e.g., the media), where they have become the norm to which other groups are unfairly compared. This kind of institutionalized structure grants me access to power because I am White and well educated. Furthermore, I fit the cultural norm because I am *cisgender*, which means that my biological sex (female) matches my gender identity (woman). I also am privileged to be (temporarily) able-bodied and able-minded.

There are advantages to having privileged identities, which are difficult to notice. *Privilege blindness* (http://rationalwiki.org/wiki/Privilege) refers to a lack of awareness of such advantages, but this term can be considered culturally insensitive. Feeling like we were blind before we became aware of our privilege is obviously not the same experience had by people who are blind or people with visual impairments. A better term might be *privilege ignorance*. White antiracist activist Tim Wise has suggested that ignorance of how we are shaped racially is a sign of privilege (personal communication, October 14, 2016). White privilege can prevent us from recognizing the implications of race in the United States and beyond.

Privilege ignorance has at least two meanings: one is not knowing about one's privilege, and the other is knowing about one's privilege but ignoring it. Many people try not to think about the injustice involved in having an advantage simply by being born male, White, or heterosexual. I would include a third meaning in the definition: ignoring the responsibility that comes with having power, such as a responsibility to help address oppressive circumstances in which others may live. Although many people do nothing to overcome privilege ignorance, it is problematic when helping professionals ignore privilege.

Privilege prevents us from knowing the truth about what other people suffer, which interferes with our ability to empathize. For instance, I grew up feeling emotionally distant from the injustices experienced by African Americans. Despite my deep cultural and religious beliefs in social justice, I was not able to easily connect with their experiences. Privilege ignorance can also make it difficult to believe the discrimination experiences we are told. Many Women of Color I have met did not think they had any privilege, until they considered the social benefits of their Christian religion or heterosexual orientation. Then they realized that privilege interfered with their ability to connect with the oppression experiences of people different from them. Experience being oppressed, antioppression beliefs, and exposure to the oppression of others are not sufficient to overcome privilege ignorance. We must change who we think we are.

In this chapter, I tell the story of my changing racial identity. Becoming a White ally is just one example, and the process can be applied to any privilege. In addition, I provide an extension of Helms's (1990, 1995) model to describe how to work with male privilege, heterosexual privilege, cisgender privilege, and Christian privilege. People of Color and others will find support for becoming allies in the extended model. Acknowledging any form of privilege, expanding awareness, and reaching out to members of oppressed groups promotes social justice. Group support for becoming an ally is recommended, so I share three examples that could be modified for other issues. That is, my story refers to a White awareness group, a cross-racial dialogue group, and groups engaging in dialogues across different privileges.

CROSSING THE DIVIDE CAUSED BY PRIVILEGE

Becoming a White ally has changed my internalized sense of my racial place in the world. White racial consciousness was studied by Helms (1990, 1995), who described six different schemas or identity statuses. She described three simple identity statuses and three sophisticated identity statuses. First, simple efforts to abandon racism require sufficient *contact* with People of Color. Second, there can be a *disintegration* of previously held beliefs that Whites are superior. However, people may reject these experiences. The term for the third identity status is *reintegration,* which was previously discussed and entails conforming to mainstream society. Fourth, more sophisticated efforts to embrace a nonoppressive White racial identity include *pseudoindependence* from the status quo, which refers to tolerance of racial and cultural differences. Fifth, some White people *immerse* themselves in discovering their own racial heritage and engaging in antiracist activism. This identity status can elicit an emotional catharsis, if the person has a supportive environment or group, which is called *emersion.* Therefore, the term for the fifth identity status is *immersion/emersion.* Sixth, *autonomy* from the status quo encompasses openness to plural cultures and relinquishing racial privilege. Many White people assume they have achieved autonomy, but that is a rare occurrence (J. E. Helms, personal communication, March 27, 2008). Perhaps we should consider this identity status aspirational and, as Helms (1990) suggested, continuously work toward it.

My journey as a White ally has been supported and explained by Helms's (1990, 1995) identity statuses. They describe where I have been and where I am going, serving as a map that I have turned to many times. My Irish ancestors believed in the social equality of the People of Color they met when they immigrated to the United States (contact, disintegration), a belief that was passed down to me. However, some of my relatives gave up their beliefs to assimilate, hoping to gain upward mobility (reintegration). I was upset that they seemed to turn against oppressed groups instead of continuing to fight for their rights, so I chose to become a White ally of racial equality movements. Throughout the 1980s and 1990s, I exhibited attitudes and behaviors related to more than one identity status (Helms, 1995). For the most part, I experienced pseudoindependence and immersion/emersion at the same time. Also, it took intentional effort to change from simpler to more complex identity statuses (Helms, 1990, 1995). What follows are a few examples of how I changed.

PSEUDOINDEPENDENCE

When I first left home in the early 1980s, I went to college and majored in women's studies. Because of my father and grandfather, I felt affection for male allies I encountered in the feminist movement. In my academic program, I was inspired by intelligent female professors who described multiple oppressions as interrelated, cocreated, and inherent in institutions (Daly, 1978; Lorde, 1983; Rich, 1980). This perspective resonated with my cultural heritage and my experiences as a working-class, bisexual woman who had just left the Catholic church and become a Buddhist. I overcame internalized sexism in a feminist academic community, and I wanted all women to have the same opportunity.

As I understood the barriers inherent in a predominantly White university, I realized that it would take social change before Women of Color could experience similarly liberating environments. I wanted to devote my career to helping create that change. This is how I became an antiracist feminist (Sinacore & Enns, 2005), which emphasizes the centrality of the experiences of Women of Color. I knew it was possible to become a White ally, because I had grown up around male allies. I understood that it was my responsibility as a White person to end racism, but I did not know how I was going to do that. I needed to prepare, so I was pseudoindependent (Helms, 1990, 1995) from the status quo.

As a social worker in the early 1990s, I spent time on Native American reservations. My job was to provide in-home family interventions for violence and abuse. Children's Protective Services (CPS) referred a client accused of child neglect who reportedly had a history of refusing to speak to CPS workers. I drove out to her home on the reservation and knocked on her door, but no one answered. I knew this mother could lose her children if I left, so I stood there for a few minutes, feeling anxious. After guessing that the cultural norms might be different, I opened the door and walked in. The woman inside laughed. She had been wondering how long I was going to stand out there, or whether I would leave, like the last two workers did. The cultural norm on the reservation was to walk into other people's houses without knocking, and they would only open doors for children who were too small to reach the knobs. If CPS had removed this client's children because she did not *answer the door* (a laughable concept in that culture), that mistake would have had serious implications.

Over the years, I learned more about Odawa and Ojibwe culture. I learned the U.S. government's history of sending White Christian (i.e., Protestant and Catholic) reformers to take away the children from Native American tribes. The goal was to forcibly assimilate an entire generation at once. The children were not allowed to visit with their parents, could speak only English, and had to adapt to White culture in every way, under threat of severe punishment. Tragically, most Native American children died in such boarding schools (http://www.nrcprograms.org/site/PageServer?pagename=airc_hist_boardingschools).

I had to work hard to build rapport with American Indian clients. They had good reason to mistrust me, in case I was another misguided White reformer. It didn't help that my business card featured a large cross, which was part of the logo used by the Lutheran agency that employed me. Because I was raised Catholic, I had to speak up and admit both White and Christian privilege. I had to display sensitivity to the complexity of the racist power dynamics involved, before I could expect Native American clients to confide in me.

My sense of identity seemed to shift as I was perceived differently in two cultures during this time, which is characteristic of pseudoindependence (Helms, 1990, 1995). White professional representatives of social institutions, like CPS workers, seemed to assume that I would get Indian clients to conform to the dominant culture, although this was not an option I considered. Many Indian people I met told me directly that they expected me to learn about their culture and advocate for its preservation in the face of White efforts to destroy it. I invested in allying with the American Indian movement (http://www.aimovement.org/ggc/history.html).

I already expected myself to be an advocate for my clients, which was easy enough to do in my professional role. Judges were routinely ordering alcohol-abusing teens from the reservation into Christian-based residential treatment programs far from their homes. Their parents could be charged with child neglect if they didn't comply, even if the families thought this strategy would make the problem worse instead of better. I advised the court that this approach was ineffective and retraumatizing for the Indian community. I recommended a specialized residential treatment program that emphasized Indian spirituality as part of recovery. When it was unnecessary to remove children from their home, I found outpatient options. Although I advocated for individuals to have appropriate treatment, I did not know how to create permanent change that would become institutionalized in social systems.

Teenagers from one reservation were legally required to attend the predominantly White high school. Framed posters picturing events from American history hung in each hallway. Several posters featured famous White men in the act of killing Indians. Mimicking the message of the posters, White students were threatening to kill Indian students, while hitting and stabbing them with sticks. The school officials did not listen when the Indian elders requests that the posters be removed. When asked by my clients to help, I added my White voice (sometimes that is all that White ears can hear on the issue of race) and involved people I knew through my professional connections (sharing access to power). Eventually, the posters were removed, but the school continued to tolerate White violence against Native American teenagers without intervening, despite policies that prohibited student bullying. Frustration motivated me toward political action.

IMMERSION/EMERSION

While I was an undergraduate student, in addition to gaining knowledge as described previously, I became an activist. This is typical of immersion (Helms, 1990, 1995). I attended antiapartheid protests (as shown in the movie *Cry Freedom,* a good example of how a White ally can help; Attenborough, 1987). I also joined a White Awareness group (Katz, 1978/2003). Six students from the women's studies program agreed to meet outside of school to discuss how we could use our White privilege to stop racism. After a few months, three Jewish women confronted three of us who were raised Catholic about our Christian privilege. If we were not going to address anti-Semitism in our all-White discussion group, they did not feel safe talking to us about racism.

Becoming a Buddhist had not raised my awareness of the Christian privilege I had while growing up. I learned that the work I needed to do to stay connected to my Jewish colleagues was emotional and relational. I could not solve the problem by reading the literature. I had to open myself up to understand what my colleagues' discrimination experiences felt like and become a better friend. I became aware of times that I had more privilege than they did. I stopped passively accepting (and thereby reinforcing) a status quo that caused obstacles for them but not for me. I encountered and confronted anti-Semitic attitudes and behaviors. I realized that Christian privilege is not separate from White privilege, because both identities are aspects of the dominant cultural group.

Years later, I learned more about how to take actions against racism in the doctoral program I attended. It was the late 1990s, and there was racial tension between Black and White students. I wanted to bridge that divide—not only the division that remained in my mind but also the systemic one affecting our program. An African American friend and I created a cross-racial discussion group (Gormley, 2005/2011). We had help from the creators of the Multiracial Unity program for undergraduates on campus. This program (a) was based on Baha'i religious beliefs in unity across races, (b) was trying to reduce the violence that had been erupting on campus since the 1967 race riots in Detroit, (c) was training students to have respectful cross-racial dialogues about White privilege and racism, and (d) encouraged cross-racial friendships based on equality (Thomas, Gazel, & Byard, 1999).

After listening to the painful stories that graduate Students of Color in the counseling psychology program shared in our group, I noticed more of the constant microaggressions they were experiencing. Through these stories, I realized that African American male students in our program were experiencing blatant discrimination, and I took every opportunity to speak out against such practices. At the time, I didn't fully understand why this was so emotionally painful for me, but I do remember thinking that one of my defense mechanisms (i.e., privileged entitlement) was becoming dismantled. Helms (1990) described such a powerful emotional catharsis as an essential component of immersion/emersion.

My empathy for African Americans deepened as I became viscerally aware of the repeated traumas they endured and how much the hostile environment interfered with their work. I don't know whether I could have completed my degree under such circumstances, which increased my admiration for their talent and resilience. By participating in a discussion group designed to foster inclusion of all races, I no longer felt emotional distance from the injustices that African Americans experience. I also knew what to do about racial injustice. I was determined to become an academic who creates liberating environments for Students of Color.

As a White ally, I humbly cultivate nondomination toward individuals of other races. I enjoy continuously learning and seeking out new perspectives on race, while advocating for racial equality in institutions. I notice that institutions in the United States render certain races invisible, and deadly force is used to maintain that invisibility. I mourn and protest the police killings of African American men and women (StayWoke.org, JoinCampaignZero. org, #SayHerName). The disproportionate number of Black people killed by police tells the story of racial inequity (Hall, Hall, & Perry, 2016); however, in a democracy, everyone deserves to be equally protected and served. Efforts to change law enforcement will be complicated, but they will likely involve antiracist White people working to change the minds of White people who are less familiar with racist power dynamics. I also contribute to efforts to change law enforcement by training criminal justice and forensic psychology students to critique racist systems of justice and develop socially equitable solutions.

The wisdom I pass on to the next generation was transmitted to me by many People of Color who reached out and helped me across the racial divide. This unnatural and unhealthy divide is created by the "racing-gendering" (Hawkesworth & Disch, 2016, p. 24) of our bodies (Coates, 2015). With the support to overcome privilege ignorance that I received from diversity-valuing communities, the innate beauty and worth of all race-genders has become more visible and obvious to me. My racial place in the world today is comfortably one among many. By this I mean that I acknowledge the differences in our experiences and understand the systemic vulnerability that goes along with certain identities, but I do not feel separate from other races. I seek out diversity where I live and work, and I share responsibility and sorrow over what occurs in our community.

EXTENDING HELMS'S MODEL: ALLIES BEYOND RACE AND GENDER

When a social justice movement fights for the rights of a group that is in the numerical minority (e.g., People of Color, queer or transgender people, Muslims), privileged allies help by increasing the number of people behind efforts to gain equality. Furthermore, each movement delegates different tasks to allies. Men who provide workshops to male undergraduates that clarify the difference between consensual sex and rape are examples of profeminist men (e.g., http://www.feminist.com/resources/links/links_men.html). Similarly, there are "Things White People Can Do to Be Real Anti-Racist Allies" (http://www.alternet.org/news-amp-politics/11-things-white-people-can-do-be-real-anti-racist-allies). There are organizations for straight allies who support queer rights (e.g., www.straightforequality.org). Although not as well organized, cisgender allies can certainly learn how to support transgender people (Cis Privilege Checklist, https://takesupspace.wordpress.com/cis-privilege-checklist/; 12 Cisgender Allies to Trans Causes, http://www.advocate.com/politics/transgender/2014/05/12/12-cisgender-allies-trans-causes). Christian allies can support religious pluralism (e.g., United Religions Initiatives [www.uri.org]), secular movements (e.g., Secular Coalition for America [www.secular.org]), and interfaith dialogues (Idliby, Oliver, & Warner, 2007). Furthermore, allies and activists from different movements sometimes build coalitions, working together when interests align.

As I support students who engage in this kind of work, Women of Color persistently ask why they cannot find professional resources to support their process (e.g., working with heterosexual privilege), like the resources that benefited me as a White person. Suggesting that they trust their own experience or helping them conduct new research has not been as satisfying as extrapolating concepts from Helms's (1990, 1995) model to other types of allies. This chapter presents an extended model that I created (with permission from J. E. Helms, personal communication, July 15, 2016). In part, I wanted to provide Students of Color with a map to becoming an ally of oppressed groups. Additionally, this approach has helped many kinds of students become allies, even when areas of privilege are not specified in Table 29.1.

In Table 29.1, the first two columns summarize Helms's (1990, 1995) concepts. The last three columns extend those concepts to male privilege, heterosexual or cisgender privilege, and Christian privilege. The columns are organized to correspond to social justice movements. Race is listed first because of its centrality (J. E. Helms, personal communication, August 6, 2016), and gender is listed second for similar reasons (for training guidelines, see American Psychological Association, 2002, 2007). Readers are encouraged to consider any identity statuses they may have exhibited for each of their privileged identities. References mentioned here may be of specific interest to White allies (Smith & Redington, 2010), male allies (Wiley, Srinivasan, Finke, Firnhaber, & Shilinsky, 2013), straight allies (Fingerhut, 2011; Gormley & Lopez, 2010), cisgender allies (Russell & Bohan, 2016), and Christian allies (Schlosser, 2003).

To illustrate the benefits of this extended model, I share a fictional story based on the actual experiences of several students. In a multicultural psychology course, a heterosexual, Christian, African American woman became aware of her implicit bias against lesbians and gay men. At first, she was oblivious to the social advantages of heterosexuality (contact; see Table 29.1). Later, she began to question why one sexual orientation should be considered more normal than another (disintegration; see Table 29.1). She resolved a conflict between her religious beliefs and her profession (she was interested in becoming a straight ally) by thinking about her actual values (e.g., to love one another). Although making this change was an emotional experience for her, the process also increased her empathy for people who were biased against her. She found it easier to confront prejudice she encountered as an African American woman once she understood how easily we all internalize cultural biases that favor dominant groups.

GROUP SUPPORT FOR TRANSFORMING ANY PRIVILEGE

Since 2004, I have been teaching at universities where most students are African American women or Latinas. Many remaining students are other People of Color, international students, immigrants, Muslims, first-generation college students, and queer students. When

TABLE 29.1. Extending Helms's Model: Allies beyond Race and Gender[a]

Identity Status	White Ally	Male Ally	Straight or Cisgender Ally	Christian Ally
	Letting Go of Privileged Entitlement			
Contact Denial; obliviousness; avoidance of anxiety-provoking race–gender information	Encounters different races; naïve to own prejudice; satisfied to benefit from status quo	Notices women's experiences; naïve to own prejudice; satisfied to benefit from status quo	Encounters lesbian, gay, bisexual, transgender, queer, intersexual, and asexual people; naïve to own prejudice; satisfied to benefit from status quo	Encounters religious and nonreligious diversity; naïve to own prejudice; satisfied with status quo
Disintegration Disoriented; ambivalent; suppression of race–gender information	Conflicted but more loyal to White superiority	Conflicted but more loyal to male superiority	Conflicted but more loyal to straight and/or cisgender superiority	Conflicted but more loyal to Christian superiority
Reintegration Idealizes own group; negative distortion of out-group; selective perception	Denigrates people of color; lives in White neighborhoods; blames Blacks	Denigrates and blames women; opposes the Equal Rights Amendment	Denigrates and fears queers; opposes same-sex marriage and unisex bathrooms; blames transgender people	Denigrates others; claims sole entitlement to heaven; blames Muslims
	Integrating Nonoppressive Identities			
Pseudoindependence Reshaping race–gender information to fit liberal view; selective perception	Intellectual learning about racism, racial inequities, tolerance, civil rights movements	Intellectual learning about sexism, inequality, gender role socialization, feminism	Intellectual learning about transphobia, biphobia, homophobia, queer culture, queer rights movements	Intellectual learning about religious and nonreligious traditions, religious pluralism movement
Immersion/ Emersion Hypervigilant; reeducating; searching for internally defined race–gender standards	Learns about own racial heritage and White privilege; is an antiracist activist	Learns about men and male privilege; is a profeminist activist	Learns about cisgender privilege and compulsory heterosexuality (Rich, 1980); is a queer rights activist	Learns own religion's history of domination; learns about Christian privilege; participates in interfaith dialogues or related activism
Autonomy Flexibility; complexity	Open to and invites expression of plural cultural perspectives; relinquishes unearned privileges; does not participate in oppressive practices; acts as a social change agent if needed; increasingly aware of intersectionality of identities (Crenshaw, 1991), as well as interrelationships among racism, sexism, ableism, heterosexism, ageism, and others and the need to eliminate all of them			

[a] First two of five columns adapted from Helms (1990, 1995) and reprinted with permission from SAGE Publications, Inc. ©1995.

Students of Color trust me enough to share that they are experiencing oppression in our educational programs, I know that I am bridging the divide caused by White privilege. This is my responsibility as a teacher, mentor (Gormley, 2013), and professional representative of institutions (i.e., the university, academia, the field of psychology, and the helping professions).

I believe that I am successfully creating liberating academic experiences for People of Color when I hear them described as: "transformative, empowering, and life changing," which is how one student described training she received in my multicultural psychology course. The training approach I use is similar to what social justice movements offer, especially those that propose starting within the movement to train ourselves to be more sensitive to the differences among us and to multiple forms of oppression (e.g., BlackLivesMatter.com; www.creatingchange.org). When diverse groups of people work well together to seek justice, the change effected in institutions is more likely to benefit more than one oppressed group.

Students of all races, genders, sexual orientations, and religions are included in diversity-valuing training strategies in my classes and research teams. Because we all have some privilege (i.e., educational privilege), we all share a common interest in uncovering privilege ignorance (e.g., through taking Implicit Associations Test, http://www.understandingprejudice.org/iat/). None of us want privilege ignorance to interfere with the multicultural competence or effectiveness of our clinical work or professional responsibilities. Typically, each group member selects one or two privileges to work on, setting goals for the semester. In addition, we learn from and teach each other. Learning how to ally with at least one unfamiliar oppressed group helps students learn a process that they can apply to other groups in the future.

Group discussions about Table 29.1 often focus on intersectionality (Crenshaw, 1991; https://www.washingtonpost.com/news/in-theory/wp/2015/09/24/why-intersectionality-cant-wait/). Everyone tries to integrate identities related to their own race, gender, sexual orientation, religion, age, ability, and so on, but this process is poorly understood in psychology (Rosenthal, 2016). Take, for instance, the statement members of marginalized groups must be ashamed of who they are if they do not always disclose their identities, bisexual (e.g., Schrimshaw, Downing, & Cohn, 2016) and biracial (e.g., Korgen, 1998) people have been found to present their identities differently in different settings to avoid discrimination. The same could be true for other oppressed groups.

We also do not know how the intersections of certain identities modify their political status. For instance, heterosexual, Christian men may have significantly different experiences of privilege, depending on whether they are Black or White. And what about people like me, allies of more than one cultural group who are activists in many social justice movements? Does an understanding of one oppression translate to another, or does involvement in multiple movements hasten integration of material learned? In the future, I would like to be part of efforts in psychology to learn more about the process of integrating multiple nonoppressive identities (see bottom half of Table 29.1).

CONCLUSION

Dialogues across differences benefit society in many ways, including by producing new knowledge. For example, an international Student of Color in my multicultural psychology class wondered if faculty were treating her as though she was not intelligent because she speaks English with an accent. She conducted a survey of higher education faculty to find out. A key finding in this research was related to faculty's view of their ability to teaching culturally diverse groups of students. As faculty saw themselves as less effective to teach these students they also reported more complaints about having to teach students for whom English was a second, third, or fourth language (Brou, 2016). Perhaps more training on how to effectively teach diverse groups of students, including immigrants and English-language learners, should be institutionalized in every program that produces future higher education faculty.

Students need academic environments that support their examination of privilege and help increase their confidence in their ability to become effective allies. In educational institutions that serve large numbers of Students of Color, such as the university where I work, students have an opportunity to receive a unique form of support. For instance, in my Allies and Activists research team, a straight Student of Color initiated a conversation about the need to address homophobia in our community (i.e., a straight ally reaching out across the divide caused by her privilege). In the same meeting, a queer White student initiated a conversation about whether we should pull over to support Black drivers who have been stopped by the police (i.e., a White ally reaching out across the divide caused by his privilege).

This highly unusual experience, wherein others are reaching out to you across the divide caused by their privilege at the same time you are reaching out to them across the divide caused by your privilege helps create a safe and supportive environment for collaborative work across multiple social justice movements. Otherwise, discussions of differences can become overly focused on one issue (e.g., race), which sometimes leads to groups of people feeling more divided. Teaching all students how to overcome the divide caused by privilege helps create a microcosm of a broadly just society. This inspires and prepares students to go on to build socially just communities. At least, that is how it worked for me.

ACKNOWLEDGMENTS

I would like to thank Drs. Michele Boyer, Gloria Smith, Eugene Pernell, and Jacquelynne Eccles for their multicultural mentoring, which was both caring and challenging. I feel honored that Dr. Janet Helms permitted me to extend her model, and I am grateful to Drs. Candice Crowell and Anneliese Singh for their comments on earlier drafts. I deeply appreciate this book's editors, Drs. Sharon Anderson and Valerie Middleton, without whom I could not have distilled and articulated my experiences as well. Correspondence concerning this chapter should be addressed to Barbara Gormley, PhD, Division of Psychology and Counseling, Governors State University, 1 University Parkway, University Park, IL 60484. E-mail: BGormley@govst.edu

DISCUSSION QUESTIONS

1. Did you react emotionally to any part of this chapter? Explain. Why is emotion important? Explain. Did anything inspire you to change? Explain.

2. What other explanations might there be for the Gormley family's opposition to racial integration of schools in the 1970s? Do any of these reactions still happen today? Explain and provide examples.

3. What have we learned from the reform efforts of those who wanted Native American people to become more like White people? How does this apply today?

4. The author describes bullying and police brutality as evidence of racism. Explain whether you agree or disagree and why.

5. What structures and support systems will help you prepare for cross-racial, inter-faith, or cross-difference conversations?

6. In your setting or region, how might the extended model be used to support allies and foster discussions about intersectionality?

REFERENCES

American Psychological Association. (2002). *APA guidelines on multicultural education, training, research, practice and organizational change for psychologists.* Retrieved from http://www.apa.org/pi/oema/resources/policy/multicultural-guidelines.aspx

American Psychological Association. (2007). Guidelines for psychological practice with girls and women. *American Psychologist, 62*(9), 949–979. Retrieved from https://www.apa.org/practice/guidelines/girls-and-women.pdf

Attenborough, R. (Dir.). (1987). *Cry freedom* [Motion picture]. London, UK: Universal Pictures.

Brou, H. Z. (2016). *The influence of multicultural teaching efficacy on higher education faculty attitudes towards ELL students.* (Unpublished master's thesis.) Governors State University, University Park, IL.

Coates, T. -N. (2015). *Between the world and me.* New York, NY: Spiegel & Grau.

Crenshaw, K. (1991). Mapping the margins: Intersectionality, identity politics, and violence against women of color. *Stanford Law Review, 43,* 1241–1299. Retrieved from http://socialdifference.columbia.edu/files/socialdiff/projects/Article__Mapping_the_Margins_by_Kimblere_Crenshaw.pdf

Daly, M. (1978). *Gyn/ecology: The metaethics of radical feminism.* Boston, MA: Beacon Press.

Fingerhut, A. W. (2011). Straight allies: What predicts heterosexuals' alliance with the LGBT community? *Journal of Applied Social Psychology, 41*(9), 2230–2248. doi:10.1111/j.1559-1816.2011.00807.x

Gormley, B. (2011). A multiracial unity group for graduate students. In S. K. Anderson & V. A. Middleton (Eds.), *Explorations in diversity: Examining privilege and oppression in a multicultural society* (2nd ed., pp. 265–272). Belmont, CA: Brooks/Cole. (Original work published 2005)

Gormley, B. (2013). Feminist multicultural mentoring in counseling psychology. In C. Z. Enns & E. N. Williams (Eds.), *Oxford handbook of feminist multicultural counseling psychology* (pp. 451–464). New York, NY: Oxford University Press.

Gormley, B., & Lopez, F. G. (2010). Authoritarian and homophobic attitudes: Gender and adult attachment style differences. *Journal of Homosexuality, 57,* 525–538. doi:10.1080/00918361003608715

Hall, A. V., Hall, E. V., & Perry, J. L. (2016). Black and blue: Exploring racial bias and law enforcement in the killings of unarmed Black male civilians. *American Psychologist, 71*(3), 175–186. doi:10.1037/a0040109

Hawkesworth, M., & Disch, L. (2016). Feminist theory: Transforming the known world. In L. Disch & M. Hawkesworth (Eds.), *The Oxford handbook of feminist theory* (pp. 13–32). New York, NY: Oxford University Press.

Helms, J. E. (1990). Toward a model of White racial identity development. In J. E. Helms (Ed.), *Black and White racial identity: Theory, research, and practice* (pp. 49–66). Westport, CO: Praeger.

Helms, J. E. (1995). An update of Helms's White and people of color racial identity models. In J. G. Ponterotto, J. M. Casas, L. A. Suzuki, & C. M. Alexander (Eds.), *Handbook of multicultural counseling* (2nd ed., pp. 181–198). Thousand Oaks, CA: SAGE.

Idliby, R., Oliver, S., & Warner, P. (2007). *The faith club: A Muslim, a Christian, a Jew—Three women searching for understanding.* New York, NY: Atria Books.

Ignatiev, N. (2009). *How the Irish became White.* New York, NY: Routledge. (Orignial work published 1995)

Katz, J. H. (2003). *White awareness: Handbook for anti-racism training.* Norman: University of Oklahoma Press. (Original work published 1978)

Korgen, K. O. (1998). *From black to biracial: Transforming racial identity among Americans.* Westport, CT: Praeger.

Lorde, A. (1983). The master's tools will never dismantle the master's house. In C. Moraga & G. Anzaldúa (Eds.), *This bridge called my back: Writings by radical women of color* (pp. 94–101). New York, NY: Kitchen Table Press. Retrieved from http://bixby.ucla.edu/journal_club/Lorde_s2.pdf

Morrow, S. L., & Hawxhurst, D. (2013). Political analysis: Cornerstone of feminist multicultural counseling and psychotherapy. In C. Z. Enns & E. N. Williams (Eds.), *The Oxford handbook of feminist multicultural counseling psychology* (pp. 339–357). New York, NY: Oxford University Press.

Rich, A. (1980). *Compulsory heterosexuality and lesbian existence.* Retrieved from http://people.terry.uga.edu/dawndba/4500compulsoryhet.htm

Rosenthal, L. (2016). Incorporating intersectionality into psychology: An opportunity to promote social justice and equity. *American Psychologist, 71*(6), 474–485. doi:10.1037/a0040323

Russell, G. M., & Bohan, J. S. (2016). Institutional allyship for LGBT equality: Underlying processes and potentials for change. *Journal of Social Issues, 72*(2), 335–354. doi:10.1111/josi.12169

Schlosser, L. Z. (2003). Christian privilege: Breaking a sacred taboo. *Journal of Multicultural Counseling and Development, 31*, 44–51. doi:10.1002/j.2161-1912.2003.tb00530.x

Schrimshaw, E. W., Downing, M. J., & Cohn, D. J. (2016, June 8). Reasons for non-disclosure of sexual orientation among behaviorally bisexual men: Non-disclosure as stigma management. *Archives of Sexual Behavior.* http://dx.doi.org/10.1007/s10508-016-0762-y

Sinacore, A. L., & Enns, C. Z. (2005). Diversity feminisms: Postmodern, women-of-color, antiracism, lesbian, third-wave, and global perspectives. In C. Z. Enns & A. L. Sinacore (Eds.), *Teaching and social justice: Integrating multicultural and feminist theories in the classroom* (pp. 41–68). Washington, DC: American Psychological Association.

Smith, L., & Redington, R. M. (2010). Lessons from the experiences of White antiracist activists. *Professional Psychology: Research & Practice, 41*(6), 541–549. http://dx.doi.org/10.1037/a0021793

Thomas, R. W., Gazel, J., & Byard, R. L. (Eds.). (1999). *Building community across racialized lines: The Multiracial Unity Project at Michigan State University* (Unity Studies Monograph Series, Monograph Number 1). East Lansing: Michigan State University, Urban Affairs Programs.

Wiley, S., Srinivasan, R., Finke, E., Firnhaber, J., & Shilinsky, A. (2013). Positive portrayals of feminist men increase men's solidarity with feminists and collective action intentions. *Psychology of Women Quarterly, 37*(1), 61–71. doi:10.1177/0361684312464575

CHAPTER 30

YES, I SEE YOU'RE COMMITTED TO THE CAUSE . . . BUT WHERE'S YOUR CREDIBILITY, AND WHY THAT ANGST?

David MacPhee

begin this chapter with two questions that have been central to my journey from growing up in a homogenously White, rural environment, with little appreciation for human diversity, to becoming an educator deeply committed to inclusion and multiculturalism yet sometimes tentative about whether I—a privileged, White male—am in a position to address with authority stereotypes and –isms. This self-reflective journey is characterized in about equal measure by missteps and "aha" moments, both of which stem from the interplay of lived experience and academic knowledge:

- Can a middle-class youth recognize his privilege without being immersed in a low-income environment?
- Can a White man comprehend racism viscerally if he has not been a visible minority in another culture or has not witnessed it in action?

BACKGROUND

Two figure/ground experiences in my youth had a formative influence on my perception of privilege. First, I grew up in a small, blue-collar town in Idaho that was dependent on mining and forestry, and my parents were White, educated professionals. Second, many of the families I knew—all White—were regular churchgoers who believed in the Golden Rule and that God loves all people. Although they might sprinkle everyday conversation with ethnic jokes and slurs, paradoxically they gave to causes that served culturally diverse and low-income people. Most of these families were generous and compassionate and would be offended to be called bigots.

Neither my ethnicity nor social class was obvious to me until I went to a private college where I was less worldly and wealthy. My battered 1954 bread truck advertised to all that I was a "hick from the sticks." I was in daily contact with People of Color for the first time, the novelty of which made me uncomfortable. Flashbacks to age 5 bubbled to the surface when, on my first trip to an urban, multicultural city, I pointed to an African American man in the grocery line ahead of us and asked my father, in a preschooler's stage voice, "What's that?"

This naiveté made me more self-conscious in graduate school when I became good friends with a Black woman and several Jewish women. Paralyzing internal debates about protocol leaked out in ways that might have been amusing but in hindsight were close to appalling. *How much can I ask about what it's like to be Black (or Jewish)? Is it acceptable to talk about prejudice and racism? Is* Jew *a slur, or should I say* Jewish people*? Is it* Black *or* African American*? Am I an ignorant bumpkin or just garden-variety naïve? How can I become less naïve if I don't ask forthright questions? How much should I expect others to rectify my ignorance, even if my intentions are sincere?*

DEVELOPING AWARENESS

A handful of events and experiences shaped my perceptions of privilege and also my commitment to equality and interest in diversity. First, few of my high school classmates attended a university, and all were middle-class kids. The women had to work much harder than I did for respect and success in school and their careers, especially if they went into law or engineering. I had assumed that I did well in high school because of native intelligence and hard work, not because I was middle class, White, and male. The social comparison processes that happened in college taught me that I had underestimated the role of opportunity structures (Bronfenbrenner & Morris, 2006), those experiences provided by families, schools, and society that allow certain predispositions to flourish. If my White, lower middle-class parents had not emphasized reading, encouraged involvement in extracurricular activities, and saved faithfully for college, I might have taken quite a different path.

A second experience involves where I grew up. Rural life shapes attitudes that are pertinent to everything from voting patterns to consumer habits, and also perceptions of privilege. Brooks (2001) observed "that most [rural] people don't think sociologically. They don't compare themselves with faraway millionaires who appear on their TV screens. They compare themselves with their neighbors" (p. 62) who tend to have a comfortable standard of living. As a result, there is little class consciousness. Attending a liberal arts college compelled me to think about social class for the first time because the framework for making social comparisons was so different there—a waking up to a different worldview (Harro,

2013). This experience of dissonance, between the (mis)perceived world and reality, is both unsettling and a necessary catalyst of development:

> In the absence of dissonance, this dimension of identity [that which is normative in the broader culture] escapes conscious attention. . . . It is the targeted identities that hold our attention and the dominant identities that often go unexamined. (Tatum, 2013, p. 7)

Thus my liberal arts education and my college peers brought into focus the status conferred upon me by being White and middle class; awareness of male privilege developed only later.

Another formative experience was religion. I was privileged to have several ministers who taught a gospel of caring for humanity but especially for those who are oppressed. My maternal grandparents, both ministers, were outspoken opponents of the neo-Nazis who lived in a compound a few miles from their home. This moral compass was put to the test with other relatives who used the Bible to justify racism and intolerance for people who are gay. Such incidents crystallized for me the hypocrisy of professing belief in Christian principles while at the same time bestowing grace on only a privileged few and that out-groups—all of whom were different from me—are a threat to people who share privileged status.

My sense of White male privilege was honed by *Masculus hostilis*. This subspecies, the hostile male, vocalizes his displeasure with gender equity and multiculturalism in shrill diatribes (Schmidt, 1997) and in clippings posted on his office door that defend White male privilege in college admissions, hiring, and the exclusion of women, scholars of color, and other disenfranchised groups not part of "the canon" that is defined by privilege. His table-pounding rants at faculty meetings are directed at those groups of people he believes are "given too much that is not earned" and his disparaging remarks about faculty research that focuses on gender and diversity. It is anger directed at those who threaten his status (Craig & Richeson, 2014; Plaut, Garnett, Buffardi, & Sanchez-Burks, 2011), rather than the angst of self-doubt. What I have learned from a few *Masculus hostilis* colleagues is that equality really does matter; otherwise, it would be a nonissue. Perhaps there would be greater acceptance of the social-justice agenda if more of us (White males) were outspoken in support of it (see Smith, 1998).

INFUSIONS OF INSIGHT

As my adolescent self-awareness blossomed, I too wanted to be judged by the content of my character, not by my lack of sophistication in navigating a multicultural world with which I had limited experience. This is the crux of multicultural education for those of us from more privileged backgrounds: how to channel our interest in the topic—an interest motivated by relevance to one's career or by commitment to social justice—despite occasionally feeling inept in knowing how to behave and talk about it. When issues of privilege and difference have been relatively invisible in one's personal history, angst and stereotyping are predictable consequences of confronting such topics in the classroom or in social interactions with out-group people (Hardiman, Jackson, & Griffin, 2013; Islam & Hewstone, 2001). However disruptive this cognitive dissonance may feel, it may prompt self-reflection and self-education that initiate the cycle of liberation (Harro, 2013).

I became more conscious of my commitment and angst when I participated in two curriculum-infusion projects at Colorado State University. The first project focused on gender and the second on multicultural diversity. The predominately White faculty participants wrestled with how to *talk*—not just teach—about prejudice, privilege, and the importance of diversity. If we were uncomfortable talking with colleagues who we knew to be committed to the cause, how could we face a class of students who might be dubious about, if not downright hostile to, the principles we espoused?

These projects drew attention to issues of social class and culture and the undercurrent of power. The intellectual component was invigorating because a few fundamental processes explained disparate behavior patterns across people, class, culture, and time. Yet fieldwork with Hispanic and American Indian families (MacPhee, Fritz, & Miller-Heyl, 1996) and with indigenous people in Australia and Belize left me with a lasting, visceral appreciation for my privileged status. Inadequate housing and food, limited opportunities, and despondency often were rooted in patriarchy and colonialism; and by birthright, I was one of the oppressors.

Despite this growing awareness of power and privilege, I have not completely relinquished my belief that the United States is a meritocracy (see Akamatsu, 2001; Banaszynski, 2001). I find myself suggesting to students that children from low-income families would have a brighter future if they just worked hard in school and their parents were more involved, which ignores a host of sociocultural forces arrayed against upward mobility (Lee & Burkman, 2002; Lopez, Gurin, & Nagda, 1998). For example, children of less advantaged class origins need to show substantially more merit than advantaged children to achieve the same level of success as adults (Breen & Goldthorpe, 1999). One lesson for me is that my limited firsthand experience with oppression hampers my ability to fully appreciate opportunities denied to others.

Membership in the privileged class is a double-edged sword for the diversity educator because the emotional labor can be painful. I attended seminars in which White males were scapegoated for a number of social ills, a tactic that left me feeling disempowered from seeking a systemic solution to those ills. At one conference workshop, the only White person in the room (me) was asked to take part in a role-play in which I was publicly humiliated as a way to turn the tables so that I could feel the sting of prejudice. An occasional class went up in flames when a few vocal students were critical of my attention to diversity issues and I lacked the skill to defuse the tension (for examples, see MacPhee, Oltjenbruns, Fritz, & Kreutzer, 1994). The common thread in such incidents is that I felt blamed—for being a privileged White male and for trying to redress social injustices—which provoked in me resentment, frustration, and guilt. The literature on privilege suggests that these feelings, particularly collective guilt, are normal when in-group members think about their privileged status (Branscombe, 1998). In some cases, such angst may be adaptive because it links consideration of privilege with positive attitudes toward and actions on behalf of social justice (Banaszynski, 2001; Harro, 2013).

Credibility can also be a thorny issue for a professor from the privileged class. As a developmental psychologist, I have no formal academic training in women's studies, cultural anthropology, or sociology. On more than a few occasions, I groped for concepts and connections that were not yet second nature, but I found solace in the suggestion that multicultural competence requires professors to abandon their all-knowing façade and acknowledge their vulnerability and ineptitude (Vacarr, 2001).

More frustrating for me was the opinion of some students and writers that I had no business talking about issues with which I had little direct experience, regardless of my commitment to the cause. Recent commentaries on this issue assert that people from privileged classes must take responsibility for questioning beliefs and practices that support dominance and discrimination (e.g., Harro, 2013; Jacques, 1997). Research on social persuasion further supports a role for the White male teacher because attempts to influence others' understanding of privilege are more successful when made by in-group members (Kappen, 2000). It does seem self-evident that a person of dominant identity should refrain from talking about the *phenomenology* of oppression—how it is experienced personally—unless it is prefaced with "Other people report that the. . . ." But I don't agree that lived experience is the only legitimate source of knowledge—a form of parochial reasoning (Tittle, 2011)—even though it can enrich what is taught.

CONCLUSION

Why would a White male professor enthusiastically pursue social justice in the face of such obstacles? Edge (2002) argued that the ability to embrace diversity is necessary to experience compassion, and compassion is a foundation of social justice. Aside from experience with diversity, the impulse for social justice can also be nurtured through community service, religious education, and discussions of moral and ethical issues. Additionally, certain values coincide with involvement in social justice activities, particularly the importance attached to influencing others and viewing one's work as an expression of beliefs and values (Treitel, 2000).

The conversion experiences I have described may also require some figure/ground contrasts. For instance, can a middle-class youth recognize his privilege without being immersed in either poor or wealthy contexts? Can a White man comprehend racism viscerally if he has not been a visible minority in another culture or witnessed racism—such as racial slurs shouted from a passing car? Is a husband truly aware of patriarchy until there is marital conflict around his limited contributions to household labor, as I (MacPhee & MacPhee, 2000) and others (e.g., Coltrane, 2000) have written about? All of these examples suggest that power and oppression are relatively invisible to the dominant group until that privilege is challenged; and for this reason, it is inevitable that multicultural education provokes angst in students and teachers alike.

DISCUSSION QUESTIONS

1. Discuss how the "invisibility of privilege" might be made evident to professionals (teachers, counselors, social workers, psychologists, human services) from

privileged backgrounds. Are there ways to create awareness without also fostering guilt (personal or collective) and defensiveness?

2. Should angst arise in a training seminar, how would you get to the source, and how might it be addressed constructively?

3. Is it necessary to have firsthand experience (such as a minority, with oppression) to teach with authority? Explain your response. How would you bring these issues alive in the classroom? How might the White males in the group effectively work toward social justice? How are students likely to react to the topic of social justice in your setting? Explain and elaborate on how you might address those reactions.

4. A colleague claims to no have the background in sociology or anthropology to address issues related to diversity and social status. How might you respond? What suggestions might you make?

5. How would you defuse a class that is "going up in flames" as the result of (a) accusations of political correctness? (b) bringing up diversity and privilege issues? (c) anger that some peers deny there is a problem? (d) not understanding why some sit tight lipped, with arms crossed?

6. Brainstorm teaching strategies that would illuminate ways to address issues such as (a) women have less power and (b) Youth of Color have less opportunity to achieve and highlight implications for practice.

REFERENCES

Akamatsu, N. N. (2001). The talking oppression blues: Including the experience of power/powerlessness in the teaching of "cultural sensitivity." *Journal of Feminist Family Therapy, 11,* 83–97.

Banaszynski, T. L. (2001). *Beliefs about the existence of White privilege, race attitudes, and diversity-related behavior.* (Unpublished doctoral dissertation). Yale University, New Haven, CT.

Branscombe, N. R. (1998). Thinking about one's gender group's privileges or disadvantages: Consequences for well-being in women and men. *British Journal of Social Psychology, 37,* 167–184.

Breen, R., & Goldthorpe, J. H. (1999). Class inequality and meritocracy: A critique of Saunders and an alternative analysis. *British Journal of Sociology, 50,* 1–27.

Bronfenbrenner, U., & Morris, P. A. (2006). The bioecological model of human development. In W. Damon (Series Ed.) & R. M. Lerner (Vol. Ed.), *Handbook of child psychology: Vol. 1. Theoretical models of human development* (pp. 793–828). New York, NY: Wiley.

Brooks, D. (2001). One nation, slightly divisible. *Atlantic Monthly, 288*(5), 53–65.

Coltrane, S. (2000). Research on household labor: Modeling and measuring the social embeddedness of routine family work. *Journal of Marriage and Family, 68,* 1208–1233. doi:10.1111/j.1741-3737.2000.01208.x

Craig, M. A., & Richeson, J. A. (2014). More diverse yet less tolerant? How the increasingly diverse racial landscape affects White Americans' racial attitudes. *Personality and Social Psychology Bulletin, 40,* 750–761. doi:10.1177/0146167214524993

Edge, R. (2002). One middle-age White male's perspective on racism and cultural competence: A view from the bunker where we wait to have our privilege stripped away. *Mental Retardation, 40,* 83–85.

Hardiman, R., Jackson, B. W., & Griffin, P. (2013). Conceptual foundations. In M. Adams, W. J. Blumenfeld, C. Castaneda, H. W. Hackman, M. L. Peters, & X. Zuniga (Eds.), *Readings for diversity and social justice* (3rd ed., pp. 26–35). New York, NY: Routledge.

Harro, B. (2013). The cycle of liberation. In M. Adams, W. J. Blumenfeld, C. Castaneda, H. W. Hackman, M. L. Peters, & X. Zuniga (Eds.), *Readings for diversity and social justice* (3rd ed., pp. 618–625). New York, NY: Routledge.

Islam, M. R., & Hewstone, M. (2001). Dimensions of contact as predictors of intergroup anxiety, perceived out-group variability, and out-group attitude: An integrative model. In M. A. Hogg & D. Abrams (Eds.), *Intergroup relations: Essential readings* (pp. 383–395). Philadelphia, PA: Psychology Press.

Jacques, R. (1997). The unbearable whiteness of being: Reflections of a pale, stale male. In P. Prasad, A. J. Mills, M. Elmes, & A. Prasad (Eds.), *Managing the organizational melting pot: Dilemmas of workplace diversity* (pp. 80–106). Thousand Oaks, CA: SAGE.

Kappen, D. M. (2000). *Acknowledgement of racial privilege, endorsement of equality, and feelings of collective guilt via ingroup versus outgroup influence.* (Unpublished doctoral dissertation). University of Kansas, Lawrence.

Lee, V. E., & Burkman, D. T. (2002). *Inequality at the starting gate: Social background differences in achievement as children begin school.* Washington, DC: Economic Policy Institute.

Lopez, G. E., Gurin, P., & Nagda, B. A. (1998). Education and understanding structural causes for group inequalities. *Political Psychology, 19,* 305–329.

MacPhee, D., Fritz, J., & Miller-Heyl, J. (1996). Ethnic variations in personal social networks and parenting. *Child Development, 67,* 3278–3295.

MacPhee, D., & MacPhee, M. (2000). The post-feminist (domestic) labor union. *Journal of Feminist Family Therapy, 12*(1), 77–79.

MacPhee, D., Oltjenbruns, K. A., Fritz, J. J., & Kreutzer, J. C. (1994). Strategies for infusing curricula with a multicultural perspective. *Innovative Higher Education, 18,* 289–309.

Plaut, V. C., Garnett, F. G., Buffardi, L. E., & Sanchez-Burks, J. (2011). "What about me?" Perceptions of exclusion and Whites' reactions to multiculturalism. *Journal of Personality and Social Psychology, 101,* 337–353. doi:10.1037/a0022832

Schmidt, A. J. (1997). *The menace of multiculturalism: Trojan horse in America.* Westport, CT: Praeger.

Smith, R. W. (1998). Challenging privilege: White male middle-class opposition in the multicultural education terrain. In R. C. Chavez & J. O'Donnell (Eds.), *Speaking the unpleasant: The politics of (non)engagement in the multicultural education terrain* (pp. 197–210). Albany: State University of New York Press.

Tatum, B. D. (2013). The complexity of identity: "Who am I?" In M. Adams, W. J. Blumenfeld, C. Castaneda, H. W. Hackman, M. L. Peters, & X. Zuniga (Eds.), *Readings for diversity and social justice* (3rd ed., pp. 6–9). New York, NY: Routledge.

Tittle, P. (2011). *Critical thinking: An appeal to reason.* New York, NY: Routledge.

Treitel, N. P. (2000). *Anti-racist practice by White psychologists.* (Unpublished doctoral dissertation). California School of Professional Psychology, Oakland.

Vacarr, B. (2001). Moving beyond polite correctness: Practicing mindfulness in the diverse classroom. *Harvard Educational Review, 71,* 285–295.

GLOSSARY

ACCULTURATION: cultural modification of an individual, group, or people by adapting to or borrowing traits from another culture; also a merging of cultures as a result of prolonged contact. Acculturation does not presume that one culture will eliminate the other, nor that the two will coexist in harmony, although these are possibilities.

AGEISM: a form of systematic stereotyping and discrimination against people simply because of their age.

ALLY: a person who takes some action to oppose oppression of a group of which he or she is not a member. For example, an Asian American who challenges a racist joke that targets African Americans is acting as an ally to the African American community.

ASSIMILATION: the process wherein members of one culture opt to (or are "forced" to) relinquish their own values and traditions in order to adopt those of the new or host culture. Thus assimilated individuals are not motivated to maintain their original cultural identity.

AVERSIVE RACISM: (Dovidio, Gaertner, Kawakami, & Hodson, 2002; Kovel, 1970): an attitudinal adaptation that results from an assimilation of an egalitarian value system with prejudicial and racist beliefs. In aversive racism as applied to White folks, one consciously endorses egalitarian values and denies negative feelings toward People of Color. There is no evidence of blatant discrimination. Racist behavior is often unintentional and attributed to nonracial factors. Despite an absence of racist intentions, racist *outcomes* still occur. Aversive racism results in nondiscriminatory behavior in situations in which doing the "right" thing is obvious but racist behavior when the situation is ambiguous. For example, Dovidio and Gaernter (2000) found that when both Black and White applicants are weakly qualified for a job, there is no evidence of discrimination in hiring practices. White research participants reject both candidates. When Black and White applicants are both moderately qualified, there is a slight but nonsignificant preference for White applicants. However, when Black and White candidates are both *highly qualified*, then a strong preference for the White candidate is seen. The term *aversive* refers to the tension and anxiety experienced by White people when they are interacting with People of Color. It also refers to the aversion that White people have the notion that their thoughts or actions might be racist.

BISEXUAL: term for a person who has orientations for intimacy toward both men and women.

CISGENDER: denoting or relating to a person whose self-identity conforms with the gender that corresponds to their biological sex; not transgender.

CLASSISM: the systematic assignment of worth on based on social or economic class (as paired with socio-economic statues and level of poverty). A socially constructed system that creates a dominant group and subordinated groups that then determines social privilege. It includes prejudice, discrimination, unfair, and differential treatment based on social class or perceived social class. Classism includes the systematic oppression of subordinated class groups to advantage and strengthen the dominant class groups. Policies and practices are set up to benefit class-privileged people at the expense of those who have less class privilege, resulting in drastic income and wealth inequality and causing basic human needs to go unmet.

CLOSETED: hidden; most commonly used to refer to keeping one's sexual orientation secret; the opposite of *out*.

CORE CONDITIONS: Rogers' (1957) proposal that there are three necessary and sufficient conditions for therapeutic change: (a) congruence, (b) unconditional positive regard, and (c) empathy. Generally speaking, congruence refers to one's ability to be authentic and genuine in a relationship. Unconditional positive regard refers to nonjudgmental acceptance of another person. Empathy occurs when one enters another person's frame of reference and uses reflection of feeling to communicate an accurate understanding of that frame.

CULTURE: defined as the sum of a shared set of attitudes, values, goals, customs, beliefs; ways of thinking, behaving or working that distinguishes one group of people from another group of people or society. Culture is transmitted through language, behavior, material objects, ritual, institutions, art, and so on.

DISABILITY, DIFFERENTLY ABLED, ABLEISM: some of the terms/terminology used to identify quality or state of being physically, mentally, and/or emotionally able and/or capable. The Americans with Disabilities Act (ADA) defines a person with a disability as a person who has a physical or mental impairment that substantially limits one or more major life activity. The ADA also makes it unlawful to discriminate against a person based on that person's association with a disability.

EGO-DYSTONIC: term used to describe when a person's thoughts, impulses, and behavior are felt to be repugnant, distressing, unacceptable, or inconsistent with their self-conception.

ETHNICITY: an ethnic or social group that shares a common and distinctive culture, religion, language, and so on.

ETHNOCENTRICISM: evaluation of other peoples/cultures according to preconceptions originating in the standards and customs of one's own culture.

GAY: term used for/by a person whose primary orientation for intimacy is toward people of the same sex. Progressive literature most often uses the term *gay* to refer to men and *lesbian* to refer to women, to denote that these are two distinct groups rather than one group being a subcategory of the other group.

GENDER: the social construction of masculinity or femininity as it aligns with designated sex at birth in a specific culture and time period.

GENDER IDENTITY: claims individuality that may or may not be expressed outwardly and may or may not correspond to one's sexual anatomy.

GENDER VARIANT/QUEER: terminology used by people who find other gender categories constraining. Their gender identities and/or expression are consciously not consistent with conventional standards for masculine or feminine behavior or appearance. Some identify as a blend, as androgynous, or as neither gender.

HETEROPHOBIA: the irrational fear of being perceived as heterosexual.

HETEROPHOBIC: someone who internalizes and/or externalizes an irrational fear of heterosexuals.

HETEROQUEER: a person, couple, or multiple partners in a relationship that identify and/or are perceived as queer yet one or more of those partners has heterosexual privilege.

HETEROSEXISM: the system of values that promotes heterosexual relationships to the exclusion of other kinds of relationships (e.g., platonic friendships, gay and lesbian relationships); beliefs, behaviors, or systems that discriminate against people who are lesbian, gay, bisexual, transgender, or queer, based upon a view of heterosexuality as normal and healthy, whereas other sexual orientations and gender expressions are viewed deviant and unhealthy. The norm of heterosexual sexual identity being the dominant socially accepted romantic-, sexual-, or emotional-based relationship that then places all other forms of attraction as subordinate.

HOMOPHOBIA: an irrational fear of, aversion to, or discrimination against homosexuality or homosexuals.

HOMOPREJUDICE: negative judgments and/or stereotypes about gays and lesbians; preferred by some over the term *homophobia*.

HUMAN RIGHTS: by the fundamental rights that humans have by virtue of being human. Human rights are based on the principle of respect for the individual. The fundamental assumption is that each person is a moral and rational being who deserves to be treated with dignity.

INSTITUTIONALIZED DISCRIMINATION: the unjust and discriminatory mistreatment of an individual or group of individuals by society and its institutions as a whole, through unequal selection or bias, intentional or unintentional; as opposed to individuals making a conscious choice to discriminate

INTERSECTIONALITY: an understanding of identity that recognizes the multiple ways in which identities intersect with one another. This approach does not view identities in an additive sense but rather sees all aspects of an individual's experience combining concurrently to produce a particular position in the world that may involve both privilege and disadvantage.

INTERDISCRIMINATION/INTERGROUP DISCRIMINATION: the phenomenon whereby factions of a single group develop conflict against each other as by-products of competition and prejudice.

INTRADISCRIMINATION/INTRARACIAL DISCRIMINATION/INTRARACIAL DISCRIMINATION: Oppression, suppression, hate, dislike, or distrust of another person or group of the same race based on physical characteristics such as skin color (light vs. dark), hair texture, nose size, and so on but also tribal and cultural reasons, as well as differences in caste or class.

LESBIAN: a person who typically identifies as a woman who is romantically, sexually, and/or emotionally attracted to other people that identify as women.

LGBTQIA: acronym used to indicate *lesbian, gay, bisexual, transgender, queer/questioning/intersex/ally*. In some cases the Q may stand for individuals questioning their status.

MACROAGGRESSION: actions that are meant to exclude, either by action or omission. Large-scale or overt aggression toward those of a different race, culture, gender, and so on.

MERITOCRACY: a society in which people are rewarded solely based on merit. In a true meritocracy, the conditions of one's birth (race, class, sex, etc.) would have no effect on one's chances to succeed.

MICROAGGRESSION: a subtle but offensive comment or action directed at a nondominant group that un/intentionally or un/consciously reinforce a stereotype (i.e., "I don't see you as Black"). Term used by Columbia professor Derald Sue to refer to brief and commonplace daily verbal, behavioral, or environmental indignities, whether intentional or unintentional, that communicate hostile, derogatory, or negative slights and insults toward others.

OPPRESSION: Oppression is the systematic, ongoing, pervasive injustice and subordination by members of the identified or acknowledged dominant status toward an individual or individuals who are not members of the identified dominant status. Whereas privilege opens doors or provides opportunities for individuals of the dominant culture or status, oppression prevents those opportunities from being accessible to those who are not identified or acknowledged as part of the dominant culture or status.

OUT: commonly used term to refer to one who is open about one's sexual orientation; the opposite of *closeted*.

PHOBIA: a persistent, abnormal, strong or irrational/illogical fear/dislike, or aversion; prejudice against a specific person, group, thing, or situation (e.g., Islamaphobia, Muslimophobia, atheist/atheophobia).

PRIVILEGE: a right or immunity granted as a peculiar benefit or advantage, often taken for granted by members of dominant cultures or statuses.

QUEER: which once was derogatory, is now used to explain a complex set of sexual behaviors and desires.

RACISM: Racism is based on power and is a belief that a specific race is superior or inferior to another race. This belief about superiority or inferiority is predetermined by biological characteristics .

RHEUMATOID ARTHRITIS: an autoimmune form of arthritis causing chronic joint inflammation, pain, and damage.

SEX: the medical assignment of "male" or "female" based upon the external genitalia that an individual possesses at birth. The biological sexes are commonly seen as mutually exclusive, and it is often believed that a person's assigned sex dictates their gender expression, chromosomal, and hormonal makeup.

SEXISM: the socially constructed system that creates a dominant group and subordinated groups based on how one is labeled at birth, anatomy, and other biological factors that then determine social privilege. In US culture, men are the dominant group, whereas women are subordinated. People who identify as gender queer, transgender, and those in transition are further subordinated.

SEXUAL IDENTITY: a person's self-description of the romantic, sexual, and/or emotional relationships with another or others such as heterosexual, gay, lesbian, bisexual, asexual, and so on. Much like gender identifications, sexual identity labels are constantly being created to both unite communities and divide members from others.

SEXUAL ORIENTATION: an inborn, enduring emotional, romantic, affectionate, and sexual attraction to another person; sexual orientation falls along a continuum ranging from exclusively heterosexual to varying degrees of bisexuality to exclusively homosexual (lesbian or gay). Sexual orientation is not determined by behavior (e.g., sexual intercourse between two men, two women, or a man and a woman) but by primary affectionate attraction and how one self-identifies.

SOCIAL JUSTICE: a broad term for action intended to create genuine equality, fairness, and respect among peoples (https://www.uml.edu/docs/Glossary_tcm18-55041.pdf).

STIGMA: a mark of shame or discredit; an identifying mark or characteristic.

STRUCTURAL DISCRIMINATION: (also known as structural inequality, systemic discrimination, or institutional racism) occurs in a society when an entire network of rules and practices disadvantages nondominant groups while serving at the same time to advantage the dominant group.

TOLERANCE: sympathy, indulgence, and/or willingness to accept behavior and/or beliefs that are different from one's own, even if one disagrees with or disapproves of those beliefs or behaviors.

TRANSFORMATIONAL LEARNING: processes that result in fundamental changes in how people see themselves and the world.

TRANSGENDER: an "umbrella term" for someone whose self-identification, anatomy, appearance, manner, expression, behavior, and/or other's perceptions of challenges traditional societal expectations of congruent gender expression and designated birth sex.

TRANSITION: the period of time when a person is electing to move from one gendered category to another via social expressions, labels, clothing, mannerisms, voice control, and so on. Transitioning may include but is not limited to taking hormones, accessing surgeries, and engaging in other such changes; until the individual feels comfortable with their body, expression of their gender, and are perceived by others consistently and correctly.

TRANSPHOBIA: the irrational fear of trans and gender queer people by others.

TRANSSEXUAL: individuals whose designated sex at birth does not match their personal sex/body identity and who, through sex reassignment surgery and hormone treatments, may seek to change their physical body to match their gender identity. Transsexuals can be male to female (MTF) or female to male (FTM). Transsexuals' sexual identification can be heterosexual, gay, lesbian, bisexual, or other.

WELL-MEANING WHITE PERSON (WMWP): one who consciously despises racism, but possesses hidden racist attitudes and fears that impede the development of authentic relationships with people of color. WMWPs have an investment in differentiating themselves from blatant racists and oppressive institutions, to support the belief in themselves as a person who is caring and humane. Despite an expressed commitment to equality and justice, there is little evidence of *antiracist* practices and rarely an examination or ownership of one's own racism and prejudice.

XENOPHOBIA: an irrational fear of foreigners or strangers or others who are different from oneself.

Sources: https://www.merriam-webster.com/dictionary; www.dictionary.com;
https://en.wiktionary.org/wiki/macroaggression;
http://www.businessdictionary.com/definition/human-rights.html
https://explorable.com/intergroup-discrimination
https://www.adl.org/racism

INDEX

Tables are indicated by an italic *t* following the page number.

intersections of race, gender, sexuality, and class, 74–78
lack of training for counselors of Color, 51, 56
lesbian counselor educator, 173–180
multicultural competence, 47–48, 56, 68–69, 71
multiracial people and, 121–124
oppression of the spirit, 55–62
sexism and perspective on male rape, 223–227
strengths-based, 264–266
supervisory behavior in successful multicultural supervision, 66–71
within-group prejudice, 64–71
Covert racism (CR), 16, 143, 279, 281, 296
CPS (Children's Protective Services), 302–303
Credibility of privileged class, 315–316
Crenshaw, Kimberle, 257
Critical consciousness, 30, 189, 237
Critical disability theory, 146
Critical race theory, 67
Crosley-Corcoran, G., 141
Cultural attunement approach, 121
Cultural capital, 74–75, 78, 80
Cultural humility, 7, 121–124, 296
Culture, defined, 320

Dandridge, Dorothy, 270
Darity, W, 269
David, E. J. R., 49
David, L. E., 124
Davis, Kathleen M., 127–128, 140–150
Davis, Ossie, 270
Defense of Marriage Act, 218, 220
Deification of normality, 241
Deines, Helen G., 100, 113–124
Delgado-Romero, Edward A., 33–34, 37–43
Dennis, H., 201
Determinism, 213
Developmental disabilities, 245
Diagnostic and Statistical Manual of Mental Disorders (DSM), 105, 174
Differently abled, defined, 320
Difficult dialogues, 6, 15, 237
Disability, defined, 233–234, 320
Disabled persons, 278
  biopsychosocial model of disability, 146
  critical disability theory, 146
  defined, 144
  hidden disabilities, 145
  socioeconomic and ability privilege, 140–147
Disintegration phase of Helm's (and extended) model, 301, 307t
Disorienting experiences, 117–118
Dissonance phase of WRID, 11

Diversity hiring, 38
Double binds of racism, 16
Double consciousness, 280
Down syndrome, 245
Du Bois, W. E. B., 280

Economic oppression, 26, 143–144
Edge, R., 316
Education and academia
  classism and, 196–198
  class oppression and privilege, 130–131, 133–136
  conflicting messages for women about, 197–198
  issues of sexual identity in, 177–178
  navigation of oppression, power, and privilege in academia, 85–96
  racism and, 276–284, 302–303
  sexism and, 196–198, 210, 212
  socioeconomic status and, 142
  using educational privilege to navigate oppression, 173–179
  White privilege and, 279–281
Edwards, K. M., 226
Edwards, L. M., 115
Ego-dystonic, 174, 320
Elder, G. H., 100
"Embracing the Teachable Moment: The Black Gay Body in the Classroom as Embodied Text" (Alexander), 257–258
Empowerment process, 212–213
Ericksonian model of storytelling, 59
Erikson, E. H., 208
Ethical Principles of Psychologists and Code of Conduct (APA), 19
Ethnicity, defined, 320
Ethnocentrism, 18, 96, 320
Eurocentrism, 280, 283
Evans, S. A., 235–236
Everything You Always Wanted to Know About Sex but Were Afraid to Ask (Reuben), 103
"Examining Race and Class" exercise, 123

Familismo, 41–42
Fein, S., 243
Female Masculinity (Halberstam), 156
Feminism, 212, 299, 302, 305
First-order change, 10
Fiske, S. T, 190
Food stamps, 130, 174
Freire, Paulo, 30, 96

Gang membership, 70
Gay, defined, 320. *See also* LGBTQIA
Gender, defined, 320

Intradiscrimination (intraracial discrimination; intraracial discrimination), 85–86, 263, 273, 321
Introspective phase of WRID, 11, 13
In-vitro amniocentesis tests, 245
Ivankovich, Karla, 229, 240–247
Ivey, A., 56

Jackson, Andrew, 196
Jackson, K. F., 121–122
Jackson Williams, D., 47
Jenkins, L., 124
Johnson, A., 47
Johnson-Ahorlu, Robin, 66
Jones, R. P., 26
Jordan, June, 29

Kane, G., 77–78
Kawewe, Saliwe M., 34–35, 85–96
Kellogg Foundation Racial Healing Initiative, 121
Kendall, F. E., 11
Kennedy, John F., 299
Key model, 219–221
Kivel, Paul, 123
Koslow, D. R., 117–118, 123
Kramer, Allison L., 184, 217–219
Kurasini International Education Center, 91–92

LaFromboise, T., 49–50
Langer, Carol L., 184, 206–214
Langer, David, 208–210
Language, 39, 46, 280
Laveria, Tato, 42
LCP (life course perspective), 100, 113
Lee, Spike, 281
Leonardo, Z., 276
Lesbian, defined, 321. See also LGBTQIA
Levy, B. R., 190
Levy, S. R., 187
Lewis, Mel Michelle, 257–258
Lew, M., 225
LGBTQIA
    assumed privilege and, 102–109
    Black queer pedagogy, 254–259
    cisgender privilege in gay male context, 164–170
    close relationship between lesbian and heterosexual woman, 217–219
    defined, 321
    homosexuality and assumed privilege, 102–109
    intersectionality in counseling, 74–78
    marriage of lesbian and transman, 153–157
    marriage rights, 75–76, 108–109

professional counselor educator, 173–180
    societal messages, 103
Lichaw, Felice, 34, 64–71
Life course perspective (LCP), 100, 113
Linehan, Marsha, 70
Longhurst, T., 236
Loomis, Colleen, 127, 129–139
Loving v. Virginia (1969), 119
Lummis, D. C., 142

Macdonald, J. L., 187
MacPhee, David, 288, 312–316
Macroaggressions, 281, 321
Madrid, Arturo, 116
Mahmoud, V. M., 16
Male privilege, 314
Male rape, 223–227
Malott, K. M., 122
Mar, Keith, 11–12, 14
Marriage, 243–244
    interracial, 118–119
    of lesbian and transman, 153–157
    LGBTQIA rights, 75–76, 108–109
    sexism in, 208–210
    terminology, 154–155
Masculus hostilis, 314
Mason, L. B., 235–236
Matthew Shepard and James Byrd Jr. Hate Crimes Prevention Act of 2009, 218
McClure F. H., 52
MCD (multicultural dialogue), 10–14, 28
McIntosh, Peggy, 17
Megivern Foster, Deborah, 1–2, 25–30
Mencius, 49
Mental health services. *See also* Counseling
    catering to nonheterosexual people, 77
    inequality of, 5
Meritocracy, 66, 71, 315, 321
Miami University of Ohio, 115–116
Microaggressions, 6, 18, 40, 94–95, 169, 281, 293, 321
Microinvalidations, 18
Middleton, Kianna M., 251, 253–260
Middleton, Valerie A., 5–6, 251–252, 261–268
Miller, Geri, 183–184, 195–205
Minnich, Elizabeth, 5
Minority stress theory, 175–179
Mixed heritage people. *See* Multiracial people
Mock, Matthew R., 287, 289–296
Moraga, Cherríe, 122
MS (multiple sclerosis), 231–234
"Multicultural and Social Justice Counseling Competencies" (Ratts et al.), 191

Multicultural Change Intervention Matrix, 10
Multicultural competence, 15, 47–48, 68–69, 71, 121, 191, 232, 237, 308, 316
Multicultural dialogue (MCD), 10–14, 28
Multicultural Guidelines on Training, Education, Research, Practice and Organizational Change for Psychologists (APA), 19
Multiple sclerosis (MS), 231–234
Multiracial people
　ambiguous ethnicity, 37–43
　assumed privilege and, 39, 113–124
　challenged descriptors, 114–115
　choice, 117–118
　context in United States, 118–121
　in counseling practice, 121–124
　identity development, 116–117
　understanding and experiencing racial privilege, 113–118
Multiracial Unity program, 304

NAACP Youth chapter, 266
Naiveté phase of WRID, 11
Narcissism, 16–17, 221
Nash, G. B., 119
National Association of Social Workers, 86, 105, 121
National Board of Certified Counselors, 51
National Career Development Association (NCDA), 191
National Institute of Mental Health, 187
National Latina/o Psychological Association (NLPA), 40–42
National Urban League Youth chapter, 266
Neill, T., 226–227
Nelson, T. D., 190
Neville, H. A., 15–16
North, M. S., 190

Obama, Barack, 107, 119, 218
Olson, A., 179
Oppression, defined, 321
Overt racism, 16, 39, 94–95, 279, 281, 296

Palmore, E., 190
Pedersen, P. B., 56
Pedrotti, J. T., 115
Peila-Shuster, Jacqueline J., 183, 185–189, 192
People's Institute for Survival and Beyond, 121
People with disabilities (PWD). *See* Disabled persons
Perfectionism, 17–18
Personal ageism, 201
Pettitt, Jessica, 151, 153–157
Phobia, defined, 321

Pieterse, A. L., 235–236
Poitier, Sidney, 270
Polkah-Toe, Sametra, 251–252, 261–266
Pollack, W., 225
Poverty, 196. *See also* Socioeconomic status
　classism and, 27
　identity and, 26
　prevalence of, 140
　suicide and, 26
　types of, 142
　White privilege and, 25–30, 141
Power analyses, 300
Priester, Paul E., 229, 240–247
Private schooling, 278–280
Privilege blindness and privilege ignorance, 300–301, 308
Privilege, defined, 321
Privilege package, 201–203
Proposition 8, 218
Pseudoindependence phase of Helm's (and extended) model, 301–303, 307*t*
Psychosocial Costs of Racism to Whites Scale, 16
Psychosocial developmental phases, 208
PWD (people with disabiliies). *See* Disabled persons

Queer, 163, 169. *See also* LGBTQIA
　Black queer pedagogy, 254–259
　coming out as, 163
　defined, 162, 254–255, 321
Queer consciousness, 109
Queer Phenomenology (Ahmed), 257

Racial/Cultural Identity Development Model, 57
Racial identity development. *See* White racial identity development
Racial privilege. *See also* White privilege
　acknowledging and challenging, 113–124
　allies and activism, 299–309
Racism
　aversive, 9, 319
　Black queer pedagogy, 254–259
　covert, 16, 143, 279, 281, 296
　defined, 321
　double binds of, 16
　in education, 276–284, 302–303
　ethnic beauty in western society, 261–266
　internalized, 66–67, 120–121
　intersectionality of sexism and, 281–282
　overt, 16, 39, 94–95, 279, 281, 296
　personal compassion in situations involving, 289–296
　skin color, 269–274
　socioeconomic status and, 276

Rawlings, S. A., 236
Reintegration phase of Helm's (and extended) model, 299–301, 307*t*
Resistance/immersion phase of WRID, 11, 58
Resolution on Poverty and Socioeconomic Status (APA), 129
Re-storying, 115
Reverse discrimination, 6, 26, 281
Rheumatoid arthritis, 186, 321
Ridley, C., 70
Riggle, E. D. B., 179
Riggs, Damien W., 34–35, 74–78
Risner-Butner, A., 235–236
Robinson, Linda, 252, 269–274
Robinson, T., 220, 263
Rodriguez, Richard, 116
Rogers, C. R., 12, 106
Rosenwasser, P., 235
Rostosky, S. S., 179
Rubin, M., 244

Salett, E. P., 117–118, 123
Samuels, G. A., 121–122
Sanchez, D. M., 122
Schaefle, S., 122
School Daze (film), 281–282
Scott, D. A., 220–221
Second-order change, 10
Sedgwick, Eve, 254–255
Self-awareness, 30, 46–47, 71, 191, 313–315
Self-forgiveness, 204
Self-reflexivity, 59–60
September 11, 2001 terrorist attacks, 293–294
SES. *See* Class oppression and privilege; Socioeconomic status
Sex, defined, 322
Sexism, 195–201
    benevolent, 207
    defined, 322
    in education, 196–198, 210, 212
    in employment, 199–200, 209–212
    impact of being born female, 206–214
    intersectionality of ageism and, 200–201
    intersectionality of classism and, 196–198
    intersectionality of racism and, 281–282
    male rape, 223–227
    marriage and children, 208–210
Sexual identity, defined, 322
Sexual orientation, defined, 322
Sexual orientation disturbance, 105
Shepard, Matthew, 217–218, 221
Shih, M., 122
Shockley, Muriel, 11–12, 14

Silencing, 123
Silver spoon, 132
Sisterhood Agenda, 266
Sloan, Tod S., 134
Smedley, B. D., 276
Social cognitive theory, 244
Socialization process, 3–4, 7, 224–225
Social justice, defined, 322
Social location, 9–10
Social Security Disability Insurance (SSDI), 144–145
Social stigma theory and stigma management, 176, 241, 244
Socioeconomic status (SES), 127–128. *See also* Class oppression and privilege
    ability privilege and, 140–147
    defined, 127
    economic oppression, 143
    education, 142
    hierarchical perspective of, 140–141
    homelessness, 141–142
    mortgage lending, 142
    racism and, 276
    skin color and, 269–270
    socioeconomic discrimination, 26
    socioeconomic survivor guilt, 143–144
    style and, 147
    unemployment, 142
Spanierman, L. B., 15–16, 246
Spencer, Michael, 27
Spencer, S. J., 243
Spirit and oppression, 55–62
    adjustment to cultural oppression, 57
    self-reflexivity, 59–60
    storytelling, 59
Square dancing, 162–170
SSDI (Social Security Disability Insurance), 144–145
Stanford University, 114–116
Stereotype threat, 186, 189
Stewart, L., 246
Stigma, 173–179, 240–241, 244, 322
Storytelling, 59
Strengths-based counseling, 264–266
Strong, S., 179
Structural discrimination (structural inequality; systemic discrimination; institutional racism), 322
Sue, D., 11, 18, 47, 57, 196, 200, 204, 226
Sue, D. W., 11, 18, 47, 56–57, 196, 200, 204, 226
Suicide, 26, 56, 61, 106
Swindler, L., 12